T0389698

A Companion to William of Saint-Thierry

Brill's Companions to the Christian Tradition

A SERIES OF HANDBOOKS AND REFERENCE WORKS ON THE
INTELLECTUAL AND RELIGIOUS LIFE OF EUROPE, 500–1800

Edited by

Christopher M. Bellitto (*Kean University*)

VOLUME 84

The titles published in this series are listed at *brill.com/bcct*

A Companion to William of Saint-Thierry

Edited by

F. Tyler Sergent

BRILL

LEIDEN | BOSTON

Cover illustration: A Cistercian monk at Sorø Abbey, a 12th-century monastery in Sorø, Denmark (southwest of Copenhagen and Roskilde). Founded as a Benedictine house in the 1140s, it became Cistercian in 1162, after which the abbey church was built in brick romanesque modeled after Fontenay. The image itself, original to the Cistercian abbey church, is located on the north aisle side of the northwestern pier in the transept. The abbey church and the medieval artwork are in excellent condition and still in use (although no longer Catholic). Photograph ©Tyler Sergent.

Library of Congress Cataloging-in-Publication Data

Names: Sergent, F. Tyler, editor.
Title: A companion to William of Saint-Thierry / edited by F. Tyler Sergent.
Description: Leiden ; Boston : Brill, 2019. | Series: Brill's companions to
   the Christian tradition, ISSN 1871-6377 ; volume 84 | Includes
   bibliographical references and index.
Identifiers: LCCN 2018059677 (print) | LCCN 2019004905 (ebook) | ISBN
   9789004392502 (ebook) | ISBN 9789004313552 (hardback : alk. paper)
Subjects: LCSH: William, of Saint-Thierry, Abbot of Saint-Thierry,
   approximately 1085-1148?
Classification: LCC BX4705.G7464 (ebook) | LCC BX4705.G7464 C66 2019 (print)
   | DDC 230/.2092--dc23
LC record available at https://lccn.loc.gov/2018059677

Typeface for the Latin, Greek, and Cyrillic scripts: "Brill." See and download: brill.com/brill-typeface.

ISSN 1871-6377
ISBN 978-90-04-31355-2 (hardback)
ISBN 978-90-04-39250-2 (e-book)

Contents

Acknowledgements

I wish to express my deepest gratitude to each of the authors who contributed to this volume with careful and thorough work. In addition, special thanks to Julian Diehl, editor at Brill and creator of this series, for discussing and accepting the initial project proposal, and very special thanks to Christopher Bellitto, series editor at Brill, who patiently and painstakingly, with wisdom and support, guided me and the project through to completion. My colleagues and dear friends, Marsha L. Dutton and Dwayne A. Mack, provided essential mentoring and scholarly advice without which this volume may not have come to fruition—thank you both sincerely. To my Berea College Writing Group friends and colleagues, thank you for helping keep me focused and on task. Thank you to David York, my teaching and research assistant, who diligently helped with the bibliography, and Tyshaun Johnson, my teaching and research assistant, who helped with the tedious task of enumerating the index. Personally, I wish to dedicate my work on this volume to the memory of Frederick W. Norris (1941–2016), patristics scholar, global church historian, MA advisor, and remarkable human being, and of Katherine C. Christensen (1956–2018), medievalist, colleague, and dear friend. On behalf of myself and all the contributing authors, let me convey our gratitude to the living community of Cistercian monks and nuns who not only carry on the monastic traditions of the past but who exemplify that which William of Saint-Thierry theorized and experienced in his life and writings.

Abbreviations

c.	*circa*, around
cf.	Compare
diss.	Dissertation
(ed.)	Editor(s)
edn.	Edition
esp.	Especially
ET	English translation
Fol(s).	Folio(s)
ln.	Line, lines
MHD	*Mittelhochdeutsch*, Middle High German
n.	Note, notes
nr.	Number
Pr(a)ef.	*Prefatio*, preface
Prol.	*Prologus*, prologue
rpt.	Reprint
§	Section, sections
tract.	*Tractatus*, tractate
trans.	Translator
vol(s).	Volume(s)
Vlg.	Vulgate
Vita Ant	*Vita antiqua*, Life of William of Saint-Thierry

The Works of William of Saint-Thierry

Adv Abl	*Disputatio adversus Petrum Abælardum*
Aenig	*Aenigma fidei*
Brev com	*Brevis commentatio*
Cant	*Expositio super Cantica Canticorum*
Cant Amb	*Super cantica canticorum ex operibus sancti Ambrosii*
Cant Greg	*Excerpta ex libris sancti Gregorii super Cantica Canticorum*
Contemp	*De contemplando Deo*
De err	*De erroribus Guillelmi de Conchis*
Ep frat	*Epistola [aurea] ad fratres de Monte Dei*
Ep Geof et Bern	*Epistola ad Gaufridum Carnotensem episcopum et Bernardum abbatem Clarae-vallensem* (Preface to Adv Abl)

Ep Rup	*Epistola ad domnum Rupertum*
Exp Rom	*Expositio in epistolam Pauli ad Romanos*
Med	*Meditativæ orationes*
Nat am	*De natura et dignitate amoris*
Orat	*Oratio domni Willelmi*
Phys an	*Physica animae/De natura animae*
Phys corp	*Physica corporis/De natura corporis*
Resp	*Responsio abbatum auctore Willelmo abbate Sancti Theodorici*
Sac alt	*De sacramento altaris liber*
Spec fid	*Speculum fidei*
Vita Bern	*Sancti Bernardi vita prima*

Serials

CC	Corpus Christianorum series. Turnhout, Belgium: Brepols, 1953–
CCCM	Corpus Christianorum, Continuatio Mediaevalis
CCSL	Corpus Christianorum, Series Latina
CF	Cistercian Fathers series. Spencer, MA; Washington, DC; Kalamazoo, MI; Collegeville, MN, 1970–
CS	Cistercian Studies series. Spencer, MA; Washington, DC; Kalamazoo, MI; Collegeville, MN, 1968–
CSEL	Corpus scriptorum ecclesiasticorum latinorum, Vienna, 1866–
NPNF	Nicene and Post-Nicene Fathers. New York: Christian Literature Publishing Company, 1886–1900; rpt., Peabody, MA: Hendrickson, 1994.
PG	J.-P. Migne, Patrologiae cursus completus, series graeca, 162 vols. Paris, 1857–1866.
PL	J.-P. Migne, Patrologiae cursus completus, series latina. 221 vols. Paris, 1844–1864.
SBOp	*Sancti Bernardi Opera*. 8 volumes. Ed. J. Leclercq, H.M. Rochais, C. H. Talbot. Rome: Editiones Cistercienses, 1957–1977.
SCh	Sources chrétiennes series. Paris: du Cerf, 1941–

Notes on Contributors

David N. Bell

is Professor Emeritus of Religious Studies and Dean of Theology in the Faculty of Theology at Memorial University (Newfoundland). He is also a Fellow of the Royal Society of Canada. His research encompasses Europe, Asia, and Egypt and range in time from the early years of Christianity to the 21st century. He has published more than two dozen books, over a hundred articles, and a great number of book reviews. His main areas of interest are the history of medieval libraries, medieval intellectual history, and Coptic Christianity.

Thomas X. Davis, OCSO

is the abbot emeritus of the Cistercian Abbey of Our Lady of New Clairvaux, Vina, CA. He has translated for Cistercian Publications William of Saint-Thierry's *The Mirror of Faith* (1979) and *The Nature and Dignity of Love* (1981). Presently he is preparing a new translation of the *Meditations*. Relating to Cistercian architecture, he facilitated the reconstruction of the Cistercian Chapter House of Santa Maria de Ovila (Trillo, Spain 1190–1220) at New Clairvaux.

E. Rozanne Elder

was for many year Editorial Director of Cistercian Publications and Director of the Institute of Cistercian Studies at Western Michigan University, Kalamazoo. Now Professor Emerita of History, she is working on a translation of and commentary on the documents relating to Peter Abelard's second condemnation.

Brian Patrick McGuire

taught at Copenhagen and Roskilde Universities, Denmark, 1972–2012. His books include *The Cistercians in Denmark* (Cistercian Publications, 1982), *Friendship and Community 350–1250* (Cornell University Press, 1988), *The Difficult Saint: Bernard of Clairvaux* (Cistercian Publications, 1991), *Jean Gerson and the Last Medieval Reformation* (Penn State University Press, 2005) and several historical studies in Danish. Presently he is working on *Bernard of Clairvaux: An Intimate Biography*.

Glenn E. Myers

is Professor of Church History and Theological Studies at Crown College, Minnesota, and the author of *Seeking Spiritual Intimacy: Journeying Deeper with Medieval Women of Faith* (InterVarsity, 2011). He has published articles on the history of Christian spirituality in *Studies in Spirituality, Cistercian Studies*

Quarterly, and *Zondervan's Dictionary of Christian Spirituality* (2011), as well as presented various papers at the International Congress on Medieval Studies.

Nathaniel Peters

earned his PhD at Boston College and is a Lecturer at Columbia University and the Executive Director of the Morningside Institute, New York City. Currently with F. Tyler Sergent he is translating William's *Letter to Rupert of Deutz, On the Sacrament of the Altar, and On the Errors of William of Conches* for Cistercian Publications.

Aage Rydstrøm-Poulsen

is Dean of the Institute of Culture, Language, and History, and Chair of the Department of Theology at the University of Greenland and former president of the same university. He is author of *The Gracious God:* Gratia *in Augustine and the Twelfth Century* (Akademisk, 2002) and has published on William of Saint-Thierry and Richard of Saint-Victor. He is presently preparing a new translation of Richard of Saint-Victor's *De Trinitate* for Dallas Medieval Texts and Translations.

F. Tyler Sergent

is Assistant Professor of History and General Studies at Berea College, Kentucky. Recently, he has co-edited with Aage Rydstrøm-Poulsen and Marsha L. Dutton, *Unity of Spirit: Studies on William of Saint-Thierry* (Cistercian Publications, 2015) and co-authored with Marsha L. Dutton, "The Cistercian Order" in the Oxford Bibliographies Online (Oxford University Press, 2018). Currently with Nathaniel Peters he is translating William's *Letter to Rupert of Deutz, On the Sacrament of the Altar, and On the Errors of William of Conches* for Cistercian Publications.

Introduction

F. Tyler Sergent

William of Saint-Thierry's biography proves elusive, yet as scholarship on William has shown, including the contents of this volume, his contribution to western intellectual history—and specifically Christian monastic tradition—rests on his insightful thought as explicated in his twenty-one extant writings.[1] This is not to say that his life did not in itself have impact in his own day. As Adriaan Bredero asserted in his presentation at the Abbey of Saint-Thierry colloquium in 1976, William stood "at the crossroads of the monastic currents of his time".[2] Yet William was no bystander. From the source material we have, he was actively involved and deeply participatory in monastic reform movements both Benedictine and Cistercian; in controversies of theological dogma, including Christological and Eucharistic debates; and in staunch reaffirmation of historical monastic practices, the tropes of desert monastic devotion, and rigorous observation of the Rule of Benedict. Most significantly, William stands out for his own place within this inherited monastic tradition, particularly through his progressive assertion of original monastic thought in the context of his own contemporary spirituality from the stages of spiritual progress to the ultimate deification of the soul.

This present volume attempts to provide an overview and introduction to the life, works, thought, and influence of William of Saint-Thierry (c. 1080–1148). As such, we have gathered an international group of current Cistercian and William scholars to explore, elucidate, and address anew each of these areas while at the same time engaging previous established scholarship that remains relevant, accessible, and insightful.

1   An Overview of William of Saint-Thierry

> Come, let us go up to the mountain of the Lord, and to the house of the
> God of Jacob, and he will teach us his ways[3]

---

1   See the Works of William of Saint-Thierry, 229–34 in this volume for Latin editions, recent translations, and dating of these writings.

2   Adriaan Bredero, "William of Saint Thierry at the Crossroads of the Monastic Currents of His Time," in *William, Abbot of St. Thierry: A Colloquium at the Abbey of St. Thierry*, trans. Jerry Carfantan, CS 94 (Kalamazoo, MI: Cistercian Publications, 1987), 113–37. The article was originally published in French in 1979 under the title *Saint Thierry. Une abbay de VIᵉ au XXᵉ siecle. Actes de colloque international d'Histoire monastique.*

3   *De Contemplando Deo* (Contemp), 1, CCCM 88:153. ET: *On Contemplating God, Prayer, Meditations*, trans. Sr. Penelope [Lawson], CSVM, CF 3 (Kalamazoo, MI: Cistercian Publications, 1977), 36. William here quotes Isaiah 2:3.

© KONINKLIJKE BRILL NV, LEIDEN, 2019 | DOI:10.1163/9789004392502_002

William begins perhaps his earliest work, *De contemplando Deo* (*On Contemplating God*) with these words. In a meaningful way, this quotation summarizes the overall content of William's writings and monastic life: his constant effort to meet God, not just in the here and now, but where God is, "the mountain of the Lord". For William, to ascend this mountain and to encounter God in profound, albeit fleeting, ways this side of eternity is indeed possible. William's commitment to monastic life, combined with his near lifelong writing career, demonstrate as well his commitment to seeking, finding, and enjoying God. For William, this journey follows a particular path along distinct stages of progress that were defined by various degrees of intellectual as well as spiritual perception and understanding. From his earliest work through to his last, *Vita prima Bernardi* (*First Life of Saint Bernard*, Book 1),[4] William's conceptual depiction of this journey remains constant through his own lifelong experience on this path, although as we shall see his depth of understanding and his descriptive nuance continuously sharpen and focus the image of that journey for the reader and ultimately also the image of the triune God William sought to know, to love, and with whom to be unified. This is the William the reader will be acquainted with through this volume.

William also was pulled—and, it must be noted, sometimes willingly inserted himself—into controversies regarding monastic life and practice as well as contemporary controversies of theological doctrine. Although he lamented the vicissitudes his abbatial office had thrust upon him, he still actively stood at the crossroads that these controversies illuminated during the first half of the 12th century. Although himself a Benedictine or "black monk" at the time, William did not approve of what he saw as the Cluniac attack on the Cistercian "white monk" reforms, and so he pleaded with his Cistercian friend, Bernard, abbot of Clairvaux, to respond and refute the Cluniac accusations. After a time, in 1125—no doubt taking longer than William would have liked—Bernard did so in a letter addressed to Abbot William of Saint-Thierry but aimed at Abbot Peter [the Venerable] of Cluny.[5]

Related to his resonance with the Cistercian reform—vis-à-vis his admiration of Bernard and the monastic life at Clairvaux—William was himself involved in reform efforts within the Benedictine order. In 1131, he successfully introduced a General Chapter of Benedictine abbots in the diocese of Reims in imitation of the Cistercian practice. This particular innovation met with resistance, both from within the order and from the ecclesial hierarch,

---

4   Although William wrote the first version of the *Life of Bernard of Clairvaux* between 1145 and his own death in 1148, subsequent authors, Arnold of Bonneval (Book 2) and Geoffrey of Auxerre (Books 3–5), wrote significant additions after Bernard's death in 1153.

5   For details on the *Apologia ad Guillelmum Abbatem*, see Conrad Rudolph, "The Scholarship on Bernard of Clairvaux's *Apologia*," *Cîteaux – Commentarii Cistercienses* 40.1 (1989): 69–110.

Cardinal Matthew of Albano, the papal legate of the region, who wrote in opposition to the practice, and to whom William in turn wrote the *Responsio abbatum* in perhaps 1132.[6] William's direct action and intervention were successful and managed to garner support for the reform work within the Benedictine houses, at least in his own diocese.

Among the theological and doctrinal controversies William addressed—there are at least three interventions we know of—the condemnation of Peter Abelard stands out most for its historical significance for 12th century theological paradigms and for the way in which William orchestrated it from behind the scenes, once again through his friend Bernard of Clairvaux. William's concern over Abelard's Trinitarian theology and its implications for redemption fueled Bernard's attack on Abelard, which culminated in Abelard's public condemnation at the Council of Sens in 1141.[7] In this case, William beforehand had also written a *Disputation against Abelard* addressed to Bernard, in which he considered and rejected Abelard's views point by point.[8] The tide against Abelard did not recede until after the condemnation and Abelard's death at Cluny that same year. Even so, William still saw fit to write *Speculum fidei* (*The Mirror of Faith*) to assist monastic minds to avoid the errors, as he saw them, of Abelard and to develop a proper faith that would illuminate the path to God.[9]

The first of the other two interventions into theological discourse came earlier in William's career during his abbacy at Saint-Thierry (1119/20–1135). It involved Rupert of Deutz and his treatise on the Eucharist which William found lacking, if not heretical, in its distinction between the substance and the species of the sacrament. At first William wrote a letter to Rupert voicing his concerns to him directly, abbot to abbot.[10] Perhaps not satisfied with that alone, William

---

6   For Cardinal Matthew's letter, see CCCM 89:93–102; for William's *Responsio abbatum auctore Willelmo abbate Sancti Theodorici*, see CCCM 89:103–11.

7   For scholarly literature on the date of the synod, see E. Rozanne Elder's chapter, "William of Saint-Thierry and the Renewal of the Whole 'Man,'" 110, n. 7 in this volume.

8   *Disputatio adversus Petrum Abaelardum* (Adv Abl), CCCM 89A:17–59 (PL 180:249–282). E. Rozanne Elder is presently working on an English translation of Adv Abl and other documents relating to the second condemnation of Abelard.

9   Spec fid, CCCM 89A:81–127 (PL 180:365–398). For analysis of William's role in the controversy with Abelard, see E. Rozanne Elder, "Introduction," William of St. Thierry, *The Mirror of Faith*, CF 15 (Kalamazoo, MI: Cistercian Publications, 1979), xi–xxxi; and Piero Zerbi, "William and His Dispute with Abelard," in *William, Abbot of St. Thierry: A Colloquium at the Abbey of St. Thierry*, trans. Jerry Carfantan, CS 94 (Kalamazoo, MI: Cistercian Publications, 1987), 181–203.

10   *Epistola ad domnum Rupertum*, CCCM 88:47–52 (PL 180:341–346). Nathaniel Peters and I are currently working on an English transation of this letter along with translations of *De sacramento altaris* and *De erroribus Guillelmi de Conchis* for Cistercian Publications (CF 82).

proceeded to write his own treatise, *De sacramento altaris* (*On the Sacrament of the Altar*), the first work on Eucharistic theology among Cistercian writers.[11]

The final theological controversy William addressed came at the same time as the issue with Peter Abelard, after William had left Saint-Thierry and joined the Cistercian house at Signy (1135). William now concerned himself with the Trinitarian theology of William of Conches, which he found misleading and dangerous, even accusing William of Manichaeism, that is, of embracing a dualism of good and evil in the psychosomatic person and thereby reflecting an unacceptable dualism in creation. He intervened not with a letter to William of Conches himself but to his longtime friend, Bernard of Clairvaux.[12]

The recurring theme in each of these incidents is William's relationship with Bernard of Clairvaux, beginning with his first encounter—by William's own account a profound and life-changing event[13]—all the way until his final effort, near the end of his own life to write the hagiography of Bernard, whom William clearly viewed as a living saint. Bernard not only inspired William's monastic reform efforts but also William's desire to leave his Benedictine community and join the New Order himself, something Bernard did not approve. As influential as Bernard was on William, we are curiously pressed to find direct influence of Bernard on William's thought and writings. In the shadow of his famous friend, William retained his own identity and originality that he articulated so well in his own writings.

What might we conclude about William the man, the monk, and the writer from these vignettes of his life? William was indeed in the middle of the crossroads of 12th-century monastic life, both in his public role as abbot and in his private, interior life as a monk. From his spiritual and theological writings—the bulk of his works—we can see that, in spite of his public and polemical activities, he always desired above all else to seek and find God, to "go up to the mountain of the Lord" and be united with God and God alone:

> When the will mounts on high, like fire going up to its place, that is to say, when it unites with truth and tends toward higher things, it is *amor*. When it is fed with the milk of grace in order to make progress, it is

---

11   Sac alt, CCCM 88:53–91 (PL 180:344–366).

12   *Epistola de erroribus Guillelmi de Conchis*, CCCM 89A:61–71 (PL 180:333–340).

13   *Vita prima Bernardi* (Vita Bern) 33–34, CCCM 89B:58–59. ET: William of Saint-Thierry, Arnold of Bonneval, Geoffrey of Auxerre, *The First Life of Bernard of Clairvaux*, trans. Hillary Costello, OCSO, CF 76 (Collegeville, MN: Cistercian Publications, 2015), 38–40. For analysis of this meeting, see Marjory Lange, "Mediating a Presence: Rhetorical and Narrative Strategies in the *Vita Prima Bernardi*," in *Unity of Spirit: Studies on William of Saint-Thierry in Honor of E. Rozanne Elder*, (eds.) F. Tyler Sergent, Aage Rydstrøm-Poulsen, and Marsha L. Dutton, CS 268 (Collegeville, MN: Cistercian Publications, 2015), 117–43, esp. 138–40.

delectio. When it lays hold of its object and keeps it in its grasp and has enjoyment of it, it is *caritas*, it is unity of spirit, it is God...[14]

These words from William's most widely dispersed treatise, the *Letter to the Brothers of Mont Dieu* (*The Golden Epistle*), provide a summary of William's spiritual and intellectual desire to encounter God, to become united with God, and to "become not God but what God is".[15] Not only does this accurately describe the heart of William, it also represents the central theme (now come full circle) that we see throughout William's three decades of spiritual writings, from his first *On Contemplating God* to his last *The Golden Epistle*.

2   William of Saint-Thierry Scholarship Overview

Scholarship on William has for the most part come in the form of numerous articles, translations, editions, conference papers, but only a few monographs and collected essays. For more than a century now, William scholarship has successfully identified William's authentic works, produced Latin editions of all of his works, published translations (primarily French and English) of most of his works, explicated William's thought, investigated his sources, and provided historical analysis and context for understanding William in his own time and place while also fitting William into the broader Christian history and more specifically Cistercian monastic tradition, past and present.[16]

William scholarship might properly be categorized into two periods: early and recent. If we arbitrarily define the early period up through the 1950s, prominent scholars include Jean-Marie Déchanet, Marie-Madeleine Davy, Jacques Hourlier, and André Wilmart. Up to the 1950s, access to William's writings was limited primarily to the *Patrologia Cursus Completus* (Patrologia Latina) of J.-P. Migne. Although all of William's works were available in this monumental collection of Latin texts, they were not all correctly attributed. Thus, the responsibility for identifying William's complete corpus fell to scholars of

---

14   *Golden Epistle* (Ep frat), 235, CCCM 88:276. *Epistola ad fratres de Monte Dei* (*Epistola Aurea*), CCCM 88:223–289 (PL 180:307–364). ET: William of St. Thierry, *The Golden Epistle: A Letter to the Brethren of Mont Dieu*, trans. Theodore Berkeley, CF 12 (Kalamazoo, MI: Cistercian Publications, 1980).

15   Ep frat, 263, CCCM 88:282.

16   For an overview of (selective) scholarship on William from 1976 to 1998, see Paul Verdeyen, SJ, "En quoi la connaissance de Guillaume de Saint-Thierry a-t-elle progresse depuis le Colloque de 1976?," *Revue des sciences religieuses* 73 (1999): 17–20. For a detailed summary of William scholarship from 1998 to 2008, see Aage Rydstrøm-Poulsen, "Research on William of Saint-Thierry from 1998 to 2008," *Analecta Cisterciensia* 58 (2008): 158–69.

this early era. André Wilmart's seminal article in 1924 helped to accomplish this essential task.[17] More accurate and useful Latin editions of William's works began to be published especially in the 1950s through the painstaking work of M.-M. Davy and Jacques Hourlier.[18]

Jean-Marie Déchanet stands out as the first major scholar to analyze William's writings and thought—and to speculate, sometimes erroneously, on William's sources—in a way that set the course for future William studies, so much so that one cannot seriously study William today without engaging and demonstrating familiarity with Déchanet's work. In addition to numerous articles spanning from the 1930s to the 1960s, Déchanet published the first major influential monograph on William in 1942.[19] Although many of Déchanet's conclusions about William's thought, and especially his sources and influences, have been rejected by subsequent scholarship, Déchanet's place within William scholarship still remains formative and notable.

The recent era from the 1960s to the present has seen an eruption of scholarly articles, some monographs and collected essays along with critical editions of all of William's works, most of which have also been translated into English, French, and a few other languages. There are too many scholars devoted to William studies in the recent era to name, and many have been prolific for producing editions of William's works and especially analyzing William's thought.[20]

Among particular recent accomplishments furthering William scholarship is the publication of William's works in critical editions from 1989 to 2011 in six volumes in the *Corpus Christianorum Continuatio Mediaevalis* series from Brepols Publishers.[21] Although earlier editions remain useful—and according

---

17   André Wilmart, "La seri et la date des ouvrages de Guillaume de Saint-Thierry," *Revue Mabillon* 14 (1924): 156–67.

18   See the Works of William of Saint-Thierry in this volume for the editions produced by Davy and Hourlier.

19   J.-M. Déchanet, *Guillaume de Saint-Thierry, l'homme et son oeuvre* (Bruges: Charles Beyaert, 1942); so important was this work that an English version was published thirty years later as *William of St.-Thierry: The Man and His Work*, trans. Richard Strachan, CS 10 (Spencer, MA: Cistercian Publications, 1972). André Adam's monograph in 1923 was the first dedicated to William's life and works, but it lacked the long-term significance of Déchanet's; see Adam, *Guillaume de Saint-Thierry. Sa vie et ses oeuvres* (Bourg: Impr. Du Journal de l'Ain, 1924).

20   For a bibliography of scholarly works on William up to 2004, especially focused on the recent era, see F. Tyler Sergent, "A Bibliography of William of Saint Thierry," in *Truth as Gift: Studies in Medieval Cistercian History in Honor of John R. Sommerfeldt*, (eds.) Marsha L. Dutton, Daniel M. LaCorte, and Paul Lockey, CS 204 (Kalamazoo, MI: Cistercian Publications, 2004), 457–82.

21   Volumes 86 (1989), 87 (1997), 88 (2003), 89 (2005), 89A (2007), 89B (2011). Each is listed in this volume with full bibliographical information in the Works of William of Saint-Thierry, 229–34.

to some scholars, superior[22]—having all of William's works available in this one series increases accessibility for scholars and students of William alike. The bulk of these new editions has been produced by Paul Verdeyen, SJ, of the University of Antwerp.[23] This present volume relies on these critical editions (except where noted otherwise).

In the last three decades or so of scholarship, only two original English language books have been published on William. The first, David N. Bell's monograph on the Augustinian nature of William's spirituality from 1984, remains essential scholarship for anyone investigating William's intellectual framework.[24] The second and more recent publication, a collection of essays in honor of E. Rozanne Elder published in 2015, provides new perspectives on William's writings and thought, although only five of the nine chapters focus exclusively on William, while the other four emphasize William as compared to Bernard of Clairvaux's thought or the portrait of Bernard in William's *Vita prima Bernardi*.[25] As a result of this paucity of English language scholarly books, this *Companion to William of Saint-Thierry* fulfills the need for more book-length scholarly publications on William and provides an overview with in-depth research that will be useful for both scholars and students, while it also benefits from the existing scholarship, including the now available critical editions of William's corpus of writings.

3   Companion to William of Saint-Thierry

The chapters in this book represent scholarship that spans the last fifty years of William studies and include both established and new scholars among the international contributors. Each chapter offers new, original research, informed by up-to-date scholarship, and addresses one or more categories typically incorporated into each volume of this Brill series: life, works, thought, and influence of the historical figure. In the first chapter, Brian Patrick McGuire introduces us to William of Saint-Thierry's life and works by sketching a biography, based on careful analysis of the *Vita antiqua* (*Life of William of*

---

22   See David N. Bell's chapter, "The Mystical Theology and Theological Mysticism of William of Saint-Thierry," 70, n. 14 in this volume plus Bell's published reviews of these editions.

23   Notable as well among these newly published volumes are reproduced earlier Latin editions by Stanislaus Ceglar, Albert Poncelet, SJ, Antony Van Burink, and Christine Vande Veire.

24   David N. Bell, *The Image and Likeness: The Augustinian Spirituality of William of St. Thierry*, CS 78 (Kalamazoo, MI: Cistercian Publications, 1984).

25   *Unity of Spirit: Studies on William of Saint-Thierry in Honor of E. Rozanne Elder*, (eds.) F. Tyler Sergent, Aage Rydstrøm-Poulsen, and Marsha L. Dutton, CS 268 (Collegeville, MN: Cistercian Publications, 2015).

Saint-Thierry), and setting forth a chronology of his life as a monk and writer. Through this chronology of William's life and works, we are also provided the historical and intellectual context for each work in William's corpus. McGuire astutely emphasizes William's relationship with Bernard of Clairvaux and its importance in William's life from their first meeting until William's death, as well as William's essential role in our understanding of Bernard through the *Vita prima Bernardi*.

In my own chapter, I provide a brief overview of the scholarly questions and debates over the sources that influenced William's written works and his thought. The assertions made in the early period of William scholarship, particularly by Jean-Marie Déchanet, that William could access and relied directly on Greek Christian sources went unchallenged until the recent period of scholarship, most notably in the work of David N. Bell. His careful and critical analysis of William's Augustinian and overall western intellectual framework—along with direct source material in quotations from, allusions to, and clear influence by Augustine's writings—demonstrated definitively that William did not rely on eastern Greek sources for his intellectual and spiritual views. The debate has not ended here: there still remains the need to determine in specific detail what other western sources apart from Augustine that we might identify as influential on William. Using two examples of key terms in William's writings, *ratio fidei* ("reason of faith") and *fruitio* ("enjoyment"), I show that western medieval authors from the intervening centuries between Augustine and William also provided source material for him, including Hilary of Poitiers, John Scotus Eriugena, Gregory the Great, Paschasius Radbertus, and Rabanus Maurus.

David N. Bell's chapter explicates in depth the central contribution of William's thought and works: mystical theology and theological mysticism. He provides historically grounded and practical definitions for both terms in order to situate William within his fundamental context: the Christian monk in search of God in prayer and life. The spirituality that comes from William's theological mysticism is neither Marian nor Christocentric; rather, it is Augustinian and built on the foundations of the human being having been created in the image and likeness of God (Gen 1:26), the doctrine of the Trinity, and the power of love ("a vehement, well-ordered will")[26] for accessing God, for experiencing God, and ultimately for being united with God.

Aage Rydstrøm-Poulsen provides much needed scholarly attention to William's work *De natura animae* (*On the Nature of the Soul*) and the concept of the human soul found there. William's understanding of the soul, once again, begins with the scriptural precept that human beings were created in the image and likeness of God (Gen 1:26); in medieval anthropology, the image resides in the human soul, which is rational. Reason in itself can lead one to

---

26   Contemp, 14; CCCM 88:162–163.

the good or the bad, and so the rational soul, influenced by the Holy Spirit, is key to guiding human reason. In addition, the human soul is a kind of trinity with memory, deliberation, and will. The desired result is that the soul and God become "one in love, one in beatitude, one in immortality and incorruption, one even in some way the divinity itself".[27]

E. Rozanne Elder addresses William's view of the renewal of the human person—the process of redemption and salvation—along the spiritual path toward God. She explains this central aspect of William's thought within the context of his *Disputatio adversus Petrum Abaelardum* (*Disputation against Peter Abelard*) and the Trinitarian issues regarding faith and salvation that Abelard's views aroused in William. While analyzing William's point by point arguments against Abelard and the questions he raised, Elder demonstrates that William's writings, and thus his thought, after this encounter were directly influenced by these questions as William determined to provide adequate answers that Abelard, in William's estimation, had failed to do. Of particular concern was the question of how Christ's death as a sacrifice to God was redemptive for humankind. William's last three theological (and spiritual) treatises were *Speculum Fidei* (*The Mirror of Faith*), *Aenigma Fidei* (*The Enigma of Faith*), and *The Golden Epistle*. All responded to this very question and articulated most fully William's theory of redemption, carefully integrated with his view of the soul's ascent to God. Although William and Abelard held several ideas in common, a key difference between the two writers lay in their goal: Abelard sought *scientia* ("knowledge") and William sought *sapientia* ("wisdom").

Thomas X. Davis, OCSO, provides what few can, a perspective on William's relevance to contemporary spirituality formed from a lifetime study of William from within the communal life and ascesis of the Order of Cistercians of the Strict Observance. He articulates the theological and spiritual legacy that William offers, especially in his concept of participation in the Trinitarian life through human *concientia*, defined as both conscience and consciousness. Davis begins with the critical question that Jesus posed to his disciples: "Who do you say that I am?"[28] For believers within the Christian community, this remains always a central, contemporary, and essential question to be answered so that one's faith in Jesus as the Christ—whether a 12th-century monk or a 21st-century student—has a concrete foundation on which to be built. To put this into William's intellectual and faith-based framework, Davis focuses on William's teaching about how Christ dwells within a person by faith and grace and how the effects of this indwelling restore and transfigure the person's life based on the image and likeness to God with which human beings were created (Gen 1:26)—by now a familiar touchstone for William's readers. For William, faith and

---

27   *On the Nature of the Soul* (Phys an), 107, CCCM 88:141.
28   Matt 16:13, Mark 8:27, Luke 9:18.

the work of Christ further manifest in experiential participation in the Trinity. Thomas X. Davis's chapter provides the first thorough analysis of *conscientia* in William's thought. Davis crafts this chapter by masterfully and comprehensively pulling from William's writings to show William's own analytical, developing— yet consistent—understanding of *conscientia* and its significance in William's conceptualization of spiritual progress and union with God.

Nathaniel Peters offers a welcome investigation into Eucharistic theology, a part of William's thought rarely addressed within the scholarship. Peters's analysis naturally begins with William's Eucharistic text, *De sacramento altaris* (*On the Sacrament of the Altar*), but it also takes into consideration William's other works up through and including the *Golden Epistle*. In this way, we have the first English language holistic treatment of William as a sacramental theologian. Central themes addressed by Peters include the presence of Christ in the Eucharist and how it is received both physically and spiritually; the Eucharist as church (body of Christ); how the sacramental participation in the Trinity is a provisional foretaste of eternal participation and union with God; and the image of the kiss from the *Song of Songs* that William employs to describe the union and participation found in the sacrament. Putting William's sacramental theology into the larger context of his overall mystical theology helps to elucidate both and to illuminate the significance of the Eucharist throughout William's *corpus*.

The final chapter investigates William's influence in the later Middle Ages as Glenn E. Myers explores in detail how William's teachings on spiritual progress, participation in the Trinity, and ultimate mystical union with God can be found in the sermons of the 14th-century German Dominican Johannes Tauler, a concrete example of William's *Golden Epistle* as a source and direct influence on a later medieval writer. To accomplish this, Myers guides the reader steadily through the process by which Tauler would have read William's text in manuscripts readily available, then shows precisely—in spite of the language transition from William's Latin to Tauler's Middle High German—where Tauler's sermons rely directly on passages from the *Golden Epistle*. Myers's contribution affords us a thorough accounting of how William's concept of spiritual union informed and helped to form Tauler's own understanding of this culmination of the spiritual journey.

The reader will undoubtedly recognize that within the different categories by which this volume looks at William of Saint-Thierry—his life, works, thought, and influence—there are certain recurring and overlapping themes. This is quite appropriate. For the historical person of William provides us with an intellectual world and spiritual insights that permeate each facet of his life and career as a 12th-century monk and writer. Indeed, the elements of his intellect and spirituality transcend his own time and place.

CHAPTER 1

A Chronology and Biography of William of Saint-Thierry

Brian Patrick McGuire

1 Introduction

There is perhaps only a single date in the life of William of Saint-Thierry which is more or less certain, that of his death on 8 September 1148.[1] Otherwise we are left to conjectures and erudite research discussions in order to determine how his life developed and when he wrote the spiritual works that are probably more available today than at any time since the 12th century. It is important to realize that William is very much a product of 20th century scholarly research. Within a few decades of his death, his name was all but forgotten, except at the abbey of Signy, and his works were attributed to other writers, and especially to Bernard of Clairvaux.[2] When the Paris theologian Jean Gerson in the 1390s warned his students against speculative theology and recommended mystical theology, he referred to Bernard of Clairvaux but actually was recommending William.[3] It is only in the 17th century that the learned Bernard Tissier made it clear that it was William and not Bernard who had written the *Letter to the Brothers of Mont Dieu*, known as the *Golden Epistle*.[4] Later this attribution was challenged, and it is only with the tireless work of the Benedictine scholar André Wilmart that the writings of William were established and given approximate datings.[5] Although Wilmart's findings are not all followed today, he gave scholarship a point of departure for the text editions of the last decades. In this study I will be for the most part following the datings provided

---

1 Paul Verdeyen, "Introduction Generale," xxiii, in *Guillelmi a Sancto Theodorico Opera Omnia*. CCCM 86 (Turnholt: Brepols, 1989). References to the works of William will be to the Corpus Christianorum edition, abbreviated as CCCM with the volume number and page.

2 See Jean-Marie Déchanet, "Introduction," *The Golden Epistle*, CF 12 (Kalamazoo, MI: Cistercian Publications, 1980), ix–xiii.

3 Brian Patrick McGuire, *Jean Gerson and the Last Medieval Reformation* (University Park, PA: Pennsylvania State University Press, 2005), 137.

4 Déchanet, "Introduction," *Golden Epistle*, x.

5 André Wilmart, "La série et la date des ouvrages de Guillaume de Saint-Thierry," *Revue Mabillon* 14 (1924): 157–67.

by Paul Verdeyen, who spent years preparing the critical editions of all of
William's works now available in the *Corpus Christianorum Continuatio Mediaevalis* series.[6]

2   The Witness of the *Vita Antiqua*

Probably some decades after William's death, a monk of Signy composed a
brief *vita* of William. The *Vita antiqua* was first published in 1908 and is now
available in a critical edition, as well as in English and French translations.[7]
It is a hagiographical work, but so far as we know it was not used in any process of canonization. Part of the text was later mutilated and lost, so we lack
some essential passages about William's early life. Another problem is that
the author apparently did not know William personally but depended for his
narrative on what he was told by those who had been close to him. The work
has been mainly used for fishing out "facts" about William, but I think it needs
to be considered as a whole in terms of what it tells about William's inner life,
his visions and search for the mystical life.

I borrow here from David Bell's translation, which also provides an excellent
introduction to the work. The surviving text tells us that William was born
in Liège, *clarus gen(ere)*, a phrase usually translated as "of noble parentage,"
but I wonder if the phrase should be pushed this far. Could it not simply be
a hagiographical convention and not necessarily a clear statement about
William's family? At this point was originally mentioned a certain Simon, and
scholarship has discussed ever since whether the man was William's brother,
but the relationship seems to me unclear, and I would prefer to leave the
matter open. The surviving text, however, tells how Simon later became abbot
of St. Nicholas aux Bois, while William became abbot of Saint-Thierry. Thus
our author passes quickly over the first decades of William's life and arrives at
1121, which is probably the date for his election at Saint-Thierry.

I will return later to William's probable activities in the first two decades
of the 12th century, but for the time being I think it best to follow the thread of
the *vita* in order to understand how a Cistercian monk of Signy remembered the
man. We find here a reminder that medieval people had different priorities

---

6 Most recently, Paul Verdeyen, "La chronologie des œuvres de Guillaume de Saint-Thierry,"
   Ons geestelijk erf (2011): 190–203.
7 *Vita antiqua* (Vita ant). First published in A. Poncelet, "Vie ancienne de Guillaume de
   Saint-Thierry," *Mélanges Godefroid Kurth*, vol. 1 (Liège, 1908), 85–96. Now available in CCCM
   89:117–22. The French translation is in Paul Verdeyen, *Guillaume de Saint-Thierry, premier auteur mystique des anciens Pays-Bas* (Turnhout: Brepols, 2003), 138–50. ET: David N. Bell, "The
   Vita Antiqua of William of St. Thierry," *Cistercian Studies* [*Quarterly*] 11 (1976): 246–55.

than our own. For them "facts" in terms of names and dates were much less important than the recollection of what took place in the inner lives of the persons they portrayed. Our author tells how William on a journey was overcome with a desire to sleep. Lying down under a roadside tree, he had a vision of a woman "who gently took his head with her own hands and rested it in her lap." William felt a "holy and spiritual joy" and when he got up again, he had no need to complete his journey but "returned to the place from which he had started out."[8] This must be Saint-Thierry, where William is said to have "taught the Christian life and the monastic rule in words, and demonstrated them by example."[9] Our author has used a familiar cliché and indicated that he had no special knowledge about William's life as abbot.

The next section introduces Bernard and William's friendship with him. "This same Bernard wrote him many letters and also a book, *On Grace and Free Will,* and that work called *The Apology* was also intended for him."[10] William is said to have been attracted to Bernard and the Cistercian life: "Stirred by the purity of the order and inflamed with the desire for solitude and spiritual quiet," he left his abbacy "and at Signy assumed the habit of that holy poverty."[11] Our author makes no mention of what we know from Bernard's own letters: that William first asked his friend if he could become a monk of Clairvaux, but Bernard refused him. But the transition is seen as traumatic, for the source mentions how William's "brethren and fellow abbots" went to the archbishop of Reims to get him to return to Saint-Thierry. At this point William received another vision of Mary, who encouraged him to remain where he was. But William was still in doubt, especially because of the demands of Cistercian asceticism in terms of diet and manual labor. William confided in a friend and prayed for help, and thereafter the harsh way of life became attractive to him. Hardly was this trial over when William became very ill. His prior was caring for him and had a vision of "a certain venerable lady", probably Mary, who called herself "the Lady of Bazoches".[12] She gave the prior furs to cover William, and these apparently cured him. The *vita* also gives us some limited insight into William's everyday life at Signy. Because of his age and weakness, he could not fully participate in manual labor, but he did help out in piling manure into a cart. He insisted on using not a shovel but his bare hands.

At this point our author lists the works written by William, a fairly complete review, and then speaks of his death and a post-mortem vision of William

---

8   Vita Ant, CCCM 89:117. ET: Bell, "*Vita Antiqua,*" 248.
9   Vita Ant, CCCM 89:117: "Ubi cum vitam christianam et monasticam disciplinam verbo doceret, exemplo monstraret...." ET: Bell, "*Vita Antiqua,*" 249.
10   Vita Ant, CCCM 89:117. ET: Bell, "*Vita Antiqua,*" 249.
11   Vita Ant, CCCM 89:117. ET: Bell, "*Vita Antiqua,*" 249.
12   Vita Ant, CCCM 89:119. ET: Bell, "*Vita Antiqua,*" 250–51.

experienced by a brother of Signy. The writer almost apologizes for the fact that when he originally was told about William, he did not intend to write a hagiography: "I did not then intend to write them [the stories] down and I did not take pains to search out the many other stories."[13] Now that he had decided to do so, his source was no longer available to him. This statement indicates that our author conveyed what he had heard from someone who had known William.

The *Vita antiqua* is an important source for William because it indicates that he was remembered at Signy with fondness and even love. Stories of his visions of Mary, his manual labor, and his illnesses were conveyed from one generation to the next. At the end of the narrative, our author especially notes how William "joined himself to a stricter order for the sake of a greater love of purity and certainty of salvation."[14] What William did before he arrived at Signy is of secondary importance for our author. It is his friendship with Bernard and his joining Signy that are points of departure for this celebration of William's Cistercian life.

3   The Early Years (1075?–1115)

William's year of birth is given, without hesitation, as 1075 by Paul Verdeyen in his useful chronology for William of Saint-Thierry from 2011.[15] In an earlier treatment from 1989 he admits that "it is not easy to establish an exact chronology of the life of William."[16] He points out that André Wilmart and Jean-Marie Déchanet prefer 1085, while Ludo Milis, after a careful review of the facts, lands on 1075–80 but concedes that this is "nothing more than the result of conjecture."[17] I can only conclude that we simply do not know, and it should be sufficient to say that William was born in the last decades of the 11th century.

There is no doubt that William was born at Liège, for this is established in the original *vita*. Liège had been since Carolingian times an ecclesiastical

---

13   Vita Ant, CCCM 89:122. ET: Bell, "*Vita Antiqua*," 255.
14   Vita Ant, CCCM 89:122. ET: Bell, "*Vita Antiqua*," 255.
15   Paul Verdeyen, "La chronologie des œuvres," 190. The best treatment I have found for William's origins is Ludo Milis, "William of Saint Thierry: His Birth, His Formation, and His First Monastic Experiences," in *William. Abbot of St. Thierry. A Colloquium at the Abbey of St. Thierry*, Cistercian Studies 94 (Kalamazoo, MI: Cistercian Publications, 1987), 9–33, esp. 16–20. This volume is a translation of *Saint-Thierry. Une abbaye de Vie au XXe siècle*, from 1979.
16   Verdeyen, "Introduction", CCCM 89, v.
17   Milis, "William of Saint Thierry," 20.

center and a place of learning. Some scholarship has claimed that Liège by the end of the 11th century was in intellectual decline,[18] but it seems clear that a boy learning Latin would not have needed an advanced state of studies. What matters is that William, probably together with his companion Simon, left Liège and entered monastic life at the abbey of Saint Nicaise in Reims. According to the *vita* they first studied here but then "took on the habit of religion."[19] This was a decisive step: William left the world of the cathedral schools and instead committed himself to a monastic vocation, a calling that he would follow for the rest of his life. But his writings reveal that he kept in contact with the world of the schools and could be quite critical of it.

Verdeyen admitted in 1989 that the reason for William's monastic vocation "escapes us."[20] But he assumes that William, probably together with his brother or friend Simon, studied liberal arts both at Liège and Reims.[21] Verdeyen compares William's monastic and intellectual formation to that of Bernard. I think it needs to be added here that William grew up in a time of crisis and change in the Western Church. The Gregorian reform was still having an impact, and there was a yearning for a return to the sources of Christian life in the New Testament. Northern France and what today is Belgium were the sites of a dynamic new clerical and monastic culture.[22] We concentrate today especially on the "schools" of Laon and Chartres, but virtually every cathedral had its own masters and often ambitious reforming bishops. It must have been an exciting time to be alive for a young man who was curious about learning and at the same time felt attracted to the monastic life.

The date for William's entrance at Saint Nicaise is conjectural, but in his most recent work Verdeyen has given it as about 1105.[23] What is certain, as Verdeyen points out, is that Saint Nicaise was "a flourishing and fervent community."[24] The abbot was known for his devotion to the Rule of Saint Benedict, and even

---

18   Milis, "William of Saint Thierry," 14–15.

19   Vita Ant, CCCM 89:117. ET: Bell, "*Vita Antiqua*," 248.

20   Verdeyen, "Introduction," CCCM 89, vii.

21   The question of William's education has been debated frequently, yet the early assertion that William studied at Laon has never been demonstrated. To the contrary, the prevailing view for two decades now is that he likely received his liberal arts education in Liège and his theological education (or more liberal arts) at Reims, as noted by Verdeyen. See also Milis, "William of Saint Thierry," 21–23.

22   There are numerous studies of the rise of scholastic culture in Western Europe, but I have been especially inspired by R.W. Southern, *Scholastic Humanism and the Unification of Europe*, vol. 1: Foundations (Oxford: Blackwell, 1995).

23   For further details on the reforming efforts at Saint Nicaise and William's entrance, see Milis, "William of Saint Thierry," 23–25.

24   Verdeyen, "Introduction," CCCM 89, viii.

if we have no writings of William from this period, it is safe to conclude that he here completed his monastic formation, at least prior to his first meeting with Bernard of Clairvaux. The entrance of Bernard into the life of William should not overshadow the fact that the monk of Saint Nicaise was probably in his forties before he visited the abbot of Clairvaux.

4   William and Bernard (1116?–1145)

It would be a mistake to attribute William's profound spiritual insights to Bernard alone, but there is no doubt that the first and subsequent contacts with the abbot of Clairvaux had a deep influence on William's inner life. William told the story of the first meeting in his own hagiography of Bernard, what became the first book of the *Vita Prima*: "It was at that time that I began to be a regular visitor at Clairvaux and to see him."[25] William came with "another abbot," who must have been the abbot of Saint Nicaise, Joran. He felt totally overwhelmed by the sight of the man and "overflowed with such affection for that man ... I would have desired nothing more than to remain with him forever and be at his disposal."[26] William was overwhelmed by Bernard's ascetic life but also appalled by the lack of sensible care given the abbot in his illness. William says he stayed with Bernard for a few days and found here "the ancient ways of our fathers the Egyptian monks." This was for him "the golden age of Clairvaux."[27]

There is no doubt that the meeting with Bernard changed William's life and gave him a focus and a goal that he set for himself during the remainder of his life. For him Bernard represented the incarnation of the monastic life, and he later did his best to spend as much time as possible with Bernard. Best known is the story of how Bernard during yet another bout of illness invited William to Clairvaux, when William also was sick.[28] The two of them had time to discuss the Song of Songs and how it is to be understood, an inspiration both to Bernard's sermons and to William's writings on the Song. But William admitted in his narrative that there was a struggle between the two friends, because when he felt sufficiently strong to return to his monastery, Bernard saw to it that William again became ill. Bernard got his way and made sure that there was more time for spiritual conversations.

---

25   Vita Bern, I.33. ET: *The First Life of Bernard of Clairvaux*, trans. Hilary Costello, OCSO, CF 76 (Collegeville, MN: Cistercian Publications, 2015), 38.
26   Vita Bern, I.33. ET: *The First Life of Bernard*, 38.
27   Vita Bern, I.35. ET: *The First Life of Bernard*, 40.
28   Vita Bern, I.59–60. ET: *The First Life of Bernard*, 61–64.

Paul Verdeyen has placed the first meeting between William and Bernard at 1118–1119, while Verdeyen dates William's convalescence at Clairvaux to 1124.[29] As so often in medieval history, exact dates are hard to come by, but what matters here is that we know William found his way to Clairvaux and experienced the charismatic powers of Bernard. We do not know, however, if he returned to Clairvaux or met Bernard personally at a later date, and our ignorance means that when William in the mid-1140s was writing his biography of Bernard, he was basing his portrait of the man and his monastery on what he had himself experienced some decades earlier.[30]

During Lent of 1121, William was elected abbot of Saint-Thierry, a Benedictine house outside of Rheims.[31] He thus left a city monastery for one in the nearby countryside, and it was to be expected by his surroundings that he would have kept the post the rest of his active life. But his first meeting with Bernard had brought about a strong desire to enter into the new monasticism of Cîteaux and probably to become a monk of Clairvaux. Because of William's new desire, we can get a fuller impression of the person he had become in his devotion to Bernard. He must have written his friend of his desire. We do not have William's letter, but Bernard's answer exists, in which he warns William against resigning his abbatial post:

> If I am to say what I think, I must tell you that, unless I am mistaken, it is something I could not advise you to attempt and you could not carry out … I say hold on to what you have got, remain where you are, and try to benefit those over whom you rule. Do not try to escape the responsibility of your office while you are still able to discharge it for the benefit of your subjects.[32]

This letter must have been a blow to William, but he remained as abbot of Saint-Thierry until 1135, at which time he found his own Cistercian home at

---

29   Paul Verdeyen, "La chronologie des œuvres," 193. Ceglar, however, puts this second meeting at 1128. See Stanley Ceglar, "The Date of William's Convalescence at Clairvaux," *Cistercian Studies Quarterly* 30.1 (1995): 27–33, esp. 30–31.

30   Perhaps, however, in the heat of the Abelard controversy in 1140, there was a meeting of the two men. See below.

31   See the careful calculation of Stanislaus Ceglar, "William of Saint Thierry and His Leading Role at the First Chapters of the Benedictine Abbots (Reims 1131, Soissons 1132)," in *William, Abbot of Saint Thierry: A Colloquium at the Abbey of St. Thierry*, trans. Jerry Carfantan, CS 94 (Kalamazoo, MI: Cistercian Publications, 1987), 46, n. 47.

32   Letter 86, dated to 1123, in *Sancti Bernardi Opera*, vol. 7, (eds.) Jean Leclercq and Henri Rochais (Rome: Editiones Cistercienses, 1974) (SBOp). ET: Bruno Scott James, *The Letters of St Bernard of Clairvaux* (Kalamazoo, MI: Cistercian Publications 1998), 128. (Letter 88 in James).

Signy. Verdeyen has pointed to one of William's *Meditations* as indicating his dissatisfaction with his way of life at Saint-Thierry.[33] Part of the passage reads thus: "A shepherd who is not a hireling, even though he lays down his life for the sheep, scarcely meets all their needs. But it is a very serious thing for him to be in charge of the flock, when he cannot give it profitable service ... O that a superior might know his own limitations! Woe is us for this, for we have sinned."[34] The language is too general to be applied specifically to William's situation, but it is certainly possible that he was reflecting on a sense of inadequacy.

Perhaps the best indication of the complex relationship between Bernard and William is another letter, probably from this same period in the 1120s when he was considering resigning. Bernard was responding to a now lost letter of William's, and the context allows us to surmise that William had accused Bernard of loving him less than he, William, loved Bernard. The abbot of Clairvaux turned the tables on William and told him he did not know what he was claiming: "You may be right when you say that my affection for you is less than yours is for me, but I am certainly certain that you cannot be certain."[35] The letter is a rhetorical masterpiece, but it also contains what appears to me genuine expression of affection. Bernard told William that he did care about him: "Why do you try to reach me and complain that you are not able? You could reach me if you but considered what I am; and you can reach me still whenever you wish, if you are content to find me as I am and not as you wish me to be."[36]

Just at this critical time in the mid-1120s, William was involved with Bernard in the latter's formulation of an attack on Cluniac practices, and so William was sent the work, the *Apologia*, as Bernard's fulfillment of the abbot of Saint-Thierry's wish: "Spurred on by the need for action, mine is the painful position of having no alternative but to comply.... How can I possibly keep quiet when I hear your complaints?"[37] A few years later Bernard dedicated to William his treatise *On Grace and Free Will*. Its prologue is dedicated to William and perhaps reflects conversations in which they had engaged at Clairvaux.[38] At every step of the way in the 1120s, the abbot of Saint-Thierry and the abbot

---

33   Verdeyen, *Guillaume de Saint-Thierry, premier auteur*, 31.

34   *Meditation* 11.7-8. ET: Sister Penelope, in *On Contemplating God, Prayer, Meditations*, CF 3 (Kalamazoo, MI: Cistercian Publications, 1977), 160–61. CCCM 89:65, §16 and 17. The section divisions are different in the Latin text than in the English translation.

35   Letter 85, SBOp, 7:220. ET: James, *The Letters of St Bernard*, 125 (Letter 87).

36   Letter 85, SBOp, 7:222. ET: James, *The Letters of St Bernard*, 127.

37   *An Apologia to Abbot William, Sancti Bernardi Opera*, vol. 3 (Rome: Editiones Cistercienses, 1963), 81 (SBOp). ET: *Cistercians and Cluniacs: St. Bernard's Apologia to Abbot William*, trans. Michael Casey, CF 1A (Kalamazoo, MI: Cistercian Publications, 1970), 33.

38   SBOp, 3:165.

of Clairvaux seem to have been in contact with each other, intellectually, spiritually, affectively. But Bernard insisted that William keep his distance and preserve his vocation, while William sought ever more contact and closeness. By the time the 1130s came and Bernard took on his star role in solving the papal schism (1130–1138) by supporting Pope Innocent II against Antipope Anacletus II, their contact could not continue, and so it is fascinating that in the 1140s William chose to take on the writing of Bernard's hagiography. By then he was looking back on the good old days of the 1120s, as we shall see when I consider the *Vita Prima* more closely. But for the time being I will turn to William's earlier literary works, as a guideline to the development of his life. I will present each work individually and provide a few remarks about its content, without going into detail. In this way, I hope to provide a sense of the intellectual and spiritual interests that characterized the last decades of William's life.

5   William at Saint-Thierry

There is no reason to doubt that William was literarily active as a monk of Saint Nicaise, but the earliest extant work of his belongs to his abbacy at Saint-Thierry. *On Contemplating God* (*De contemplando Deo*) was written, according to Verdeyen, between 1121 and 1124.[39] It is a fully formed work of the spiritual life, written by a man mature in his thinking. His reflections regularly turn into prayers, in the same manner as we can find in Bernard's Sermons on the Song of Songs. We may ask whether Bernard was influenced by William in this respect, but of course both of them could have drawn on the writings of Saint Augustine, especially his *Confessions*, which are an extended prayer to God.

Much longer is *The Nature and Dignity of Love* (*De natura et dignitate amoris*), starting out with the assertion that the art of arts is the art of love: *ars est artium ars amoris*.[40] William reviews the different types of love and speaks of the image of the Trinity within us. Ever trained in the schools, he carefully distinguishes between *affectus* and *affectio*. For William, *affectus* is a persevering relationship of love to the good, while *affectio* is a fickle attachment to anything.[41] The work can be looked upon at times as almost autobiographical in terms of William's own spiritual development, as when he speaks of the "special school of charity," which seeks solutions "not by reasoning" but "by experience."[42]

---

39   Verdeyen, "La chronologie des œuvres," 200.

40   Nat am, 1, CCCM 88:177. ET: *The Nature and Dignity of Love*, trans. Thomas X. Davis, CF 30 (Kalamazoo, MI: Cistercian Publication, 1981), 53.

41   Nat am, 28. ET: *The Nature and Dignity of Love*, 70.

42   Nat am, 26, CCCM 88:198: "Haec est specialis caritatis schola ... solutiones non ratiocinationibus tantum, quantum ratione et ipsa rerum veritate et experientia terminantur."

On the Sacrament of the Altar (*De sacramento altaris*) is a polemical work, attacking the Eucharistic theology of the distinguished Rupert, abbot of Deutz. Wilmart in 1924 dated it to about 1128, while Verdeyen places it at 1127.[43] Thanks to the work of John van Engen we can see this work in its full context.[44] Rupert had distinguished between the body of Christ (*Corpus Domini*) and the body of sacrifice (*Corpus sacrificii*), a definition that William found to be almost heretical. He preferred the traditional distinction between the hidden substance, the body and blood of Christ, and the visible species of bread and wine. Rupert narrowly escaped a formal condemnation.

The Prologue of the work is a brief letter to Bernard, one more indication that during these years William was living and thinking in regular contact with his friend. He told Bernard that he had taken his arguments (*rationes*) from the statements of the Fathers and especially from Augustine. Now he had decided to bring these ideas together into a whole, and he asked Bernard to correct the result, so that "my work also may be yours, since what I have done you will have corrected."[45] William concluded that what he issued forth would be more the words of the Fathers than his own, but a review of his sources indicates that the text is very much his own synthesis. The work takes up forty pages in the *Corpus Christianorum* edition. The work reveals how William had been trained in the schools and had brought his learning with him into the monastery. He asks how a Christian is to approach the faith, and what faith is.[46] He defines the visible appearance in the sacrament of the body of the Lord and uses Boethius to express what in the sacrifice is according to nature and what is above nature. He warns that not all who receive the body of the Lord corporally from participation in the sacrament of the altar are filled spiritually with heavenly blessings and grace.[47] In the later part of the treatise he is moving towards a fuller definition of the term sacrament. The last few pages are a pastiché of statements about the Eucharist from the Fathers, especially Augustine.

---

43   Verdeyen, "La chronologie des œuvres," 198. John Van Engen provides a much earlier alternative dating; see Van Engen, "Rupert of Deutz and William of Saint-Thierry," *Revue bénédictine* 93 (1983): 326–36. An English translation is in progress: William of Saint-Thierry, *Letter to Rupert of Deutz, On the Sacrament of the Altar, and On the Errors of William of Conches*, trans. with intro. F. Tyler Sergent and Nathaniel Peters, CF 82 (Collegeville, MN: Cistercian Publications, forthcoming).

44   John Van Engen, *Rupert of Deutz* (Berkeley: University of California Press, 1983), 136–58.

45   Sac alt, Prol., "...et meum opus et vestrum sit,– cum ego fecerim, vos correxeritis....," CCCM 88:53.

46   Sac alt, Prol., "Quomodo christiano expediat accedere ad fidem, et quid sit ipsa fides," CCCM 88:53.

47   Sac alt, 8, CCCM 88:68.

It is my impression that William put aside the work before it was completely finished and so chose to leave behind this amalgam of patristic *sententiae*. In these pages we find the imprint of the debates about the Eucharist that had raged in the cathedral schools since the time of Berengar (d. 1088).[48] Until theologians could make use of the Aristotelian distinction between substance and accidents, various inadequate formulae were suggested to explain how the body and blood of Christ could exist together with or independently of the bread and wine. William chose to join the discussion, apparently because he was worried that Rupert's distinctions were contrary to the faith. If we try to characterize the theological writings of this period according to a rigid distinction between scholastic and monastic theology, we are bound to oversimplify the synthetic union of faith and understanding that we find in such a treatise.

The twelve *Meditations* cover the entire period from 1125–1137, at least according to Verdeyen.[49] They are found in a single manuscript, probably written at Saint-Thierry. They are the fruit of William's *lectio divina*, for each of them takes its point of departure in a Psalm verse. In the first *Meditation* William considers God's foreknowledge and predestination. The second *Meditation* deals with the Trinity, beginning with Psalm 33:6: "Come unto him and be enlightened and your faces shall not be ashamed." *Meditation* 3 concentrates on William's longing to see God and the joy that vision will bring. *Meditation* 4 asks for the gift of prayer and describes William's former state of desolation. There may be an autobiographical element in this section: "Therefore, O Lord, I hid myself among the trees of paradise, therefore I fled away to dark places ... not from you, Lord, but to you and abode in the wilderness. And there I wait for you."[50]

Meditation 5 considers the different kinds of prayer and the sight of Christ on the cross. *Meditation* 6 describes the joy of the blessed, "these blessings that were hidden in your secret heaven through the ages." *Meditation* 7 emphasizes longing to see God: "My heart has spoken of you and my face has sought you," while *Meditation* 8 turns to the kiss and embrace of the Bridegroom and the Bride in the Song of Songs, one of William's favored themes in his later

---

48   For background, see Étienne Gilson, *Christian Philosophy in the Middle Ages* (London: Sheed and Ward, 1955), 615, n. 41.

49   *Meditationes devotissimae (Med)*, CCCM 89:3–80. ET: *On Contemplating God, Prayer, Meditations*, trans. Sister Penelope [Lawson], CF 3 (Kalamazoo, MI: Cistercian Publications, 1977), 77–190. Verdeyen, "La chronologie des œuvres," 197.

50   Med 4.5, "Ideo, Domine, abscondi me intra ligna paradisi, ideo refugi in tenebras meas ... non tamen a te, sed ad te, et mansi in solitudine. Ibi te exspecto....," CCCM 89:21. ET: *Meditations*, 112.

writing. *Meditation* 9 takes stock of William's wayward affections, "There is in me, O Lord, so vast and dense a mass of misery." *Meditation* 10 considers the incarnation and passion of Christ, while *Meditation* 11, as mentioned, may possibly be autobiographical about William's desire to lay aside his post.

In *Meditation* 12 he confesses his sins and expresses his longing for God ("...give me the water of wisdom to drink," Sir 15:3). His seeking the love of God takes on a dimension that reminds me of Anselm of Canterbury's prayers, but William's source, aside from biblical language itself, is probably Augustine: "So then I find you in my love, O Lord, but O that I might always find you there!" (*Invenio igitur te, Domine, in amore meo, sed utinam semper inveniam*).[51] It is impossible to read these *Meditations* without being touched by the depth and power of William's desire for union with God. Even if it is problematic to see his language as autobiographical, his use of the Psalms and the Wisdom literature of the Old Testament express yearning for God's presence.

Also from these years is the *Brevis Commentatio* on the Song of Songs. Verdeyen dates it to 1124–1125,[52] but it may actually reflect the conversations between William and Bernard when they both were ill and convalescing at Clairvaux. This would place the work during Lent of 1128.[53] William speaks of the delights that come in contemplation and the sweetness of the humanity of Christ. He chooses various themes from the Song and provides more a theological exposition than a meditation on the text. Song 2:4 "The king led me into the wine cellar" is interpreted as being brought into the fullness of love. William "only" reaches Song 2:5. He has broken off before completing his commentary, but he never promised to get through the entire text. This is his first attempt with the Song, which became a central concern of his intellectual and spiritual life.

6   William and Monastic Reform

Recent work on William has shown him to be more than a spiritual writer and theological polemicist. He contributed to an attempt to reform monastic life in the ecclesiastical province of Rheims, and he sponsored the first "chapter" of Benedictine monks there. Stanislaus Ceglar has shown William "and his leading role at the first chapters of the Benedictine abbots, Reims 1131, Soissons

---

51   Med 12.17, CCCM 89:79. ET: *Meditations*, 177.
52   Verdeyen, "La chronologie des œuvres," 198.
53   Ceglar, "The Date of William's Convalescence," 30–31.

1132."[54] Ceglar's research indicated that the language of these sources indicates William's authorship. The first chapter, during or immediately after the Council of Reims (October 1131) took place at Saint-Thierry itself. For the second chapter, Bernard was invited but could not attend. We do, however, have a letter from him showing his support of what the abbots were doing. Here is Bernard at his most enthusiastic, but not sufficiently so for him to have left Clairvaux for Soissons:

> I am vexed with my affairs because they prevent me from attending your meeting. But it is only my body they hinder, not my spirit, for neither the long distance nor my crowd of cares can impede my spirit and prevent me from praying for you, applauding you, and resting amongst you.[55]

Ceglar published the minutes of the first chapter, which begin: *Haec est societas inter abbates Remis constituta.*[56] One of the main concerns is the office, how the Psalms are to be sung *morose et cum devota distinctione* ("scrupulously and with devout attention"). So that there be enough time for the office, some of the Psalms are to be cut short. The purpose here may have been to come to terms with Cluniac practices, which added more and more prayers and made it necessary to rush through in order to fulfill the daily quota. This intention offended the papal legate, Cardinal Matthew of Albano, who wrote a long letter to the abbots and criticized them for their policies. The following year, 1132, at a chapter held at Soissons, the abbots formulated a reply, which was authored by William. "We profit not from having sworn to the customs of Cluny, but to the law and Rule of Saint Benedict."[57] The Rule comes first, and the customs had to be adapted according to the language of the Rule: "...we venerate all customs everywhere which are subject to the Rule...."[58] Besides the general principle of the importance of keeping to the Rule, there are a number of detailed descriptions of everyday life, as an insistence on the importance of manual

---

54   Ceglar, "William of Saint Thierry and His Leading Role," 34–49, followed by the Latin texts of *Acta* of the Chapter at Reims (51–64), the letter of Cardinal Matthew of Albano to the abbots (65–86) and the *Responsio abbatum* by William of Saint-Tierry (87–112). See also E. Rozanne Elder, "Guillaume de Saint-Thierry et le chapitre bénédictin de 1131," in Nicole Boucher, *Signy l'abbaye et Guillaume de Saint-Thierry*, (ed.) Nicole Boucher, (Signy l'Abbaye: Association des amis de l'abbaye de Signy, 2000), 487–504.

55   Letter 91, SBOp, 7:239. ET: James, *Letters of St. Bernard*, 140 (as Letter 94).

56   Ceglar, "William of Saint Thierry and His Leading Role," 51.

57   Ceglar, "William of Saint Thierry and His Leading Role," 89: "Profitemur nos non in consuetudines Clunacenses iurasse, sed in legem et regulam sancti Benedicti."

58   Ceglar, "William of Saint Thierry and His Leading Role," 89: "...et veneramur omnes ubique consuetudines quae regulae subserviunt familiarius."

labor.[59] The William who formulated such a prescription is the same monk who according to his *vita* insisted on unloading manure with his bare hands! The response also mentions the content and quality of the conversations monks have with each other and recommends the Carthusians for their *verba ... spiritualia, verba aedificationis et caritatis* ("spiritual speech and words of edification and charity"), in contrast with the Cluniacs.[60] William was thus already aware of Carthusian life and spirituality and on the way to his famed *Golden Letter* to the Carthusians of Mont Dieu.

William's leadership of the Benedictine abbots of the province of Reims during these years needs to be seen in terms of his fascination with Bernard and with Cistercian life in general. In the summer of 1135 he entered Signy as a simple monk and thus gave up the office that Bernard had insisted he should keep.[61] His choice fulfilled an old ambition, even though it meant that he left behind the responsibilities that Bernard had insisted he must not shirk. It would be worthwhile for a future scholar to look at William's contribution to the Benedictine chapters in terms of Cistercian influence. William was inspired not only by his meeting with Bernard but also by a general attraction to Cistercian monasticism. At Reims and Soissons he and his fellow abbots sought to legislate for a monastic way that combined the best in the Cistercian and Carthusian vocations and limited Cluniac observances. But a few years later, in 1135, it was not enough for William to admire the Cistercians from a distance. He became one.

7   William's Writings 1124–1139: from Saint-Thierry to Signy

These years brought not only an involvement with monastic reform. William continued his involvement in interpreting the Song of Songs, following up on his *Brevis Commentatio*. He compiled two works that are basically summaries of what the Church Fathers Ambrose and Gregory had provided for the Song.[62] Recent research, however, has shown that the two works do not follow the same method. Marc DelCogliano has found that in the Ambrosian commentary, William's method is analogous to the cutting and pasting one does with a text in a word processor. William takes blocks of text from Ambrose, while the Gregorian florilegium weaves together passages and creates "a single

---

59   Ceglar, "William of Saint Thierry and His Leading Role," 95.
60   Ceglar, "William of Saint Thierry and His Leading Role," 99.
61   Ceglar, "William of Saint Thierry and His Leading Role," 46, n. 47.
62   *Excerpta de libris beati Ambrosii et Gregorii super Cantica Canticorum* (Cant Amb and Cant Greg), CCCM 87:205–444.

logical unit."[63] So the result is more a synthesis than a collection of excerpts. DelCogliano, nevertheless, shows that William provides a prologue for the Ambrosian texts which indicates his own ideas and interpretation of the work. So the Ambrosian florilegium "affords a peek into William's thinking that the Gregorian florilegium does not."[64]

In his *Golden Epistle's* prologue, where William listed his writings, he mentioned how Bede already had borrowed from Gregory's commentary on the Song of Songs: "For Bede, as you know, made his collection of extracts into the last book of his commentary on the Song."[65] Today, such a collection of texts is not looked upon as pure scholarship, but in the 12th century a florilegium of extracts was considered to be a worthwhile intellectual activity. According to Verdeyen, both works belong to 1124–25, a time when William was deeply involved in his duties as abbot of Saint-Thierry.[66]

The *Exposition on Romans* (*Expositio super epistolam ad romanos*) exists in a single manuscript (Charleville BM 49).[67] Verdeyen thinks it was written between 1130 and 1137. This would be a work that William brought with him and completed at Signy after beginning it at Saint-Thierry. William was influenced by Saint Augustine's exegesis of Paul, but also by Origen's in the translation made by Rufinus. Verdeyen speaks of a "renaissance of Origen" in Western Europe in the 12th century.[68] William's preface indicates that he did not intend to make his own analysis but from the start intended to use Augustine and Origen. He explains that he wanted to experience "joy in contemplating God's grace" (*contemplandae gratiae Dei iocunditas*).[69] He opens the first book with a prayer.[70] The work is very much what Jean Leclercq spoke of as monastic theology,[71] for it is a meditation on the text of Paul, as understood by Church

---

63   Mark DelCogliano, "A Fresh Look at William of Saint-Thierry's Excerpts from the Books of Blessed Ambrose on the Song of Songs," in *Unity of Spirit: Studies on William of Saint-Thierry*, (eds.) F. Tyler Sergent, Aage Rydstrøm-Poulsen, Marsha L. Dutton, CS 268 (Collegeville, MN: Cistercian Publications, 2015), 37–59, esp. 43.

64   DelCogliano, "A Fresh Look at William," 59.

65   Ep frat, Prol., CCCM 88:226–27. ET: *The Golden Epistle*, trans. Theodore Berkeley, OCSO, CF 12 (Kalamazoo, MI: Cistercian Publications, 1980), 7.

66   Verdeyen, "La chronologie des œuvres," 199.

67   Exp Rm, CCCM 86:3–196. ET: *Exposition on the Epistle to the Romans*, trans. John Baptist Hasbrouck, (ed.) John D. Anderson, CF 27 (Kalamazoo, MI: Cistercian Publications, 1980). Verdeyen's "Introduction Generale" to CCCM 86 contains valuable research results until 1989, but some of his datings he revised in his 2011 article, "La chronologie des oeuvres."

68   Verdeyen, "La chronologie des œuvres," 197.

69   Exp Rm, Prol., CCCM 86:3. ET: *Exposition on the Epistle to the Romans*, 16.

70   Exp Rm, I.1.1, CCCM 86:6. ET: *Exposition on the Epistle to the Romans*, 19–20.

71   Jean Leclercq, *The Love of Learning and the Desire for God: A Study of Monastic Culture*, trans. Catharine Misrahi (New York: Fordham University Press, 1982).

Fathers. Such meditations at the time lead to prayers and recall Anselm of Canterbury's meditations. It would probably be most accurate to characterize such a work as a prolonged *lectio divina*, a careful, thoughtful, meditative reading of a Bible text, as seen through earlier commentaries but sifted through the writer's own heart and mind.

In becoming a simple monk at Signy, William freed himself from the administrative obligations that would have taken up his day, but at the same time he committed himself to a regime of labor in a new monastery. Advanced in age by now, William may have been spared the most demanding labor. William had an intellectual and spiritual agenda and was apparently able to carry it out in his new surroundings.

For years, William had dealt with the language of the Song of Songs, and after his arrival at Signy he began the *Commentary on the Canticle* for which he long had been preparing.[72] Verdeyen dates it between 1136 and 1139 and says it is William's "principal work".[73] I do not think this work can be singled out as such, but I agree with Verdeyen's statement that "the personal commentary is the mature result of a veteran interpreter of the Fathers".[74] William opens with a prayer to the Trinity. He proceeds with what is more an exposition than a commentary. The fruit of *lectio*, but not *lectio* itself. There are ten pages of preliminaries before he reaches the actual text of the Song of Songs and the first verse: "Let him kiss me with the kiss of his mouth". The style emphasizes the consolation to be found in the Song. We are made in the image of God and have departed from that image.[75] At times William begins a section with a prayer, as "*O amor amorum*".[76] He reaches Song 3:2, "I sought him and did not find him", and here stops. In the meantime a novice had apparently brought with him to Signy a treatise of Abelard, and so William turned to other concerns.

It is important in looking at such works of monastic theology to remember that they were not intended to be exhaustive commentaries. William provided a meditation on the Song, the result of decades of careful *lectio* not only of the work itself but also of earlier commentaries on it. William's work is also the result of his conversations with Bernard, and future scholarship will have to look more carefully at Bernard's *Sermons on the Song of Songs* and compare their content with William's commentaries.

---

72 Cant, CCCM 87:19–133. ET: *Exposition on the Song of Songs*, trans. Mother Columba Hart, OSB, CF 6 (Kalamazoo, MI: Cistercian Publications, 1970).

73 Verdeyen, "La chronologie des œuvres," 196.

74 Verdeyen, "La chronologie des œuvres," 196: "Le commentaire personnel est donc le fruit mûr d'un patrologue chevronné."

75 Cant, 66, CCCM 87:51 (§ 62). ET: *Exposition on the Song of Songs*, 53.

76 Cant, 143, CCCM 87:97 (§ 139). ET: *Exposition on the Song of Songs*, 114.

8   William at Signy

In 1140 William wrote a letter both to Bernard and to the papal legate, Geoffrey of Chartres. His target was the theology of Peter Abelard, whose form and content he found to be out of touch with the writings of the Fathers: "Peter Abelard ... teaches new things, writes new things and his books cross the seas, surmount the Alps and his new statements on faith and new teachings are brought through provinces and kingdoms."[77] William warned against Abelard's descriptions of the persons of the Trinity, including the question of the procession of the Holy Spirit. He claimed that Abelard saw the Holy Spirit as the Platonic soul of the world. He also attacked Abelard on the doctrine of the redemption, in claiming that Christ did not suffer in order to free us from the devil's yoke.[78]

William sought to involve Bernard in the matter and sent him his treatise. Bernard's response was measured: "I am not in the habit of trusting much my judgment ... I suggest that it would be worth our while to meet somewhere, as soon as we have an opportunity and discuss the whole thing."[79] There probably was a meeting, and then in 1141 the Council of Sens, where Abelard was condemned without being allowed to have a hearing. If we examine the fullest statement of Bernard's understanding of Abelard's teaching, called a letter but really a treatise, it is apparent that he was for the most part simply taking William's criticism and making it his own.[80] He trusted in the theological acumen of his friend and took it for granted that what worried William should worry him. In this exchange, which sadly brought the rejection of a theology only half understood, we see a continuing bond between William and Bernard.

Perhaps the decision of the Council of Sens enabled William to put aside his concern with Abelard. In any case the first half of the 1140s was fruitful for him in terms of his writings. His work *On the Nature of the Body and the Soul* (*De natura corporis et animae*) Verdeyen originally placed at an early point, in the course of William's monastic formation, but in his 2011 article he corrected his dating and dated it between 1143 and 1145.[81] It is different from William's

---

77   Ep Geof et Bern, 1, CCCM 89A:13. Adv Abl, Pref.

78   Adv Abl, 7, "Quod Christus non ideo assumpsit carnem et passus est, ut nos a iugo diaboli liberaret," CCCM 89A:42. For analysis of William's critique in this work of Abelard's views, see E. Rozanne Elder's chapter, "William of Saint-Thierry and the Renewal of the Whole 'Man,'" in this volume, pp. 109–30.

79   Letter 327, SBOp 8:263. James, *Letters of St. Bernard*, (Letter 236).

80   Letter 190, SBOp 8, addressed to Pope Innocent. Not translated in James, *Letters of St. Bernard*.

81   Verdeyen, "La chronologie des œuvres," 195.

other works because it deals with the physical world in terms of the functions of the body. As Bernard McGinn has pointed out in his introduction to the English translation, the work has "fundamental importance in a general evaluation of William's theology."[82] Such a treatise reveals the breadth of William's interests: he did not limit himself to Biblical commentaries but was eager to consider the relationship of body and soul according to what he found in the Fathers.

   The Mirror of Faith (*Speculum Fidei*)[83] and *The Enigma of Faith* (*Aenigma Fidei*)[84] were both written between 1142 and 1143, again according to Verdeyen, but here he is close to the dating originally provided by Wilmart (c. 1144 and 1145).[85] William described these works at some length in his *Golden Epistle's* prefatory letter. He claims that the first "is straightforward and easy", while the second has "a summary of the grounds and the formulations of faith … and is a little more obscure."[86] William claimed here in all modesty that he wrote these works in order to avoid idleness (a reference to Benedict's Rule), for his old age and bad health "prevent me from taking part in the common work."[87]

   We meet here a person who was trying to define the meaning of his life in terms of what he wrote, and it is not accidental that we have two lists of William's works—the first his own from *The Golden Epistle*, the second in his hagiography. William wanted the world to know what he had created, and although he appealed to a central monastic concern about avoiding idleness, he really could do little else than create one literary work after another. The course of his life had by now for decades been focused on dealing with theological questions in the context of monastic *lectio*. Now in his last years, he could describe how we believe. He recommended that the person in doubt simply embrace Christ crucified: *Tu vero amplecere Christum crucifixum.*[88] He addresses the faithful soul and encourages her to follow love and not to try to understand. We are a long way from Anselm's "faith seeking understanding", but for William, faith creates joy (*Habe in fide certa gaudium certum*).[89] Faith is the answer, and this

---

82   *Three Treatises on Man. A Cistercian Anthroplogy*, (ed.) Bernard McGinn, CF 27 (Kalamazoo, MI: Cistercian, 1977), 29.

83   Spec fid, CCCM 89A:81–127. ET: *The Mirror of Faith*, trans. Thomas X. Davis, CF 15 (Kalamazoo, MI: Cistercian Publications, 1979).

84   Aenig, CCCM 89A:129–191. ET: *The Enigma of Faith*, trans. John D. Anderson, CF 9 (Kalamazoo, MI: Cistercian Publications, 1973).

85   Verdeyen, "La chronologie des œuvres," 194. See Wilmart, "Les série et la date des ouvrages," 163.

86   Ep frat, 7, CCCM 88:226. ET: *Golden Epistle*, 5.

87   Ep frat, 7, CCCM 88:226. ET: *Golden Epistle*, 5.

88   Spec fid, 57, CCCM 89A:104.

89   Spec fid, 104, CCCM 89A:121.

relatively brief work captures the essence of William's trusting devotion in the goodness of God and the love of Christ for the faithful soul.

If the *Mirror of Faith* is a prayerful meditation on the meaning of faith, the *Enigma of Faith* is a more abstract theological exposition of the Trinity. It depends for a large part on Augustine and shows how we come to resemble God through the process of similitude based on the divine image imprinted on the human soul.[90] William explains, "And it is there that we become more like God as we progress more in knowledge and love of God. To the extent that we see God by knowing and loving God", yet similitude in this life is imperfect compared to the next.[91] So long as we are in the body, we wander from God. At times, William allows his discourse to turn to prayer, as in quoting Psalm 72:26, *Domine Deus cordis mei et pars mea in aeternum* ("Lord God of my heart and my share in eternity"), where he continues in his own words, "The end of all my desire and the destination of my intention."[92] Much of the work, however, takes its point of departure in the *De Trinitate* of Augustine, and in the last sections the personal element of prayer is absent and William quotes liberally from Boethius and Augustine.

Time and again in William's writings there is a disciplined theological and analytical element, going back to the Fathers, together with a prayerful, meditative, reflective element, probably the result of his years of *lectio divina*. This approach was naturally different from the more purely analytical one of Peter Abelard. In the course of the 12th century the method of question and answer that had originated at the school of Laon became dominant, especially in Paris, and however much William and Bernard questioned some of its results, they could not stop its advance. But William and Bernard should not be seen as dinosaurs about to be extinct: monastic theology in its careful meditation on Scripture does have an analytical element, and it would persist beyond the 12th century. It investigates the basis for belief but in this process does not go as far as scholastic theology. William questioned Abelard's methodology and results, but the scholastic and the monastic approaches are, in fact, not all that distant from each other.[93]

Another manifestation of William's campaign against the new learning is his *De erroribus Guillelmi de Conchis*, probably from 1143. Recently a brother who was leaving the world came to us with one of this master's books, entitled *Summa philosophiae*, explains William at the start of this brief treatise, which

---

90   Aenig, 6, CCCM 89A:132. ET: *Enigma of Faith*, 39 (§ 5).

91   Aenig, 6, CCCM 89A:132. ET: *Enigma of Faith*, 39 (§ 5).

92   Aenig, 24, "...finis omnis desiderii mei, et destinatum intentionis meae," CCCM 89A:143. ET: *Enigma of Faith*, 54 (§ 22).

93   See Brian Patrick McGuire, "Bernard of Clairvaux," in *The History of Western Philosophy of Religion*, (eds.) Graham Oppy and Nick Trakakis (Durham, UK: Acumen, 2009), 109–20.

is formulated as a letter to Bernard.[94] So far as we know, Bernard never replied to it, but according to Verdeyen such a text shows that William "did not appreciate the scholasticism taking form in the cathedral schools."[95] This assertion may be slightly exaggerated. William makes clear here not that he opposed the new scholasticism but that he criticized a tendency to turn theology into philosophy. He wanted to return to the teachings on the Trinity found in the Fathers, especially in Augustine. Besides William of Conches's dealings with the Trinity, William of Saint-Thierry criticized his understanding of the creation story, according to which humankind was made not by God but by nature, and then his soul was given him by God. William of Conches was made out to be a Manichean, "saying that the soul of man was created by the good God and his body by the prince of darkness."[96]

It seems William of Saint-Thierry was here exaggerating the remarks of his rival. In my experience the teachings of William of Conches are extremely difficult to decipher, and so they were easy to distort. The monk of Signy in old age looked more and more at the contemporary intellectual scene with disdain, but at least this time around, Bernard did not join him. One can speculate why, and the banal reason may have been that the abbot of Clairvaux did not have time, in the midst of his endless activities, to engage in another campaign against an alleged heretic.

9   The Golden Epistle and First Life of Bernard

The last two of William's compositions are the best known and hardly need any introduction. *The Golden Epistle* (*Epistola aurea*) has been placed at 1144–45 and the first book of the *Vita Prima* belongs to the last years of William's life, 1145–48.[97] *The Golden Epistle*, more properly called *Letter to the Brothers of Mont Dieu*, was intended for the younger brothers of the Carthusian community "that they may perhaps find ... something that will serve to console their solitude and spur them on in their holy resolution."[98] In his prefatory letter William reviewed the contents and titles of his literary production, providing almost an "access to the texts" that must have been intended not only for the Carthusians but for posterity: "Read all these works then; and if you are not the first to do so, at all events be the last if you will have it so."[99]

---

94   De err, 1, CCCM 89A:61.

95   Verdeyen, "La chronologie des œuvres," 195.

96   De err, 8, CCCM 89A:70.

97   Verdeyen, "La chronologie des œuvres," 194.

98   Ep frat, Prol., 2, CCCM 88:225. ET: *Golden Epistle*, 3–4.

99   Ep frat, Prol., 14, CCCM 88:227. ET: *Golden Epistle*, 7.

William made it clear that his enthusiasm for the community of Mont-Dieu was due to the fact that its members were bringing "to our Western darkness and French cold the light of the East and that ancient fervor of Egypt for religious observance."[100] As an old man he could still become enthusiastic about monastic communities that lived up to his ideals, and he spoke of how he would seek out the brothers and "run to meet them, O my soul, and run with them in the joy of the Holy Spirit."[101] The work is full of aphorisms and striking expressions that summarize William's concerns: "Do not be careless then, do not linger on the way. A long journey remains for you to accomplish. For you have undertaken the loftiest of professions."[102] "Rather in fear and trembling work out your salvation."[103] "Understand what I say, for the Lord will give you understanding."[104] "The man who has God with him is never less alone than when he is alone."[105] Only someone who had lived the monastic life to the full and at the same time experienced the call of the desert could have written in this manner, with such insight and learning. Here we find a William who could embrace others and who did not need to be polemical.

The last product of William's pen is the first book of the hagiography of Bernard of Clairvaux, the *Vita prima*. This work has had an enormous influence in shaping perceptions of Bernard, but it needs to be remembered that William drew on a previous work, the so-called *Fragmenta* brought together by Bernard's secretary Geoffrey of Auxerre. But William's biography of Bernard is not just a compilation of Geoffrey's descriptions. As Hilary Costello points out in introducing his superb translation of the *Vita Prima*, William "as a highly skilled author ... wove these materials on Bernard's life into an original narrative, combining the sources he had at hand with his own reminiscences of close friendship with Bernard."[106] Costello refers especially to the time that William and Bernard spent together "in the little hut on the grounds of Clairvaux."[107] But he does not answer the next question that arises: Did William in his last years ever return to Clairvaux in order to interview not only Bernard but also his brothers? There is no evidence for such physical contact, and it seems as if the last face-to-face meeting would have been in connection with Abelard's theology, probably in 1140. Thus the *Vita prima* would appear to be an old, sick

---

100   Ep frat, 1, CCCM 88:228. ET: *Golden Epistle*, 9.
101   Ep frat, 1, CCCM 88:228. ET: *Golden Epistle*, 9.
102   Ep frat, 15, CCCM 88:231. ET: *Golden Epistle*, 14.
103   Ep frat, 21, CCCM 88:232. ET: *Golden Epistle*, 16; cf. 1 Tim 1:15.
104   Ep frat, 24, CCCM 88:233. ET: *Golden Epistle*, 17; cf. II Tim 2:7.
105   Ep frat, 30, CCCM 88:234. ET: *Golden Epistle*, 19. Cf. Ambrose of Milan, Letter 49.1 and Cicero, *De Officiis*, 3:1 (*Golden Epistle*, 17, n. 69).
106   Costello, "Introduction," *The First Life of Bernard*, xviii.
107   Costello, "Introduction," *The First Life of Bernard*, xiv.

man's recollections, together with the written sources he had in terms of the *Fragmenta.*

William provides in his Preface to Book One of the *Vita prima* a clear indication why he valued Bernard so highly, for he says that thanks to him "the renewal of the Church in our time has blossomed anew."[108] At the end of this section he expresses hope that others will take up the task of describing Bernard after his death. They will "do better and more worthily what I myself have attempted."[109] In this statement William indicated that he knew Bernard would outlive him, and so he took the step of writing hagiography while the saint was still alive. William thereby indicated his debt to Bernard and desire to make his life available to others. At the same time William hid from view the fact that Bernard's everyday life and actions in recent years were outside his ken. Despite this limitation, William's segment of Bernard's *vita* has become the point of departure for all future biographies of the saint. Clearly, he managed to capture the restless vitality and deep spirituality of the abbot of Clairvaux.

A recent study of William and Bernard has cast new light on the *Vita prima.* E. Rozanne Elder points out that William in writing about Clairvaux was looking back with nostalgia on what he had experienced decades earlier with Bernard and thus was implicitly criticizing the way the monastery had developed. William admired what we might call primitive monasticism, while Clairvaux had grown by leaps and bounds into a flourishing, busy monastery. Without saying a harsh word, William was comparing the Clairvaux of the 1120s with the Clairvaux of the 1140s and hinting that something important had been lost. "The Clairvaux of 'today,' a quarter century later, did not apparently affect William in the same way."[110]

10   Summary: A Restless Life Seeking God

William's life and writings manifest the dynamism and ambition of Western Europe in the first decades of the 12th century. In this energy there was what Jean Leclercq so aptly has termed the love of learning and the desire for God. William was born into favorable circumstances at Liège and was able to attend cathedral schools and then to enter a Benedictine house at Reims, Saint Nicaise.

---

108   Vita Bern., Prol., CCCM 89 B:31, "...per quem ecclesiam temporis nostri in antiquum apostolicae gratiae et virtutis decus voluisti reflorere...." ET: *The First Life of Bernard,* 1.
109   Vita Bern., Prol., CCCM 89B:32. ET: *The First Life of Bernard,* 3.
110   E. Rozanne Elder, "The Influence of Clairvaux: The Experience of William of Saint-Thierry," *Cistercian Studies Quarterly* 51.1 (2016): 55–75, esp. 72.

The exact date of his birth and of his monastic conversion eludes us, but the consensus is for approximately 1075 and 1112. The next decisive moment in his life was his first meeting with Bernard on the outskirts of the Clairvaux property, in 1118 or 1119. In the winter of 1121 he was elected abbot of Saint-Thierry outside of Reims, a post he held until he gave it up in 1135.

At Saint-Thierry William began to compose and publish works that on the one hand reflect monastic *lectio* and on the other more speculative treatments of theological questions. Thus we have *The Nature and Dignity of Love* and *On Contemplating God* in the first category and *On the Sacrament of the Altar*, in opposition to Rupert of Deutz, in the second. These belong to the 1120s, while his *Meditations*, which I consider to be his finest work, may have been written over a longer period, from 1125–1137. Here as in much else I follow the conclusions of Paul Verdeyen, but I warn the reader that this scholar does not always justify his results.

It was also at Saint-Thierry that William began to approach the Song of Songs and to use it as a primer of spiritual love. Presumably, in the mid-1120s, he used Ambrose's commentary on the Song and then Gregory the Great's as points of departure for his own reading. Probably in 1128 he allowed Bernard to summon him at a time when both abbots were ill. Their conversations are described in the *Vita prima*, and these talks apparently provided the foundation for the *Brevis Commentatio*.

William's life combined spiritual meditations with theological writings. At one point he served as a monastic legislator, for he was apparently instrumental in bringing the Benedictine abbots of the province of Reims into a chapter that tried to reform their habits and bring them into greater harmony with the Rule of Saint Benedict. This effort from 1131–32 brought about resistance from a cardinal who championed Cluniac monasticism, and so we find William defending his choices on behalf of his fellow abbots.

In 1135 William resigned his abbacy and entered the newly established Cistercian house of Signy. In the last fourteen years of his life he was extremely productive, and it is at the end of the 1130s he wrote his fullest Commentary on the Song of Songs, left incomplete because he felt obliged to turn to an attack on Abelard for his writings on the Trinity and the Redemption. The polemical William also appears in opposing William of Conches. While William managed to recruit Bernard against Abelard, the abbot of Clairvaux kept his distance when William of Saint-Thierry appealed for his assistance against William of Conches.

Probably in the early 1140s William composed his *Mirror of Faith* and *The Enigma of Faith*, beautifully written and balanced statements on the meaning of faith and interpretations of the Trinity, based especially on Augustine.

Enigma can perhaps be seen as William's indirect answer to Abelard on the Trinity. Meanwhile his concern for the contents of monastic life and a yearning back to the lives of the Desert Fathers led him to write to the Carthusians of Mont-Dieu about their vocation. What later became known as the *Golden Epistle* became one of the most accessible and popular of William's writings. It can be dated to the 1140s.

Finally, we have his homage to Bernard, the first book of the *Vita prima*, the *First Life*, making use of the notes of Geoffrey of Auxerre but putting them together into a fuller portrait of the man who had become William's close friend. When William died on 8 September, probably in 1148, he had left behind works of both monastic and pre-scholastic theology. He was a restless soul, a seeker, a man ever looking for a better way of life, and so it was inevitable that he came to challenge and offend other scholars and monks—and even a cardinal. It is only today, after so many centuries, thanks to decades of scholarly work and publication, that we can grasp the extent of his writings, even though his *Sentences* appear to be lost.[111] But we have more than enough to guarantee William's place in the history of Christian spirituality and monastic life.

---

111   Wilmart, 167.

CHAPTER 2

William of Saint-Thierry's Sources and Influences: *Ratio Fidei* and *Fruitio*

F. Tyler Sergent

1   Introduction

The process of determining influence and source material between authors of different periods, especially when separated by several centuries, poses difficulties and pitfalls. Parallels in thought, quotations, or allusions to earlier writings do not necessarily demonstrate direct source material. During the Middle Ages florilegia were common and could, therefore, be the literary source rather than the complete text of another author's work, a fuller expression of the author's thought. Yet 12th-century authors certainly did use earlier texts, both patristic and medieval, for their own intellectual formation and as direct source material, and thus influence, for their own writings. For William of Saint-Thierry, the 12th-century Benedictine abbot who became a Cistercian monk, the question of sources has been addressed by several scholars for more than six decades. Although we have a more accurate understanding of William's sources and influences as a result, questions still remain unanswered, leaving more work to be done.

William of Saint-Thierry, as a cathedral school trained lifelong monk, read patristic and early medieval authors, and many of these quotations have been identified by editors of critical editions and translators of William's writings. In order to help the reader understand the challenges and results of investigating William's sources, let me provide an historiographical overview of the scholarly debates surrounding the question of his sources, citing key protagonists and their ultimate findings, and then using two key terms in William's writings—*ratio fidei* (reason of faith) and *fruitio* (enjoyment)—suggest some additional authors who may well have provided source material for William's understanding of these two terms. We will find that William of Saint-Thierry read and gleaned terms and concepts from earlier patristic and medieval sources (primarily from the West but also from the Greek East in Latin translation), while at the same time, he applied these terms judiciously and creatively for his own purposes to express and explicate his overall teaching on the soul's journey to God and the necessary stages this trajectory must follow to reach its end, union with God.

© KONINKLIJKE BRILL NV, LEIDEN, 2019 | DOI:10.1163/9789004392502_004

2   William's Sources: Historiography

David Bell, in his excellent book, *The Image and Likeness*, published in 1984, provides a summary and analysis of scholarly literature on William up to 1983.[1] It supplements a similar analysis of William scholarship Bell published in a thorough article in 1982.[2] Both of these analyses, along with articles published in 1979 and 1981,[3] focus on the question of William's literary sources and intellectual influences, as does the whole of these two publications. At the time Bell was researching and writing these important studies, Dom Jean-Marie Déchanet had been the recognized scholarly authority on William's life and thought, as Bell himself mentions.[4]

Déchanet and Bell constitute two formidable and opposite poles with regard to identifying the sources and influences that appear in William's writings. Déchanet intuitively identifies a variety of sources for William's thought, including eastern (Greek) authors.[5] Bell methodically analyzes William's writings and other texts to "re-assess the relative importance of eastern and western thought in William's spirituality and re-direct our attention back to the work of Augustine of Hippo."[6] As a result, Bell definitively demonstrates Augustine's foundation in William's writings and thought, supplanting many of Déchanet's assertions toward other significant sources, eastern and western.

In his 1981 article, "The Alleged Greek Sources of William of St Thierry," Bell makes direct criticism of Déchanet's arguments for William's Greek sources. In particular, Bell convincingly argues against Déchanet's conclusions that

---

1   David N. Bell, *The Image and Likeness: The Augustinian Spirituality of William of St. Thierry*, CS 78 (Kalamazoo, MI: Cistercian Publications, 1984), 13–20.

2   David N. Bell, "William of Saint-Thierry and John Scot Eriugena," *Cîteaux – Commentarii Cistercienses* 33 (1982): 5–28.

3   David N. Bell, "Greek, Plotinus, and the Education of William of Saint-Thierry," *Cîteaux – Commentarii Cistercienses* 30 (1979): 221–48, and Bell, "The Alleged Greek Sources of William of St. Thierry," in *Noble Piety and Reformed Monasticism*, (ed.) E. Rozanne Elder, Studies in Medieval Cistercian History VII, CS 65 (Kalamazoo, MI: Cistercian Publications, 1981), 109–22.

4   Bell, *Image and Likeness*, 13.

5   See Jean-Marie Déchanet, *William of St Thierry: The Man and His Work*, trans. Richard Strachan, CS 10 (Spencer, MA: Cistercian Publications, 1972), 151–55; Déchanet, *Aux sources de la spiritualite de Guillaume de Saint-Thierry* (Bruges: Beyaert, 1940); Déchanet, *Guillaume de Saint-Thierry, aux sources d'une pensees* (Paris: Beauchesne, 1978); Déchanet, "Guillaume et Plotin," *Revue du Moyen Âge Latin* 2 (1946): 246–60; Déchanet, "Introduction," *The Golden Epistle: A Letter to the brethren at Mont Dieu*, trans. Theodore Berkeley, The Works of William of St. Thierry, CF 12 (Kalamazoo, MI: Cistercian Publications, 1980), ix–xxxiii, esp. xxiv, xxxiii; and Déchanet, "Introduction," *Exposition on the Song of Songs*, trans. Columba Hart, The Works of William of St. Thierry 2, CF 6 (Kalamazoo, MI: Cistercian Publications, 1970), vii–xlviii, esp. xxviii–xxxix.

6   David N. Bell, "The Alleged Greek Sources," 109.

William relied heavily on Gregory of Nyssa, Origen, Plotinus, and that William's "works carry the unmistakable imprint of eastern thought."[7] Bell categorizes Déchanet's arguments into three: first, the image and likeness of the soul in relation to God; second, the epistemology of love for the human soul toward God; and third, "the assimilatory power of love."[8]

In the first category, Déchanet looks to Gregory of Nyssa to provide William's concept as to how the imprint of the Trinity on the soul makes possible for the soul to be drawn into "the ineffable Trinitarian movement" and thus into participation with the God.[9] At the same time, Déchanet also rejects the possibility that Augustine expresses this same concept. This is Bell's main criticism, and thus he shows precisely how this concept of participation through the image and likeness appears in Augustine's writings (especially *De Trinitate*), and demonstrates that William need not go beyond his western inheritance to find this concept.[10]

In the second category, Déchanet again looks to Gregory of Nyssa as the source for William's thought on "how God is known in and through love."[11] Once again, Bell shows where William's notion of how loving God is a way of knowing God—since the love from God that dwells within the soul is the Holy Spirit, who is also God, is the means by which one loves God—also appears in Augustine's *De Trinitate*.[12]

Within the final category is Déchanet's assertion that Plotinus, the 3rd-century architect of Neoplatonism, provides the source for William's concept of love as assimilatory, meaning that by loving, the lover becomes like the beloved; in other words, by loving God one becomes like God, through assimilation to God.[13] As seen above, this concept also has an antecedent in

---

7   Déchanet, *Aux Sources*, 73.

8   David N. Bell, "The Alleged Greek Sources," *passim.*

9   Déchanet, *Aux sources*, 15.

10   Bell, "Alleged Greek Sources," 110–11.

11   Jean-Marie Déchanet, *William of St. Thierry: The Man and His Work*, trans. Richard Strachan, CS 10 (Spencer, MA: Cistercian Publications, 1972), 50–51.

12   Bell, "Alleged Greek Sources," 112.

13   Déchanet, *William of St Thierry*, 74; Déchanet, *Aux sources*, 18–21; Déchanet originated this idea in his 1946 article, "Guillaume et Plotin," and thirty years later, he continued to assert the same conclusion that William read and was influenced by Plotinus's *Enneads*. This early article compares William's Latin with Plotinus in French translation, and although it shows clearly the parallels in thought, as Bell correctly argues, the article does not provide critical evidence that William relied on Plotinus. Déchanet admits that the question would be much simplified if one could assume that William read Greek: "Gillaume connaissait-il le grec? Si nous pouvions repondre affirmativement, le probleme serait beaucoup simplifie," 260, n.26; especially since no Latin manuscript of the *Enneads* is known in the 12th century.

Augustine, which Bell points out decisively, and therefore no need exists to look to Greek sources for concepts developed among western writers.[14]

On the question of William's access to the Greek language—of obvious importance for his alleged use of Greek sources not available in Latin translation—Bell methodically examines where William might have learned the language.[15] After considering the possibilities for Greek in the Liège-Laon and Reims region of France, from the Carolingian renaissance to William's day, he concludes that William "would have had great difficulty in acquiring even a rudimentary knowledge of the Greek language" because "there is no evidence for any Greek orientation in his education and early training, whether at Reims or Laon."[16] Since the most recent assessment puts William's education at Reims, the opportunity for Greek language is even more bleak since "there was no one at the school who knew Greek."[17]

Bell's final retort to Déchanet's later assertions that William was "a disciple of" and "profoundly influenced" by John Scotus Eriugena[18] appears in his 1982 article, "William of Saint-Thierry and John Scot Eriugena."[19] Here he addresses two parts of the question: "(a) whether William really was influenced by Eriugena, and (b) if he was, to what extent he was so influenced."[20] Déchanet's view presupposes William's education at Laon under Anselm, who, according to Déchanet, was devoted to John Scotus.[21] Besides the issue that William was likely educated at Reims instead, Bell demonstrates that Anselm's "devotion" to John the Scot cannot be substantiated, especially since Anselm's copy of John the Scot's expositions on the Gospel of John was anonymous[22]—thus he may not have been aware he was reading John Scotus Eriugena—and the foundational aspects of these expositions (commentary and homilies) are Augustinian.[23]

---

14   Bell, "Alleged Greek Sources," 112–13.

15   Bell, "Greek, Plotinus, and the Education of William of St Thierry," 225–30.

16   Bell, "Greek, Plotinus," 230.

17   Bell, "Greek, Plotinus," 232. See also John R. Williams, "The Cathedral School of Reims in the Time of Master Alberic, 1118–1136," *Traditio* 20 (1964): 93–114.

18   Déchanet, *Aux sources*, 23–59, 75, n. 3, "ce disciple d'Erigene." Other authors also accepted this assertion: Odo Brooke, "William of St. Thierry's Doctrine of the Ascent to God by Faith," *Recherches de théologie ancienne et médiévale* 30 (1963): 181–204, 33; (1966): 283–318, esp. 299, n. 68, and Brooke, "The Theology of William of St Thierry: A Methodological Problem," *Cistercian Studies* [*Quarterly*] 6.3 (1971): 263, n. 7 (Bell cites this article as "*CS* 4," p. 5, n. 2.); and Brooke, "Introduction," *Guillaume de S. Thierry, La contemplation de Dieu*, (ed.) and trans. Jacques Hourlier, SChr 61 (Paris: du Cerf, 1968), 41–43.

19   Bell, "William of Saint-Thierry and John Scot Eriugena," *Cîteaux – Commentarii Cistercienses* 33.1 (1982): 5–28.

20   Bell, "William and John Scot," 6.

21   Déchanet, *William of St Thierry: The Man and His Work*, 3.

22   Bell, "William and John Scot," 11.

23   Bell, "William and John Scot," 11–12.

Yet Bell admits that copies of John the Scot's works were readily available in monasteries, both Cistercian and Benedictine, in and around Reims.[24]

Bell's strongest criticism aims at the specific citations of John the Scot that Déchanet finds in the writings of William. Of these eleven, Bell says, six are Eriugena's translation of Gregory of Nyssa; of the remaining five, two were abandoned by Déchanet, two others are only "assonances," leaving only one possible direct citation of John Scot Eriugena.[25] Bell, however, considers two possible texts in William and concludes that William may have taken interest in John Scotus Eriugena but that he would have done so with caution, that William indeed was not a "disciple of" John the Scot, and that "Déchanet's assessment is certainly over-enthusiastic."[26]

Alongside these two lie other notable scholars who comment on William's influences and possible sources, including John D. Anderson, E. Rozanne Elder, and Thomas Michael Tomasic.[27] In his introduction to the English translation of William's *Enigma of Faith*, John D. Anderson addresses the issue of William's sources specifically in this work. Along the same line as Bell, Anderson criticizes Déchanet's quest for Greek sources based on William's language by showing how these same terms and ideas are found in western authors.[28] He points out that, while Déchanet says that William's opening line to the text comes from Origen's *Commentary on Romans*, Hilary of Poitiers's *Tractate on Psalm 129* is the actual source. Other examples of likely sources Anderson identifies for terms such as *supersapere*, *supereminens*, and *supercoelestis* include scripture, Ambrose, Augustine, Jerome, Leo the Great, and Isidore of Seville, and not Pseudo-Dionysius as concluded by André Fracheboud in the *Dictionnaire de spiritualité*.[29] Specific sources that Anderson identifies within William's *Enigma of Faith* include Hilary of Poitiers's *On the Trinity*; Augustine's

---

24   Bell, "William and John Scot," 15–16.

25   Bell compiles "some two dozen passages" cited by Déchanet, Brooke, and Hourlier as evidence of John the Scot's influence on William, then divides them into three categories, the last category, (C) "those which may indeed indicate a familiarity with the works of John the Scot," contains only two such passages; Bell, "William and John Scot," 20.

26   Bell, "William and John Scot," 28.

27   Two other scholars from the same time period, Anne Saword and Adele Fiske, also address the question of William's sources, yet neither adds any original contributions to the answer. See Anne Saword, "Note on William of St. Thierry's Use of Gregory of Nyssa's Treatise *On the Making of Man*," *Cistercian Studies* [*Quarterly*] 9.4 (1974): 394–98 and A. Fiske, "William of St. Thierry and Friendship," *Cîteaux – Commentarii Cistercienses* 12 (1961): 5–27.

28   John D. Anderson, "Introduction," William of St. Thierry, *The Enigma of Faith*, trans. John D. Anderson, CF 9 (Kalamazoo, MI: Cistercian Publications, 1973), 17–18.

29   Anderson, "Introduction," 18. See *Dictionnaire de spiritualité*, vol. 3 (Paris, 1957), 329–40, s.v. "Les cisterciens." Cited in Anderson.

On the Trinity, On the Literal Meaning of Genesis, Tractates on John, On True Religions, On Christian Doctrine, Letters, 92, 120, 147, and 170, possibly *The City of God, On the Merits and Forgiveness of Sins, Against Julian,* and his *Enarrationes ad Psalmos*; Leo the Great's *Sermons* 76 and 77; Boethius' *One Person and Two Natures* and *On the Trinity*; and Isidore of Seville's *Etymologies*. Anderson also notes that all but one of these authors were represented in the library at Signy, where William resided for the last thirteen years of his life.[30]

Anderson also considers two specific problems regarding William's sources in this work: first, the divine names (*nomina divina*); and second, the phrase *ratio fidei*.[31] Once again, he shows that William—rather than relying on Pseudo-Dionysius' *On the Divine Names* as "some scholars" declared "rather hastily" —borrowed from Augustine's *On the Trinity* for the "concepts, terminology, and divisions of the Divine Names."[32] William uses *ratio fidei* "no less than twenty-two times in the treatise,"[33] and the phrase appears in Romans 12:6 as well as Hilary's *On the Trinity*, Gregory the Great's *Moralia in Job*, Anselm of Canterbury's *Cur Deus Homo*, and Bernard of Clairvaux's *Sermons on the Song of Songs*. With so many Latin occurrences, there is little need to look to Greek sources for this phrase.[34]

In his 1976 article, "The Use of Greek Sources by William of St Thierry Especially in the *Enigma Fidei*," Anderson provides a detailed analysis to supplement his assertions published in the introduction discussed above.[35] Once again he strongly criticizes the conclusions of Déchanet's (and others') search for Greek sources in William's writings, and—in an unveiled accusation that Déchanet's research presumed its own findings—Anderson describes his purpose: "This paper, by presenting the results of a detailed investigation of one treatise, suggests the need for a critical reexamination of William's other works based on close textual scrutiny, and free from *a priori* commitments to the presence of Greek influences in the Cistercian author under examination."[36]

---

30   Anderson, "Introduction," 20. Although he does not provide specific reference citations in the introduction, he does provide footnotes throughout the translation identifying these texts and possible sources in William's text.

31   Anderson, "Introduction," 21.

32   Anderson, "Introduction," 21.

33   Anderson, "Introduction," 22. As will be seen below, William uses the phrase six more times in five other works, and thus twenty-eight times altogether.

34   Anderson, "Introduction," 23–24. He also provides specific textual references in each author's work.

35   John D. Anderson, "The Use of Greek Sources by William of St Thierry Especially in the *Enigma Fidei*," in *One Yet Two: Monastic Tradition East and West,* (ed.) M. Basil Pennington, CS 29 (Kalamazoo, MI: Cistercian Publications, 1976), 242–53.

36   Anderson, "The Use of Greek," 243. This provides the context for my research and studies of *ratio fidei* and *fruitio* below.

After giving several examples of Greek sources erroneously identified in William's writings (not just *Enigma of Faith*) and providing the actual western sources,[37] including once again Augustine and Hilary of Poitiers, Anderson addresses "the problem of misunderstanding Greek theology" that he sees in Jacques Hourlier, Odo Brooke, and Déchanet, the same scholars who erroneously identified these Greek sources in William.[38] And this problem of misunderstanding exacerbated the issue of seeing Greek thought in William where it does not exist. Anderson concludes:

> Until proven otherwise, William, in the *Enigma* at least, must be seen as a Latin writer in the Latin West drawing upon the tradition of his Latin heritage which admittedly includes some translations from the East. But emphasis must be placed on William's known use of Augustine, Gregory, Hilary, Boethius, Leo, etc. and not on his supposed use of Dionysius or the Cappadocians.[39]

E. Rozanne Elder addresses directly the question of William's sources within his Christology, and at the same time she provides new approaches to the issue and new criticisms to the old methodologies.[40] Elder begins with a restatement and critique of Déchanet's hypothesis—and those who had assumed this hypothesis as fact—that "William enjoyed a singular and probably first-hand knowledge of Origen and Gregory of Nyssa, of Pseudo-Denis through Eriugena, and even of Plotinus."[41] As part of the critique, Elder cites Pierre Courcelle's methodology for determining an author's sources: the first entails finding "doctrinal similarities," which are too unreliable, and the second entails identifying "textual parallels," which provide stronger evidence.[42] Both Déchanet and Hourlier employed these methods to find all of the alleged Greek sources in William, and yet these "parallels" in thought and text have not demonstrated William's direct knowledge of Greek authors.

More than mere parallels in ideas, language, vocabulary, and even nominal citations is required to demonstrate direct textual sources. Not even William's

---

37   Anderson, "The Use of Greek," 244–45.
38   Anderson, "The Use of Greek," 246–47. Bell leveled the same criticism at Déchanet and Louis Bouyer; see "Alleged Greek Sources," 110–11.
39   Anderson, "The Use of Greek," 253.
40   E. Rozanne Elder, "William of Saint Thierry and the Greek Fathers: Evidence from Christology," in *One Yet Two: Monastic Tradition East and West*, (ed.) M. Basil Pennington, CS 29 (Kalamazoo, MI: Cistercian Publications, 1976), 254–66.
41   Elder, "William and the Greek Fathers," 254.
42   Elder, "William and the Greek Fathers," 255. See Pierre Courcelle, *Les lettres grecques en occident de Macrobe a Cassiodore*, 2nd edn. (Paris, 1948), cited in Elder.

use of specific Greek terms, such as *theophania, theotokos*, and *theoria* prove his reliance on Greek texts since these also appear in other Latin authors, including Jerome.[43] Regarding vocabulary, Elder points out that although William used the term *satisfacere* in reference to Christ's death—implying familiarity with his older contemporary, Anselm of Canterbury, and his satisfaction theory of atonement from *Cur Deus Homo*—William himself admits in his *Disputation against Peter Abelard* that indeed "he had not in fact read Anselm," "that he did not understand his theory, and that he half disagreed with as much of it as he had heard of."[44] Even when William cites his sources, Elder shows, it does not indicate direct contact with the literary source itself. For example, William cites Cyril of Alexandria in his *On the Sacrament of the Altar*, but the quotation appears in so many other 12th-century writers that the source is more likely a florilegium than Cyril directly.[45]

Elder then turns to manuscript evidence in order to see what texts were readily available to William at Saint-Thierry and Signy to help determine what sources he may have used, and she provides a list of nineteen Greek authors (in Latin translation) appearing in manuscripts "conceivably" accessible to William.[46] Yet as she quickly points out, the availability of a manuscript does not necessitate its use, nor does the absence of a manuscript indicate its inaccessibility.[47] For true access to William's sources, one would have to look at the very manuscript William used in order to see precise wording, language, or peculiarity William would have read and possibly borrowed, and modern edited or critical editions of the works listed in the 12th-century catalogues may lack these elements.[48] Still, the collection and copying of these Greek authors for the libraries at Saint-Thierry and Signy could signify something of William's "enthusiasm for what he knew of the Eastern tradition," thereby influencing his Cistercian confreres in a way additional to his own writings.[49]

A few years later, in her introduction to the English translation of William's *Mirror of Faith*, Elder explains the influence Peter Abelard had on William's thought.[50] It was not, however, the kind of influence seen by Augustine or

---

43   Elder, "William and the Greek Fathers," 257.
44   Elder, "William and the Greek Fathers," 257. Cf. Adv Abl, VII, PL 180:274D (CCCM 89A:48), cited in Elder.
45   Elder, "William and the Greek Fathers," 258.
46   Elder, "William and the Greek Fathers," 258, n. 14.
47   Elder, "William and the Greek Fathers," 262.
48   Elder, "William and the Greek Fathers," 263.
49   Elder, "William and the Greek Fathers," 266.
50   E. Rozanne Elder, "Introduction," William of St. Thierry, *The Mirror of Faith*, trans. Thomas X. Davis, OCSO, CF 15 (Kalamazoo, MI: Cistercian Publications, 1979), xi–xxv.

other possible sources in William's writings. William, preoccupied with what he thought were serious errors in Abelard's methodology, wrote both his *Enigma of Faith* and *Mirror of Faith* in the light of Abelard's "faulty foundation."[51] Elder writes, "Abelard casts a long, unmistakable shadow across each [work], for William, while not mentioning him by name, grappled constantly with his teachings, his approach to revelation and his uncanny—and to William incomprehensible—academic ability to divorce himself from faith in order to elucidate faith."[52] Specifically, Abelard seems to have had impact on William's understanding of virtue, sacrament, authority, reason, and love.[53] This kind of influence, however, is negative in the sense that William formulated his thought in opposition to Abelard's thought, and as such is different from the sources and influences positively informing William's thought and appearing in his writings. Yet certainly this impact of Abelard's thought is no less important, given that William not only wrote his *Disputation* as a direct attack on Abelard's theology but also these two weighty treatises, *Enigma of Faith* and *Mirror of Faith*, so late in his career.[54]

Thomas Michael Tomasic focuses on William's sources in two excellent articles, one on the Neoplatonic elements within William's spiritual worldview, or "mysticism," as Tomasic writes, and the other on exploring the influence of John Scotus Eriugena.[55] This article stands out from all other previous studies for its methodology. Tomasic used a computer analysis to compare source texts with William's writings to determine, by mathematical probability, whether or not a given source text appeared. One quantitative result of this method is

51   Elder, "Introduction," xiii.

52   Elder, "Introduction," *Mirror of Faith*, xiii.

53   Elder, "Introduction," *Mirror of Faith*, xvi–xv.

54   *Disputatio adversus Petrum Abaelardum* (Adv Abl) was written just after Abelard's condemnation at the Council of Sens in 1141 (for further discussion on the date of the council and the scholarship, see E. Rozanne Elder's chapter, "William of Saint-Thierry and the Renewal of the Whole 'Man'," in this volume, esp. p. 110, n. 7). William began these two treatises, writing them both within the time frame of 1142–1144. For the dates of William's works, I follow Paul Verdeyen, "Introduction," *Expositio super epistolam ad Romanos*, CCCM 86 (Turnout: Brepols, 1989), xxiv–xxxi. For two of William's works, *On the Sacrament of the Altar* and the *Letter* to Rupert of Deutz, I follow instead John Van Engen, "Rupert of Deutz and William of St. Thierry," *Revue bénédictine* 93 (1983): 332.

55   Thomas Michael Tomasic, "Just How Cogently Can One Argue for the Influence of John Scotus Eriugena on William of Saint-Thierry?" in *Erudition at God's Service*, (ed.) John R. Sommerfeldt, Studies in Medieval Cistercian History XI, CS 98 (Kalamazoo, MI: Cistercian Publications, 1987), 185–94. Another excellent article by Tomasic investigates more generally the Neoplatonic elements within William's thought and spiritual worldview, "Neoplatonism and the Mysticism of William of St.-Thierry," in *An Introduction to the Medieval Mystics of Europe* (Albany, NY: SUNY Press, 1984), 53–75.

Tomasic's discovery that fifty-one per cent of William's *On the Nature of the Body* "was reproduced either verbatim or by extraordinarily close paraphrasing from Gregory's [of Nyssa] *De hominis opificio* [*On the Making of Humankind*], and that significant iterations from Gregory appear in other works, but only those William wrote after his *De natura corporis et animae*."[56] This conclusion, of course, serves mainly to provide additional evidence for Déchanet's significant discovery in 1938 that William borrowed extensively from Gregory of Nyssa's *On the Making of Humankind* for his own *On the Nature of the Body and the Soul*.

The more original contribution to William studies is Tomasic's detailed application of computer textual analysis of a large corpus of John the Scot's writings, including translations of Pseudo-Dionysius and Maximus the Confessor, compared with the full corpus of William's writings.[57] The results suggest that William did not incorporate Pseudo-Dionysius or Maximus in his writings at all, but that in all probability, he did borrow from *Periphyseon* at least six and up to twelve times altogether.[58]

In a final analysis of the scholarship relating to William's sources and influences, Bell fittingly concludes, "That Déchanet swung the scale too far to the orient is not, I think, in doubt; the extent to which it should be swung back again has not yet been precisely determined."[59] Apart from a few hints and suggestions for William's sources that have been offered periodically since then (as highlighted above), the state of the question that David Bell described in this way in 1981 remains largely unchanged today within William scholarship. The debate continues.

Thus the last fifty years of William scholarship investigating and debating William's sources has resulted, in brief, in these views:

(1)   William formed his religious worldview and specific aspects of his thought and language with Augustine as a major source and influence.

(2)   William took interest in at least two Greek writers, Gregory of Nyssa and Origen, in Latin translations by John Scotus Eriugena and Rufinus, respectively, since William did not read Greek.

---

56   Tomasic, "Just How Cogently ... Eriugena," 185.

57   For the comparison, Eriugena's texts included *Periphyseon* and translations of *On the Divine Names*, *The Mystical Theology*, *The Celestial Hierarchy*, *The Ecclesiastical Hierarchy*, and the *Ten Letters* of Pseudo-Dionysius, along with the *Ambigua* of Maximus the Confessor. Tomasic, "Just How Cogently ... Eriugena," 187.

58   Tomasic, "Just How Cogently ... Eriugena," 193. He also provides the caveat that the absence of Pseudo-Dionysius and Maximus in William's texts, as determined by the computer program, does not provide absolute evidence that William did not read and was not influenced by these writers' texts in translation.

59   Bell, "Alleged Greek Sources," 116.

(3)   William seems also to have used John Scotus's own writings as a source, though infrequently.
(4)   William also relied on Boethius, infrequently.
(5)   There remains some suspicion that William may have used Cassian as a source, who could have provided indirect access to other eastern influences, including the desert monks and the Cappadocians, though no one has yet provided a complete analysis of this.[60]
(6)   William read and likely borrowed from Gregory the Great, Ambrose of Milan, Leo the Great, and Hilary of Poitiers, although to what degree is unknown since the detailed analyses remain to be done.

I would add that the dates of the authors listed above leave a great number of centuries between the source material and William's 12th-century writing career. This leaves open and largely unaddressed the possibility of many medieval authors from the 6th through the 11th centuries as William's sources, as the following studies show.

3   William's Sources: *Ratio Fidei* and *Fruitio*

In order to contribute to the scholarly discussion regarding William's sources and influences, I will explore in detail two terms, central to William's understanding of spiritual life and progress on the path toward God: *ratio fidei* and *fruitio*. Each term has a biblical connection, as we will see, and describes William's view on a specific stage of the soul's journey toward God. By exploring the origin and literary transmission of each term and then William's usage of it, we will investigate what tradition William inherited and what of this inheritance he utilized—or did not utilize—as a source that influenced his own thought, language, and writings.[61]

---

60   I have demonstrated that William at least knew Cassian's *Conference* 10 based on each monk's unique interpretation of John 17:21 regarding spiritual union between the individual soul and God and II Cor. 5:16 on the incarnation of Christ. See F. Tyler Sergent, "Cassian and William of St. Thierry on the Incarnation and Spiritual Union," presentation at the Cistercian Studies Conference in the International Conference on Medieval Studies, Western Michigan University, Kalamazoo, MI, 13 May 2011. William also knew *Conference* 7, I argue, based on their shared usage and context for the term *arrha*, which both writers describe as 'foretaste of heaven,' unique in the literary tradition. See F. Tyler Sergent, "*Arrha*: The Pledge and Foretaste," in "'Signs of Spiritual and Divine Realities': The Sources and Originality of William of Saint Thierry's Ascetic Language." Ph.D. diss., Roskilde Universitet, Denmark, 2009, 54–78.
61   The tool used for identifying the terms' origins and appearances in historical documents is the "Library of Latin Texts," LLT-A Centre Traditio Litterarum Occidentalium (Turnhout: Brepols, 2001–2018) www.brepolis.net.

3.1   *Ratio Fidei*

The phrase *ratio fidei*, the reason of faith, has its origin for Latin Christianity in the Latin version of the New Testament in Romans 12:6, which reads, "*secundum rationem fidei*."[62] The context is the diversity among members within the unified body of Christ. The full verse translates as, "And having different gifts according to the grace that is given to us, either prophecy, *according to the reason of faith*, or ministry, etc...." The patristic interpretive tradition tended to read this as though it were "*secundum mensuram fidei*," "according to the measure of faith." We can see this from Rufinus's versions of Origen, to Cassian, to Augustine and Jerome, and many others;[63] the phrase itself even appears in the *Rule of Master* (9.48). The original Greek version reads, "κατὰ τὴν ἀναλογίαν τῆς πίστεως,"[64] and translates as, "according to the proportion of faith," which fits logically with the Latin tradition of "*mensuram fidei*" and is the likely intent of the Pauline text.

One other version of this verse also appears in the Latin tradition through Augustine, who quotes this verse as "*secundum regulam fidei*," "according to the rule of faith," in his *On Christian Doctrine*,[65] but this is unique to him. John Anderson has suggested that William's concept for *ratio fidei* comes directly from Augustine's phrasing, combined with the original biblical context, rather than the majority patristic tradition for this biblical phrase, an hypothesis tested below.

The phrase *ratio fidei* itself appears ninety-seven times up to the mid-12th century in the writings of forty different authors. William himself contributes thirty-one of these, nearly one third of the total. If we exclude direct quotations of the biblical verse, it appears eighty-four times, and William provides thirty of these since he quotes the verse only once.[66] By comparison, the next most prolific use by a single author is six by Peter Abelard and five by Origen. These quantitative statistics at least imply that the phrase is important in William's writings and thought, to a degree greater than to his predecessors.

---

62   *Biblia Sacra Iuxta Vulgatam Versionem* (Stuttgart: Deutsche Bibelgesellschaft, 1983). There are no variants.

63   For example, an 11th-century manuscript of an anonymous 9th-century commentary on Pauline books cites Origen by name and explains that *ratio fidei* is equal to "*fidei mensuram*." *Ad Ephesios* 1, 9.3, in *Expositiones Pauli epistularum ad Romanos, Galathas et Ephesios e codice Sancti Michaelis in periculo Maris, Expositiones Pauli epistularum*, (ed.) G. de Martel, CCCM 151 (Turnout: Brepols, 1995).

64   *Novum Testamentum Graece*, Nestle-Aland, 27th ed. (Stuttgart: Deutsche Bibelgesellschaft, 1996). There are no variants.

65   Augustine, *De doctrina Christiana*, 4.20.

66   As an observation, the only other author with nearly as many uses as William is Thomas Aquinas with twenty-eight, a century after William.

Even though William only quotes Romans 12:6 one time—not surprisingly in his *Exposition on Romans*—we will begin there because he relies on Origen (via Rufinus) for his initial comments on this verse. From Origen's *Commentary on Romans*,[67] William learns that the Greek version of Romans 12:6 uses "ἀναλογία," and so William, in his commentary, provides the Latin phrase *secundum analogiam fidei*, a rendering of this verse unique to him.[68] Origen's text simply reports that the original Greek word is "ἀναλογία" but does not translate or transliterate it into Latin. Instead, it uses *ratio fidei* for the Greek and then equates this with *mensuram fidei*.[69] Having written "*analogiam fidei*," William then predicates this "*analogia*" with "*rectam fidei regulam*," "the right rule of faith." Speaking of the gift of prophecy, William writes:

> ...it is the most important of the gifts, provided it is truly lived according to the 'analogy of faith,' for this is what the Greek text has. But often pestilences are found in the thrones of churches and vipers' dens in the desert, when they try to be wiser than is fitting and do not proceed according to the analogy, that is, the right rule of faith...[70]

This describes the proper use of spiritual gifts. Using this text along with a quotation from Augustine's *On the Trinity* in William's *Enigma of Faith*, Anderson concludes that William takes his basic meaning of *ratio fidei* from Augustine's *regulam fidei*. The quotation mentioned addresses the intra-trinitarian relationships of the three persons:

> Therefore it is not the Father himself who is the Son, nor the Son himself who is the Holy Spirit. With my whole attention directed on this rule of faith (*regulam fidei*), Lord, I will seek your face and continually search for your face as much as I can and as much as you render me capable of doing.[71]

In this passage of the *Enigma of Faith*, however, William uses Augustine's words to describe a basic tenet of Christian doctrine and thus Christian belief: the

---

67   Origen, *In Epistulam Pauli ad Romanos explanationum libri*, 9.3.
68   I found, however, that John Scotus Eriugena's Latin translation of Maximos the Confessor's *Quaestiones ad Thalassium* twice uses the phrase "*secundum analogiam fidei*" (Ad Thal, 29).
69   Origen, *In Epistulam Pauli*, 9.3.
70   Exp Rm, VII.12:6, CCCM 86:168–169. ET: *Exposition on the Epistle to the Romans*, trans. John Baptist Hasbrouck, (ed.) John D. Anderson, CF 27 (Kalamazoo, MI: Cistercian Publications, 1980), 234.
71   Aenig, 23, CCCM 89A:145. ET: *The Enigma of Faith*, trans. John D. Anderson, CF 9 (Kalamazoo, MI: Cistercian Publications, 1973), 55–56. Cf. Augustine, De Trin, 15.28.

three in one Trinity as expressed in the creeds, and this he calls the *regulam fidei* not *ratio fidei*. To strengthen this point, a few lines later, William writes:

> Therefore I have here everything concerning the Lord my God for which I was searching for some time. I have it free from tormenting questions, insidious sophistry, and noisy arguments; namely, what it is that the Father is, the Son is, and the Holy Spirit is. This is my faith about God because it is the catholic faith.[72]

Rather than the meaning found here, simply the "rule of faith" as basic Christian doctrine, for William's development of *ratio fidei*, I suggest that Anderson is mistaken because William is using these phrases in these two texts in two different ways with two different meanings. First is the proper use of spiritual gifts, and second is the basic tenets of Christian belief; one from Origen, one from Augustine. William goes on then to use *ratio fidei* throughout the remainder of the *Enigma of Faith* in yet a third way, which we will analyze in detail.

Although William mentions *ratio fidei* one time each in his *Disputation against Abelard*, his *Letter on the Errors of William of Conches*, his *Exposition on the Song of Songs*, and his *Mirror of Faith*, not until his *Enigma of Faith* does he thoroughly develop the meaning of this phrase and fit it into his overall understanding of faith, theology, and spiritual life. The *Mirror of Faith* and *Enigma of Faith* are two formidable theological texts that William wrote in tandem and in reaction to what he thought were errors in Peter Abelard's theology, even interrupting his *Exposition on the Song of Songs*, arguably the heart of his spiritual writings, to do so. The two texts together provide detailed elaboration on another Pauline text, First Corinthians 13:12: "For now we see through a mirror in an enigma, but then, face to face. Now I know in part, but then I shall understand fully, even as I have been fully understood." William's two works draw their titles from this verse and the two metaphors, *speculum* (mirror) and *aenigma*.

The *Mirror of Faith* and *Enigma of Faith* form one work in two books. As William himself describes them:

> ...divided into two books, the first of which, because it is straight forward and easy, I titled the *Mirror of Faith*; the second, because it will be found to contain a summary of the grounds and formulations of faith according to the words and thought of the catholic fathers and is a little more obscure, the *Enigma of Faith*.[73]

---

72   Aenig, 24, CCCM 89A:145. ET: *The Enigma of Faith*, 56.

73   Ep frat, Preface, 7, CCCM 88:226. ET: *The Golden Epistle: A Letter to the Brethren at Mont Dieu*, trans. Theodore Berkeley, OCSO, CF 12 (Kalamazoo, MI: Cistercian Publications, 1980), 5.

The *Mirror of Faith* explicates the importance of faith, hope, and love and the role of grace and the Holy Spirit to enlighten these "powers" (*vires*), each of which is necessary for the others to be effectual. As William notes, faith without hope and love is no power (*vis*) because even the demons believe.[74] These powers together can lead a person to knowledge and vision of God. The *Enigma of Faith* focuses on the object of faith, hope, and love; knowledge and vision: God, and specifically the mystery of the Triune God.

William uses *ratio fidei* twenty-five times in the *Enigma of Faith* alone. Quantitatively, this suggests some significance of phrase for William's theology since this is his major theological work. To understand William's *ratio fidei*, one must first understand William's *ratio*, "reason." Reason and love provide two important ways for knowing God. William explains that these are the "two eyes of the soul": "love gives life to reason, and reason gives light to love."[75] Reason alone sees what God is not; love sees what God is.[76] Reason and love both need to be guided rightly when it comes to matters of faith, and there is great potential for error if either is allowed to wander off on its own. Curiosity and speculation only invite the possibility of error because human reason and human love, on their own, tend to set as their object that which is not God. And this is where divine assistance and cooperation become essential. Through the Holy Spirit grace illumines and guides both reason and love so that they may properly be directed toward God as their common object. In this process, the weak soul (*anima*) becomes a strong soul (*animus*).[77]

Reason can only take one so far. One can use reason to think about God, and this "first knowledge concerning God," as William calls it, can be rational "according to the reason of faith" (*secundum ratio fidei*).[78] But this is not perfect

---

74 Spec fid, 2, CCCM 89A:81. ET: *The Mirror of Faith*, trans. Thomas X. Davis, CF 15 (Kalamazoo, MI: Cistercian Publications, 1979), 5–6.

75 Cant, 92, CCCM 87:67. ET: *Exposition on the Song of Songs*, trans. Mother Columba Hart, OSB, CF 6 (Kalamazoo, MI: Cistercian Publications, 1969), 74.

76 Nat am, 21, CCCM 88:193. ET: *The Nature and Dignity of Love*, trans. Thomas X. Davis, CF 30 (Kalamazoo, MI: Cistercian Publications, 1981), 77–78.

77 Ep frat, 198. CCCM 88:270. ET: *The Golden Epistle*, 94. William's rationale for changing from feminine to masculine I think is quite different from the classical Platonic idea (e.g., Plotinus and Origen) in which the original and divine state of the soul (ψῠχή) is feminine, and as the soul "falls" into embodiment, it becomes "cool" (ψῦχος, a masculine adjective in Greek). As the soul returns to God, it "warms" in the divine presence. But neither author uses a masculine Greek word to refer to "soul"; it is always ψῠχή. William has in mind a more gender-oriented metaphor in which the masculine symbolizes strength and the feminine weakness, not uncommon in medieval thought. Yet the gendered difference between *anima* and *animus* is not literal but metaphorical. The progression from *anima* to *animus* to *unitas* also has resonance with Plotinian Neoplatonism. See Tomasic, "Neoplatonism and William of St.-Thierry," 65–67.

78 Aenig, 38. CCCM 89A:153. ET: *The Enigma of Faith*, 69.

knowledge, William argues, because even those who "believe not as they should," those whose faith has taken a wrong turn, have this level of knowledge.[79] Describing it further, William declares:

> This is that knowledge of God which the Psalmist says [Ps 18:3] night declares to night; that is, human to human, flesh and blood to flesh and blood, and sometimes unbeliever to unbeliever. It is far removed from the wisdom and the word which day does not declare but rather pours forth to day, or spiritual person to spiritual person, or the Holy Spirit ... to the spirit of any holy person.[80]

This greater knowledge "should be sought after by all without exception" because it is necessary for the growth and development of one's faith if such knowledge is "managed according to the reason of faith" (*ratio fidei*).[81]

William makes a distinction between human reason (*humana ratio*)[82] and *ratio fidei*. He says that in human matters, reason acquires faith, but that in divine things, faith must come first—his own statement echoing Anselm's *fides quaerens intellectum*—and faith forms "its own type of reason" (*sui generis rationem*).[83] But this reason of faith does not reject human reason *per se* but instead adopts what is good and adapts it to faith's own rules (*suis regulis*).[84]

Through this *ratio fidei* the church establishes both its language for and understanding of God. William says that even though words like "Trinity," "*homoousia*," and "consubstantial" are not found in scripture, still through the reason of faith, these words came to describe what has always been true. The reason of faith is what provides the means—the cooperation between human reason, divine revelation, and pious authority—for establishing these tenets of faith. In other words, the rule of faith—the credal beliefs of Christianity—are established through the reason of faith.[85] Therefore the reason of faith is the means for establishing the rule of faith and parameters for belief. Thus *ratio fidei* and *regulam fidei* are not the same in William's thought.

For William, however, human reason and the reason of faith are not merely cerebral exercises. His concern always remains the spiritual life and the soul's journey toward union with God. He writes:

---

79   Aenig, 38. CCCM 89A:153. ET: *The Enigma of Faith*, 69.
80   Aenig, 38. CCCM 89A:153. ET: *The Enigma of Faith*, 70.
81   Aenig, 38. CCCM 89A:153. ET: *The Enigma of Faith*, 69.
82   Aenig, 41. CCCM 89A:154. ET: *The Enigma of Faith*, 73.
83   Aenig, 41. CCCM 89A:158. ET: *The Enigma of Faith*, 73.
84   Aenig, 43. CCCM 89A:159–60. ET: *The Enigma of Faith*, 76.
85   Aenig, 48. CCCM 89A:163. ET: *The Enigma of Faith*, 80.

God first of all formed the first man in his image and likeness and then breathed into his face the breath of life and he was made a living soul.... We proceed even now with fear and trembling to fall prostrate and cry out, 'Holy Trinity, in your presence, O Lord our God, you have made us! You cause us to pray and entreat that you not permit us to err in any way in the contemplation of or belief in that form to which we seek to be conformed.'[86]

What can we conclude, then, about *ratio fidei* in William's thought and possible influences on this thought? First, William takes the biblical phrase as found in the Vulgate and multiple sources, and instead of following the majority patristic usage and reading *ratio* as *mensura*, he keeps the term *ratio* and develops *ratio fidei* by starting with reason and then adding faith. In this way he develops the concept of a faith-reason that is a human reason transformed by divine illumination. This fits very well with his other transformative concepts and language regarding stages of spiritual life, weak soul to the strong soul, human love to divine love, etc. For William, this *ratio fidei* becomes the tool for seeking and finding knowledge of God and for keeping this search within the proper bounds of orthodox Christian faith.

Second, although the *Enigma of Faith* is full of many and often lengthy allusions and verbatim quotations from Augustine's *On the Trinity*, William does not take the concept of *ratio fidei* directly from Augustine, and certainly not from this work (Augustine never uses the term *ratio fidei* here). On the one occasion in which Augustine uses *ratio fidei*, in his *Against Fortunatus the Manichee*,[87] he uses it as synonymous with "rule of faith," the same way he uses *regulam fidei* in *On the Trinity*. As influential as Augustine is for William's Trinitarian theology, both metaphysical and spiritual, he is not the source for William's *ratio fidei*.

Can we find, then, a source for William's *ratio fidei* among the other twenty-seven authors who use the phrase? All of the fifty-five occurrences (not counting William) fall into four categories: (1) equating *ratio fidei* with *mensura fidei*,[88] (2) *ratio fidei* meaning "cause" or "grounds for" one's belief,[89] (3) *ratio*

---

86   Aenig, 74. CCCM 89A:181–182. ET: *The Enigma of Faith*, 104–05.
87   Augustine, *Contra Fortunatum Manichaeum*, 3.
88   Apponius, Rufinus, Origen (via Rufinus), Cassiodorus, Eucherius, Cassian, Jerome, Augustine, Burginda, Bede, *Rule of the Master*, Benedict of Aniane, Frowin, Jerichus of Auxerre, Hrabanus Maurus, Peter Lombard, Sedulius Scotus, and two anonymous commentaries on the letters of Paul.
89   Agobard of Lyons, Berengar of Tours, Anselm of Canterbury, Peter Abelard, Bernard of Clairvaux.

fidei as synonymous with *regula fidei*,[90] and (4) *ratio fidei* as a faculty of reasoning, enacted on by faith, assisted by God, that helps one to understand correctly essential matters of the faith.

The only authors to use the term in this last way, one that most resembles
William's use, include Hilary of Poitiers, Gregory the Great, and Paschasius
Radbertus. Among the other twenty-four authors, we can categorize some as
more likely sources than others for William based on time period, proximity,
and accessibility of the author's writings. To this group, I add Bernard of Clairvaux and Peter Abelard who, as we have seen elsewhere in this volume, were
influential on William in other ways, if not directly on his thinking and writing.
This provides us six antecedent authors to William who are possible candi-
dates to supply source material for him.[91]

In his prefatory Book 1 of *On the Trinity*, Hilary of Poitiers (d. 367) summarizes the content of his work. When discussing book three, he speaks of faith's
ability to comprehend certain truths Jesus taught concerning himself and the
Trinity, and he says that rationality (*rationabilis*) and knowledge (*scientia*) assist faith in this. He then writes, "Nor ought it to be supposed that the understanding of God's power can be apprehended without the reason of faith [*ratio
fidei*]."[92] Hilary does not say specifically that *ratio fidei* is what establishes the
truths of faith, but he does seem to think of it as a faculty for understanding
and a faculty that complements human rationality and knowledge and that
is necessary for understanding important truths of the faith, or what other
authors might call the rule of faith, the confession of faith. It is possible that
this concept could have inspired or at least informed William's view and use
of *ratio fidei* as the essential means to establishing the rule and confession of
faith.

---

90   Only Augustine and Agobard. Agobard used it in one of his strongly anti-Semitic texts,
      On the Baptism of Slaves of Jews (*De baptismo mancipiorum Judaeorum*), written in 823,
      to mean "cause" or "rationale" for the faith. See Karl Radl, *Semitic Controversies: A Daily
      Blog about Jews and Judaism*, "An English Translation of Agobard of Lyons" 'De Baptismo
      Judaicorum Mancipiorum,' posted 24 March 2013, http://semiticcontroversies.blogspot
      .com/2013/03/an-english-translation-of-agobard-of.html, accessed 23 July 2018. Agobard,
      De Bapt Jud Manc (CCCM 52, ln. 79; L. Van Acker, 1981).

91   Berengar of Tours (c. 1010–1088) also uses the term in his *Rejoinder against Lanfranc*
      (*Rescriptum contra Lanfrannum*), but this particular text is difficult to understand, was
      not published in Berengar's lifetime, and exists in only one manuscript. So I will exclude it
      from this study on these grounds that William would not likely have known of it. Berengar
      of Tours, Rescr. Lanf., 1 (ln. 1618), 2 (ln. 793, 1241) (CCCM 84, R.B.C. Huygens, 1988). For de-
      tails about the manuscript, see Toivo J. Holopainen, *Dialectic and Theology in the Eleventh
      Century* (Leiden: Brill, 1996), 77 and 77 n. 1.

92   Hilary of Poitiers, De Trin, I.22 (CCSL 62).

Gregory the Great (d. 604) uses *ratio fidei* one time, and it appears in his lengthy *Moralia in Job*.[93] Commenting on Job 1:3, which says that Job had 7000 sheep and 3000 camels, Gregory says that we too have 7000 sheep when we "feed the innocent thoughts within our breast in a perfect purity of heart with the food of truth which we have sought."[94] We too have 3000 camels when "all that is high [*altum*] and crooked [*tortuosum*] in us has been subjected [*subditur, subdo*] to the reason of faith [*rationi fidei*] and, by our own accord and in our desire for humility, is bent [*inclinator*] at the foot of [*sub*] knowledge of the Trinity."[95] Two terms here express the same idea as William's when Gregory explains the role of *ratio fidei: subdo* in Gregory and *redigo* in William. Although not identical words, they express the same idea that certain human faculties and possessions must yield to *ratio fidei* in order to have the proper understanding and knowledge of essential tenets of the faith. Gregory may possibly provide the source for William's understanding and use of *ratio fidei* in this context.

Paschasius Radbertus (c. 790–860), the 9th-century abbot of Corbie, uses *ratio fidei* one time in his *On the Body and Blood of the Lord* (*De corpore et sanguine Domini*). He says that when one seeks to understand the "order of the divine nature" (*ordo naturae*), "reason will yield and the truth remains beyond human reason, just as the force and efficacious power of the divine nature is entrusted, in every way, to the reason of faith (*ratione fidei*), granting that one who receives it is of a good life, because the doubt of the mind prevents understanding of the sacrament."[96] Along the same line as William, Paschasius contrasts human reason and reason of faith, using *ratio fidei* as a faculty of understanding that is beyond human reasoning and capable of grasping divine truth. Therefore, he too is a possible source for William's own concept of *ratio fidei*.

Peter Abelard (1079–1142), the catalyst for William's concept of *ratio fidei*, uses *ratio fidei* in his *Commentary on Romans* 12:6–7 and connects *ratio* with *discretio* (discretion) and *discerno* (discernment).[97] The context for discernment is what one teaches of the faith to different hearers; like Paul, one must discern "what is fitting ... to those according to their capacity [*capax*]." He uses

---

93   Gregory the Great, *Moralia in Job* (Moralia), I.28 (CCSL 143). ET: *Moral Reflections on the Book of Job*, vol. 1, trans. Brian Kerns and intro. Mark DelCogliano, OCSO, CS 249H (Collegeville, MN: Cistercian Publications, 2014).

94   Gregory, Moralia, I.28. ET: vol. I.39.

95   Gregory, Moralia, I.28. ET: vol. I.40.

96   Paschasius Radbertus, De corp sang Dom, 1, "Ubi si naturae ordo requiritur succumbit ratio et tamen manet extra humanam rationem facti veritas ita ut in ratione fidei vis deitatis et potestas efficax modis omnibus redatur quia dubietas mentis licet bonae vitae sit qui accipit excludit ne ad huius sacramenti intelligentiam pertingat," CCCM 16:ln. 165.

97   Peter Abelard, Comm Rom, IV.12, CCCM 11:ln. 64–89.

discretion in a similar way. Both ways of describing *ratio fidei* by Abelard here relate to the specific content of the Pauline passages: ministering to believers through teaching and preaching and using one's *ratio fidei* to discern what is appropriate to the audience. And thus it differs from William's use in the *Enigma of Faith.*

Bernard of Clairvaux (1090–1153) uses the phrase *ratio fidei* in his Letter 189 to Pope Innocent regarding Peter Abelard.[98] He argues that the *ratio fidei* ought not to be handed over to human reasoning (*humanis ... ratiunculis*) for discussion (i.e., the council of Sens) because the *ratio fidei* is "supported by a certain and firm truth..."; it is not up for discussion (and in Bernard's view, Abelard's writings already condemned him regardless of the hearing). This use of the phrase may be similar to William's own usage, but it also seems very much like those who speak of the reason of faith with the meaning of cause or rationale for the faith rather than the means for establishing the faith, as William uses the phrase. The old 19th-century English translation of Mabillon's edition of Bernard's letters even translates *ratio fidei* as "grounds of the faith" in this text.[99] I agree, and thus Bernard is not a source for William on this point.

There may be no definitive precedent that William clearly followed or specific author we can say with certainty influenced William directly for his understanding of *ratio fidei*. Hilary, Gregory, and Paschasius come closest, and each of them diverges from the prevailing use of *ratio fidei* in both the patristic and medieval periods. Hilary's *De Trinitate* enjoyed wide dispersion, and John Anderson shows William's familiarity with this text in the first paragraph of the *Enigma of Faith.*[100] As others have shown, Gregory the Great's *Moralia in Job* was also widely available in the 12th century. In this case, *ratio fidei* undergoes transformation from the "measure of faith" (the biblical context), to a faculty of understanding matters of faith (Hilary, Gregory, and Paschasius), and finally to the essential means (forming its own type of reason: *sui generis rationem*) for establishing the central tenants of faith and keeping human reason in line with the rule of faith—that is William's contribution to the tradition.

3.2   *Fruitio*

The term *fruitio* appears first in the 4th century and is transmitted to the 12th in an exclusively Christian context and with a strict meaning of "enjoyment."[101]

---

98   Bernard, Letter 189, SBOp, 8:14 ln. 18.

99   Jean Mabillon, *The Life and Works of Bernard of Clairvaux*, 2nd edn., trans. Samuel Eales (London: John Hedges, 1889), 546.

100   John Anderson, "Introduction," 17, 35 n. 2.

101   *Fruitio* does not appear in Classical Latin. Lewis and Short's Latin dictionary defines *fruitio* as "enjoyment" and indicates that it comes from the deponent verb *fruor* while listing

But it appears only rarely in the 4th century, infrequently in the 8th and 9th centuries, and afterwards not until the 12th century. The first part of this study identifies the origin of *fruitio,* traces it up to the 12th century, and determines the context and definition transmitted into the 12th century at which time William makes prolific use of the term throughout his writings. The second part describes William's language of fruition and how it fits within his understanding of spiritual life, and then makes some conclusions about influence and transmission of the term.

The earliest Latin author[102] to use the term *fruitio,* Jerome (*c.*340–420),[103] does so only twice (and in the same sentence) in his *Commentary on the Letter to Philemon,* written in 388,[104] commenting on Philemon 20 ("And so, brother, I will enjoy you in the Lord..."[105]).[106] The verb *fruor* appears eleven times in the Vulgate, including Philemon 20. I suggest that Jerome, if the originator, forms his word *fruitio* from this verb. A noun formed from a verb usually comes from the fourth principle part (the perfect passive participle).

Jerome as the earliest occurrence. Lewis and Short, *A Latin Dictionary* (1879; reprint, 1996) s.v. "fruitio, -onis, f." Niermeyer's medieval Latin lexicon provides "possession" as a medieval meaning in addition to "enjoyment," and says that the phrase *fruitio Dei* can also refer to the "beatific vision," and it also indicates that the term appears only after 200 CE, yet Niermeyer offers no specific references for *fruitio,* neither a time period nor geographic area for its usage. J.F. Niermeyer, *Mediae Latinitatis Lexicon Minus* (1993), s.v. "fruitio, -onis, f."

102　The earliest author in whose writings *fruitio* can be found is Irenaeus (c.130–200), the 2nd-century philosopher and Christian apologist, whose original Greek largely exists only in later Latin translations. His *Adversus Haereses* is in a 4th-century Latin translation. *Fruitio* appears three times in this text. In each case the 4th-century translator uses *fruitio* in a similar context with the exact same meaning: the happy fruition of what God gives to those who, living just and virtuous lives, love and follow God. See *Ante-Nicene Fathers, Vol. 1 The Apostolic Fathers, Justin Martyr, Irenaeus,* (eds.) Alexander Roberts and James Donaldson (1885; rpt., Peabody, MA: Hendrickson Publishers, 1994) 311–12, with some Greek fragments of book 1 (of 5) extant in quotations by subsequent authors, including Hippolytus (d. *c.*236) and Epiphanius of Salamis (d. 403). For the Latin version, see Irenée de Lyon, *Contre les heresies,* Livre V-2, Sources chrétiennes 153, (eds.) Adelin Rousseau, Louis Doutreleau, sj, and Charles Mercier (Paris: du Cerf, 1969).

103　Augustine's use of *fruitio* appears in Sermon 255 *In Diebus Paschalibus* only in a paragraph heading: "Duae vitae in Martha et Maria adnumbratae. Unum necessarium. Dei fruitio erit beatis bonorum omnium loco," which translates as, "The two lives accounted in Martha and Mary. One is necessary. The enjoyment of God will be a place blessed of all good things." Sermon 255, 26 "De alleluia," VI.6. PL 38:1188. The meaning and context for *fruitio* match the 4th-century Latin version of Irenaeus' seen above, though this sermon dates somewhere between c. 400 and 425, certainly later than Jerome's use.

104　NPNF, vol. 6, *Jerome: Letters and Selected Works,* 2nd Series, (eds.) Philip Schaff and Henry Wace (1893; rpt., Peabody, MA: Hendrickson Publishers, 1995), xxv.

105　"Ita frater ego te fruar in Domino..." Quoted in Jerome's commentary, also matching verbatim with his later Vulgate translation.

106　Jerome, *Commentariorum in Epistolam ad Philemon Liber Unus.* PL 26:615.

Since *fruor* is deponent, it has only three principle parts: present active in-
dicative (*fruor*), present active infinitive (*frui*), and the perfect active indica-
tive (*fructus sum* or *fruitus sum*).[107] The common noun in Classical Latin for
"enjoyment" is *fructus* (*-us*, masculine, fourth declension) taken from the
third principle part of *fruor*. Jerome, however, seems to form *fruitio* from
the optional third principle part, *fruitus sum*, which provides the noun base
(*fruiti-*) from the verb stem (*fruit-*) that could form *fruitio* (*-onis*, feminine,
third declension), fitting the *-tio* nouns, and thus having the same meaning as
fructus but different gender and declension.[108] This analysis is my own conjecture because I find no other lexicographical explanation.

Jerome uses *fruitio* simply to mean "enjoyment," but the "enjoyment"
(*fruitio*) in the biblical text is not an egocentric fruition of base things, rather
specifically the fruition that comes only in God and in the things God offers.
His apparent need to clarify godly fruition as distinct from other types of enjoyment (*fructus*) is what Jerome provides for the subsequent Christian literary
tradition, and indeed the term itself is peculiar to Christianity.

Not only was Jerome not particularly enamored with his new word, using
it only twice, nor was anyone else for 300 years because the next occurrence
of *fruitio* appears only in the 8th century with Alcuin of York (c.730–804), the
great headmaster of the cathedral school in York (778), the palatine school in
Aachen (782), and abbot of Saint Martin's in Tours (796). He uses it only once
in his *Tractatus super ad Philemonem Epistolam* and then in a near-verbatim
quotation from Jerome's commentary on Philemon cited above.[109] The variants are minor and in no way affect the direct relationship between these two
authors' texts. But Alcuin's transmission, though unoriginal, may have contributed to the following century's continuation with this term.

Three contemporary authors of the 9th century use *fruitio*: Rabanus Maurus (c.780–856), Paschasius Radbertus (c.790–c.860), and John Scotus Eriugena
(c.810–c.877/79). Rabanus Maurus, abbot of Fulda (822) and then archbishop
of Mainz (847), studied under Alcuin at Tours. Not surprising, Rabanus follows
his teacher's use of *fruitio* by quoting the exact same section from Jerome's
commentary on Philemon as Alcuin in his own commentary on Philemon.[110]

---

107   Lewis and Short, *A Latin Dictionary*, s.v. "fruor."
108   The same can be seen in the participle of *fruor*, *fructus -a, -um* and *fruitus -a, -um*, from
         which the participial stem of the latter is also *fruit-*.
109   Alcuinus, *Opusculum Septimum. Tractatus super Tres S. Pauli ad Titum, ad Philemonem, et
         ad Hebraeos Epistolas*. PL 100:1030. Though he does not quote Jerome's following sentence
         that also uses *fruitio*, for whatever reason. This of course could mean that Alcuin's copy of
         Jerome's commentary lacked this phrase or that Alcuin chose to leave it out, or that the
         sentence could have been removed by a later copyist or redactor.
110   Rabanus Maurus, *Enarrationum in Epistolas beati Pauli*.

Rabanus's quotation is longer and closer to Jerome's original than is Alcuin's and includes both occurrences of *fruitio* by Jerome. Because the variants in Jerome's text as quoted in Rabanus differ entirely from those in Alcuin's work, I suggest that Rabanus is working directly from a copy of Jerome rather than a copy of Alcuin.

Rabanus distinguishes himself in the transmission of *fruitio* by using it fourteen times (compared with three times at most by all earlier authors). These all appear in his commentary on the letters of Paul.[111] A few representative examples from the fourteen occurrences will demonstrate how he uses *fruitio*:

> ...fruitionem futurorum bonorum ... (PL 112:483)
>> "fruition of future good things"

> ...aeternae vitae et futurae gloriae fruitionem assecuti. (PL 112:532)
>> "fruition of eternal life and future glory"

> ...et quod magnorum bonorum fruitionem exspectent potiri credentes. (PL 112:569)
>> "fruition of great good things"

> ...possint etiam promissorum bonorum assequi fruitionem. (PL 112:638)
>> "fruition of promised good things"

Three examples use a form of *bonum*, indicating that the "enjoyment" (*fruitio*) relates to the good or good things. However, the exception speaks explicitly of fruition "of eternal life and future glory," fruition of heaven.[112] Rabanus is the first author to make frequent use of *fruitio* and also explicitly to refer to heaven.

Paschasius Radbertus was born in Soissons and before 820 he joined the monastery of Corbie where he was made abbot (843–c.851).[113] Among his various works is one theological treatise, *De Fide, Spe, et Charitate* in which he uses the term *fruitio*.[114] He writes, "But no one knows the good perfectly because it is not loved perfectly and not at first understood unless believed. For fruition of the highest good is charity."[115] That Paschasius links *fruitio* and *caritas*, in a

---

111   Rabanus Maurus, *Enarrationum*, PL 112:483–708.
112   Where "futurorum bonorum" is equivalent to "futurae gloriae" and "promissorum bonorum."
113   Though a deacon he was never ordained priest.
114   Paschasius Radbertus, *De Fide, Spe et Charitate*, PL 120:1387–1489.
115   Paschasius Radbertus, De Fide, PL 120:1454. "Sed nullum bonum perfecte noscitur, quod non perfecte amatur, et prius nec intelligitur, nisi credatur. Fruitio enim summi boni charitas est."

maxim of sorts, anticipates a theme of monastic theology found in William's writings. Paschasius transmits the traditional meaning and usage of *fruitio*, as the enjoyment of something good.

John Scotus Eriugena, who wrote most of his works in the 860s in the region of Rheims (where William spent most of his life), uses *fruitio* twice, both in his *De divisione naturae*.[116] The first appears in a quotation he translates from Gregory of Nyssa's *De Imagine*.[117] The second occurs later in this work and is from Eriugena himself:

> And the ancient enemy may not have access to the man of the spirit (the soul, I say, made in the image of God), unless first implanted in the corporeal sense ... the delight of the soul, as if through that very serpent he might separate the corporeal sense in the way the soul might consent to destructive material things by taking delight and misapplied fruition in the corporeal sense...[118]

Eriugena's own use of *fruitio* is different from previous occurrences because he adds "misapplied" (*perabusiva*) to describe improper "fruition." This does not change the meaning for *fruitio* because when *perabusiva* is taken into account, as if he says "this is not proper *fruitio*," it means that proper *fruitio* is directed to something other than "destructive material things."[119] In addition, his clear definition of *fruitio* as enjoyment of the good only, is narrowed like Jerome's, to specialized or sanctified fruition. After John Scotus, *fruitio* seems forgotten, based on its absence in extant texts, in the 10th and 11th centuries.[120]

---

116 Johannis Scoti, *De Divisione Naturae Libri Quinque*, written c.865–870.

117 John Scotus, Div Nat, PL 122:847. One of Gregory of Nyssa's works known to have been translated from Greek into Latin by John Scotus Eriugena.

118 John Scotus, Div Nat, Bk 4, "Neque antiquus hostis ad virum animae, animum dico ad imaginem Dei factum, accessum haberet, nisi prius per insitam corporeo sensui, qui est veluti quaedam mulier, animi delectationem, quasi per quendam colubrum ipsum corporeum sensum seduceret: quemadmodum neque animus in rerum materialium perniciosa delectatione et perabusiva fruitione corporeo sensui consentiret, si prius in ipso superba praesumptio non praecederet," PL 122:847; written c.865–870.

119 For example, nourishment from Scripture as described in his quotation from Gregory of Nyssa.

120 The term *perfruitio*, meaning "enjoyment to the fullest" appears once in Peter Abelard, *Sic et Non* (PL 178:1587B), c.1120, and in Hugh of Saint Victor's *De sacramentis Christianae fidei*, VIII.ix. (PL 176:611C), c.1134, in which he quotes this phrase verbatim from Abelard. *Expositio moralis in Abdiam*, erroneously attributed to Hugh, contains *fruitio*. See Rebecca Moore, "Hugh of St. Victor and the Authorship of *In Threnos Jeremiae*," *Journal of Religious History* 22.3 (1998): 255–69 (esp. 256 n.4 and 258 n.12), in which she also cites five other scholars who challenge the authenticity of this commentary on Obediah, including Beryl

Altogether from the 4th to the 12th centuries, we have at most twenty-six occurrences of the term *fruitio* prior to William's own writings (excluding pseudo-Hugh of Saint Victor). By comparison, William is enamored with the term because he uses it forty times, twenty-five alone in his *Expositio super Canticum canticorum*. In his earliest work, *De contemplando Deo*, written between 1121–1124, a short text comprised of a lengthy prayer, he uses *fruitio* five times. Writing about the vicissitudes of contemplation, the contrast between being with God in prayer and the other times when we "fall to the ground" and become "foreigner[s]" in a strange land,[121] William is given a word of hope: "There is love of desire and love of fruition. Love of desire merits a certain vision, vision merits fruition, fruition merits perfection of love."[122] He finds consolation in this answer, which he calls a foretaste of God's Spirit and promise, but does he speak of the ultimate fulfillment, enjoyment of perfected love in this life or the next? The answer given is the foretaste (*arrha*) in this life, yet the fulfillment of what the answer promises may be found only in the next life.

A few paragraphs later, William mentions again the foretaste of union with God, which is brief and is the "silence in heaven" that allows the mind to linger on the experience. But he then explains that only in eternal and blessed life is fruition perfected and perpetual.[123] Toward the end of the text, William describes ultimate spiritual union as "such conjoining, such adherence, such fruition of sweetness" that in it the prayer of Jesus is fulfilled, "that they may be one in us ... just as you and I are one" (John 17:21).[124] Without exception, William always (and frequently) interprets this prayer of Jesus as the union between the individual soul and God. Thus in his earliest work, he speaks of *fruitio* only a few times, but each time referring to the eternal fruition of the next life.

In his next work, *De natura et dignitate amoris*, written just after *De contemplando Deo*, William uses *fruitio* four times. He says that the mind is the place of the soul in which we enjoy God. And this enjoyment (*fruitio*), is a divine savor (*sapor*), from which wisdom comes. He links *sapor* and *sapientia* quoting

---

Smalley, Heinrich Denifle, P. Glorieux, Artur Michael Landgraf, and F. Vernet. Based on his authentic writings, Hugh never used the term *fruitio*, and therefore is not a link in the transmission of the term. Richard of Saint Victor does use the term *fruitio*, twelve times in his *Explicatio in Cantica canticorum* (PL 196:405), but this work post-dates William by at least a decade.

121   Contemp, 5, CCCM 88:156. ET: William of St. Thierry, *On Contemplating God, Prayer, Meditations*, trans. Sr. Penelope [Lawson], CF 3 (Kalamazoo, MI: Cistercian Publications, 1977), 43.

122   Contemp, 5, "Amor desiderii meretur ... visionem, visio fruitionem, fruitio amoris perfectionem," CCCM 88:157. ET: *On Contemplating God*, 43. The Latin reads beautifully and simply.

123   Contemp, 7, CCCM 88:160. ET: *On Contemplating God*, 49.

124   Contemp, 11, "...tantaque fit conjunctio, tanta adhaesio, tanta dulcedinis tuae fruitio," CCCM 88:164. ET: *On Contemplating God*, 56.

Psalm 24:9 "Taste and see that the Lord is good." This tasting, William writes, is
the word of God here and now, and it is also a foretaste of the world to come.[125]

William explains that now, the contemplation and fruition of divinity is the
foretaste and initiation into the blessedness of the future. This is part of the
glorification of the body begun in this life that will be received fully in the next
life.

> For as they seem to have already in this life a foretaste and to be initiated
> into the happiness of the life to come in holiness of life, in the glorifica-
> tion of the inner person, in the contemplation and fruition of divinity,
> so too they receive in this life some glorification of their bodies that they
> will there receive fully.[126]

William uses *fruitio* a bit differently here than he had previously—one need
not wait until the ultimate union with God, the eternal, heavenly blessedness
in order to experience a certain fruition in this life. There are steps that bridge
the gap between the full fruition of divine union and the metaphorical foreign
land of exile,[127] and along the way one may experience the fruition of both the
progress one makes and the foretaste God grants.

William's next usage of *fruitio* appears in his *Meditativae orationes*
(*Meditations*), begun around 1130. Through desiring the vision of God, with
good intentions, one "rejoices in the Holy Spirit in contemplation and fruition
(*fruitio*) of Your [God's] very own truth (*ipsius veritatis tuae*)."[128] He does not
say one must attain the vision of God before one can experience some fruition;
rather, in contemplation, in the Holy Spirit, one has fruition of some aspect
of God, whether the Highest Good, the Word of God, a foretaste of union, etc.

Then describing the seven steps of the soul's ascent to God in his *De natura
corporis et animae* (*On the Nature of the Body and the Soul*), written in 1138, William says that the seventh is "the very vision and contemplation of truth, no
longer a step but a permanent state (*gradibus pervenitur*) to which the previous
steps lead." He writes, "One who enjoys (*fruitur*) alone understands what are
the joys and what is the fruition of the true and highest good."[129] This seventh

---

125   Nat am, 28, CCCM 88:199. ET: *The Nature and Dignitiy of Love*, 88.

126   Nat am, 43, CCCM 88:210. ET: *Nature and Dignity of Love*, 106.

127   Contemp, 5, CCCM 88:156. ET: *On Contemplating God*, 43.

128   Med, 7.6, CCCM 89:44. ET: *On Contemplating God, Prayer, Meditations*, trans. Sr. Penelope
      [Lawson], CF 3 (Kalamazoo, MI: Cistercian Publications, 1977), 136.

129   Phys an, 14. CCCM 88:144. ET: *Three Treatises on Man: A Cistercian Anthropology*, (ed.)
      Bernard McGinn, trans. Benjamin Clark, OCSO, CF 24 (Kalamazoo, MI: Cistercian Publica-
      tions, 1977), 150.

step or stage is echoed again and given more description in William's latter work, *The Golden Epistle*, in which he writes:

> For thus is the way God is to be loved. For *amor* is a vehement will toward God; *dilectio* [is] a clinging to or joining with [God]; *caritas* [is] fruition of [God]. But unity of spirit with God, for the person whose heart is raised on high, is perfection of the will progressing toward God, when it no longer merely wills what God wills, and is not just a great *affectus* but a perfected *affectus* so that it cannot will except what God wills.[130]

Here William speaks of what is possible in this life because he goes on to say in the next paragraph that in this process, one becomes "what God is: holy," and "in the future, fully blessed"; and that God *is* one's holiness and blessedness, the source of one's "present holiness" and one's "future blessedness."[131]

In his *Mirror of Faith*, written between 1142 and 1144, just before *The Golden Epistle*, William puts *fruitio* into his broader understanding of the human person and spiritual progress. He explains that the mind is created for eternity and through the mind's understanding, which comes through the senses (e.g. reading, hearing, etc.), and its knowledge, which comes from wisdom that is natural through creative grace (what we all have from our nature as human beings) and enlightened through illuminating grace (what we receive from God through the Holy Spirit), the mind becomes open (*capax*) to eternity and through fruition becomes a participant (*particeps*) in eternity.[132] By nature, human beings have a certain likeness to eternity and divinity, the image of God that comes through God's creative grace. But one's ability to recognize the things of eternity depends on one's knowledge through human reason and wisdom, which can mistake the bad for the good unless enlightened by

---

130 Ep frat, 257, "Sic enim diligendus est Deus. Magna enim voluntas ad Deum, amor est; dilectio, adhaesio sive conjunctio; caritas, fruitio. Unitas vero spiritus cum Deo, homini sursum cor habenti, proficientis in Deum voluntatis est perfectio, cum iam non solummodo vult quod Deus vult, sed sic est non tantum affectus, sed in affectu perfectus, ut non possit velle nisi quod Deus vult," CCCM 88:281. ET: *The Golden Epistle*, 94.

131 Ep frat, 258, "quod Deus est, sint sancti, futuri plene beati ... nec aliunde hic santi nec ibi futuri beati, quam ex Deo qui eorum et sanctitas and beatitudo est," CCCM 88:281. ET: *The Golden Epistle*, 94.

132 Spec fid, 24, "Menti siquidem ad eternitatem create, ut eius per intelligentiam sit capax, per fruitionem particeps, quasi naturali quadam affinitate conjuncta videntur, que eterna sunt ac divina, ...Nam et si invisibilia forte cogitare non poterit sic tamen eorum cognitio rationi humane concreta est.... Inquibus tametsi habet natura appetitum ex gratia creante, non tamen ea perfecte dinoscit, nisi ex gratia illuminante, nec apprehendit nisi Deo donante...," CCCM 89A:112. ET: *The Mirror of Faith*, 59.

the Holy Spirit so it can discern the good from the bad—this is illuminating grace.[133] William explains here that the fruition of things eternal and divine is the means by which we participate in the things eternal and divine, and this is what we experience here and now as part of our nature, given by God's grace, and part of our spiritual progress, also granted by God's grace.

William explains too that as one comes closer to God, human words are not only insufficient but become impediments to understanding divine realities. However, illuminated love (*amor illuminatus*) speaks inwardly to God and is better than human words, as is humble devotion through piety, through prayer, through understanding, which is "the very fruition of reality, when *affectus* and grace converse, faith and understanding respond to each other, hope and reality agree, mercy and truth meet one another, justice and peace kiss each other."[134] We can experience this because what we understand, we can grasp without obscurity, and what we do not understand we grasp through faith which nourishes love.[135] Once we progress to this point beyond human language, which relies on faith and love, the experience is fruition of reality, when everything comes together not just for knowledge, not just for understanding, but for enjoyment, fruition.

William's *Expositio super Canticum canticorum* (*Exposition on the Song of Songs*), written in 1138, erupts, as it were, with *fruitio*, using it twenty-five times throughout. One major point William makes here, and not elsewhere in his works, is that fruition is mutual between God and the human soul. Three times he explains how the fruition of each one's love, the fruition of each one's embrace, each one's union brings mutual joy.[136] Commenting on Song 2:7, "The voice of my Beloved," William writes, "And this very same voice becomes both the voice of the Bridegroom to the Bride and the voice of the Bride to the Bridegroom, in the joy of mutual conjoining and fruition in which they constantly converse and answer one another."[137]

At times William is not entirely clear whether he refers to fruition here and now or in the eternal life to come, and I suggest that this lack of clarity may reflect William's own uncertainty and the vicissitudes of contemplative life,

133   Spec fid, 24, CCCM 89A:112. ET: *The Mirror of Faith*, 59.

134   Spec fid, 32, "...ipsa rei fruitio ubi colloquitur affectus et gratia, respondent sibi fides et intellectus, spes et res conveniunt, *misericordia et veritas obviant sibi, justitia et pax se osculantur* (Ps 84.11)," CCCM 89A:125. ET: *The Mirror of Faith*, 83.

135   Spec fid, 32, CCCM 89A:125. ET: *The Mirror of Faith*, 83.

136   Cant, 138, 142, 154. ET: *Exposition on the Song of Songs*, 111–12, 113–14, 126–27.

137   Cant, 142, "Fitque vox ipsa et Sponsi ad Sponsam, et Sponsae ad Sponsum, in gaudio mutuae conjunctionis et fruitionis in quo jugiter sibi loquuntur et respondent," CCCM 87:97. ET: *Exposition on the Song of Songs*, 113–14.

perhaps even his own experience. The kiss from Song 1:1 is certainly the attainment of full fruition, as he writes, "The kiss will know its fullness when, eye to eye, embrace to embrace, full and abiding fruition shall be attained."[138] Relating back to his initial question in his first work, *On Contemplating God*, about the love of desire and the love of fruition, William comments on Song 1:6, "Lest I begin to wander after the flocks of your companions," writing, "For there is the love of desiring and the other, the love of fruition. Certainly the love of desire burns even in the darkness, but does not illuminate; but love of fruition is wholly in the light because fruition itself is the light of the loving."[139] Is being "wholly in the light" a metaphor for spiritual life now or for the future enjoyment alone? He does not clarify this for us here. However, William uses *fruitio* to explain the fruition of the Bride, the soul, that may be experienced in this life and also that will come in the fullness of the next life.

William's language of *fruitio* contains the meanings and contexts of the tradition he received: 4th-8th centuries, enjoyment of good things in this life, and from the 9th century, enjoyment of heaven. Since Paschasius Radbertus and Rabanus Maurus are the only authors, prior to William, who write about *fruitio* as enjoyment of heaven and not just enjoyment of something good in this life, William may have relied on either or both for this innovated meaning. Although I found no direct literary link to demonstrate this, the lack of any other texts with this content create some probability that William knew and relied on one or both of these authors to inspire this specific meaning and usage of *fruitio*.

William comes very close to Paschasius Radbertus' phrase, "Fruitio enim summi boni caritas est,"[140] "For *fruitio* of the Highest Good is *caritas*," when in *The Golden Epistle*, he writes that fruition of God is *caritas*.[141] The phrase is not an exact quotation or even allusion, and it requires some syntactical analysis: "Magna enim voluntas ad Deum, amor est; dilectio, adhaesio sive coniunctio; caritas, fruitio."[142] "For *amor* is a vehement will toward God; *dilectio* [is] a clinging to or joining with [God]; *caritas* [is] fruition of [God]." However, in the syntax of the phrase, the verb "to be" (*est*) and the object "God" (*Deum*) are both distributed from the first phrase to the subsequent phrases, including the

---

138   Cant, 98, "fiet que osculum plenum, cum oculo ad oculum, amplexum ad amplexum plena fiet et perpetua fruitio," CCCM 87:72. ET: *Exposition on the Song of Songs*, 80.

139   Cant, 60, "Nam alius est amor desiderantis, alius fruentis. Amor quippe desiderii etiam in tenebris ardet, sed non lucet; amor vero fruentis totus in luce est, quia fruitio ipsa lux amantis est," CCCM 87:48. ET: *Exposition on the Song of Songs*, 48.

140   Paschasius Radbertus, De Fide. PL 120:1454.

141   Ep frat, 257, CCCM 88:281. ET: *The Golden Epistle*, 94.

142   Ep frat, 257, CCCM 88:281. ET: *The Golden Epistle*, 94.

last one predicating *fruitio* and *caritas*. This is not a near quotation of Paschasius, even if the idea itself is very close and particular to these two authors. Yet this predication of *fruitio* and *caritas*, together with connection between *fruitio* and heaven detailed above, suggests William's familiarity with Paschasius Radbertus or at least his idea of connecting *fruitio* and *caritas* in this way.

William also uses *fruitio* one time that differs from all others but for John Scotus Eriugena, when he writes, "It is evident that the soul, as it were, when weakened by the senses of the body that are outside of itself and by the delights of bodily pleasures all around, feeds its own sensuality by fruition of these [bodily delights]."[143] The language is similar to what John Scotus Eriugena calls "misapplied fruition in the corporeal sense,"[144] and what William simply describes as misapplied fruition on account of the corporeal senses. Although the language is not similar enough to indicate a direct relationship between the two texts, the idea and meaning of the two texts are precisely the same and unique to these two authors, which does indeed suggest a connection between William and this passage in Eriugena. That William does quote from Eriugena's *On the Division of Nature* elsewhere in his *On Contemplating God*, strengthens the argument.[145]

Within William's own thought, *fruitio*, enjoyment, is systematized, generally speaking, and appropriated to each stage of spiritual life and progress. At the beginning, guided by natural reason with which we are all endowed by our created nature, we may have enjoyment of the right or the wrong things, the spiritual or the sensual. Once we progress and our natural reason is enlightened by the Holy Spirit through illuminating grace, we may discern the good from

---

143 Ep frat, 46, "scilicet cum anima quasi extra se per sensus corporis circa dilectorum delectationes corporum affecta, eorum fruitione pascit, vel nutrit sensualitatem suam," CCCM 88:237. ET: *The Golden Epistle*, 27.

144 Johannis Scoti, *Div Nat*, Book 4, "Neque antiquus hostis ad virum animae, animum dico ad imaginem Dei factum, accessum haberet, nisi prius per insitam corporeo sensui, qui est veluti quaedam mulier, animi delectationem, quasi per quendam colubrum ipsum corporeum sensum seduceret: quemadmodum neque animus in rerum materialium perniciosa delectatione et *perabusiva fruitione corporeo sensui consentiret*, si prius in ipso superba praesumptio non praecederet," PL 122:847. Italics for emphasis.
"And the ancient enemy may not have access to the man of the spirit (the soul, I say, made in the image of God), unless first implanted in the corporeal sense, which is like a certain woman, the delight of the soul, as if through a certain serpent itself he might separate the corporeal sense in the way the soul might consent to destructive material things by taking delight and *misapplied enjoyment in the corporeal sense*, if at first prideful presumption does not proceed in the soul." My translation, italics for emphasis.

145 See Contemp, 8, where William quotes from John Scotus Eriugena's *De divisione naturae* I.7. This quotation, however, may have come from a florilegium. See Bell, *The Image and Likeness*, 127 n.10.

the bad and have enjoyment of the good things, of the highest good, of truth itself. Further on we might even, in contemplation, be granted a foretaste of that eternal union with God, and experience the enjoyment, if only temporarily, of what is to come. Finally, once hope is fulfilled and the eternal union is realized, we then will experience the enjoyment of the eternal, heavenly blessedness.

The overwhelming traditional usage employs *fruitio* to mean enjoyment of something good in this life. The only three exceptions to this appear in the 9th century. Paschasius Radbertus is the only one who predicates *fruitio* and *caritas*, as does William in a very similar phrase with the exact same meaning.[146] Paschasius and Rabanus Maurus are the only authors who apply *fruitio* to the enjoyment of heaven. William does the same. One or both authors likely influenced William on this idea. Only John Scotus Eriugena says that *fruitio*, when it is misapplied, can also come from sensual pleasures rather than only spiritual ones. William follows this line of thought and agrees. Although William does not use the same language as John Scotus in this text, the two concepts are the same and unique to these two writers, and therefore we have a likely probability that John Scotus influenced William on this particular point.

4 Conclusion

What we may conclude is that William, as he has with other terms and concepts,[147] takes the biblical phrase, *ratio fidei*, modifies it from its original context, and under influence of others in the literary tradition, redefines it for his own purpose, and applies it to his own new context. In the other example, William's usage of *fruitio* fits more squarely within the established use of the term as seen in the literary transmission beginning in the 4th century and received into the 12th century. Thus he simply takes what he has received and applies it to his own writings and thought, unchanged. In the final

---

146   Paschasius, De Fide, PL 120:1454, and William, Ep frat, 257.

147   For a study of William's unique concept for *unitas spiritus*, see F. Tyler Sergent, "*Unitas Spiritus* and the Originality of William of Saint-Thierry," in *Unity of Spirit: Studies on William of Saint-Thierry in Honor of E. Rozanne Elder*, 144–70, (eds.) F. Tyler Sergent, Aage Rydstrøm-Poulsen, and Marsha L. Dutton, CS 268 (Collegeville, MN: Cistercian Publications, 2015); for the longer version of the *unitas spiritus* study and similar studies of the terms *arrha* and *sensus amoris*, see Sergent, "'Signs of Spiritual and Divine Realities'". I argue that William's use of *arrha* comes from Cassian, while *sensus amoris* is an entirely original term and concept coined by William himself.

analysis, we have here two examples of two different ways in which William chose his sources, utilized them, and appropriated them into his own thinking and writings. The study of these two terms lets us reiterate early suggestions for William's sources, including Hilary of Poitiers, Gregory the Great, and John Scotus Eriugena, and then to potential sources, we can also add the names Paschasius Radbertus (for both terms) and Rabanus Maurus.

CHAPTER 3

The Mystical Theology and Theological Mysticism of William of Saint-Thierry

David N. Bell

1   Introduction

There are two terms in the title of this paper which require explanation. One is "mysticism"; the other is "theology." The first is simple: by "mysticism" I mean, within the Christian tradition, an unmediated, experiential contact with the Trinitarian God in and through the Holy Spirit, made possible by the incarnation of the same God in the person of Jesus of Nazareth. This is not an experience of God in and through the sacraments or any other intermediary, but the direct experience of God himself, to the extent that human nature can endure it. The second term—"theology"—is rather more complicated. As John Kleinz said many years ago, "To the great medieval philosophers the journey of the mind to God was the supreme consideration of any theory of knowledge. The knowledge of God was not only the crown of their metaphysical specu-lations; it was paramount throughout their greatest works."[1] Or, putting it another way, for William of Saint-Thierry and virtually everyone else up to and including Thomas Aquinas and Bonaventure, the experiential knowledge of God was the logical end of the theological quest. What Kleinz says of Hugh of Saint-Victor was true of all: "all the roads of reason and revelation should end in the contemplation of God."[2] William, therefore, was at one with the Venerable Bede whose definition of theology was simple: *Una ergo et sola est theologia, id est, contemplatio Dei*, "Theology, therefore, is one thing and one thing alone: the contemplation of God."[3]

---

1 John P. Kleinz, *The Theory of Knowledge of Hugh of Saint Victor* (Washington, D.C.: Catholic University of America Press, 1944), 105.

2 Kleinz, *Theory of Knowledge*, 117.

3 Bede, *In evangelium Lucae*, III.X, "Una ergo et sola est theologia, id est, contemplatio Dei, cui merito omnia justificationum merita, universa virtutum studia postponuntur," PL 92:471D. Exactly the same definition appears in Bede's *Homilia LVII in die Assumptionis Mariae*, PL 94:421A, with *theoria* instead of *theologia*. See also n. 10 below. Provided there are no sig-nificant variants, I have generally cited Latin and Greek texts according to the volume and column number of the PL and PG. Then reason is simple: all the volumes are freely available

William's theology was monastic theology, or, putting it more accurately, it was one of a variety of monastic theologies, all of which shared the same goal and which led to the same end.[4] But this sort of theology cannot be divorced from spirituality, a term which is far wider and far harder to define than "mysticism." As Paul Clogan put it, it is "a subject on which an inordinate amount of nonsense has been and continues to be written,"[5] but if we think of spirituality simply as "the combination of praying and living,"[6] we shall be sufficiently close to the thought of William. We must remember too, that, as Norman Tanner has pointed out,

> For medieval people there was far less of a distinction between the outer and the inner aspects of religion than for us today.... Medieval people thought and expressed themselves largely by what they did, and therefore their external activities were the key to, indeed for the most part *were*, their inner piety.[7]

William's theology expressed itself naturally in his Christian life, and his Christian life was a natural expression of his search for God.[8]

---

online and the interested reader can bring up a text in a matter of seconds. It should also be pointed out that not all recent so-called critical editions are as reliable as they should be.

4   See Jean Leclercq, "The Renewal of Theology," in *Renaissance and Renewal in the Twelfth Century*, (eds.) Robert L. Benson and Giles Constable with Carol D. Lanham (Toronto: University of Toronto Press, 1991), 69–87. This article presents a more accurate view of the blurred relationship between monastic and scholastic theology first propounded by Leclercq more than thirty years earlier in his *L'Amour des lettres et le désir de Dieu. Initiation aux auteurs monastiques du Moyen Âge* (Paris: Éditions du Cerf, 1957; rpt., 2008).

5   Paul M. Clogan, preface to *Medievalia et Humanistica: Studies in Medieval and Renaissance Culture*, N.S, 4 "Medieval and Renaissance Spirituality" (Denton: North Texas State University, 1973), vi. See also the intriguing paper by Stuart Rose, "Is the Term 'Spirituality' a Word that Everyone Uses, But Nobody Knows What Anyone Means by it?," *Journal of Contemporary Religion* 16 (2001): 193–207, and the rejoinder by Stephen Hunt, "'Spirituality': A Word that Everyone Uses and Some Believe that They Know What it Means," *Implicit Religion* 18 (2015): 107–31.

6   Geoffrey Wainwright, "Types of Spirituality," in *The Study of Spirituality*, (eds.) Cheslyn Jones, Geoffrey Wainwright, and Edward Yarnold (New York/Oxford: Oxford University Press, 1986), 592; see also 604–05.

7   Norman Tanner, "Piety in the Middle Ages," in *A History of Religion in Britain: Practice and Belief from Pre-Roman Times to the Present*, (eds.) Sheridan Gilley and W.J. Sheils (Oxford: Blackwell, 1994), 71.

8   Thus, to say that "William's theology was secondary to his Christian life" (Aage Rydstrøm-Poulsen, "The Way of Descent: The Christology of William of Saint-Thierry," in *Unity of Spirit: Studies on William of Saint-Thierry in Honor of E. Rozanne Elder*, (eds.) F. Tyler Sergent, Aage Rydstrøm-Poulsen, and Marsha L. Dutton, CS 268 [Collegeville, MN: Cistercian Publications/ Liturgical Press, 2015], 86), is to misunderstand the nature of that theology.

This is not to say, of course, that William was not well trained in what we would now call systematic theology. He had been soundly educated at Reims and quite possibly at Liège—Laon is pure speculation[9]—and, when he needed to use it, he had an admirable command of scholarly style and rhetoric. If, with Evagrius Ponticus, we define a theologian as one who truly prays and one who truly prays as a theologian,[10] then it would be foolish to compare William and Bernard, but only the most blinkered admirer of Bernard could fail to admit that, in his scholarly learning and in his understanding of the complexities of the ideas of Rupert of Deutz, Peter Abelard, and William of Conches, William was Bernard's superior.[11] What I mean by "mystical theology," therefore, is a quest to know God by both thinking and doing—living the Christian life with all its demands and difficulties—which finds its culmination in the experiential knowledge of God. And by "theological mysticism" I mean a mysticism which is far from being merely emotive or simply a search for altered states of consciousness, but a doctrine of the knowledge of God firmly rooted in and leading logically from certain well-established theological principles. But before we examine those principles, let us say something of what William's theological mysticism is not, for in this he stands in marked contrast with Bernard and, indeed, with almost all other 12th-century Cistercians.

2   Mystical Theology

First of all, William's mystical theology is not Marian. The Mother of God plays hardly any role in his thought.[12] There is the rather lovely story, recounted in the late 12th-century life of William, of his dream-meeting with Our Lady of Bazoches, who gently took William's head in her hands and rested it on her bosom. "And although the blessed man realized that this had occurred in his sleep, he nevertheless sensed such a holy and spiritual joy that he could not

---

9   For a full discussion, see Ludo Milis, "William of Saint Thierry, his Birth, his Formation and his First Monastic Experiences," in *William, Abbot of St. Thierry: A Colloquium at the Abbey of St. Thierry*, trans. Jerry Carfantan, CS 94 (Kalamazoo: Cistercian Publications, 1987), 9–33.
10   Evagrius, *De oratione* 60, PG 79:1179B (there attributed to St. Nilus).
11   See, for example, Jean Châtillon, "William of Saint Thierry, Monasticism, and the Schools: Rupert of Deutz, Abelard, and William of Conches," in *William, Abbot of St. Thierry*, 153–80, and Pietro Zerbi, "William of Saint Thierry and his Dispute with Abelard," in *ibid.*, 181–203. One could compile an extensive bibliography on this matter, but Châtillon's admirable paper alone proves the point.
12   See Jacques Delesalle, "La Vierge Marie dans les œuvres de Guillaume de Saint-Thierry," in Jean Longère *et al.*, *La Vierge dans la tradition cistercienne. 54ᵉ session de la Société Française d'Études Mariales, Abbaye Notre-Dame d'Orval, 1998* (Paris: Éditions Médiaspaul, 1999), 97–107.

recall ever having experienced the like before."[13] There is also a passage in the *Speculum fidei* where the Mother of the Lord is described as "a special sign of faith" (*speciale fidei signum*),[14] but there is very little else.[15] Mary's role in the writings of Bernard and Aelred is dramatically different.

The second thing we may say about William's theological mysticism is that it is not Christocentric. To be sure, Christ is its foundation, inasmuch as without the incarnation and redemption the flow of grace would have remained interrupted, we would still be in our sins, and spiritual progress would be utterly impossible.[16] William staunchly followed anti-Pelagian Augustine in his view of the total depravity of human beings as a consequence of the first sin, and equally staunchly followed him in his belief that of our own power, we can only fall.[17] Human nature, says William, "is so corrupted and fallen through sin that the human will is free only to do evil. It can do nothing good save by liberating grace."[18] Christ, therefore, is, quite simply, the essential and unique basis for the Christian life, but whereas Aelred, Bernard, and others will dwell longingly and lovingly on Christ's humanity and the events of his Passion, these, for William, are but stepping-stones to a much more apophatic understanding.

---

13 David N. Bell, "The *Vita Antiqua* of William of St Thierry," *Cistercian Studies* [*Quarterly*] 11 (1976): 248; Freddy Le Brun, "*Vita Antiqua Willelmi Sancti Theoderici* d'après le manuscrit latin 11782 de la Bibliothèque Nationale de Paris," in *Signy l'Abbaye et Guillaume de Saint-Thierry. Actes du Colloque international d'Études cisterciennes 9, 10, 11 septembre 1998, Les Vieilles Forges (Ardennes)*, (ed.) Nicole Boucher (Signy l'Abbaye: Association des Amis de l'Abbaye de Signy, 2000), 444–45.

14 Spec fid, 59, CCCM 89A:104. As requested by the volume editor, I have cited William according to the editions in CCCM. It must be observed, however, that these editions are not always satisfactory, and the critical apparatus limited. I should also add that all translations in this paper are my own.

15 A more positive assessment of the place of Mary in William's work appeared in Georges Bavaud, "Guillaume de Saint-Thierry, docteur de l'Assomption?," *Revue Bénédictine* 70 (1960): 641–51, but Bavaud's assessment depends on whether he is correct in attributing the pseudo-Augustinian sermon *Ad interrogate* (PL 40:1141–48) to William. The evidence for this is thin, and, in my view, the attribution most unlikely. On the other hand, it must be remembered that none of William's sermons for the great Marian feasts—the Annunciation, Visitation, and so on—has been preserved, so we are working with limited resources.

16 On William's Christology, see the very sound studies by E. Rozanne Elder, "The Christology of William of Saint-Thierry," *Recherches de théologie ancienne et médiévale* 58 (1991): 79–112, and "Christologie de Guillaume de Saint-Thierry et vie spirituelle," in *Signy l'Abbaye*, 575–87. These are based on Dr. Elder's doctoral dissertation "The Image of the Invisible God: The Evolving Christology of William of Saint-Thierry" (Ph.D. diss., University of Toronto, 1972). See also n. 8 above.

17 Augustine, *Enarratio in Psalmum* 129.1, PL 37:1696. See further David N. Bell, *The Image and Likeness: The Augustinian Spirituality of William of St Thierry*, CS 78 (Kalamazoo, MI: Cistercian Publications, 1984), 59.

18 Adv Abl, 6, CCCM 89A:40.

This is all part of William's doctrine of pure prayer, and follows quite logically from his essentially Augustinian theology. Augustine distinguishes three levels of vision: corporeal, spiritual, and intellectual.[19] *Corporalia* are simply those created physical or corporeal objects we see with our everyday eyes. *Spiritualia* are those images we see with the "spirit," which here means no more than the mind—i.e., those mental objects we see with the eyes of our imagination. They range from imaginary creatures like basilisks through dream-images to the psychedelic wonders of the book of Revelation. But the *intellectualia* are experienced through the *intellectus*, the highest level of human reason, and they are wholly extra-conceptual, beyond all forms and images. Given that the human intellect is the mark of our creation in the image of God, it is our business to use that intellect to apprehend the *intellectualia*, and anything less than that, says William, is idolatry.[20] Dwelling on the events of Christ's humanity— the scene in the manger, the crucifixion, the print of the nails—may actually hinder true spiritual prayer and, William says so:

> But if we sometimes clasp the feet of Jesus[21] in our prayer, and develop a certain quasi-corporeal affection for the form of his humanity, on the grounds that it is one person with the [divine] son of God, we do not err, but we do, nevertheless, retard and hinder spiritual prayer, as he himself tells us: "It is expedient for you that I depart. Unless I go away, the Paraclete will not come to you (Jn 16:7)."[22]

What William means here is that our imaginary vision of Jesus' physical form must be put aside if one is to pray to him truly in the Spirit, for spiritual prayer, as we have seen, is beyond all images. He quotes the same verse in his commentary on the Song of Songs and explains there what he means:

> "It is expedient for you that I depart"—that is, that I remove from your sight the mask (*persona*) of my humanity—"for unless I go away, the Paraclete will not come to you." For as long as someone praying thinks of anything corporeal in him to whom he prays, he prays devoutly (*pie*), but not wholly spiritually (*non omnino spiritualiter*).[23]

---

19 See Bell, *Image and Likeness*, 67–68, 94–96. Augustine explains the matter in lucid detail in his *De Genesi ad litteram,* XII.III.6-XVII.38, PL 34:455–69.

20 For a full discussion and English translation, see David N. Bell, "The Prayer of Dom William: A Study and New Translation," in *Unity of Spirit: Studies on William of Saint-Thierry*, 25–28.

21 Cf. Matt 28:9.

22 Orat, 7, CCCM 88:170. ET: Bell, "Prayer of Dom William," 35.

23 Cant, 15, CCCM 87:26.

Nevertheless, even though such prayer is not wholly spiritual, it may yet lead the soul to more exalted realms. By thinking of all the good that Christ has done for us, says William, we may be led suddenly or unexpectedly (*repente*) beyond good things to the Highest Good itself (William, again, is echoing Augustine[24]), and the Highest Good is beyond all *corporalia* and *spiritualia*. By a superabundance of grace, the soul experiences the Second Person of the Trinity *sicuti est*, "as he is,"[25] which is the foretaste of the Beatific Vision, and which leads us into those rarefied realms into which we must now venture. This final stage, we might add, is not within our power to attain. We may and must do all that we can to prepare ourselves for it, but only God can bring it about.

So if William's theological mysticism is not Marian and not Christocentric, what is it? It is based, firmly and logically, on three essential theological principles. The first is God's own words in Genesis 1:26, "Let us make human beings to our image and likeness (*ad imaginem et similitudinem nostram*)." The second is Augustine's doctrine of the Trinity, and especially the nature and function of the Holy Spirit. And the third, which also comes from Augustine, is that love is will, and that it is by love that we cleave to God. Let us examine these principles in a little more detail.

William's doctrine of our creation *ad imaginem et similitiudinem Dei* is rooted in Augustine,[26] and, as we may see from the magisterial work of Robert Javelet,[27] it was a doctrine shared by virtually every theologian of the 12th century. In William's case, however, it was elaborated with great skill by the ideas of Gregory of Nyssa (*c.* 335–394), whose treatise *De opificio hominis* had been translated by John Scot Eriugena as *De imagine*.[28] This is especially clear in

---

24   "This is good and that is good, but why add more and more? Remove the 'this' and 'that,' and try to see the Good itself. Then you will see God, not good by a good other than himself, but the good of all good.... For the good that the soul must seek is not that above which it is to fly by judging, but that to which it is to cleave by loving. And what can this be but God?" (Augustine, *De Trinitate*,VIII.4, PL 42:949); Bell, *Image and Likeness*, 52.

25   Med X.8-9, CCCM 89:59–60. 1 John 3:2 reads "We know that when he shall appear, we shall be like him: because we shall see him as he is (*similes ei erimus: quoniam videbimus eum sicuti est*)." This is a key text for William.

26   See Bell, *Image and Likeness*, Chapters I and III, *passim*.

27   Robert Javelet, *Image et ressemblance au douzième siècle. De saint Anselme à Alain de Lille* (Paris: Letouzey & Ané, 1967), two volumes, of which the second contains a wealth of notes.

28   The influence of Gregory was first noticed by Dom Jean-Marie Déchanet in 1938–39: "Aux sources de la doctrine spirituelle de Guillaume de Saint-Thierry: 1, Saint Grégoire de Nysse," *Collectanea O.C.R.* 5 (1938–39), 187–98, 262–78, reprinted in Déchanet's *Aux sources de la spiritualité de Guillaume de Saint-Thierry. Première série d'études* (Bruges: Charles Beyaert, 1940), 25–59. For Eriugena's translation, see Maieul J. Cappuyns, "Le 'De imagine' de Grégoire de Nysse traduit par Jean Scot Érigène," *Recherches de théologie ancienne et médiévale* 32 (1965): 205–62. See further Anne Saword, "Notes on William of

William's *De natura corporis et animae,* a rather neglected work which testifies to the impressive breadth of William's reading.

It is in that very work that we read that when God created human beings, he gave them being (*esse*), which they share with stones, "seed life" (*vita seminalis*), which they share with plants and trees, sensual or animal life (*vita sensualis sive animalis*), which they share with beasts, "and he even added rational life (*vita rationalis*) with the angels."[29] William has borrowed this not from Gregory but from Claudianus Mamertus, who has borrowed it from Augustine,[30] but it was a common and well-known theme. Its implications, however, are momentous.

Of ourselves we are nothing. If we exist, if we *are*, it is only because we have been granted existence by God; but since God is Supreme Being, anything that *is* bears—to that tiny trifling extent—a likeness to God. As William puts it, God is the "principal essence" of every created thing.[31] A stone, therefore, has a certain likeness to God simply because stones *are*, but stones are not images of God. Plants and trees and animals have greater likeness, but neither are they images of God. For something to be a true image of God, it must be invisible, formless, immortal, and rational, and the only thing that fits all these qualifications is the human soul. Everything else may show "traces" of God— Augustine uses the term *vestigia Dei*, which appears in the book of Job[32]—but only human beings are created in his image.[33]

Putting it another way, all created things participate to some extent in God, and each level of participation includes those that come before it. Stones participate in being; plants and animals in being and sensing; human creatures in being, sensing, and rationality. And it follows from this that the *imago Dei* in

---

St Thierry's Use of Gregory of Nyssa's Treatise *On the Making of Man,*" *Cistercian Studies* [*Quaterly*] 9 (1974): 394–97; Anne Saword, "Man as the Image of God in the Works of William of St Thierry," in *One Yet Two: Monastic Tradition East and West. Orthodox-Cistercian Symposium, Oxford University, 26 August–1 September 1973,* (ed.) M. Basil Pennington, CS 29 (Kalamazoo, MI: Cistercian Publications, 1976), 267–303 (a useful study); Bernard McGinn, "Introduction," *Three Treatises on Man: A Cistercian Anthropology,* (ed.) Bernard McGinn, CF 24 (Kalamazoo, MI: Cistercian Publications), 35–41; and Thomas M. Tomasic, "Just How Cogently is it Possible to Argue for the Influence of St. Gregory of Nyssa on the Thought of William of Saint-Thierry?," *Recherches de théologie ancienne et médiévale* 55 (1988): 72–129.

29   Nat corp, 58, CCCM 88:123.

30   See Bell, *Image and Likeness,* 90, n. 3.

31   Ænig, 66, CCCM 89A:170.

32   Job 11:7. See Bell, *Image and Likeness,* 46, 90. Gregory the Great's commentary on this verse is illuminating, and there is no doubt that William had read it or had heard it read: see Gregory the Great, *Moral Reflections on the Book of Job,* vol. 2, Books 6–10, trans. Brian Kerns, CS 257 (Collegeville, MN: Cistercian Publications, 2015), 348–50 (X.viii.13).

33   See, for example, Nat corp, 82–87, CCCM 88:132–34. This whole section is heavily dependent on Gregory of Nyssa.

us cannot be lost. If it were to be lost, we would immediately cease to exist, for not only would we lose our rationality, but our very being. This idea is clearly set out in Augustine, and was a commonplace of 12th-century theology.

But Genesis 1:26 tells us that we were created by God to his image *and likeness*, and the word "to"—*ad* in Latin—is important here. It implies a process, a development, whereas "*in* his image and likeness" might imply something rather more static. But if the image cannot be lost, this is certainly not the case with the likeness. The likeness can indeed be lost, and it is lost through the corruption and depravity of sin. Every time we put our self-will before God's will, every time we love ourselves more than our Creator, every time we sin (and sin is the product of self-love and self-will) we distort the image, though the image itself always contains within itself the idea of and the potential for likeness.[34] Through sin we have entered the "region of unlikeness," the *regio dissimilitudinis*, a well-known term among the 12th-century *spirituels*,[35] and one which William uses three times.[36]

So let us now be logical. Through sin and self-will, we have all become unlike images of God, for if we say we have no sin, then we deceive ourselves and the truth is not in us (1 Jn 1:8). If, then, we can in some way restore the lost likeness and let the image shine forth in its true splendor, we may—simply by looking into ourselves—see an image of our Creator.

But there is more to it than this. Just as the image is distorted and deformed through sin, so it is re-formed through virtue. Every good work that we do, however trifling, is a move in the right direction, though no good work is possible without grace. Furthermore, just as we *are* only by participation in God's being, and just as our reason is what it is only by participation in God who, as Bernard of Clairvaux tells us, is "unchangeable reason" (*incommutabilis ratio*),[37] so our virtues are what they are only by participation in God's virtues, or, more accurately, in the virtues which are God. Augustine makes it clear that, for God, "to be" is the same as "to be great" or "to be wise" or "to be just" or to be anything else.[38] If, then, we ourselves are good, just, merciful, truthful, and so on—in other words, if, through grace, we are or try to be virtuous—these virtues are not ours by right any more than our being is ours by right. We are good in his goodness, wise in his wisdom, truthful in his truth, and so on, and the more virtuous we become, the greater is our likeness to the source of all virtues, which is God. So not only may we see in ourselves the image of God, we also become

---

34   See Bell, *Image and Likeness*, 46–47.

35   See Javelet, *Image et ressemblance*, I, 266–85. The expression first appears in Augustine, *Confessiones*, VII.X.16; PL 32: 742.

36   Nat am, 34, CCCM 88:203; Med IV.9, CCCM 89:22; Nat corp, 118, CCCM 88:145.

37   Bernard, *De consideratione*, V.XI.24, SBOp 3:486.

38   See Bell, *Image and Lkeness*, 47, n. 109.

like God, and through this ever-developing likeness, we regain, once more, the likeness to the image we lost in the Fall. It will be a long and hard process, and, in a passage directly dependent on Gregory of Nyssa, William says so. We might have remained perfect images, he tells us,

> if, through malice, nature had not been corrupted in its beginning. For this reason we are born like beasts, and the image of our Maker cannot shine forth in us immediately, nor without great and long labors.[39]

This principle, that we can know God by being like God, is the essence of the doctrine of connatural knowledge,[40] and it leads us directly to a consideration of the second basic premise on which William's theological mysticism is founded: the Holy Spirit in the Trinity.

3   Single and Double Procession

The earliest view of the way in which the Holy Spirit came into being is invariably referred to as Single Procession. That is to say, the Father eternally generates the Son, and through the Son the Father puts forth the Holy Spirit. The simplest analogy is water from a reservoir being channeled through a series of pipes to the faucets in our homes. Single Procession remains the view of the Orthodox Churches. Augustine's idea, as we find it set forth in his great *De Trinitate*, was quite different.[41] Here the Father eternally generates the Son, and then the Father and Son together bring into being the Holy Spirit. The technical term here is Double Procession, since both Father and Son contribute equally to the procession of the Spirit. It is rather like a modern car battery: the Father is the positive terminal, the Son is the negative terminal, and the Holy Spirit is the electric current flashing between them.

---

39   Nat corp 58, CCCM 88:123; Saword, "Notes on William of St Thierry's Use," 395 (710B-C).

40   See the brief and penetrating study by Odo Brooke, "Towards a Theory of Connatural Knowledge," *Cîteaux – Commentarii Cistercienses* 18 (1967): 275–90, reprinted in Odo Brooke, *Studies in Monastic Theology*, CS 37 (Kalamazoo, MI: Cistercian Publications, 1980), 232–49.

41   One could compile a substantial bibliography on Augustine's doctrine of the Holy Spirit, but this is obviously not the place to do it. Reference to two works will suffice: first, the old but sound study by Ferdinand Cavallera, "La doctrine de saint Augustin sur l'Esprit saint à propos du *De Trinitate*," *Recherches de théologie ancienne et médiévale* 2 (1930): 365–87, and 3 (1931): 5–19, and secondly the recent study by Luigi Gioia, *The Theological Epistemology of Augustine's* De Trinitate (Oxford: Oxford University Press, 2008), Chapter 6 "The Holy Spirit and the Inner-Life of the Trinity."

The Holy Spirit, in other words, is the mutual interaction of Father and Son—whatever is common to them both—and is so substantially. He is their mutual and common holiness, goodness, kindness, grace, peace, fellowship, will, delight, joy, happiness, embrace, communion, and blessedness,[42] but—above all—the Holy Spirit is the mutual love of Father and Son, the love which proceeds from them both and which is common to them both.[43] He is, in fact, their very unity. "The Holy Spirit", says Augustine,

> consists of the same unity and the same equality. For whether he is the unity of both [Father and Son], or the holiness, or the love—and therefore the unity because he is the love, or therefore the love because he is the holiness—it is clear that he is not one of the two. For through him the two are conjoined, through him the begotten [Son] is loved by the One who begets him and loves him who begot him, and through him "they preserve unity of spirit in the bond of peace" (Eph 4:3), not by virtue of participation but by their own essence, not by the gift of any superior, but by what they are.[44]

This is precisely William's view. For him, too, the Holy Spirit is whatever is common to Father and Son: *quidquid commune est eorum*.[45] And just as "God is spirit"[46] so it follows that all three Persons of the Trinity are spirit, but

> although each of them is spirit, and certainly holy, the Holy Spirit, who is common to the two, is properly designated by that name which is common to both. And just as he is common to both, so he is whatever is common to them: their divinity, charity, sweetness, blessedness, and so on.[47]

And as to the Holy Spirit as the actual unity of Father and Son, William quotes, almost word for word, the very passage from *De Trinitate* V.7 we have just translated.[48]

---

42   For all these terms with illustrative texts, see Cavallera, "La doctrine de saint Augustin," 367–87 *passim*. For all the terms listed in Latin, see Bell, *Image and Likeness*, 58.

43   See, for example, Augustine, *De Trinitate*, xv.10, PL 42:1064, and xv.27, PL 42:1079–80. For the Holy Spirit in general, see the whole of the sixth book of the *De Trinitate*.

44   Augustine, *De Trinitate*, V.7, PL 42:927–28. See also Gioia, *Theological Epistemology*, 130, who refers to this passage, quite rightly, as "crucial."

45   Adv Abl vi, cccm 89A:29; Ænig 97, cccm 89A:189; Exp Rom I.1:24, cccm 86:22.

46   John 4:24, *Spiritus Deus est*.

47   Ænig 97, cccm 89A:189.

48   See n. 44 above. See Ænig 98, cccm 89A:189–90.

4   The Life of Virtue

So let us now return for a moment to the life of virtue. As we have said, if we are good, we are good only by participation in the goodness of God, who is the Highest Good, if we are wise, we are wise in his wisdom, and so forth. We are what we are by participation in God; without that participation we are nothing. But participation in God is participation in God as Trinity. The great Athanasius was perfectly correct when, in opposition to those who denied the divinity of the Holy Spirit, he stated that when the triune God acts, he acts as a unity.[49] But the corollary to this is that when the one God acts, he acts as a Trinity, and that is what we have here. We do not just participate in God—William is neither Jew nor Muslim—but our participation in God the Father proceeds through God the Son, whose incarnation and redeeming death restored the flow of grace and made all such participation possible, and it is effected by, in, and through God the Holy Spirit, who is not only the communion and union of the Trinity within itself, but our communion and union with that same Trinity.

Thus, if we are to tread the path of virtue and restore the lost likeness, if we are to let the image of God shine forth once again in us as it did before the Fall, this is possible only through grace, and grace is the Holy Spirit. By grace we can become ever more like God, and "likeness to God is the whole of human perfection."[50] "For this alone were we created and do we live: that we might be like God, for we were created to his image."[51]

In the human creation, however, there is more than one likeness to God—not just the likeness of virtue—and before we proceed to the third and last of the basic premises which are the foundation of William's theological mysticism, we need to say a word about it. I am speaking here about what we might call the natural likeness, namely, that "as God is everywhere in his creation and everywhere whole, so too is every living soul in its body."[52] This is the likeness of ubiquity. Furthermore, although God is always in his own heaven, since his own being is his own heaven, when he dwells in us, we become his heaven.[53] But in that case, asks William in his third Meditation: "If

---

49   Athanasius, *Ad Serapionem* 1.28, PG 28:596A: "The Father does all things through the Word in the Holy Spirit: thus the unity of the Holy Triad is preserved."

50   Ep frat, 259, "Et haec hominis perfectio est, similitudo Dei," CCCM 88:281.

51   Ep frat, 259, "Propter hoc enim solum et creati sumus et uiuimus, ut Deo similes simus. Ad imaginem enim Dei creati sumus," CCCM 88:281.

52   Ep frat, 260, CCCM 88:281. See further the much more detailed discussion in Phys corp, 61–66, CCCM 88:124–126 (to line 808).

53   Med, VI.11, CCCM 89:36. See also Bell, "Prayer of Dom William," 28–29. William is again drawing on Augustine: see Bell, *Image and Likeness*, 101, n. 62.

you are with me, why am I not with you?"[54] The answer is simple. We *are* with him since we are his image, and, as we have seen, the image can never be lost. We are *not* with him because the image is distorted and because what I have called elsewhere our "latent participation" in God[55] has not been actualized. It is simply the difference between standing in the sun with your eyes closed, and opening your eyes. It makes no difference to the presence of the sun.

This idea, that the ubiquity of the soul in the body is similar to the ubiquity of God in creation is borrowed by William directly from Augustine, though the concept of God as "everywhere present and everywhere whole" (*ubique praesens et ubique totus*) was a theological commonplace in the 12th century.[56] Likewise, William also borrows directly from Augustine the idea that it is not just to God that the embodied soul has a certain similarity, but to God the Trinity. Augustine himself offered a wide variety of Trinitarian analogies in the human being,[57] but the most important of these was undoubtedly that of memory (*memoria*), intellect (*intellectus*), and love (*amor*) or will (*voluntas*).[58] In William *memoria* remains *memoria*, *intellectus* appears also as *intelligentia* or *ratio*, and *amor* as *dilectio* or *voluntas*.[59] Inasmuch as these are three distinct and separable qualities which, of necessity, always act inseparably, so in any human action we may see a likeness of the Trinity itself at work.

If all had gone as God had planned, this "lesser created trinity" (*creata trinitas inferior*)—William's words—would have cleaved indissolubly to "the unity of the highest and creative Trinity,"[60] and the human creation might have enjoyed unending felicity. But this was not to be. The new inhabitants of the new world were seduced and led astray by the variety of created things, and lost that conscious participation in God which was their gift at creation. They entered, in other words, the "region of unlikeness" which we mentioned above. So how were they and how are we to restore that lost likeness? The answer to

---

54   Med, III.4, CCCM 89:15.

55   See Bell, *Image and Likeness*, 32–33.

56   In Augustine, see *Epistola* 155.13, PL 33:672, *In evangelium Johannis tractatus* 75.4, PL 35:1830, and *Enarratio in Psalmum* 86.9, PL 37:1107–08. For a sound discussion of the principle (borrowed by Augustine from the Platonists), see Olivier Du Roy, *L'Intelligence de la foi en la Trinité selon saint Augustin: Genèse de sa théologie trinitaire jusqu'en 391* (Paris: Études augustiniennes, 1966), 469–70.

57   For a complete list, see Du Roy, *L'Intelligence de la foi*, 537–40.

58   For a convenient account in English, see John E. Sullivan, *The Image of God: The Doctrine of St. Augustine and its Influence* (Dubuque: The Priory Press, 1963), Chapter IV. But the longer and seminal discussion in Michaël Schmaus, *Die psychologische Trinitätslehre des hl. Augustinus* (Münster in Westfalen: Aschendorff Verlag, 1927; rpt. with new intro. and *Nachwort*, 1967) retains its value.

59   See Bell, *Image and Likeness*, 103, n. 71.

60   Nat am, 3, CCCM 88:180.

that question leads us now to the third and final premise on which William's theological mysticism is founded. What premise? The premise of love, which is none other than will, and love and will are none other than the Holy Spirit:

5   Love, Will, and the Holy Spirit

> As to this love of which we are speaking, we must not conceal the place of its birth, from which it possesses its lineage of distinguished nobility, nor the place from which it arises. First of all, its birth-place is God. There it is born, there nourished, there developed. There it is a citizen, not a stranger, but one who belongs there. Love is given by God alone, and in him it remains, for it is due to none other than him and for his sake. For if we discuss its birth, when God the Trinity created human beings to his image, he formed in them a sort of likeness of the Trinity (*quamdam Trinitatis similitudinem*), in which, too, the image of the Creator Trinity was to shine out. Through this [image], since like naturally returns to like, these new inhabitants of the world—had they so willed—might have cleaved indissolubly to God their Creator.[61]

Here, the "sort of likeness of the Trinity" is the "lesser created trinity" of memory, reason, and will,[62] and this statement of William is to be found in one of his earliest works, the *De natura et dignitate amoris*. Love is the key to the restoration of the lost likeness, for as Augustine said, it is by love that we cleave to God.[63] So what is love?

First of all, there are, in Latin, three words for love: *amor, dilectio*, and *caritas*. *Amor* is the general term and may be used for any kind of love, selfless or selfish, good or bad. *Dilectio* is almost always used for love which is directed toward a virtuous end. John Burnaby calls it "the love of conscious preference."[64] *Caritas* or "charity" always and without exception refers to the highest and most perfect form of love, and when, in the Latin text of 1 John, we read that "God is love," the word for "love" is *caritas*. And when, in the same verse, we are told that "whoever does not love does not know God," the verb for "to love" is *diligere,* from which derives *dilectio*.[65] We shall have more to say on *caritas* in a moment.

---

61   Nat am, 3, CCCM 88:179–180.
62   See Nat am, 3, CCCM 88:179–180.
63   See n. 24 above, but the idea is common.
64   John Burnaby, *Amor Dei. A Study of the Religion of St. Augustine* (London: Hodder & Stoughton, 1938; rpt., 1947), 115.
65   The verb from which *amor* is derived is *amare*, but there is no verb from which *caritas* is derived. It is associated with *carus*: dear, beloved, costly, precious, valued, high-priced.

Secondly, love and will are the same thing. This is pure Augustine and is taken over directly from him by William. Augustinian love, in other words, is no warm fuzzy emotional enthrallment, but the laser-beam of the focused will. Love, says William, following Augustine, is "vehement will"[66] or "a vehement well-ordered will,"[67] though he also borrows, apparently from John Scot Eriugena, a different definition, in which the love of the rational soul is described as "a movement or a quiet abiding or an end," in which the will neither seeks anything other than what it is, nor judges it worth seeking.[68]

If, then, love and will are fundamentally the same, it follows that self-love and self-will are also fundamentally the same, and this brings us once again to the restoration of the lost likeness. The essential reason why the likeness has been lost is because human beings have put their own self-love and self-will before that of God—as we have said, sin arises from self-love and self-will—and the way back to God obviously lies in eradicating our own love and will and putting in their place the love of God and the desire to do his will. Bernard put the matter very clearly in saying that the soul, which was created *recta* or "upright" has become *curva*, "bent, crooked," by turning away "from heaven, to which God had erected him, to bow himself down to the earth to which his animal nature attracts him."[69] Self-love/self-will is, at basis, "idolatry, self-adoration, and revolt against God":

> There, then, is the root of all the evil. Reason, setting itself above God, has perverted its own power of choice, warped its capacity to rejoice only in the good and introduced disorder into the will.[70]

A well-ordered will (*voluntas bene ordinata*[71]) is, on the contrary, a will which is directed to God and God alone, and it is the responsibility of every human being

---

66   Med, XII.20, CCCM 89:76, and Spec fid 19, CCCM 89A:89, define *amor* as "uehemens uoluntas." Nat am, 4, CCCM 88:180, defines it as "uehemens in bono uoluntas" (see n. 90 below).
67   Contemp, 14, "...uehemens et bene ordinata uoluntas," CCCM 88:162–63.
68   Contemp, 11, "Est enim amor animae rationalis, sicut dicit quidam seruus tuus, motus uel quieta statio, uel finis, in id ultra quod nil appetat, uel appetendum iudicet uoluntatis appetitus," CCCM 88:160. John Scot Eriugena, *De divisione naturae*, I.74, "Amor est naturalis motus omnium rerum, quae in motu sunt, finis quietaque statio, ultra quam nullus creaturae progreditur motu," PL 122:519B. William may have found the definition in a florilegium: see Bell, *Image and Likeness*, 127, n. 10. For yet other definitions of love, see Bell, *Image and Likeness*, 127–28.
69   Étienne Gilson, *The Mystical Theology of Saint Bernard*, trans. A.H.C. Downes (London/New York: Sheed & Ward, 1940; rpt., Kalamazoo, MI: Cistercian Publications, 1990), 54.
70   Gilson, *Mystical Theology*, 57–58.
71   See n. 67 above.

to undertake the long and difficult path which will lead to this end. It is no easy task, but the overcoming of self-centeredness, egocentricity, and self-love lies at the basis of virtually every spiritual tradition, Christian and non-Christian alike. In the Christian tradition, and in the Augustinian Christian tradition in particular, this arduous pilgrimage is wholly impossible without grace, and grace is the Holy Spirit.[72]

It will be remembered, however, that the Holy Spirit is not only grace, but whatever is common to Father and Son, and here we come to the crux of the matter. If the Holy Spirit is not only grace but also the mutual love of Father and Son and their very unity, what does this mean for us? Let us follow for a moment William's thought in his early *De contemplando Deo*, written not later than 1124.[73] We shall shortly see how these ideas reach their culmination in the last of William's works, the letter addressed to the Carthusian brethren of Mont-Dieu.

About halfway through the *De contemplando Deo*, William utters a fervent prayer to God that if he loves anything at all, he should love it for the sake of God. "For when I love something for your sake (*propter te*), it is not the thing itself that I love, but *you* for whose sake I love what I love!"[74] Indeed, it is this gift of loving God and being loved by God which is the basis of salvation, and that salvation is to be seen in the love which Christ showed for us—a love which led to an agonizing death on a cross. By this love he incites us to love him—William quotes 1 John 4:19 "we love because he loved us first"[75]—but not because Christ needs our love. No. "But because we could not be what you made us [to be] except by loving you."[76]

William now distinguishes the way in which we love God from the way in which God loves us. We love him (the verb is *diligere*) by an "impulse of love"—an *affectus amoris*, which is a singularly rich term in William[77]—which

---

72 See generally the useful study by Giuseppe Como, *Ignis amoris Dei. Lo Spirito Santo e la transformazione dell'uomo nell'esperienza spirituale secondo Guglielmo di Saint-Thierry* (Milan: Ed. Glossa, 2001).

73 See Jacques Hourlier, "Introduction", *The Works of William of St Thierry, Volume One: On Contemplating God, Prayer, Meditations*, trans. Sister Penelope [Lawson], CF 3 (Kalamazoo, MI: Cistercian Publications, 1977), 11–13.

74 Contemp 12, CCCM 88:161.

75 Contemp 12, CCCM 88:161, and 13, CCCM 88:162.

76 Contemp 12, CCCM 88:161

77 See Wolfgang Zwingmann, *Der Begriff* Affectus *bei Wilhelm von St. Thierry* (Ph.D. diss., Pontifical Gregorian University, Rome, 1964). A major portion of this dissertation was published as two articles in 1967: "*Ex affectu mentis*. Über die Vollkommenheit menschlichen Handelns und menschlicher Hingabe nach Wilhelm von St. Thierry," *Cîteaux – Commentarii Cistercienses* 18 (1967): 5–37, and Zwingmann, "*Affectus illuminati*

God has put, placed, introduced, or inserted (the verb here is *indere*) into us. But this cannot be the case with God, who, by nature, is impassable—beyond all passions and the ebb and flow of voluntary or involuntary impulses. God cannot be "moved" or "affected" by loving us. In philosophical terms, his love for us cannot be "accidental,"[78] in the sense of something extraneous to himself, but must be in some way substantial. And so William asks the pertinent question, "How then do you love us if you do not love us with love?"[79] Here is his answer:

> Your love is your goodness, Supremely Good and Supreme Good,[80] the Holy Spirit proceeding from the Father and the Son, who, from the beginning of creation, was borne over the waters[81]—that is, floating over the souls of the children of men—offering himself to all, drawing all things to himself by breathing into them and breathing upon them, by keeping harmful things away, by supplying those which are useful, uniting God to us and us to God. For in this way your Holy Spirit itself, who is called the love of the Father and Son, and unity, and will, indwells us by his grace and implants in us the love (*caritas*) of God. Then, joining him to us through this [love], he unites us to God through the good will that he breathes into us. In us, this vehement good will is called love (*amor*), by which we love what we ought to love, namely, you! For love is nothing other than vehement and well-ordered will.[82]

This is a dense passage—dense passages are not uncommon in William[83]—but what William is saying may be reduced to three simple statements. (1) God

---

        amoris. Über das Offenbarwerden der Gnade und die Erfahrung von Gottes beseligender Gegenwart," *Cîteaux – Commentarii Cistercienses* 18 (1967): 193–226. See also Thomas X. Davis's appendix to his translation of *William of Saint Thierry: The Mirror of Faith*, CF 15 (Kalamazoo, MI: Cistercian Publications, 1979), 93–95, and Bell, *Image and Likeness*, 128–133. I do not always agree with Zwingmann.

78   Contemp, 14, "numquid accidenti uel incidenti amoris affectu amas quos amas; et aliquo in aliquo afficeris, qui omnes et omnia facis?" CCCM 88:162. This is the language of the Schools.

79   Contemp, 14, CCCM 88:162.

80   See n. 24 above.

81   Gen 1:2.

82   Contemp, 14, CCCM 88:162–163.

83   As Sister Penelope Lawson said many years ago, William often "tries to say too much at once, and a sentence that is overcharged in Latin is inevitably more so in our own less succinct tongue." (*The Meditations of William of St Thierry: Meditativae Orationes*, trans. A Religious of C.S.M.V. [Sr Penelope Lawson] [London: A.R. Mowbray, 1954], 103).

loves us substantially, in that his love for us is himself in the person of the Holy Spirit. (2) The Holy Spirit implants in us or commits or entrusts to us—the verb is *commendare*—the love of God. And (3) through this love, which is also will and unity, we are united by grace (which is also the Holy Spirit) to the Father and Son. In other words, the actualization of our participation in God (which is the restoration of the lost likeness), which takes place in and through God the Holy Spirit, must ineluctably lead to union with God and, since the Holy Spirit is unity, will, and love, it must also lead to our love being united with God's love and our will with God's will. William does not quite say this in this particular passage, though he certainly implies it, but we are still at the early stages of his developing mystical theology and his thought, in some areas, is still hesitant, "encore flottante" as Robert Thomas put it.[84]

William is "flottante," for example, in his approach to the Holy Spirit as our love for God. If the Holy Spirit indwells us as our love, then our love for God is the Holy Spirit. If the Holy Spirit implants this love within us or entrusts it to us, that would seem to imply that our love for God is not the uncreated third person of the Trinity, but something created in us. There was, in fact, a dispute in the 12th and 13th centuries on precisely this point. Is our love for God uncreated love, *dilectio increata*, or created love, *dilectio creata*? William unquestionably tends in the direction of uncreated love, and in his later works leaves us in no doubt on the matter.[85] Peter Lombard, that classic authority, would agree with him. Others—Abelard, for example, or Rupert of Deutz— did not, and the idea that our love for God was a created love would find canonical expression in the writings of Thomas Aquinas.[86]

A similar hesitancy may be seen in the *De natura et dignitate amoris*, written at about the same time as the *De contemplando Deo*.[87] The broad themes are similar: love is the natural *pondus*—we might translate this anachronistically as "gravitational attraction"—which draws us back to God (this is pure Augustine[88]), love/will is the third element of the Trinitarian image in our

---

84   Robert Thomas, *Notes sur Guillaume de Saint-Thierry* (Chambarand: Pain de Cîteaux, 1959), III, 74.

85   See Bell, *Image and Likeness*, 133–47.

86   See the very sound account of the dispute in Artur M. Landgraf, *Dogmengeschichte der Frühscholastik* (Regensburg: Friedrich Pustet, 1952), I, 220–237.

87   For a discussion of the relative dates of Nat am and Contemp, see David N. Bell, "Introduction," *William of St Thierry: The Nature and Dignity of Love*, trans. Thomas X. Davis, CF 30 (Kalamazoo, MI: Cistercian Publications, 1981), 18–19. The usual view is that Contemp preceded Nat am; my own view is that it was written later. See n. 125 below.

88   See Étienne Gilson, *Introduction à l'étude de saint Augustin* (Paris: J. Vrin, 2003 [2nd ed.]), 173–77. The *locus classicus* in Augustine is *Liber confessionum*, XIII.ix.10, PL 32:849: *Pondus meum amor meus.*

minds and is substantially the Holy Spirit, we have lost the likeness by turning from a love of our Creator to a love of creation (we have taken as our teacher in love not God but Ovid[89]), we have wandered far in the region of unlikeness, and the *De natura et dignitate amoris* is intended to show us the way back. The path leads from a rightly-directed will to love (*amor*), from love to charity (*caritas*), and from charity to wisdom (*sapientia*), but all four—will, love, charity, and wisdom—are ultimately the Holy Spirit:

> When, by prevenient and cooperating grace, [the will] begins to cleave by its good assent to the Holy Spirit, who is the love and will of the Father and Son, it begins vehemently to will what God wills and what memory and reason suggest it should will, and by vehemently willing it becomes love. For love is nothing other than a vehement will for the good.[90]

This, as we have said, is no easy task, but God is aware of this and so, to prevent us from losing heart and fainting along the road, he may send us "frequent and unexpected theophanies" to revive and illumine the soul in its continual desire to progress.[91] William refers to these as *affectiunculae* "little affective experiences,"[92] and they bring comfort to the soul when they are present and torment when they are absent. On the other hand, they may also be dangerous, for some might be tempted to see them not as encouragements towards the final goal of the spiritual path but the final goal itself.[93]

For those who persevere, love (*amor*) now begins to be strengthened and illumined by grace and becomes charity (*caritas*):

> Illumined love (*amor illuminatus*) is charity: love from God, in God, [directed] to God is charity. But charity is God: God, says [St John], is charity (1 Jn 4:16). Brief praise, but it includes everything! What can be said of

---

89 As the anonymous author of the *Vita antiqua* of William tells us, the *De natura et dignitate amoris* "may be called the 'Anti-Naso,' for in it he instructs the true philosopher in what ways and stages he may and should progress in his love for God" (Bell, "*Vita Antiqua*," 252; Le Brun "*Vita Antiqua*," 454–55). Ovid's full name was Publius Ovidius Naso.

90 Nat am, 4, CCCM 88:180.

91 Nat am, 10, "Iam frequentes et improuisae theophaniae … animam continuo desiderio laborantem incipiunt refocillare et illustrare," CCCM 88:185.

92 Nat am, 10, CCCM 88:185.

93 See Bell, *Image and Likeness*, 207–10.

God can also be said of charity. Thus, when we consider [charity] according to the natures of the gift and the giver, in the giver it is the name of the substance and in the gift [the name] of the quality. But for emphasis (*per emphasim*) God is even called the gift of charity in that more than all other virtues, the virtue of charity cleaves to God and is made like him.[94]

This is yet another dense passage, and William seems to want to have the best of both worlds. On the one hand he wants to identify charity with God; on the other he wants to distinguish substantial charity (which is the Holy Spirit) from the gift or quality of charity in us. But what is the meaning of the words *per emphasim* by which even the gift of charity may itself be called God? This is a matter I have discussed elsewhere, and I suggested there that the term may reflect William's difficulty in giving a straight answer to the question of whether our charity for God is or is not the Holy Spirit:

> We are forced inexorably into answering both yes and no: yes, our love for God is the Holy Spirit, but no, not in the same sense in which the Holy Spirit is the consubstantial love of Father and Son. Our love is not the Holy Spirit by essence, nature, or substance; it is the Holy Spirit by participation.... Love, therefore, is certainly God, but not in the same sense in which God is love.[95]

By the time William wrote his commentary on the Song of Songs, this early vacillation seems to have disappeared. What is the Holy Spirit, he asks?

> He is none other than the unity of the Father and the Son of God, their kiss, their embrace, their love, their goodness, and whatever is common to both in that most simple unity. All this is the Holy Spirit, God, charity, the same both giver and gift.[96]

---

94 Nat am, 12, "...sic tamen ut considerata secundum naturas doni et dantis, in dante nomen sit substantiae, in dato qualitatis; sed per emphasim donum etiam caritatis Deus dicatur, in eo quod super omnes uirtutes uirtus caritatis Deo cohaeret et assimilatur," CCCM 88:186–87.

95 Bell, *Image and Likeness*, 139–40.

96 Cant, 91, "...quod totum est Spiritus Sanctus, Deus, caritas, idem donans, idem et donum," CCCM 87:70. And again in Cant, 128, CCCM 87:91: in the Trinity the Holy Spirit "is the majesty of the consubstantial nature, while here it is the gift of grace. There it is dignity (*dignitas*); here it is condescension (*dignatio*). Yet it is the same, completely the same Spirit (*idem tamen, idem plane Spiritus*)".

6   Wisdom – The Experience of Charity

Returning now to the *De natura et dignitate amoris*, William has brought
us from will to love to charity, and he now leads us to wisdom, which is, in
essence, the experience of charity: "First the will moves the soul to God, love
moves it further, charity contemplates, wisdom enjoys."[97] William (with many
of his confrères) now quotes Psalm 34:8 (33:9 Vlg) "Taste (*gustate*) and see that
the Lord is sweet," and then tells us, unequivocally, that "to taste (*gustare*) is to
understand (*intelligere*)."[98] It is the experiential and connatural knowledge of
God which is the culmination of the spiritual path here on earth. But William
does not elaborate on the nature of this experience. Why not? Because at
the time of writing the *De natura et dignitate amoris* William had not yet
experienced these high states. He tells us so himself:

> This is the wisdom of which the Apostle [Paul] says: "We speak wis-
> dom among the perfect" (1 Cor 2:6). We too speak of it, as those who
> have heard and not seen, as we speak about a particular city we have
> not seen, but of which we have heard many things. But someone who
> has seen it could speak about it very differently and with greater clarity
> (*expressius*).[99]

In due course, in fact, William will speak with greater clarity on a number of
themes which are not fully developed in the *De natura et dignitate amoris*: the
ideas of unity of will (*unitas voluntatis*) and unity of spirit (*unitas spiritus*), for
example, or the concept of the "illumined love" of God "which, acquiring its
own seat in the Christian soul, carries it forward toward to a certain likeness
to divine power (*quamdam diuinae potentiae similitudinem*), while making it
see that every finite and short-lived creature is as nothing in comparison to
God."[100]

   The truth of the matter is that unity of will, unity of spirit, and illumined
love are all what they are by participation in the Holy Spirit who, as we know,
is the consubstantial will, unity, and love of the Father and the Son, and that
participation takes place by grace, which is also the Holy Spirit. Here is William
in his commentary on the Song of Songs:

---

97   Nat am, 28, "Primum enim ad Deum uoluntas animam mouet, amor promouet, caritas
         contemplatur, sapientia fruitur," CCCM 88:199.
98   Nat am, 31, CCCM 88:201.
99   Nat am, 39, CCCM 88:207.
100   Nat am, 20, CCCM 88:193.

When one is effected to the likeness of his Maker, the human being is affected to God.[101] This is [to be] one spirit with God, beautiful in Beauty, good in Goodness, and it [occurs] in proportion to the strength of faith and the light of the intellect and the measure of love. One then exists in God by grace what [God] is by nature.[102]

In other words, the human creature can never become what God is by nature—that would be grave blasphemy—but what God is by participation: beautiful in his Beauty (which is the Holy Spirit), and so on. The operative force here is love/will, which, once again, is the Holy Spirit, and the process involves the whole image of God in us, namely, the threefold Trinitarian analogy of *mens*, which is the highest part of the rational soul where all this takes place, *intellectus*, and *amor/voluntas*. And finally, it all takes place by grace, which, yet again, is the Holy Spirit. And if we are beautiful in God's beauty, good in his goodness, and so forth, all we have to do is to look at ourselves and experience in our likeness to him a connatural knowledge of him. To be *unus spiritus* with God, in and through God the Holy Spirit, is the culmination of likeness and the goal of William's spirituality. But remember: William is in no way suggesting that we become God. The unity is a unity of likeness, *unitas similitudinis*, and William says so. The Holy Spirit, he tells us, in his commentary on Romans 8:27,

helps our infirmity, humbling us by training us, and, by humbling us, forming and conforming us to the countenance which we seek[103] until, renewed to the image of him who created us, one begins through a unity of likeness to be the son who is always with the father, to whom all the father's possessions belong.[104]

And again, in a very clear passage in the *Ænigma fidei*, we are told that those who have been predestined to be rapt up into the experience of the Trinity will

---

101   The contrast is between *efficio*, when the soul is passive in the hands of the Holy Spirit and *afficio*, when the soul is active by the grace of the Holy Spirit.

102   Cant, 90, "...existens in Deo per gratiam, quod ille est per naturam," CCCM 87:68.

103   Cf. Ps 26:8.

104   Exp Rom, V.8:27, "...donec renouatus ad imaginem eius qui creauit eum, per unitatem similitudinis incipiat esse filius, qui semper sit cum patre, cuius sint omnia quae patris sunt," CCCM 86:124. The last words refer to Luke 15:31, the parable of the Prodigal Son. William is not saying that by a unity of likeness we begin to be the Second Person of the Trinity who is always with the Father. The capitalization in Verdeyen's edition is gravely misleading. We may compare Ep frat, 289, "Haec enim unitas hominis cum Deo, uel similitudo ad Deum...," CCCM 88:287.

see God as he is, *sicuti est*, "and in seeing him as he is, they will be made like him (*similes ei*)."

> And there, as in the Father and the Son, where that vision is also unity, so in God and the human being, that vision will be the likeness to come. The Holy Spirit is the unity of the Father and the Son [and] is himself charity and the likeness of God and human beings.[105]

This perfected likeness, which must be effected by God, is what Bernard, but not William, would term "deification,"[106] and this is the basis for our connatural knowledge of God. It is a process that begins in this world and finds its consummation in the next; but the perfection of connatural knowledge may occasionally be experienced here below in rare moments of ecstasy. Once again, to understand this and its implications, it does not mean we become God, but, by grace, we become what God is (*quod Deus est*)[107] and this is the basis for our connatural knowledge of God. To understand this and its implications, let us glance at the third level of likeness set forth by William in his last work, the letter to the brethren of Mont-Dieu. The first two we have already considered: the first is the likeness of ubiquity (as God is everywhere present and everywhere whole in his creation, so is the soul in the body), and the second is likeness in virtue, in which, by our own free-will (through grace) we become good in his goodness, truthful in his truth, and so on. But it is in the third likeness that we see the truth of William's *dictum* that "likeness to God is the whole of human perfection."[108] There is a third likeness, says William,

> which is so close [in its resemblance] that it is called not just likeness but unity of spirit (*unitas spiritus*).[109] It makes the human person one spirit with God, not just by a unity of willing the same thing, but by a more explicit truth of virtue, as has already been said,[110] the inability to will anything else. This is called unity of spirit not only because the Holy

---

105   Ænig, 7, "...Spiritus sanctus unitas Patris et Filii, ipse etiam caritas et similitudo Dei et hominis," CCCM 89A:132.

106   William never uses either *deificari* or *deificatio*. For Bernard, see Gilson, *Mystical Theology*, 260, index, s.v. "Deification." See also Javelet, *Image et ressemblance*, I, 439–41.

107   Ep frat, 263, CCCM 88:282.

108   See n. 50 above.

109   See the very useful survey of this theme by F. Tyler Sergent, "*Unitas Spiritus* and the Originality of William of Saint-Thierry," in *Unity of Spirit: Studies on William of Saint-Thierry*, 144–70. Only William and Guerric of Igny, says Sergent, use this term "to describe the spiritual union between the human soul and God" (169), and Guerric has probably borrowed this meaning from William. See also Bell, *Image and Likeness*, Chapter V, *passim*.

110   In Ep frat, 257–258, CCCM 88:281.

Spirit effects it or inspires the human spirit to it, but because it is the Holy Spirit itself, God [who is] charity.[111] To will what God wills is already to be like God; not to be able to will anything other than what God wills is to be already what God is (*quod Deus est*), for whom "to will" and "to be" are the same thing.[112]

William's thought here may be startling, but it is no more than logical. If we are truly one spirit, *unus spiritus*, with God, our participation in the Holy Spirit has been fully actualized. But since the Holy Spirit is none other than the mutual will and love of Father and Son, it follows that in this condition our self-will/ self-love has been annihilated in the will and love of God. And since we now have no self-love/self-will left, our will can only be God's will. It is not too surprising to find that William was indeed accused of "pantheism"—meaning, in this case, that the human soul and God become identical—but this, emphatically, was never the case.[113] As Robert Javelet has said, "Participation excludes pantheism, for it indicates clearly the inferiority of the participant."[114]

But does this mean that a human being who has experienced *unitas spiritus*, and who can now will only what God wills, cannot sin? That he or she has become impeccably perfect or perfectly impeccable? It does not, for we must distinguish between willing and doing. My conscience, for example, may tell me with absolute clarity that a certain action is wrong. It *is* wrong and I know that it is wrong. But despite this, I can still use my free-will to perform the action and thereby to sin. William is perfectly aware of the statement in 1 John 3:9 that "Everyone who has been born of God does not commit sin (*peccatum non facit*), for his seed remains in them and they cannot sin (*non potest peccare*) because they have been born of God." His explanation of this is straightforward:

> [Blessed John] says "He does not sin" (*non peccatum facit*) because anyone born of God endures (*patitur*) rather than commits [sin]; "and they cannot sin"—that is, persevere in sin (*perseuerando scilicet in peccato*)[115]— since they hasten to subject the flesh, which is attacked by temptation and sin and thereby seems to serve the law of sin, to the law of God which they observe in their mind (*mens*).[116]

---

111   Ep frat 262–263, CCCM 88:282.
112   Ep frat, 258, CCCM 88:281.
113   See Bell, *Image and Likeness*, 176–77.
114   Javelet, *Image et ressemblance*, I, 139.
115   The key here is the Augustinian doctrine of the gift of perseverance; see Bell, *Image and Likeness*, 193–96.
116   Nat am, 14, CCCM 88:189.

Thus, when Peter denied Christ, he did not lose charity (for he sinned against truth rather than charity), and when David sent off Uriah the Hittite to be killed in battle, charity was "stunned" (*obstupuit*) by the violence of David's temptation, but it was not nullified.[117] Thus charity remains, and a sinful act does not abolish it.[118] And should an uncharitable thought make its way into a charitable soul, it will be wholly consumed by the fire of the love of God and, just as happens with an ordinary fire, converted into its own substance.[119]

7   Conclusion

In short, it is still possible for human beings to commit sin, though not to persevere in sinning, even though they may have experienced the high state of unity of spirit. This state, when (by grace) we have become *quod Deus est*—not God, but what God is—is as far as we can go here on earth. The vision of God, says William, is begun here "by holiness of life and by the practice of divine contemplation," but it is perfected in heaven.[120] To be *quod Deus est* is to have a true connatural knowledge of God, so far as that can be achieved in this life, and it is the culmination of love, more accurately, of the highest form of love, which is charity. The monastery is the school of charity, the *schola caritatis*,[121] but unlike the Schools outside its walls, within the monastery the studies and disputations and solutions are achieved "not only by reasoning, but by reason and the very truth and experience of things."[122]

In and through charity, which is the Holy Spirit, we experience the most comprehensive knowledge we can have, while still incarnate, of our Creator, for, as William says in a famous phrase, "love itself is knowledge," *amor ipse intellectus est*.[123] Putting it another way, we might also say that the Holy Spirit itself is knowledge, in God consubstantially, in us by participation, and I do not think there can be any doubt that William himself had been granted this rare and indescribable experience. Why indescribable? The answer is simple. If we

---

117   See Nat am, 14, CCCM 88:189.

118   This was not the view of Augustine and emphatically not the view of Thomas Aquinas: see Bell, *Image and Likeness*, 191–92, nn. 73–74.

119   See Cant, 112, CCCM 87:81.

120   Ænig 23, CCCM 89A:143.

121   See Nat am, 24–26, CCCM 88:196–198.

122   Nat am, 26, CCCM 88:198.

123   In this form, the phrase occurs only twice in William (Cant, 54, CCCM 87:47; Ep frat, 173, CCCM 88:264). In Cant, 71, CCCM 87:59 it appears as "Amor quippe Dei ipse intellectus eius est." See generally Bell, *Image and Likeness*, Chapter VI, and for the history and wide diffusion of the idea, Bell, *Image and Likeness*, 231–33.

go back to our earlier account of Augustine's threefold visionary scheme, we are speaking here of the realm of the *intellectualia*, which are beyond concepts and images and ultimately beyond thought. It is something inexpressible, something which cannot be described but must be experienced, a *certa experientia* of God's love and a sweetness beyond the ordinary understanding.[124] It follows, then, that one can remember having had the experience, but one cannot re-member—in the literal sense of putting back together again—the individual elements. William himself says so:

> And when I am eager to commit to my memory with greater accuracy the precise distinctive features (*formata quaedam liniamenta*[125]) of what I sought or received or experienced, or even to help the fleeting memory by writing them down, by this fact and by this very experience I am forced to learn what is said of the Spirit in the Gospel: "You do not know whence it comes or where it goes" (John 3:8).[126]

There is nothing new in this. It is universally agreed by all mystics of all ages that the ultimate mystical experience is indescribable, but it is curious that, having once said this, most of them then go to great lengths in trying to describe it. Only the Jewish mystics (and even among them there are exceptions) followed in the footsteps of Jesus of Nazareth before Herod Antipas. The tetrarch was eager to see Jesus and questioned him in many words, but Jesus gave him no answer (Luke 23:9). If I may be permitted a brief excursion to the Far East, the contradiction was neatly summarized by the Chinese poet Po Chü-I (772–846). His poem "On Reading Lao Tzu" is no more than four lines of seven Chinese characters each, but it puts the matter in a nutshell:

> "One who speaks does not know; one who knows does not speak":
> Such are the words of Lao Tzu.
> If Lao Tzu was one who knew,
> Why did he write five thousand characters?[127]

---

124 For all these descriptions in William, see Bell, *Image and Likeness*, 201–02.

125 *Liniamenta* or *lineamenta*: traits, distinctive characteristics, unique features.

126 Contemp, 21, CCCM 88:168. It seems to me that this may well indicate that Contemp was written later than Nat am (see n. 87 above). The implication in Nat am (see n. 99 above) is that William has not yet experienced this highest level of knowledge; the implication in Contemp is that he has.

127 Translated from the Chinese text in Reginald H. Blyth, *Zen in English Literature and Oriental Classics* (Tokyo: The Hokuseido Press, 1942), 141.

And there we must leave it. Love has brought us to the end of the path, to unity of spirit with God in and through God the Holy Spirit, but it is not for us to attempt to describe that sublime experience. *Solvitur ambulando.* Or, as William said at the very end of his letter to the brethren of Mont-Dieu, "My secret is my own, my secret is my own."[128]

---

128   Ep frat, 300, CCCM 88:289, quoting Isaiah 24:16.

CHAPTER 4

William of Saint-Thierry on the Soul

*Aage Rydstrøm-Poulsen**

1   Introduction

When William of Saint-Thierry lists his works in the Prologue to his *Epistola aureae* (*Golden Epistle; Letter to the Brethren of Mont-Dieu*), he mentions his *De natura animae* (*On the Nature of the Soul*) as the last one before the *Golden Epistle*. "There is also another work of ours,"[1] he writes, and this formulation could of course simply mean: 'by the way, there is also another work to be mentioned.' Or this could also mean that the two *opuscula*—*On the Nature of the Body* and *On the Nature of the Soul*—actually are the last ones that William wrote before his *Golden Epistle*. This would imply that the two works were written as late as 1144 and thus at the end of William's literary career. In 1989, Paul Verdeyen, however, dates the two treatises to 1138 but with some uncertainty, and he lets us know that the tradition of manuscripts only tells us that the two works have been put together and published after William's transition to Signy in 1135.[2] Bernard McGinn, in 1977, suggested that the two treatises are from "around 1140" and finds that the works might be seen as preparations for the *Speculum fidei* (*Mirror of Faith*) and *Aenigma fidei* (*Enigma of Faith*) as well as for the *Epistola aurea*.[3] On the other hand, if we follow William's own listing in the Prologue—a possibility we must not exclude—the works *On the Nature of the Body* and *On the Nature of the Soul* would be the last ones before the *Golden Epistle*. That would also make good sense, especially for *De natura animae* in which, in its concluding section, William's thought about the unity of the soul with God is in close accordance with the *unitas spiritus* theory found in the *Golden Epistle*.

---

*   This chapter is a revised edition of two presentations for the Cistercian Studies Conferences at the 48th and 49th International Congress on Medieval Studies, May 9–12, 2013, and May 8–11, 2014, Western Michigan University, Kalamazoo, Michigan.
1   Ep frat, 13, "Est etiam alium opusculum nostrum *De natura animae*...," CCCM 88:227.
2   Paul Verdeyen, "Introduction," *Expositio super epistolam ad Romanos*, CCCM 86 (Turnhout: Brepols, 1989), XXVIII.
3   *Three Treatises on Man: A Cistercian Anthropology*, (ed.) and intro. Bernard McGinn, CF 24 (Kalamazoo, MI: Cistercian Publications, 1977), 28 and n. 119. This volume includes the English translations of William's *De natura corporis* and *De natura animae* (Phys an).

2   *De natura animae*

William's own wording will, of course, be followed as closely as possible in order to give the most precise description of his original thought. However, William provides in his *De natura animae* first a definition of the soul which is not his own. Typical for his role as a 12th-century theologian, William expressly wants to avoid anything new and instead follow "the doctors of the church." Here he quotes from Cassiodorus's *De anima*, writing: "The soul is a spiritual and individual substance, created by God, giving life to the body, it is rational and immortal, but it is convertible into good and bad."[4] William puts this definition in opposition with that of "the philosophers of this world," namely, that the soul is just "a simple substance, a piece of nature, different from the bodily material and its members, and having the power of life."[5] We can notice here that the Christian definition primarily is thus different in saying that (1) the soul is created by God, (2) it is rational, (3) it is immortal, and (4) it is convertible into good and bad. As we are going to see, not least the last characteristic has extensive theological consequences to William.

William is fascinated by the body's physiological functions, but his main interest is the God-given soul which in many wondrous ways makes the complicated human person "into one living being,"[6] as he expresses it, in which the rational soul, "united directly to the body," organizes everything "artistically and orderly."[7] Here we can see, William continues, how "God, the author of nature and creator of body and soul, formed the human person in his image and likeness."[8] This sounds so perfect, but William still shares his theological anthropology with almost all his theological colleagues in the 12th century, namely that the human nature would have been perfect indeed "if nature had

---

4   *De natura animae* (Phys an), 4, 1–7, "Porro secundum nostros, id est ecclesiasticos doctores, anima spiritualis propriaque est substantia a Deo creata, sui corporis uiuificatrix, rationabilis, immortalis, sed in bonum malumque conuertibilis," CCCM 88:121; cf. Cassiodorus, *De anima*, (eds.) A.J. Fridh and J.W. Halporn, CCSL 96 (Turnhout: Brepols, 1973), 538; see *Three Treatises on Man*, 125, n. 1.

5   Phys an, 4, 1–7, "Anima, sicut philosophi huius mundi dicunt, substantia est simplex, species naturalis, distans a materia corporis sui organum membrorum et uirtutem uitae habens," CCCM 88:121.

6   Phys an, 53, "...anima a Deo data ... ex omnibus in unum uiuendi facit collationem," CCCM 88:122.

7   Cf. Phys an, 57, "Sic uitae nutriendae et confortandis naturalibus incrementis, per hanc artificialem et disciplinalem formationem statim coniuncta uirtus animae rationali ostenditur...," CCCM 88:123.

8   Phys an, 57, "...sic auctor naturae et corporis et animae conditor Deus *hominem* format *ad imaginem et similitudinem* suam...," CCCM 88:123.

not been corrupted in its beginnings through malice."[9] William even uses the strong expression about the created nature that it is nothing but a "corrupta natura," explained by the Pauline theory of the Fall, which Augustine in his later writings, as is well-known, communicated to the Western world. William states in accordance with this, "Therefore we are born like animals."[10] Accordingly, the inborn image of the Creator is hidden for William; it can only begin "to light up in us through great and continuous labors," not suddenly or at once, but humanity "is led to perfection by a long way...."[11] We can notice that William uses the passive form *ducitur* ("is led").[12] Despite this "corrupta natura," however, the human person must thank the Creator—William adds just afterwards—for "the dignity of the human condition," and the reason is pointed out at once because humanity has a soul which no other creature on earth has.[13]

However, there can be life without a soul,[14] and William is full of admiration of this, but all creation without a soul will always be missing what he calls "the perfection that comes from the gift of reason and understanding."[15] In this way, William can see the dignity of the human person already in the "corrupta natura" because the human person possesses a soul with reason and understanding. He even calls it a "perfection",[16] saying, "Therefore we say that the human soul alone is true and perfect, capable of every action."[17] Thus even though humans are born like animals and "completely governed by our senses,"[18] and the senses want to have their way, William adds,[19] the human person actually has reason, the necessary ruler within one's spirit. And here the royal language

---

9   Phys an, 58, "Quae ex principio perfecta esset, si in suo principio corrupta natura per malitiam non fuisset," CCCM 88:123.

10   Phys an, 58, "Propterea nascimur ut pecudes," CCCM 88:123.

11   Phys an, 58, CCCM 88:123.

12   Phys an, 58, "...nec continuo nec nisi cum magnis et diuturnis laboribus relucere potest in nobis factoris imago, sed longa quadam uia per materiales et pecuales animae proprietates ad perfectionem suam homo ducitur," CCCM 88:123.

13   Phys an, 59, "Sed licet quouis modo herbae et arbores uiuere uideantur, et habere animam bruta etiam quaeuis animalia, constat tamen haec omnia quamuis quouis modo uiuentia, animam non habere nec assurgere in hoc ad dignitatem conditionis humanae," CCCM 88:124.

14   Phys an, 59, "Est enim ibi uita quamuis non sit anima," CCCM 88:124.

15   Phys an, 61, "Bruta uero animalia, per motum uoluntarium et adiectionem sensuum, dignius aliquo modo uiuere uidentur quam herbae uel arbores, non tamen usque ad perfectionem quae in rationis et intelligentiae gratia consistit," CCCM 88:124.

16   Phys an, 61, "...usque ad perfectionem...," CCCM 88:124.

17   Phys an, 61, "Propterea dicimus ueram quidem perfectamque animam humanam esse solam, quae in omni ualet actione," CCCM 88:124.

18   Phys an, 61, "Bruta quippe omnino sunt suis sensibus dedita...," CCCM 88:124.

19   Phys an, 61, CCCM 88:124.

of William is introduced for the first time: "As a queen," William proclaims, "reason sits in the central castle of the city."[20]

There is no doubt that reason is the first keyword in William's anthropology. As he states, "Of its nature the rational soul is something wonderful."[21] Here William depicts an image from Gregory of Nyssa: the rational soul is like a musician who plays his instrument.[22] In William's words, "...it uses the whole body as if it were a musical instrument."[23] Or he can see the rational soul's role in another image, namely in the righteous person, which points in the direction toward heaven. Here William returns to his impressive royal appellations: it "signifies the imperial and royal dignity of the rational soul."[24] And William can add, "...the rational soul rules the reason so that it only chooses what is useful."[25]

However, we do remember William's point already in his definition of the soul, namely that it is "rational and immortal" but, nevertheless, unstable, "it is convertible into good and bad."[26] Accordingly, humans who let reason follow the desires of nature, the lust from the senses, have lost their royal dignity, William maintains.[27] These humans actually remain or become animals and have lost the image of the Creator. Just like the animals, they look toward the ground and not up to heaven. And they are unlike to God because of their passion, their pleasure, their fear and wildness, desire, and hatred. All this is so far away from the divine being which William here simply characterizes with the concept of *pulchritudo*: beauty.[28] Precisely "in the love of pleasure" we show our

---

20   Phys an, 62, "Spiritus uero hominis longe aliter. Nam sensibus dominatur, et de sensibus iudicat. Quasi enim regina sedens ratio in media ciuitatis suae arce...," CCCM 88:125.

21   Phys an, 62, "Itaque mirabile quid est animus secundum sui naturam...," CCCM 88:125.

22   Grgory of Nyssa, *De hominis opificio*, 8–10. See *Three Treatises on Man*, 131, n. 10.

23   Phys an, 65, "...ueluti organum musicum totum corpus in suos creat effectus," CCCM 88:126. Cf. Phys an, 66, "...it takes possession of the whole instrument of nature and touches each part with its intellectual operations...," "...sic et animus totum corporis organum obtinens, et intellectualibus operationibus singulas partes sicut consueuit tangens...," CCCM 88:126.

24   Phys an, 73, "Erecta hominis figura ad caelum extensa et sursum aspiciens imperialem regalemque dignitatem animae rationalis significat...," CCCM 88:129.

25   Phys an, 73, "...ut imperet animus rationi, nec patiatur quin eligat quod utile est," CCCM 88:129.

26   Phys an, 51, "...rationabilis, immortalis, sed in bonum malumque conuertibilis," CCCM 88:121; cf. n. 4 above.

27   Phys an, 73, "Huius dignitatis expertes sunt qui rationem, quae naturaliter domina est, seruire facientes desideriis naturae, libidini quae per sensus est blandiuntur seruiliter," CCCM 88:129.

28   Phys an, 74, "Huiusmodi enim homines imagine creatoris exuta, aliam induerunt imaginem terram respicientem, pecudalem, bestialem. Non enim secundum furorem hominis

"likeness to irrational beings," William states.[29] But again, reason is able to stand against this: "Certainly, reason with its reasonable desires rejects these things with all their wildness, yet with the help of human thoughts they increase."[30] Thoughts can easily serve bad purposes—William observes, for instance, that out of anger come madness, envy, lies, and treachery[31]—and such things are the result of a "degenerate rational soul."[32] So far, the situation seems not too dire for the soul; it will simply have to use its reason, and then everything will become right. But William does not think in this superficial—and Pelagian—way. With a quotation from Gregory of Nyssa he maintains that "all these things ... have entered into the human constitution from his beastly nature."[33]

The original creation of the human person was good enough. In William's words, "The Supreme Artisan indeed made our nature suitable and apt for its royal role..."[34] Correspondingly, "The rational soul is royal and lofty"; "it is free and able of its own power to command all things.... This is proper to one with royal dignity."[35] This is indeed the soul's nature: "it is by nature far removed from the rustic lowliness and degeneracy..."[36] William adds, however, following this eulogy, that this nature "seems to be a sorrowful stepmother."[37] Whereas, for instance, nature gives trees a double layer of bark for protection,[38] the human person instead is born without any protection and, in William's words,

ad Deum est similitudo, non ex uoluptate supereminenti naturae consimilatur, formido quoque et ferocitas, et ad quaedam desiderium, ad quaedam uero odium, longe sunt a diuinae pulchritudinis caractere," CCCM 88:129.

29   Phys an, 76, "Sic uoluptatis amor principium quidem habuit ex ipsa similitudine ad irrationalia...," CCCM 88:130.

30   Phys an, 76, "Haec enim et talia cognata quidem sibi abicit ratio rationabilium affectuum, sed augentur cogitationum auxilio," CCCM 88:130.

31   Phys an, 76, "Inde ex ira nascitur insania, inuidia, mendacium, insidiae," CCCM 88:130.

32   Phys an, 77, "Haec autem omnia malignae operationes degeneratis animi sunt," CCCM 88:130.

33   Phys an, 77, "Et haec omnia ... ex pecudali generatione in constitutionem hominis cointrauerunt...," CCCM 88:130.

34   Cf. Phys an, 77, "In operationem quippe regni commodam et aptam naturam nostram optimus artifex condidit, et in obseruationibus animae, et in ipsa quoque, ut iam satis dictum est, corporis figura tale praeparauit animal quale ad regnum oportunitatem haberet, scilicet non pronum in terram sed erectum in caelum," CCCM 88:130.

35   Phys an, 78, "Anima siquidem rationalis intelligens et conseruans honorem suum, regale quiddam est et excelsum" and "cum sit libera et per se potens, imperet omnibus ... quod propium regiae dignitatis est," CCCM 88:130.

36   Phys an, 78, "...se a rustica humilitate et degereratione esse longe naturaliter segregatam...," CCCM 88:130.

37   Phys an, 78, "...in aliis aliorum animantium primordiis laeta mater appareat natura, in homine solo uideatur tristis nouerca," CCCM 88:131.

38   Phys an, 78, CCCM 88:131.

"the poor human being ... is imprisoned ... and put in swaddling bands with all his members tied together"; the human person, consequently, is only free to weep and cry: "His eyes and mouth alone are left free to give vent only to tears and cries."[39] This is the sad condition of every human being, and "the son of an emperor or a king"—William continues with his royal imagery[40]—in order to remove any possible doubt. In short, this is simply the punishment of humanity, even though its only fault is having been born.[41] When the person grows up, William can state, "immediately come sickness, medicines, and finally the cares of burial. Nothing has a life or health that is more fragile..."[42] William can then summarize: "Poor humankind is brought into this life lacking everything that is useful."[43]

There is, thus, no doubt about William's thoroughly Augustinian theological anthropology. Humanity is poor and lacking everything useful. Nevertheless, and paradoxically, William continues immediately afterwards saying that the human person "possesses power over everything"![44] This begs the question: how is this possible? The answer is human reason. William explains that human reason exercises power over everything in the sense that it "masters the power of hurting all the things under it."[45] As a result, reason can avoid certain natural things or it can destroy them—William valuates negatively all irrational nature in itself—or it can make use of things. For instance, human reason can make a horse into a useful means of transportation and a dog into a useful guard when we sleep at night.[46]

This wonderful ability, *ratio*, is the cause for William's lofty praise when he exclaims, "See and embrace, O human, the dignity of your nature...!"[47] Humanity is "precious in the inner being" (*pretiosus in interior*).[48] William continues in

---

39   Phys an, 79, "Deinde miserum hominem, ut in carcere se datum intelligat, statim uincula excipiunt, et omnium membrorum nexus praeter solum oculorum et oris officium quod liberum permittitur ad lacrimas tantum et uagitus," CCCM 88:131.

40   Phys an, 79, "Et hoc qui feliciter educatur, imperatoris uel regis filius," CCCM 88:131.

41   Phys an, 80, "...flens animal a suppliciis uitam auspicans, unam tantum ob culpam, quia natus est," CCCM 88:131.

42   Phys an, 81, "...statim morbi succedunt et medicinae, et ad extremum cura sepulturae. Nullius quippe uita uel sanitas fragilior...," CCCM 88:131.

43   Phys an, 81, "...pauper homo et omnium quae ad usum sunt egemus in hanc uitam inducitur," CCCM 88:132.

44   Phys an, 82, "...imperium super omnia dicitur possidere," CCCM 88:132.

45   Phys an, 82, "...nocendi potentiam in rebus subiectis ratio humana habet subiectam...," CCCM 88:132.

46   Phys an, 82, CCCM 88:132.

47   Phys an, 84, "Vnde uide et amplectere, o homo, dignitatem naturae tuae...," CCCM 88:133.

48   Phys an, 84, CCCM 88:133.

the same high style: "...according to your inner dignity you are born to a royal estate. For to be made in the image of the Almighty what else is this than to be immediately granted a royal nature?"[49] Indeed, by this gift of the rational soul the human person participates in the highest good, God, William maintains,[50] and he makes his point even more perspicuous when he adds that "there is in us the form of all good, virtue and wisdom and anything good," and "the soul is free from any necessity and cannot be enslaved by any natural power, but it can by itself will whatever it desires, and so the power of free will shows its dignity."[51] The soul is thus exactly this free power which is not forced by anything. Indeed, William concludes, "the rational soul or the soul in general is given by God, and from the soul is our natural life."[52]

In the middle of the treatise, William summarizes the questions to be answered regarding the soul: (1) What is it? (2) Why is it? (3) How is it?[53] The answers are just as clear: (1) What it is, no one understands, but it is a spiritual or intellectual reality most like God; (2) Why it is, its goal is to live according to reason, and finally (3) How it is, it follows simply from living according to reason.[54]

Now, Williams explains, the rational life acts through three powers: rationality, a positive appetite, and a negative appetite.[55] This is in accordance with the divine image of faith, hope, and charity because, William argues, we believe what is reasonable; we hope positively, of course; and we love God and our neighbor when we hate evil.[56] But these very same powers will, by a corrupt reason, produce (1) presumptions of bad faith, heresies, instead of

---

49   Phys an, 84, "Secundum interiorem enim dignitatem in regiam natus es conditionem. Omnipotentis enim naturae imaginem fieri, quid est aliud quam continuo regalem conditam fuisse naturam?" CCCM 88:133.

50   Phys an, 86, "In eo enim quod imaginem Dei factus dicitur homo, tale est ac si diceretur quia humanam naturam participem omnis boni fecit Deus," CCCM 88:133.

51   Phys an, 86, "Est enim in nobis omnis boni forma, uirtutis, sapientiae, et omnium quae in melius possunt intelligi. In eo item quod sit liber omni necessitate animus nullique naturali potentiae subiugatur, sed per se potentem ad id quod desiderat habet uoluntatem, uirtutem scilicet liberi arbitrii, suam exprimit dignitatem," CCCM 88:133.

52   Phys an, 86–87, "Res enim est dominatu carens ac uoluntaria uirtus, quod autem cogitur uiolentiamque patitur uirtus non est. Hic animus uel haec anima a Deo datur, ab anima uero naturalis uita nostra," CCCM 88:133–134.

53   Phys an, 87, "Data autem anima quaerendum est quid sit, quare sit, quomodo sit?" CCCM 88:134.

54   Phys an, 87, "Quid sit nemo comprehendit ... quia res est spiritualis, intellectualis, Deoque simillima. Quare sit ... ut uiuat secundum rationem. Quomodo sit, ipsum exigit modum secundum rationem uiuendi," CCCM 88:134.

55   Phys an, 89, CCCM 88:134.

56   Cf. Phys an, 89–90, CCCM 88:135.

true faith, (2) lust and pride instead of hope, and (3) anger, beastly cruelty, and hatred instead of love.[57] The soul is "so powerful and wonderful, that the human intellect can hardly understand it," William repeats.[58] Yet the soul can go two ways: "miserable is the companionship of stupidity, happy is the embrace of wisdom"[59] and "the soul acts according to its various desires, joyful or painful."[60] Even though the soul has no quantity, it will always have a quality, William explains, since it follows changing desires.[61] The soul is, however, always itself, it thinks by itself and it has its free will. William stresses that "the soul is its own power.... It is by its very own substance that it thinks. And so also with the will ... the willing itself is its substance ... it is all thought ... it is all will."[62] This implies that the soul is also "totally love when it loves," but again, it can be "heavenly charity (*caritas*)" or "damnable love (*amor*)."[63] William can conclude in his typical language about the soul: "the soul is created in such a majesty and dignity to the image of its Creator...," but it is changeable and moveable—it moves through desire and therefore it needs "...the firmer stability above it that moves neither in place nor in time."[64] Here we see clearly the whole turning point in William's thought: the total necessity of God.

The soul can discover the image of its Creator in its love, thought, and memory, William points out,[65] but the soul is not created equal to God.[66]

---

57 Phys an, 92, "Rationalitas enim corrupta saepe de se generat praesumptiones, haereses, et his similia. Concupiscibilitas *concupiscentiam carnis, concupiscentiam oculorum, superbiam uitae.* Irascibilitas, iram bestialem, truculentiam, odium," cccm 88:135.

58 Phys an, 92, "In utrisque uero tam potenter, tam mirabiliter operatur, ut uix humanus hoc comprehendat intellectus...," cccm 88:135.

59 Phys an, 93, "...misera est contubernio stultitiae, beata complexu sapientiae," cccm 88:136.

60 Phys an, 96, "Agitur enim anima ... pro affectuum diuersitate delectabiliter et poenaliter," cccm 88:137.

61 Phys an, 95, "Humana autem anima quia non habet molem, non habet quantitatem; quia affectuum mutabilitati subiacet, non effugit qualitatem...," cccm 88:136.

62 Phys an, 97, "Ipsa etiam anima sua potential ... ipsa uero sua substantia est qua cogitat. Sic de uoluntate ... uelle substantia eius est ... tota cogitatio est ... tota uoluntas est," cccm 88:137.

63 Phys an, 97–98, "Si enim anima cogitans tota cogitatio est, si tota uoluntas est, profecto tota diligens tota dilectio est. Sed et Deus dilectio dicitur et est. Sed dilectio illa talis est, ut nec ipsa diligere nisi bonum.... Haec autem dilectio quae est humana anima, pro affectuum mutabilitate potest et in superiora ... caelesti caritate flagrare, et in inferiora damnabili amore defluere," cccm 88:137–138.

64 Phys an, 98–99, "Tantae maiestatis creata anima ac dignitatis ad imaginem creatoris sui..." and "...stabilius stabilimentum, quod nec loco mouetur nec tempore...," cccm 88:138.

65 Cf. Phys an, 101, "Et in hoc etiam ex aliqua parte imaginem sui conditoris in se recognoscit...," cccm 88:139.

66 Phys an, 102, "...ad similitudinem auctoris tui factus, non ad aequalitatem creatus...," cccm 88:139.

"You have been formed," William reminds his reader; therefore, you need to "withdraw from the things which are beneath you. They are less formed, less beautiful than you are. Come up to the Form that gives form so that you may become more beautiful! Constantly unite yourself to this Form, for you will receive more from its beauty the more the weight of charity presses you against it. From this you will be stabilized as the image of him from whom you took your origin."[67]

At this point in the treatise William the theologian, with his ambitious yet simple explanations, becomes even more outspoken. Truth itself is now instructing our heart, William thus declares, and our soul will hear this instruction "even though human misery is always prompt to envy, it will no longer have any reason to envy an angel."[68] For the human situation is totally changed by faith in Christ because the human person has now become one spirit with God: "For such a person and the angels and God are all one spirit, according to the Apostle [1 Cor 6:17] or they are one in God according to the Gospel [John 17:21]".[69] This happens, William explains, through the "Head of Humanity, the human Christ who was truly and perfectly united in person by Truth itself, the Son of God"; "so, let holy humanity rejoice, glorified in its Head, Christ."[70]

William's divine universe is not optional, so to speak, but the true reality. He can maintain, therefore, that "nothing exists without God the Creator"[71] which means that everything is also marked by its triune creator.[72] Consequently, the

---

67   Phys an, 103, "Recede ab his quae infra te sunt, minus formata, minusque formosa quam
      tu es; accede ad formam formatricem, ut possis esse formosior, eidemque semper adiun-
      gere, quia tanto ab illa specie amplius accipies quanto te illi maiori caritatis pondere im-
      presseris. Ab illa enim obtinebis imaginis huius indemutabilem statum, a quo sumpsisti
      principium," CCCM 88:139; cf. Phys an, 1, "The power of knowledge of the thinking person
      is hardly enough, without the help of grace, to know himself, and even this is of no value
      unless from the knowledge of what he is rises to him from whom he is, to him who is
      above him" (Quapropter, cum omni homini qui capax est rationis uix suus sufficiat sensus
      nisi adiutus a gratia ut sciat se ipsum, cum tamen hoc nichil ei conferat nisi ex hoc quod
      ipse est, ascendat ad eum a quo ipse est et qui est super ipsum), CCCM 88:103.
68   Phys an, 103, "Haec et alia loquitur ueritas ad aurem cordis, intrinsecus admonens nos.
      Quae quaecumque audit anima cum semper humana miseria prompta sit ad inuidiam,
      non habet unde inuideat angelo...," CCCM 88:139.
69   Phys an, 103, "...quia homo talis et angelus et Deus, unus iam sunt spiritus, secundum
      Apostolum; uel unum sunt in Deo, secundum Euangelium...," CCCM 88:139–40.
70   Phys an, 103–104, "...hominis caput homo Christus, in uirtutem personae ab ipsa ueritate
      a Filio Dei uere et perfecte assumptus..." and "Gaudeat itaque glorificata in capite suo
      Christo sancta humanitas...," CCCM 88:140.
71   Phys an, 104, "...nichil sine creatore Deo, ipsa scilicet sancta Trinitate, existit...," CCCM
      88:140.
72   Phys an, 105, "...ita nichil omnino esse potest et quod non unum sit et trifarium consistat,"
      CCCM 88:140.

soul is also a trinity, for it is one "in three undivided parts: memory, deliberation, and will."[73] William's universe is thus one coherent reality. Therefore he can say without reservation that "the image of the Trinity proceeds from the supreme being who is God, through the middle being which is the soul, to the lowest which are bodies...."[74] When we are notified about this reality, the soul becomes happy not only for its own beauty but also happy for its divine Form.[75] Indeed, it makes sense to direct oneself to this Form because it always makes the soul more beautiful and this is what forms the soul, William explains.[76]

This thought undoubtedly provides the key to understanding William's anthropology, which is theological in that sense that it simply encompasses the divine reality. The Creator is part of it, which is precisely evident in the soul, and therefore the human person can only become what it actually is and is meant to be in unity with its Creator. Anything else is simply a mistake and leads to destruction. Therefore, it is not just a pious and simple-minded remark but a pure logical statement when William maintains that "whatever is drawn toward God is not its own but his by whom he is drawn."[77] Thus, the human soul is drawn into the unity it already belongs in, and in this spiritual unity, the soul will do only what the Holy Spirit works in it. In William's words, "Whatever it does, not itself but the Spirit works in it.... For just as the body lives from the soul, so does the soul live from God."[78] Moreover, "The soul breathes God," William can express, "just like the human body breathes the air." Even more than that, William declares daringly, "it is totally in God," and "the soul lives as one spirit with God."[79]

In this connection, one might ask a question about William's understanding of the human will in this situation. Is it really free? The answer must be negative. The human will, according to William, will naturally follow the highest power. William clearly explains: "The will of the Father and Son, the Holy Spirit, by an inconceivable grace, with an unspeakable joy ... conforms the will

---

73 Phys an, 105, "Omnis quippe anima, sicut dictum est, tribus indiuiduis subsistit: memoria, consilio, uoluntate," CCCM 88:140.

74 Phys an, 105, "Permanat enim a summo quod Deus est, per medium quod est anima, ad imum quod sunt corpora...," CCCM 88:140.

75 Phys an, 105, "Haec omnia anima intellectu conspiciens, non iam tantum delectatur in sua formositate quam in forma formatrice...," CCCM 88:140.

76 Phys an, 105, "...cui intendendo semper efficitur formosior. Ipsum enim intendere formari est," CCCM 88:140.

77 Phys an, 106, "Quicquid enim ad Deum afficitur non est suum, sed eius a quo afficitur," CCCM 88:140.

78 Phys an, 106, "...quaecumque demum operatur, non ipsa sed *Spiritus* in ea *omnia* in omnibus *operatur*.... Sicut enim corpus uiuit ex anima, sic ex Deo uiuit anima...," CCCM 88:141.

79 Phys an, 106, "...ipsum solum iugiter spirans, sicut corpus uiuens aerem, tota manens in Deo ... unus spiritus cum eo exsistens," CCCM 88:141.

of the soul to himself, uniting its love to himself with spiritual omnipotence."[80] William makes his point crystal clear by quoting the Gospel of John 17:21 about the prayer of Christ: "'I will'"—William comments, "this means that I [Jesus] bring it about by the power of my will which is the Holy Spirit"—"'that as I and You are one' in substance, 'so they may also be one in us' by grace."[81] Finally, William concludes regarding the soul and God: "one in love, one in beatitude, one in immortality and incorruption, in a certain way, one even in divinity itself."[82]

This last statement in particular provides evidence for how close William's *On the Nature of the Soul* is to the *Golden Epistle*.[83] According to both works, the Christian's existence basically consists in a direct spiritual unity with God in Christ. This describes not only the believer's future heavenly life but also the Christian perfection already in this life. "For those who have been enabled to become sons of God have been enabled to become, not indeed God, but what God is: holy, and in the future, fully happy as God is."[84] William expressly points out on the concluding pages of his *Golden Epistola*: "…it is because the human person has become one spirit with God that he is spiritual. And this is the perfection of humankind in this life."[85]

As William sees it, the human soul is a majestic power of the human body and, by reason, the highest dignity. Nevertheless, it remains in total need of the divine in order to be useful and avoid corruption. So, in William's understanding, it is only when God as the highest power and the highest good takes over the soul that the human soul truly becomes itself as it was meant to be. In this way the royal dignity of human nature, which can rise and fall, actually is given divine dignity: God in the soul.

---

80 Phys an, 107, "Voluntas enim Patris et Filii Spiritus sanctus incogitabili gratia, ineffabili gaudio … uoluntatem eius sibi conformans, amorem eius omnipotentia spirituali sibi uiuens, in tantum cum ea unum efficitur," CCCM 88:141.

81 Phys an, 107, "Et haec est oratio Filii ad Patrem. *Volo*, id est, uoluntatis meae uirtute, qui Spiritus sanctus est, efficio *ut sicut ego et tu unum sumus* in substantia, *sic et ipsi in nobis unum sint* ex gratia," CCCM 88:141.

82 Phys an, 107, "Vnum amore, unum beatitudine, unum immortalitate et incorruptione, unum etiam quodam modo ipsa diuinitate," CCCM 88:141.

83 Ep frat, 262–263, "Cum fit homo cum Deo unus spiritus, non tantum unitate idem uolendi, sed expressiore quadam ueritate uirtutis, sicut iam dictum est, aliud uelle non ualendi" and "Cum in osculo et amplexu Patris et Filii mediam quodammodo se inuenit beata conscientia; cum modo ineffabili et incogitabili, fieri meretur homo Dei, non Deus, sed tamen quod Deus est: homo ex gratia quod Deus est ex natura," CCCM 88:282.

84 Ep frat, 258, "Quibus enim 'potestas data est filios Dei fieri' (John 1:12), data est est potestas non quidem ut sint Deus, sed sint tamen quod Deus est, sint sancti, futuri plene beati, quod Deus," CCCM 88:281.

85 Ep frat, 287, "…quia factus unus spiritus cum Deo, spiritualis est. Et haec in hac uita hominis perfectio est," CCCM 88:287.

William's treatise ends with a brief reproduction of Augustine's seven steps of the progress of the soul to reach this goal in his *De quantitate animae*.[86] After this follows a repetition of the soul's two ways: it can go up or it can go down. But neither paragraph adds anything new to what has been said already.

Thus, we can notice that William's *De anima* is not about theories about the soul but about the realities of the soul. The *anima* is the God-created spiritual substance which gives life to the body. The same *anima* is *rationabilis* and immortal and convertible into good and evil.[87] This means that the soul is able to become rational, which is the most important point to William. Accordingly, William speaks about the same human *anima* when he speaks about the life-giving power of the soul to the body, the rational activity of the soul, as well as the soul when it comes into unity with the divine Spirit.

In the first case, William uses the word *anima* about the soul in general terms; in the other case, when he speaks about the soul becoming rational he prefers the masculine form of the same word, *animus,* or he can use an expression as *anima rationalis.* He is speaking about the human soul. In the same way, when William describes the human soul as *spiritus hominis* which becomes *unus spiritus* with God in the Holy Spirit, he refers to the same human soul. Likewise, when William differentiates between the soul's powers in *memoria, consilio,* and *voluntas,* he talks about the same individual soul as a trinity of qualities. Thus, the word "individual" is precise about William's understanding of the soul in his treatise, which is a *De anima*—and not just any "De anima et animo et spiritu et intelletu et conscientia et cetera," but the one soul—as the treatise ends—"Explicit de physica animae."[88]

3   *Epistola ad Fratres de Monte Dei*

As Bernard McGinn remarks in his introduction to the English translation of the *De natura animae*, William gives "…the foundation for the profound theory of the mystical union outlined in his later works" when he talks of the soul as created in the image of God and "the unique role of the Holy Spirit in the divinization of man."[89] Accordingly, as we have seen above, William's *De natura animae* ends with a description of the soul in *unitas spiritus*.[90] When McGinn refers to "later works" it is obvious first of all to think of the *Golden Epistle.*

---

86   Augustine, *De quantitate animae*, 33.70-76. See *Three Treatises on Man*, 147, n. 38.
87   Ep frat, 51, CCCM 88:121.
88   Phys an, 121, CCCM 88:146.
89   *Three Treatises on Man*, 44, 45.
90   Phys an, 103–107, CCCM 88:139–141.

However, when reading this work, one can easily get the impression that, as Jean Déchanet notes in his introduction to the English translation (1980), the *orientale Lumen*, according to William,[91] implies that William takes over the Greek tripartite division of the human person. As Déchanet writes, "The Greek Fathers, as we know, carefully distinguished in man the body, soul, and spirit or *nous* in which was found the divine image. This trichotomy which is alien to St Bernard was taken over by William (*corpus—anima—animus*)..."[92] This trichotomy would imply that there should be a careful distinction between *anima* and *animus* in William's *Golden Epistle*. Bernard McGinn made a similar observation in his analysis of William's *De natura corporis et animae* three years earlier, in 1977, when he remarked, "While William does not make use here of the trichotomy of *anima–animus–spiritus* which was to be of importance in such later works as *The Golden Letter* it might be said that this distinction between *anima* and *animus* when coupled with the *unitas spiritus* mentioned in Section thirteen [that is, of the *De anima*] already hints in that direction."[93]

How much division is there in a "trichotomy"? It can mean both a three-way classification and an actual splitting into three parts. When the word is used, as by Déchanet, about the relationship between the body and the soul, one must say that there is a clear division. This may not be quite the case when McGinn uses the word about a division inside the human spiritual being, and we can notice McGinn's comment a few pages later that "William concludes ... that the essence of the soul is identical with its powers."[94] This must mean that the soul is understood as one essence but with different powers.

Both of these interpretations, however, can find evidence in the *Golden Epistle,* simply in the clear structure of the treatise in which William writes about the animal person, the rational person, and the spiritual person. As William writes, "...there are beginners, those who are making progress, and the perfect. The state of beginners may be called 'animal,' the state of those who are making progress 'rational,' and the state of the perfect 'spiritual.'"[95] These are "three kind of human beings," and "each is recognized by distinctive pursuits."[96] William continues in the following paragraph, which can be summarized as the animal persons are like blind ones who must be led by

---

91   See Ep frat, 1, CCCM 88:228.

92   *The Golden Epistle: A Letter to the Brethren at Mont Dieu*, trans. Theodore Berkeley, OCSO, intro. J.M. Déchanet, OSB, CF 12 (Kalamazoo, MI: Cistercian Publications, 1980), XXIV.

93   *Three Treatises on Man*, 37.

94   *Three Treatises on Man*, 43.

95   Ep frat, 41–42, "...incipientium scilicet, proficientium et perfectorum. Incipientium status dici potest animalis, proficientium rationalis, perfectorum spiritualis," CCCM 88:236.

96   Ep frat, 41–42, "...his tribus hominum generibus...," and "...sic etiam dinoscuntur ex suorum proprietate studiorum...," CCCM 88:236.

others; the rational are led by the judgment of their reason; and the perfect are led by the spirit and enlightened by the Holy Spirit.[97] Furthermore, "the first state is concerned with the body, the second with the soul, the third finds rest only in God."[98] It also appears from these same paragraphs that William is talking about people in progress. We notice the words 'beginners,' 'progressing,' and 'perfect.' Here it is all about "how far they have come, the progress of the day and the hour."[99]

Probably the best example about the relationship between *anima, animus,* and *spiritus* is found in William's point in which he says that the *animalis sensus*, the *rationalis scientia*, and the *spiritualis sapientia* can be three persons, but just as well can be present in the one and same person "in various degrees of progress."[100] The same point is repeated later in the text in which William understands the perfect and spiritual state as always abasing themselves to the rank of the beginners.[101]

William, however, is clearly not a theologian with rigid concepts. As we know, he absolutely does not want to be a philosopher, just as he remarks in the beginning of the *Golden Epistle*, Christ precisely put fishermen above philosophers.[102] As we also know, when William is talking about the most important concept in his thought, namely love, he can use the words *amor, dilectio,* and *caritas* just as it fits best into the context without following strict definitions. The same can be said about William's words about the soul, as shown in the following examples:

Paragraph 1: When William talks of his meeting with the Brethren of Mont-Dieu he talks of *anima mea*.[103] The translation says, accordingly, "soul."

Paragraph 13: The first Christians wanted to cultivate their souls. William uses the word *animus* here,[104] and the translation writes, accordingly, "soul," not "reason" or "rational soul."

---

97   Ep frat, 43, CCCM 88:237.

98   Ep frat, 44, "Primus status circa corpus se habet, secundus circa animum se exercet, tertius non nisi in Deo requiem habet," CCCM 88:237.

99   Ep frat, 42, "...quousque peruenerit, et in quo proficiendi statu singulis diebus uel horis...," CCCM 88:237.

100   Ep frat, 140, CCCM 88:257.

101   Ep frat, 190, "Perfecti ... et spirituales ... premunt se semper ac deiiciunt in id quod incipientium est," CCCM 88:268.

102   Ep frat, 7, "...philosophos mundi huius per piscatores sibi subiecit," CCCM 88:229.

103   Ep frat, 1, "...occurre et concurre anima mea...," CCCM 88:228.

104   Ep frat, 13, "...de cultu animi...," CCCM 88:230.

Paragraph 35: When William talks about the soul in its intercourse with the Word of God he chooses the expression *fidelis anima*,[105] not *spiritus* which would be expected if William held systematic concepts, and the translation reads, rightly, "the faithful soul," not "spirit."

Paragraph 74: Talks of the body which shall serve the soul. William discusses the spirit, and writes, "corpus … ad seruiendum spiritui datum est,"[106] where we might expect the more general *anima,* but the translation chooses, correctly, "spirit," here.

Paragraph 84: William talks of manual work which shall nourish the mind's taste for spiritual things, as the translation says, but William's Latin uses the word *animus*, not *mens*.[107] The translation is not wrong, but it would be more correct to choose the word "soul."

Paragraph 88: William talks about the spirit's recovering by turning to God, *spiritus* is, correctly, translated as "soul,"[108] but if there were a system, it should have been "spirit." In the same way, *animus* is—again correctly—translated with "soul" in the following paragraph 89 where *animus* is equated with *conscientia*, which is translated with the word "spirit."[109] There are other examples of the translation of *animus* with "soul,"[110] and the translation is correct, but it shows that there is no thoroughly defined terminology to be found.

When William discusses the indwelling of the Holy Spirit in the soul, the translation says "spirit" just as we should expect *spiritus* in the Latin, but William writes *conscientia*.[111] This is also the case when we read William's *unitas spiritus* theory in which *conscientia* finds itself in the middle of the Trinity,[112] just as *conscientia* is the word for the 'inner cell,' about which William writes, "My secret is my own," the last words of the *Golden Epistle*.[113]

William does, however, deliberate on definitions when he defines the soul as the incorporeal *anima* which makes the body alive and is capable of becoming

---

105 Ep frat, 35, CCCM 88:235.
106 Ep frat, 74, CCCM 88:243.
107 Ep frat, 84, CCCM 88:245.
108 Ep frat, 88, CCCM 88:246.
109 Ep frat, 88, CCCM 88:246. For a detailed discussion of *conscientia* in William's thought, see Thomas X. Davis's chapter, "The Trinity's Glorifying Embrace: *Conscientia* in William of Saint-Thierry" in this volume, pp. 131–59.
110 Cf. Ep frat, 95, 96; CCCM 88:248.
111 Ep frat, 105, CCCM 88:250; cf. Ep frat, 115, CCCM 88:252.
112 Ep frat, 263, CCCM 88:282.
113 Ep frat, 300, CCCM 88:289; cf. Isaiah 24:16.

rational.[114] When the soul is in possession of reason it is called *animus* or *spiritus*, he says, and it is now in possession of itself.[115] With this, we do get some distinctions. Yet already in the next paragraph William writes that the *spiritus hominis* was created capable of reason and in the image of God.[116] Here he talks obviously of the soul that he just defined as the *anima* which is *rationis capax*.

4   Conclusion

Just as these distinctions do not divide the soul, William's use of Augustine's explanation of the soul's character of being created in God's image confirms the unity of the soul. The soul is thus to be divided into memory (*memoria*), understanding (*intelligentia*), and love (*amor*).[117] But it is still one individual soul.

The examples in the rest of the *Golden Epistle* about the use of *animus, spiritus, conscientia,* and *anima* do not give any new information, but they confirm that the soul is the spiritual part of the individual which is life-giving to the body; is able to develop reason or intellect or mind; has memory, understanding, and will; just as it is able to love; and most importantly, it can be divinized by the presence of and unity with the Holy Spirit, which is love, so that the divine love is in the human person in the form of human love. As we have seen, this is the conclusion of both William's treatises, *On the Nature of the Soul* and his *Golden Epistle*. William's understanding of the individual soul is thus clear and coherent regarding its contents but not so in its wording.

---

114   Ep frat, 198, CCCM 88:270.
115   Ep frat, 198, CCCM 88:270.
116   Ep frat, 199, CCCM 88:270.
117   Ep frat, 210, CCCM 88:272.

CHAPTER 5

William of Saint-Thierry and the Renewal of the Whole 'Man'

E. Rozanne Elder

1 Introduction

Relieved of abbatial responsibilities in 1135, William of Saint-Thierry began at Signy to write what he may well have thought would be his final and most important work, a verse by verse commentary on the Song of Songs,[1] a text which had deeply influenced his life and thought. By listening while in the Clairvaux infirmary to Bernard speak in its terms of his experience, he had been led to comprehend meanings in the Song that he had not previously grasped.[2] After returning to Saint-Thierry, he had recorded what he had learned,[3] mused on his own "inexperience,"[4] and copied—or finished copying—extracts from the commentaries of Ambrose and Gregory the Great.[5] Then at Signy he set out to understand still better "the love of God, by which God is loved and by which God is said to be love" by exploring the love between the Bride, the rational (human) soul, and Christ the Bridegroom[6] in his own *Exposition on the Song*

---

1 Almost certainly after completing a commentary on the Epistle to the Romans he had begun at Saint Thierry. See Paul Verdeyen, "Introduction," *Guillelmi A Santo Theodorico Opera Omnia Pars 1, Expositio super Epistolam ad Romanos*, (ed.) Paul Verdeyen, SJ, CCCM 86 (Turnhout: Brepols, 1989), xxvii, and Paul Verdeyen, "La Chronologie des œuvres de Guillaume de Saint-Thierry," *Collectanea Cisterciensia*, 72.4 (2010): 427–40 and *Ons geestelijk erf,* 82.3 (2011): 190–203, here 196–97.

2 *Vita prima Bernardi* (Vita Bern), 59, CCCM 89B:74–75.

3 *Brevis commentatio* (Brev comm), CCCM 87:155–90.

4 *Meditatio* (Med), 8, CCCM 89:46–51.

5 *Epistola ad fratres de Monte Dei* (*Epistola Aurea*) (Ep frat), Prol., 11, CCCM 88:226f. From the fact that the two best manuscripts containing these florilegia, Reims BM 132 and Valenciennes BM 50, "came directly or indirectly from the abbey of Saint Thierry," Antony Van Burink and Paul Verdeyen deduce that William created them while abbot (CCCM 88:199, 387). Verdeyen dates them to 1124–1125 (Verdeyen, "La chronologie des œuvres," 417–40). William's stay at Clairvaux has been dated to January-February 1128, which contradicts the hypothesis he began them after that; see Stanislaus [Stanley] Ceglar, "The Dating of William's Convalescence at Clairvaux," *Cistercian Studies Quarterly* 30.1 (1995): 27–33.

6 *Expositio super Cantica Canticorum* (Cant), Praef., 5, "Liber ... agens de sponso ac sponse, Christo et rationali anima.... Agit enim de amore Dei, uel quo Deus amatur, uel quo ipse Deus amor dicitur...," CCCM 87:23–24.

© KONINKLIJKE BRILL NV, LEIDEN, 2019 | DOI:10.1163/9789004392502_007

of Songs. He had reached Chapter Three when, probably just before Lent,[7] he happened across two booklets of unequal length but "containing almost the same thing" entitled the "Theology of Peter Abelard."[8] Surely aware of Abelard's dubious reputation as a theologian,[9] his curiosity was piqued, and he laid aside his commentary to read them. The more he read, the more "seriously disturbed" he became.[10] His literary plans and, to some degree, his thought were changed forever. He never finished the commentary.

---

7   Lent 1140 or 1139, depending on the date of the synod of Sens at which Abelard's *Theologia* was all but condemned. The synod date originally proposed, 25 May 1141, (S. Martin Deutsch in *Die Synode von Sens* [Berlin, 1880]) was later corrected to 2 June 1140 by Elphège Vacandard ("Chronologie abélardienne: La date du concile de Sens: 1140," *Revue des questions historiques* 50 [1891]: 235–45), the date accepted by most 20th-century scholars (e.g., Giles Constable, *The Letters of Peter the Venerable*, vol. 1 [Cambridge, MA: Harvard University Press, 1967], 318–19, and C. Stephen Jaeger, "Peter Abelard's Silence at the Council of Sens," in *Scholars and Courtiers: Intellectuals and Society in the Medieval West* [New York: Routledge, 2002], 31) until Constant J. Mews presented a compelling new argument for the 1141 date and cited the concurrence of Ferruccio Gastaldelli and Pietro Zerbi (Mews, "The Council of Sens (1141): Abelard, Bernard, and the Fear of Social Upheaval," *Speculum* 77 [2002]: 342–82, esp. 347); see also Wim Verbaal, "The Council of Sens Reconsidered: Masters, Monks, or Judges?," *Church History* 74.3 (2005): 460–93.

8   *Disputatio adversus Petrum Abaelardum* (Adv Abl), *Epistola Willelmi* (Ep Geof et Bern), 2, "Duo autem erant libelli idem paene continentes, nisi quod in altero plus, in altero minus aliquando inuenietur," CCCM 89A:13. William apparently read the *Theologia* and a *liber sententiarum,* probably notes for or by students which he mistakenly thought Abelard had written. Bernard, in Letter 190 to Innocent II, mentions, in addition to the *Theologia,* his Commentary on Romans, *Scito te ipsum,* and a *liber sententiarum,* which Abelard subsequently denied having written (*Sancti Bernardi Opera,* vol. 8, (eds.) Jean Leclercq and H.M. Rochais [Rome: Editiones Cistercienses, 1977]), 26 and 40. On which books William, Bernard, and Thomas of Morigny had in what forms, see Constant J. Mews, "The Lists of Heresies Imputed to Peter Abelard," *Revue bénédictine* 95 (1985): 73–110.

9   As the new abbot of Saint-Thierry, William signed a charter issued at the 1121 synod of Soissons at which Abelard's first book on theology, *De unitate et trinitate divina,* had been condemned; see manuscript BNF Picardie 249, fol. 235. Although William never mentioned the condemnation, he alluded to it more than once by stating that Abelard was "again" teaching novel doctrine. See Michael Clanchy, *Abelard: A Medieval Life* (Oxford: Blackwell, 1997), 297, n. 46. By Abelard's account he was condemned, not for his teaching but as an example to other theologians who might presume, as he had done, to lecture on or circulate their work "without the authorization of the roman pontiff or of the [local] church" (*Historia calamitatum,* (ed.) Jacques Monfrin [Paris: J. Vrin, 1967], 87).

10   BM Charleville 67, fols. 72v–73r, edited Jean Leclercq, "Les lettres de Guillaume de Saint-Thierry à Saint Bernard," *Revue bénédictine* 79 (1969): 375–91, here 377. Adv Abl, Ep Geof et Bern, "Fateor, curiosum me fecit titulus ad legendum.... Cum enim grauiter turbarer ad insolitas in fide vocum novitates," CCCM 89A:13–15, here 13.

2   Objections to Abelardian Propositions

In a letter he dispatched to two of the most influential churchmen in France, Bernard of Clairvaux and Geoffrey de Lèves, bishop of Chartres and papal legate, he listed fourteen Abelardian propositions which in his opinion "seriously and perilously corrupt the faith of our common hope ... not minor things, but the faith of the holy Trinity, the person of the Mediator, the Holy Spirit, the grace of God, [and] the sacrament of our universal redemption."[11] While he modestly invited them to judge whether he might, perhaps, have overreacted,[12] he also sent along his notes—forty-two pages in the critical edition[13]—in which he quoted offending passages from the booklets and documented his objections to "the unusual novelties of the words about the faith and new inventions of unheard-of meanings."[14]

Of the sixteen objectionable teachings, he listed three which touched on human redemption and the dual natures of Christ:

> 1. "That Christ did not assume flesh and suffer in order to free us from the devil's yoke."[15]

Abelard had examined and dismissed this widespread theory in his *Commentary on the Epistle to the Romans*, which William quoted.[16] That William took strong exception is somewhat incongruous, not only because Abelard had made a strong case for rejecting the devil's right theory,[17] but also because William's position on it, despite his protestation, did not differ all that much from Abelard's. When he referred to the Fall of humanity in an early treatise written at Saint-Thierry, he had stated that "man perished through pride" and

---

11   Adv Abl, Ep Geof et Bern, 1, CCCM 89A:13.
12   Adv Abl, Ep Geof et Bern, 1, CCCM 89A:13.
13   Adv Abl, CCCM 89A:17–59.
14   Adv Abl, Ep Geof et Bern, 2, "Cum enim grauiter turbarer ad insolitas in fide uocum nouitates et nouas inauditorum sensuum adinuentiones,...," CCCM 89A:13.
15   Adv Abl, Ep Geof et Bern, 3, "7. Quod Christus non ideo assumpsit carnem et passus est, ut nos a iugo diaboli liberaret," CCCM 89A:14.
16   Lending support to the opinion that the second Abelardian book he had was a florilegium of student notes. For a comparison of their commentaries, based on his 2001 dissertation, see Steven R. Cartwright, "Twelfth-century Pauline Exegesis: William of St. Thierry's Monastic Rhetoric and Peter Abelard's Scholastic Logic" in *A Companion to St. Paul in the Middle Ages*, (ed.) Steven R. Cartwright (Leiden: Brill, 2012), 205–34.
17   Abelard, *Commentarial in epistolam Pavli ad Romanos* (*Commentary on the Letter to the Romans*), 2:26, *Petri Abaelardi Opera Theologica*, vol. 1, (ed.) Eligius M. Buytart, OFM, CCCM 11 (Turnhout: Brepols, 1969), 113–18.

had then been snared by the devil,[18] and that the "just man," Christ, by deceiving the ancient deceiver, had obtained a new justice.[19] He said nothing then about the devil acquiring or losing any rights, and in the *Disputatio* claimed, not that God had given the devil power over fallen humankind, but that through deceit, "the seducer took possession of the sinner," justly abandoned by God.[20] Not unlike Abelard, too, he attributed the Fall and humanity's propensity to sin, not to the devil but to humankind. In his own commentary on Romans, William asked, "Is there no other exit from sin for me except through the death of Christ your Son?" and he replied, "None," but he emphasized, not blood sacrifice, but God's love, believing that "great love had to be set against great hatred; the love of the Son against the hatred of the enemy; the love of [God] even to contempt of self against the sin of self-love."[21]

2. "That from Adam we bear not the guilt, but the punishment, of original sin."[22]

William pointed out, rather unnecessarily to churchmen in the medieval Latin tradition, that the Church Fathers, principally Augustine, had taught that in baptism the guilt is remitted,[23] but, William later reiterated, "in Christ we have been freed from sin, but not yet from the punishment of sin,"[24] which is misery.[25]

---

18   *De natura et dignitate amoris* (Nat am), 35, "Accinxit ergo se quodammodo Dei Filius, et aggressus est per humilitatem recuperare eum, qui recuperari poterat, qui per superbiam perierat. Itaque inter Deum et hominem medium se faciens, qui recedens a Deo, captus erat et ligatus a diabolo," CCCM 88:204.

19   Nat am, 37, "Occisus iustus iniuste pro iustitia nouam de inimico obtinuit iustitiam, mortis scilicet iniuste sibi illatae," CCCM 88:206.

20   Adv Abl, 7, "Potestas autem haec diaboli in homine dederit potestatem, sed mox, cum peccantem Deus iuste deseruit hominem, seductor inuasit peccatorem," CCCM 89A:44. In support, he cited an unidentified passage attributed to Augustine.

21   *Expositio super epistolam ad Romanos* (Exp Rom), III.5.7-11, CCCM 86:65.

22   Adv Abl, Ep Geof et Bern, 3, "11. Quod ab Adam non trahimus originalis peccati culpam, sed poenam," CCCM 89A:14.

23   Adv Abl, 11, "Sed in baptismo, sicut dicunt Patres, sicut supra sufficienter exposuisse diximus beatum Augustinum, culpa dimittitur, poena ad exercitium uitae huius manet, quae est mors corporis et caeterae tribulationes uitae huius," CCCM 89A:58. See Exp Rom, III.6.4, CCCM 86:78–79.

24   *Aenigma fidei* (Aenig), 22: "...jam olim a peccato liberati, sed nondum a pena peccati," CCCM 89A:142. Citing Rom 6:18, 22.

25   Exp Rom, V.8.24-26, "Nam quod in hanc uenimus miseriam, poena peccati est," CCCM 86:121.

3. "That Christ, God and man, is not a third person in the Trinity."[26]

Abelard later taxed Bernard with having misunderstood his teaching on this point, arguing that 'man,' a mortal corporeal being, cannot properly (*proprie*) be said to be God.[27] William had supported his logical refutation of Abelard's position by quoting his favorite authorities, Augustine and Gregory the Great,[28] on the unity of Christ's person, and dismissed Abelard's conclusion as redolent of Arianism, Nestorianism, and Sabellianism, separation of Christ's natures, and, to William's mind, the introduction of quaternity into the Trinity.[29]

What really got under William's skin was not so much Abelard's theological 'novelties' as a question he had posed: "How could the Apostle say that humankind is reconciled by the death of the Son of God to a God who ought to be so much the more enraged against men in that men transgressed in crucifying his Son than by disobeying his commandment and eating a bit of that one fruit?"[30]

---

26   Adv Abl, Ep Geof et Bern, 3, "8. Quod Christus Deus et homo non est tertia persona in Trinitate," CCCM 89A:14. Objections in Adv Abl, 8, CCCM 89A:51–56.

27   See *Theologia Christiana*, 4.45 (CCCM 11:285), but William's criticism seems more relevant to a passage in *Theologia Solarium* 3.76, "Homo quippe res corporea est et membris composita ac dissolubilis. Deus uero nec corporea res est nec partibus constat ut dissolui possit. Deus ergo nec caro nec homo esse proprie dicendus est.... Absit autem ut aliquam rem deum esse ponamus que non semper extiterit aut non semper deus fuerit. Hoc quippe est deum nouum uel recentem confiteri," CCCM 13:521–522. Cf. Abelard's own summary in his *Apologia contra Bernardum* (*Fragmenta*, 8–12, CCCM 11:367–368) in which he protested Bernard's failure to understand his point: Frag, 12, "...quia illae duae naturae non possunt aliquid aeternum esse, cum una earum careat aeternitate, 'deus et homo' non est aliqua in Trinitate persona," CCCM 11:368.

28   Adv Abl, 8, "Sed sicut dicit beatus Augustinus ad Euodium: 'Assumpto homine nequaquam personarum numerus auctus est, sed eadem Trinitas mansit,'" CCCM 89A:51–52. Augustine, Letter 169.8, "Haec haeresis proprie Agnoetarum est, quae olim tempore beati Gregorii in ecclesia apparuit ... sic inter caetera dicit....," *Augustinus Epistulae 124–184*, (ed.) A. Goldbacher, CSEL 44 (1904; rpt. Verlag der österreichischen Akademie der Wissenschaften, 2013), 617, and Gregory the Great, *Epistola contra Agnoetas*, 10.21, *Gregorius Magnus Registrum Epistularum*, (ed.) D. Norberg, CCSL 140A (Turnhout: Brepols, 1982).

29   Adv Abl, Ep Geof et Bern, 3, CCCM 89A:26. His objections have been discussed in E. Rozanne Elder, "The Christology of William of St Thierry," *Recherches de théologie ancienne et médiévale* 58 (1991): 79–112.

30   Adv Abl, 7, "'Quomodo,' inquit, 'Apostolus reconciliari hominem Deo per mortem dicit Filii Dei, qui tanto plus aduersus hominem irasci debuit, quanto amplius homines in crucifigendo Filium eius deliquerunt quam in transgrediendo eius praeceptum gustu unius pomi?'" CCCM 89A:43. Cf. Abelard, *Commentaria in epistulam Pauli ad Romanos*, 2.3, "Quomodo etiam nos iustificari uel reconciliari Deo per mortem Filii sui dicit Apostolus, qui tanto amplius aduersus hominem irasci debuit quanto amplius homines in

William was possibly less annoyed by the question—although in his opinion it was a topic to be pondered prayerfully, not disputed in a noisy classroom[31]—than he was exasperated by Abelard's failure to answer it.[32] Having posed the question, Magister Petrus offered no magisterial solution, but left his young, impressionable students to draw their own conclusions, possibly imperiling their orthodoxy and, therefore, their salvation, and that of still other students who would in future be taught or preached to by them.

"Then Master Peter, by-passing the stony and scandal-filled questions undiscussed (as you can read) and studiously leaving a pit of perdition grubbed up and gaping for the somewhat dull witted, turns back to the catholic sense, as if declaring himself innocent should anyone tumble into it."[33] Instead of grappling with the illogic he perceived at the center of traditional theories of the atonement, the most renown dialectician of the age had simply leapt over the yawning logical crater to a traditionally exemplarist, purely subjective, conclusion: "It seems to us," Abelard had written, "that in this we are justified in the blood of Christ and reconciled to God, that it was through his matchless grace shown to us that his Son received our nature, and in that nature, teaching us both by word and by example, persevered to the death and bound us to himself even more through love, so that when we have been kindled by so great a benefit of divine grace, true charity might fear to endure nothing for his sake."[34]

---

crucifigendo Filium suum deliquerunt, quam in transgrediendo primum eius in paradiso praeceptum unius pomi gustu?" CCCM 11:116.

31   Adv Abl, 7, "...quomodo sit hominis reconciliatio ad Deum per mortem Filii ejus, difficilis quaestio est, non agitanda in tumultu, sed pie et humiliter quaerenda in spiritu," CCCM 89A:45.

32   Clanchy has noted that "Abelard raised questions which he could not answer because he wrote as a teacher and an intellectual almost at the moment of formulating his thoughts ... in perpetual hope of coming up with the answers, even to the paradoxes of the Trinity and the Redemption and even when his books were burned" (Clanchy, *Abelard: A Medieval Life*, 269).

33   Adv Abl, 7, "Deinde magister Petrus propositas quaestiones, sicut legere poteritis, scrupulosas et plenas scandalis indiscussas praeteriens, et multo studio effossam foueam perditionis simplicioribus apertam relinquens, quasi redit ad sensum catholicum, tamquam immunem se faciens, quicumque ceciderit in eam," CCCM 89A:313.

34   *Commentaria in Epistolam ad Romanos*, 2.3, CCCM 11:117. ET: Steven Cartwright, *Peter Abelard: Commentary on the Epistle to the Romans*, Fathers of the Church Mediaeval Continuation 12 (Washington, DC: Catholic University of America Press, 2011), 167–68. William's quotation of this passage, and only this passage, from the Commentary suggests that the second *libellus* he read was a compilation of notes for or by students. See Mews, n. 8, above.

That Abelard began his magisterial non-solution to this question with *Nobis autem videtur* irritated William, too.[35] He read it, not as the prelude to a masterful determination, but as evidence that "this domestic enemy has arrogated to himself alone the teaching office in [the Church], doing in holy Scripture what he used to do in dialectics, proposing his own theories, this year's novelties; a critic, not a disciple, of the faith, a redactor, not an imitator."[36]

As irked as William was by Abelard's casual dismissal of traditional teaching and his irresponsible pedagogy, his chief criticism focused on Abelard's conclusion: "he seems to want to build a case that Christ died for nothing (*gratis*)" by implying, "if he dared," that, except as a means of arousing believers' love, "the advent of Christ into the world was not necessary."[37] Upon reflection, William may have remembered that, as abbot, he himself had taught that everything the incarnate Christ did and said was God speaking "to us in the Son, by [His] love calling forth and arousing our love for [Him]."[38] Perhaps he suspected that the scholars of Mont Sainte Geneviève were less well grounded in the faith than were the monks of Saint-Thierry; or perhaps his dismay led him subsequently to reflect more deeply on *how* Christ had redeemed humankind.

Like many of his contemporaries, William emphasized love and reason, seeing them as human means of knowing, and insisting that each perceives in its own way and that neither alone gets far in "seeing" God, whereas together they become the eye of charity, "the sight for seeing God."[39] In preaching to the

---

35   See Adv Abl, 7, "'Vt nobis,' inquit, 'uidetur.' Melius ergo ipse aliquid asseret nobis, qua in quo omnes doctores post apostolos conuenerunt et consentiunt? Meliusque aliquid ei reuelatum est, uel ipse per se adinuenit, quam quod nos docuerunt qui a Domino didicerunt?" CCCM 89A:42.

36   Adv Abl, Ep Geof et Bern, 2, "Emortuis quippe ex Ecclesia omnibus paene doctrinae ecclesiasticae magistris, quasi in uacuam rempublicam Ecclesiae domesticus irruens inimicus, singulare sibi in ea magisterium arripuit, agens in Scriptura diuina quod agere solebat in dialectica, proprias adinuentiones, annuas nouitates; censor fidei, non discipulus; emendator, non imitator," CCCM 89A:14.

37   Adv Abl, 7, "Deinde ingreditur causam cum Deo homo ingratus, et astruere uelle uidetur quod Christus gratis mortuus sit," CCCM 89A:42. Despite his criticism here, William in his own commentary on Romans 3:24-26, wrote that God manifests his justice "...gratis justificando," Exp Rom, II.3.24-26, CCCM 86:46.

38   *De sacramento altaris* (Sac Alt), 6, "Quicquid enim Redemptor noster in carne fecit, ob hoc utique fecit, ut amaretur a nobis; non quod egeret ipse nostro amore...," CCCM 88:64–65. Cf. *De contemplando Deo* (Contemp), 16, "Et quicquid fecit, quicquid dixit in terra, usque ad opprobria, usque ad sputa et alapas, usque ad crucem et sepulchrum, non fuit nisi loqui tuum nobis in Filio, amore tuo prouocans et suscitans ad te amorem nostrum," CCCM 88:161.

39   Nat am, 21, "Visus ergo ad uidendum Deum naturale lumen animae, ab auctore naturae creatus, charitas est. Sunt autem duo oculi in hoc uisu ad lumen quod Deus est uidendum

monks of Saint-Thierry, he had made this epistemology sound fairly straight-forward.[40] Life experience subsequently taught him that it was not easy. While wrestling with the decision to leave Saint-Thierry, he prayed: "You know that I want to love you ... but I do not sense, or barely sense, you; I do not see or barely see, very very rarely and very very little do I savor [you]."[41] Yet at the same time he was becoming ever more convinced that human beings were cre-ated to "see God face to face,"[42] and that God's purpose in the incarnation and passion was to restore to humankind the means of overcoming the unlikeness that deprived fallen humanity of the capacity to "seek the face of God."[43]

After dropping the Abelard problem in Bernard's lap, William did not complete his Canticle commentary, but instead wrote two treatises directed against, but not naming, Abelard. In the process he apparently prayerfully pon-dered the 'difficult question' which Abelard had posed but avoided answering. Deeply imbued with the Christian Neoplatonism of Augustine, he wove into his final works his own understanding of how Christ, the Image of the unseen God,[44] had by his incarnation and death not only elicited responsive love from human beings, but also restored the de-formed and sin-diminished sons and daughters of Adam and Eve to the likeness of God to which they had been cre-ated, thereby enabling them to "seek my face,"[45] and in the life to come "to be like God, for to the image of God were we created."[46]

Before turning his full attention to attempting to refute Abelard by writing the *Enigma of Faith* and the *Mirror of Faith*, however, he seems to have paused to return to the Canticle commentary long enough to extend, or to write, its

naturali quadam intentione semper palpitantes, amor et ratio. Cum alter conatur sine altero non tantum proficit; cum inuicem se adiuuant, multum possunt...," CCCM 88:193.

40   My impression that the work reads like chapter talks collected into a treatise was shared by the late meticulous scholar Stanley (Stanislaus) Ceglar, SDB, "William of St.-Thierry: The Chronology of His Life with a Study of His Treatise *On the nature of love*, His Author-ship of the *Brevis commentatio*, the *In lacu*, and the *Reply to Cardinal Matthew*," Ph.D. diss., Catholic University of America, Washington, DC, 1971, 318–20.

41   Med, 12.14-15, "Tu scis quia amare te uolo ... te uero non sentio [uel uix sentio], non uideo uel uix uideo, rarissime et parcissime sapio," CCCM 89:74.

42   E.g., Aenig, 5, "Visio namque facie ad faciem," CCCM 89A:130 and Aenig, 6, "Deus uidebitur sicuti est facie ad faciem," CCCM 89A:132. Seeing God face to face occurs several times in the Pentetuch, e.g. Deut 5:4, 32:30, Ex 33:17, and in 1 Cor 13:12.

43   Ep frat, 25, "Ipsa enim est professio uestra: ...quaerere ipsam faciem Dei...," CCCM 88:233.

44   Col 1:15.

45   See, e.g., Med, 9.17, "Ostende nobis quod credimus, insinua nobis quod speramus, fac fa-ciem quam faciei Dei comparemus, ut dicamus: Tibi dixit cor meum: Exquisiuit te facies mea [Ps 26:8 Vlg.]," CCCM 89:56 and Ep frat, 26, CCCM 88:233.

46   Ep frat, 209, "Ad imaginem enim Dei creati sumus," CCCM 88:281 and Ep frat, 278, "...imago Dei reformatur in homine...," CCCM 88:285.

Prologue. After what reads like a conclusion,[47] he abruptly introduces a new topic. "It is evident," he wrote, "that there are three states of men of prayer or three states of prayer: animal, rational and spiritual."[48] He then sketched out a theory of redemption which he elaborated only later in his *Letter to the Carthusians* (*Golden Epistle*) in describing the stages "by which [man] created to the image and likeness of [God]....[49] draws near by likeness to God from whom he departed by unlikeness"[50] so that human beings might contemplate the Creator, for "no one contemplates You to fulfillment, save insofar as one becomes like to You."[51]

3   William's Augustinian Foundation

William built on the foundation of Augustine's teaching that God impressed upon the human soul an indelible image of the Trinity: the faculties of memory, reason, and will.[52] As God is three persons but one substance, these three

---

47   Cant, Prol., 9, "Haec in principio praemitti oportuit...," CCCM 87:24.

48   Cant, 3.11-12, "Tres ergo status esse orantium uel orationum manifestum est: animalem, rationalem, spiritualem. Vnusquisque secundum modum suum format sibi uel proponit dominum Deum suum, quia qualis est ipse qui orat, talis ei apparet Deus quem orat. Etenim qui fideliter orat, sicut solidum quid dignum que Deo afferre semper nititur in oratione quod offerat, sic anxium habet cor ac suspectum, donec aliquatenus uideat coram quo illud deponat uel cui committat. 12. Homo uero animalis orans Deum, sed nesciens orare quemadmodum oportet, petens aliquid a Deo praeter ipsum uel ad ipsum, ut multum proficiat in ordine suo, et prudentior inueniatur in generatione sua, non ut munda sit conscientia a malis operibus et cor a prauis cogitationibus, talem se Deo offert qualis est, aliud quid scilicet praeter ipsum desiderantem ac petentem; nec alterius formae requirit Deum quam cuius ipse est, id est praeter semetipsum alia quae petitur praestantem," CCCM 87:24.

49   Gen 1:26, 27. For a thorough study of William's dependence on Augustine in this exegesis, see David N. Bell, *The Image and Likeness: The Augustinian Spirituality of William of St Thierry*, CS 78 (Kalamazoo, MI: Cistercian Pubications, 1984). For the image and likeness theme set within William's spirituality, see also Bernard McGinn, "William of St. Thierry: Spirit-Centered Mysticism," in *The Growth of Mysticism. The Presence of God: A History of Western Christian Mysticism*, vol 2. (New York: Crossroad, 1992), 225–74.

50   Ep frat, 208, "Ad imaginem et similitudinem eius conditus est; hoc est ut quamdiu uiuitur hic, quam propius potest accedat ad eum similitudine, a quo sola receditur dissimilitudine; ut sit hic sanctus, sicut ille sanctus est; in futuro beatus futurus, sicut ille beatus est," CCCM 88:272.

51   Cant, 1.1, "Domine Deus noster, qui ad imaginem et similitudinem tuam creasti nos, scilicet ad te contemplandum te que fruendum, quem nemo usque ad fruendum contemplatur, nisi in quantum similis tibi efficitur," CCCM 87:19.

52   Both varied their terminology somewhat, exchanging *amor* and *voluntas*, and *intellectus* or *consolio* for *ratio*. Augustine, *De Trinitate*, 10.11.17 (*memoria, intelligentia, voluntas*);

faculties are one in "effectivity," William had written years earlier.[53] Dim memory, "the latent presence of God in the soul,"[54] nudges the soul towards God; weakened will, "the natural appetite of the soul,"[55] is pulled between physical appetites and spiritual yearning; reason, the very sight of the mind,[56] which sets human beings above all other creatures, searches for understanding.[57] As a mark of the dignity of creatures bearing the image of the Almighty,[58] the Creator also endowed humanity with free choice, *liberum arbitrium*, the ability to will and, therefore, to love without compulsion.[59] This likeness to God makes human beings "capable of the fullness of all good,"[60] and therefore *capax Dei*. At the Fall, however, freedom of choice, "the judgment of reason in judging and discerning," was impaired and, as a result, sometimes does not choose to be guided by reason;[61] the allure of self-gratification all too often overwhelms rational discernment.[62] In Bernard of Clairvaux's terms, fallen man is free but

---

15.22.42 (*memoria, intellectus, amor*); *Sololoquia*, 12.15.24 ([*intellectus*] *scientia, voluntas*); 14.12.115 (*memoria dei, intelligentia dei, amor dei*). William, Nat am, 105 (*memoria, consilio, uoluntas*); Ep frat, 242 (*uoluntas, memoria, intellectus*). Understanding (*intellectus*) grows from the use of reason (*rationcinatio*).

53   Nat am, 3, "Et haec tria unum quiddam sunt, sed tres efficaciae; sicut in illa summa Trinitate una est substantia, tres personae," CCCM 88:180. He extended the parallel by writing that memory begets reason and that from the two of them the will proceeds.

54   Bell, *Image and Likeness*, 26. Chapters Three and Five give a full discussion of image, likeness, love, and assimilation.

55   Ep frat, 234, "Voluntas, naturalis quidam animi appetitus est...," CCCM 88:276. Bernard, by comparison, defines the will as "a rational movement protecting the senses and appetites. It holds reason as its handmaid wherever it is involved, not that it always moves by reason by that it never moves without reason, so that it does many things by [reason] against [reason], i.e. by its ministry but contrary to its counsel" (*De gratia et libero arbitrio*, 3.6): "Porro voluntas est motus rationalis, et sensui praesidens, et appetitui, Habet sane, quocumque se volverit, ationem semper comitem et quodammodo pedissequam; non quod semper ex ratione, sed quod numquam absque ratione moveatur, ita ut multa faciat per ipsam contra ipsam, hoc est per eius quasi ministerium, contrarius consilium sive judicium...," SBOp, 3:168.

56   Spec fid, 4, "Aspectus uero animae ratio est...," CCCM 89A:82.

57   William, *De natura corporis* (Phys corp), 26, CCCM 88:112.

58   William, *De natura animae* (Phys an), 84, CCCM 88:133.

59   Phys an, 86, "In eo item quod sit liber omni necessitate animus nulli que naturali potentiae subiugatur, sed per se potentem ad id quod desiderat habet uoluntatem, uirtutem scilicet liberi arbitrii, suam exprimit dignitatem," CCCM 88:133.

60   Phys an, 86, "Igitur in eo quod sit plenitudinis omnis boni capax, ad principale exemplum imago habet similitudinem," CCCM 88:133.

61   Ep frat, 199, "Nec tamen omnino amisit arbitrium, id est iudicium rationis in iudicando et discernendo, quamquam libertatem eius amiserit in uolendo et agendo," CCCM 88:270.

62   Spec fid, 13, "Ad peccatum tantum per se liberum est; qua libertate peccant omnes, quicumque delectatione uel amore peccati peccant," CCCM 89A:86.

cannot not sin, *non posse non peccare*.[63] Yet "likeness to God is humankind's perfection," and "not to want to be perfect is to miss the mark," to fall short of being fully human.[64] Those who repeatedly make self-serving choices devolve into a sub-human state, becoming like the "horse and mule which have no understanding."[65] In gratifying their whims, they fritter away their innate love (*amor*) on trifles, mindful neither of their true good nor of God.

Not surprisingly, therefore, William, in writing for Carthusian novices, gave his fullest attention to the training of the will. "The will must therefore always be nurtured with this perfection in view and love made ready. The will must be prevented from dissipating itself on alien objects, love protected lest it be defiled. For to this alone were we created and do we live, that we may be like God, for we were created in his image."[66]

Before reading Abelard, William had followed Augustine in accepting that the right use of the will was both a personal responsibility and an effect of grace.[67] After deleting Abelard for teaching that one can choose and can do good by one's own free will, without the help of grace,[68] he heightened his emphasis on faith and grace. Faith is freely chosen but not without divine aid.[69] Without creative grace, humankind would not be *capax omnis boni*; without illuminating grace, that capacity could never be actualized; without liberating grace, the will could never be sufficiently free to choose the good.[70]

---

63   Ep frat, 199, "Nec omnino amisit arbitrium, id est judicium rationis in judicando et discernendo, quamquam libertatem suam amiserit in volendo et agendo," CCCM 88:270. Cf. Bernard of Clairvaux, *De gratia et libero arbitrio*, 7.21 and *passim*, see for example 7.21, man fell from being able-not-to-sin (*posse non peccare*) to being not-able-not-to-sin (*non posse non peccare*), but can be restored to being not-able-to-sin (*non-posse-peccare*) (SBOp, 3:182). As William urged Bernard to compose this work, they may possibly have conferred on the sequence. See Bell, *Image and Likeness*, 185, for a concise summary.

64   Ep frat, 259, "Et haec hominis perfectio est, similitudo Dei. Perfectum autem nolle esse, delinquere est," CCCM 88:281; Jerome, Letter 14.7, CSEL 54:54.

65   Phys an, 118, "...efficiturque *sicut equus et mulus quibus non est intellectus* [Ps 31:9 Vlg] prudens tantum ut faciat malum, bene autem facere nesciens. Sui nulla cura, Dei nulla memoria," CCCM 88:145.

66   Ep frat, 259, "Et ideo huic perfectioni nutrienda est semper uoluntas, amor praeparandus; uoluntas cohibenda, ne in aliena dissipetur; amor seruandus, ne inquinetur. Propter hoc enim solum et creati sumus et uiuimus, ut Deo similes simus," CCCM 88:281.

67   E.g., Contemp, 19, "Est enim uirtus ... bonus usus libere uoluntatis...," CCCM 88:167. Cf. Augustine, *Retractationes*, 1.9.6; *De libero arbitrio*, 2.19.50; and William, Exp Rom, V.8.35-39, "Amor noster mentis humanae affectus est; amor Dei gratiae effectus est," CCCM 86:130.

68   Adv Abl, Ep Geof et Bern, 3, CCCM, 89A:14. On Abelard's position, see John Marenbon, *The Philosophy of Peter Abelard* (Cambridge: Cambridge University Press, 1997), 326.

69   Spec fid, 13, "Est autem fides res liberi arbitrii, sed liberati a gratia," CCCM 89A:86.

70   On *gratia liberans*, see Adv Abl, 6 (CCCM 89A:40); Spec fid, 13 (CCCM 89A:86); Ep frat, 201 (CCCM 88:271). On William's distinction between other types of grace—*gratia creans* and *gratia illuminans*, see Bell, *The Image and Likeness*, 131–32.

Because the love "naturally invested in the human soul" by the Creator, has been deflected from the God who is Love to self and to trifles which beguile our fleeting affections, it must be relearned; it must be taught by a human being.[71] Yet there is no human teacher untainted by sin. Therefore, "for us and for our salvation,"[72] God the Son became humankind's *summe magister*.[73] "The Word of God has appeared in human form for this purpose: that *as in many and various ways God* long ago *spoke to the fathers through the prophets*, so he might, in *recent days, speak to us in his Son,* that is effectually, as in his very word itself, because what he has done in him temporally and corporally he has extended to us to receive as with the hands of faith."[74]

4   The Incarnation of Christ

The incarnate Christ claimed a unique magisterial authority, declaring that "no one has seen the Father but the Son."[75] He, the image of the unseen God, came to humankind as Mediator, "wholly man because of the humanity he assumed, wholly God because God did the assuming,"[76] and he taught that "without me you can do nothing."[77] By word and deed he renewed the memory of God's love, so that by meditating on what has been "recorded by his own apostles,"[78]

---

71   Nat am, 2, "Amor ergo … ab auctore naturae naturaliter est animae humanae inditus; sed postquam legem Dei amisit, ab homine est docendus," CCCM 88:178.

72   Nicene-Constantinopolian Creed.

73   Contemp, 1, CCCM 88:153.

74   Spec fid, 118, citing Heb 1:1-2, he wrote, "Nam et ideo Verbum Dei in forma hominis apparuit, ut *multifariam multis que modis, olim Deus* locutus patribus in prophetis nouissime diebus istis loqueretur *nobis in Filio*, hoc est efficaciter, sicut in ipso Verbo suo. Quia quod temporaliter et corporaliter in eo fiebat, quasi ad suscipiendum manibus fidei porrigebat; ipsum autem Verbum, per quod *facta sunt omnia*, per corporalia et temporalia purgandis promittebat, et purgatis in aeterna beatitudine plenius contemplandum et habendum reseruabat," CCCM 89A:126. Cf. *Brevis commentatio* (Brev com), 7, CCCM 87:5; Contemp, 12, CCCM 88:161.

75   Med, 3.8, "Nemo autem videt patrem nisi filius et filium, nisi Pater [Matt 11:27]," CCCM 89:16.

76   Ep frat, 175, "Postmodum uero fide migrante in affectum, amplexantes in medio cordis sui, dulci amoris amplexu Christum Iesum, totum hominem propter hominem assumptum, totum Deum propter assumentem Deum, incipiunt eum iam non secundum carnem cognoscere, quamuis eum necdum secundum Deum plene possint cogitare," CCCM 88:265.

77   Exp Rom, VI.9.30-33, "Fides Christi est: credere in eum qui iustificat impium; credere in mediatorem, sine quo nullus reconciliatur Deo; credere in eum qui dicit: Sine me nichil potestis facere [John 15:5]," CCCM 86:141.

78   Aenig, 28, "Quod si Verbum et Sapientia Dei in hac uita nos scire uoluisset, nemo melius quam ipse per semetipsum, seu per apostolos suos hoc in mundo docuisset," CCCM 89A:146.

a person can "apprehend God in man" and in Jesus catch a glimpse of God as God is.[79] Christ enabled a greater understanding than could be grasped by reason; he revealed "a new wisdom surpassing all the wisdom of this world."[80] Reason leads to knowledge, but it is dependent on sensory evidence. Therefore, "Those who want to know him in some way as more than man do not cling too closely to the words written about him," and must couple reason with "the love by which we go to God," if they are to "pass over from faith to vision." Without love, the will intensified and focused,[81] reason is incapable of the full vision of God.[82] When Jesus "taught man that the understanding of the Godhead is beyond men, he was teaching men to think as he thinks."[83]

The more William meditated on Christ's teaching, the more convinced he became that the incarnation had not been a prelude to inevitable death. Scripture declares that "the wages of sin is death,"[84] yet it also claims that Christ was "like us in all ways except sin."[85] The human Christ neither inherited original sin nor committed personal sin; therefore he "owed nothing to the penalty of sin, that is, death."[86] Christ *chose* to share the penalty of the sin he did not share, and "by his grace, he dissolved and deleted all the transgressions which men by their own will had added to the original [sin] in which they were born."[87] If Jesus had had to die, William reasoned, the human nature assumed by the

---

79   Ep frat, 174, CCCM 88:264.
80   Spec fid, 84, "Ex quo profluxit in mundum noua sapientia, sapientia super omnem sapientiam mundi huius et stultam eam faciens...," CCCM 89A:14.
81   E.g., Contemp, 14, "Nichil enim aliud est amor, quam uehemens et bene ordinata uoluntas," CCCM 88:162–163.
82   Nat am, 21, "Sunt autem duo oculi in hoc uisi ad lumen quod Deus est ... amor et ratio," CCCM 88:193.
83   Spec fid, 20, "Cum enim diuinitatis intellectum docuit esse supra homines, suo inde modo docuit cogitare homines," CCCM 89A:127.
84   Rom 6:23.
85   Heb 4:15.
86   Adv Abl, 7, "Et Dominus qui poterat, si uellet, non mori, quia non homo tantum, sed et Deus erat, et ab omni remotissimus peccato, poenae peccati, hoc est morti, nichil debebat, sponte suscepit mortem...," CCCM 89A:48. Although in general, he leaned toward the opinion that Christ retained a choice of whether or not to die—quoting as his authority John 10:18, "I have the power of putting down my life and of taking it up again"— at times, when not concentrating on this point, William implied that mortality was an integral part of Christ's humanity, that, having accepted human nature, Christ accepted the death that ends human life. See Exp Rom, II.3.1, "Nunc autem, id est tempore gratiae, manifestata est iustitia, non legis, non meritorum, sed Dei in sanguine Christi [Rom 3:21]," CCCM 86:40; Exp Rom, I.1.4 (CCCM 86:8); Exp Rom, III.5.12 (CCCM 86:68–69); Exp Rom, IV.7.20-23, 8.3-4 (CCCM 86:102, 109). Cf. Augustine, *De peccatorum meritis et remissione*, 1.28.55 (PL 44:131).
87   Exp Rom, III.5.15, "...Christus autem etiam quae homines delicta propriae uoluntatis ad originale in quo nati sunt, addiderunt, gratia sua soluit atque deleuit," CCCM 86:73.

Eternal Son would have been identical with the nature corrupted by sin, and if it is true that "man is incapable of willing anything unless he is helped by someone who cannot will evil,"[88] it follows that without Christ's free and willing acceptance of death, the human will would have remained forever deformed, cut off from the vision of God that is salvation. When William asserted that no escape from sin is possible except through the blood of Christ,[89] it was not because he believed God the Father demanded a blood sacrifice or a substitute debtor, but because Christ by love made it possible for humankind to achieve "some likeness to that love which made God like man through the humiliation of the human condition, so that man might be made like God by the glorification of divine participation."[90] As Augustine had written some seven hundred years earlier, "just as [Christ] was mortal, not of his nature but of ours, so we shall be immortal, not of our nature but of his."[91]

William agreed with Abelard that the sacrifice of Christ does indeed evoke responsive love,[92] and he recommended spending at least an hour a day in

---

88   Exp Rom, III.6.22, "Nec potest homo boni aliquid uelle, nisi adiuuetur ab eo qui malum non potest uelle," cccm 86:89.

89   Cf. Exp Rom, III.5.7-11, "Nullus ne alius a peccato mihi exitus, nisi per mortem Christi Filii tui? Nullus," cccm 86:65. Cf. Exp Rom, I.1.4 (cccm 86:8); Exp Rom, III.5.12, 6.5-9 (cccm 86:68–69, 82); Exp Rom, IV.7.20-23, 8.3-4 (cccm 86:102, 109).

90   Ep frat, 272, "...proficiat in aliquam similitudinem amoris illius, qui Deum similem fecit homini per humiliationem humane conditionis, ut hominem similem Deo constituat per glorificationem divinae participationis," cccm 88:284.

91   Augustine, *Enarrationes in Psalmos*, 146.5.11, ccsl 40, line 45. The libraries of both Saint-Thierry and Signy contained copies of the *Enarrationes*, not surprisingly in monasteries in which psalms formed the Work of God. Charleville BM mss 202, three volumes, originally at Signy, is dated to the second half of the 12th century by Anne Bondéelle Souchie, *Bibliothèques cisterciennes dans la France Médiévale: Répertoire des Abbayes d'hommes* (Paris: cnrs, 1991), 286–93, esp. 290; Saint Thierry mss 41–42 (undated by Bernard de Montfaucon, *Bibliotheca bibliothecarum manuscriptorum nova*, vol. 2 [Paris, 1739], 1233). Although the work does not appear in the 11th-century library catalogue (Reims BM, ms E.331), mss 41 survives as Reims BM 85 (E 262) and is dated by the cataloguer to the 11th century.

92   Sac Alt, 6, "Quicquid enim Redemptor noster in carne fecit, ob hoc utique fecit, ut amaretur a nobis; non quod egeret ipse nostro amore, qui bonorum nostrorum non eget, per omnia sufficiens ipse sibi, sed quia, quos beatos facere susceperat, nisi eum amando non poterant esse beati ... Ideo que non solummodo amore, quo nos prior dilexit, sed omnimodis amoris obsequiis, ut amaretur a nobis....," cccm 88:64–65. See also Contemp, 16, "Et quicquid fecit, quicquid dixit in terra, usque ad opprobria, usque ad sputa et alapas, usque ad crucem et sepulchrum, non fuit nisi loqui tuum nobis in Filio, amore tuo prouocans et suscitans ad te amorem nostrum," cccm 88:161. See Med, 6.7, "Amor enim ad te, Domine, in nobis illuc ascendit, quia amor in te ad nos huc descendit. Quia enim amasti nos, huc descendisti ad nos. Amando te, illuc ascendemus ad te," cccm 89:34.

meditating on the passion.[93] But the suggestion that the incarnation had no other purpose he found unacceptable. Relying utterly on Christ's promise in the Gospel that he has gone to prepare a place for his disciples,[94] William believed that human beings, having chosen to cooperate in being renewed and redeemed by the perfect man who is the eternal Image of God, "will be worthy of dwelling in eternity and dwelling in Christ and in the Father, to be with him in whom he is."[95]

> All the things said and done by the Word of God are to us a single word; all the things which we read, hear, say, and ponder about him call us to that one [Word] either by eliciting love or inciting fear; they send us to that One of whom many things are said and nothing is said, because no one arrives at that which is unless he who is sought come to meet us and shine his face upon us and illuminate his own face so that we may know in the light of his face where we are going.[96]

Having had to learn 'here,' on earth, not to cling too tightly to Jesus the teacher,[97] but to pass over to the contemplation of the divine Son,[98] William did not expect 'there,' in the life to come, to see the human Jesus.[99] God incarnate is forever true God and true man, but William seems to have found the

---

93   Ep frat, 115, CCCM 88:252. For William's connection between meditation on Christ's passion and his Eucharistic theology, see Nathaniel Peters's chapter, "The Eucharistic Theology of William of Saint-Thierry," in this volume, pp. 160–95, esp. 177–83.

94   John 4:13.

95   Spec fid, 114, "Ferat que patienter quamdiu mundatur, et dignam se faciat, quae crebrius admittatur, diutius immoretur, ubi et aliquando in aeternum habitare mereatur; ut possit esse in Christo ubi ipse est et in Patre esse cum illo in quo ipse est," CCCM 89A:124.

96   Spec fid, 121, "Omnia ergo facta uel uerba Verbi Dei unum nobis uerbum sunt; omnia quae de eo legimus, audimus, loquimur, meditamur, siue prouocando amorem, siue incutiendo timorem, ad unum nos uocant, ad unum nos mittunt, de quo multa dicuntur et nichil dicitur, quia ad id quod est non peruenitur, nisi occurrat ipse qui quaeritur, et illuminet uultum suum super nos, et illustret faciem suam, ut in lumine uultus eius sciamus qua gradiamur," CCCM 89A:127.

97   Ep frat, 36, "Cella terra sancta et locus sanctus est, in qua Dominus et seruus eius saepe colloquuntur, sicut uir ad amicum suum; in qua crebro fidelis anima Verbo Dei coniungitur, sponsa sponso sociatur, terrenis caelestia, humanis diuina uniuntur," CCCM 88:235.

98   Spec fid, 118–119, CCCM 89A:126.

99   Spec fid, 118, "Ubi sicut Christus non secundum hominem cognoscetur, sic et hic a desiderantibus aliquatenus eum supra hominem cognoscere, uerbis quae de eo sunt non nimis inhaereatur, sed eis quasi nauigio a fide ad speciem transeatur," CCCM 89A:128. Cf. Bernard, *De diligendo Deo,* 40, "Nemo ibi si cognoscet secundum carnem quia caro et sanguis regnum dei non possidebunt," SBOp, 3:153.

idea of the human Jesus, as it were, strolling around heaven an indefensible separation of his unconfused and inseparable human and divine natures.[100] In the afterlife he anticipated gazing in adoration upon the Trinity, "the one God from whom we exist, through whom we exist, in whom we exist; from whom we departed, to whom we became dissimilar, by whom we were not permitted to perish. This is the source to whom we return, the form which we follow, the grace by which we are reconciled, the One by whose doing we were created, the likeness by whom we are re-formed to oneness, and the peace by which we cleave to oneness. This is the reality in which alone we should delight."[101]

The likeness to God in which humankind had been created but had deformed, the love which humankind had squandered, the vision of God from which Adam and Eve had been cast out, he believed, has been restored in the unbegotten *imago genita* who is *homo perfectus*.[102] Human beings 'there' will participate in Christ in the "likeness to God of which the apostle John says in his letter: *We shall be like him because we shall see him as he is.*"[103] "There to know or to see God will be to be like God (*similis ei*). And to be like him will be to see and to know him. This perfect knowledge will be eternal life, a joy which no one will take away from the person who has it."[104]

This, to William's mind, was the purpose of the incarnation: the restoration of humankind to the likeness of God with which the first human beings had

---

100   See Exp Rom, VI.11.36, "Trinitas enim Deus unius eiusdem que naturae atque substantiae, non minor in singulis quam in omnibus, nec maior in omnibus quam in singulis.... Et haec omnia nec confuse unum sunt, nec distincte tria sunt; sed cum sint tria, unum sunt; cum sint unum, tria sunt," CCCM 86:161. See Aenig, *passim*, for William's fullest treatment of the Trinity.

101   Exp Rom, VI.11.36, "Quare ipsum donum Dei cum Patre et Filio aeque incommutabile colere et tenere nos conuenit, unius que substantiae Trinitatem, unum Deum a quo sumus, per quem sumus, in quo sumus, a quo discessimus, cui dissimiles facti sumus, a quo perire non permissi sumus; principium ad quod recurrimus, formam quam sequimur, gratiam qua reconciliamur, unum quo auctore conditi sumus, et similitudinem eius per quam ad unitatem reformamur, et pacem qua unitati adhaeremus. Haec est res, qua sola frui debemus," CCCM 86:163. On the Trinitarian theology of William, see Odo Brooke, *Studies in Monastic Theology*, CS 37 (Kalamazoo, MI: Cistercian Publications, 1980), 87–127.

102   Adv Abl, 8, "Incarnatus enim Vnigenitus Dei factus que pro nobis homo perfectus....," CCCM 89A:52.

103   1 John 3:2.

104   Spec fid, 107, "Ibi mutua cognitio Patris et Filii, unitas est; hic hominis ad Deum similitudo, de qua dicit apostolus Iohannes in epistola sua: Similes ei erimus, quoniam uidebimus eum sicuti est. Similem enim ibi esse Deo, uidere Deum siue cognoscere erit; quem in tantum uidebit siue cognoscet qui cognoscet uel uidebit, in quantum similis ei erit; in tantum erit ei similis, in quantum eum cognoscet uel uidebit. Videre namque ibi seu cognoscere Deum, similem est esse Deo; et similem ei esse, uidere seu cognoscere eum est," CCCM 89A:122.

been endowed. For this, God the Son became human, for, "as we read in Job, 'The man who regards his own exemplar (*species*) does not sin.'"[105] And the Mediator, possessing as man unimpaired memory, reason, and will, exalted man "to the likeness of the godhead"[106] through "the glory of divine participation" and made it possible for human beings in the life hereafter to have a nature which will be above fallen human nature, but short of divine,[107] by becoming "by grace what God is by nature"[108]—a phrase which attracted later attention.

5   The Question of Salvation

Latin theologians of later centuries leveled accusations of pantheism and "heterodox mysticism" at the, then unknown, author of the *Letter to the Carthusians* (William's *Golden Epistle*)[109] and, more recently, allegations have been made that William found his ideas in Eastern Christian sources.[110] As

---

105   Ep frat, 174, "Est quippe in forma mediatoris, in quo, sicut legitur in Iob, uisitans homo speciem suam non peccat," CCCM 88:264. Cf. Aenig fid, 17, "Similiter contuemur et lumen ipsum, quo cuncta ista discernimus, speciem scilicet aeternae rationis...," CCCM 89A:139.

106   Ep frat, 272, 273 "...ut hominem similem Deo constituat per glorificationem diuinae participationis.... [273] ut hominem exaltet usque ad similitudinem diuinitatis," CCCM 88:284.

107   Spec fid, 101, "...non quidem in naturam diuinitatis, sed tamen in quamdam supra humanam, citra diuinam...," CCCM 89A:120.

108   Ep frat, 272, "...quousque amor proficiat in aliquam similitudinem amoris illius, qui Deum similem fecit homini, per humiliationem humanae conditionis, ut hominem similem Deo constituat per glorificationem diuinae participationis," CCCM 88:284.

109   Statements in the *Golden Epistle* were criticized as "heretical mysticism" with "a suspicion of pantheism" by the early 20th-century French scholar, Pierre Pourrat, *La spiritualité chrétienne*, vols. 1–4 (Paris: Gabalda, 1918–1928); Vol. 2 ET: *Christian Spirituality in the Middle Ages*, trans. S.P. Jacques (London: Burns, Oates, and Washbourne, 1924), 130–31. As precedent, he cited the 14th-century Parisian scholar, Jean Gerson, *Sermo de humilitate factus in coena Domini* (*Joannis Gersonii opera omnia*, vol. 3 [Antwerp, 1706], 1125) (Pourrat, 130, n. 2). Unaware that William was the author of Ep frat and of other works now known to be his, Pourrat was unable to balance his "heterodoxy" against other treatises. Although Pourrat notes (130, n. 1) that Jean Mabillon attributed Ep frat to William of Saint-Thierry, not until 1924 did André Wilmart decisively identify William as the author and, on the basis of the preface to the Letter, restored his name to his other works. Wilmart, "La préface de la lettre aux frères de Mont-Dieu," *Revue bénédictine* 36 (1924): 229–47 and Wilmart, "La série et la date des ouvrages of Guillaume de Saint-Thierry," *Revue Mabillon* 14 (1924): 157–67.

110   J.-M. Déchanet, "Autour d'une querelle fameuse, de l'Apologia à la Lettre d'or," *Recherches de théologie ancienne et médiévale* 20 (1939): 3–34, esp., 19–20, and J.-M. Déchanet, *Guillaume de Saint-Thierry: aux sources d'une pensée* (Paris: Beauchesne, 1978), 8, 62, 74, 78–79, 120.

William has become more widely studied, both hypotheses have faded.[111] Salvation as participation was not typical of early 12th century soteriology; *participatio* in William's sense was never used by Abelard, for example, or, so far as I know, by his scholarly colleagues.[112] Yet William's belief that, just as all 'being' is participation in God who is Being, and that human salvation must be a still greater and enduring participation, was neither unique in the West nor heterodox. He could have found the idea in a small but not insignificant number of Latin patristic works, among them Saint Augustine's *Enarrationes in Psalmos*,[113] and in the writings of some monastic contemporaries.[114] Among these was Rupert, the Benedictine abbot of Deutz, whose *De diviniis officiis* William read and felt free to correct.[115] It is not altogether improbable that he read others of Rupert's works and that, as both had come from Liège, they might, just possibly, have known each other. William, perhaps cautiously, did not use the verb *deificare* or the noun *deificatio*, although both Augustine[116] and Bernard of Clairvaux[117] did.

---

111   Apart from his familiarity with Gregory of Nyssa's *De hominis opificio*, many supposed Greek sources have been found to be taken from Latin writers. See e.g., David N. Bell, "The Alleged Greek Sources of William of St Thierry," in *Noble Piety and Reformed Monasticism: Studies in Medieval Cistercian History VII*, (ed.) E. Rozanne Elder, CS 65 (Kalamazoo, MI: Cistercian Publications, 1981), 109–22, and John D. Anderson, "The Use of Greek Sources by William of St Thierry, Especially in the *Enigma Fidei*," in *One Yet Two: Monastic Theology East and West*, (ed.) M. Basil Pennington, CS 29 (Kalamazoo, MI: Cistercian Publications, 1976), 242–54. For summary of the scholarly debate over William's Greek sources, see F. Tyler Sergent's chapter, "William of Saint-Thierry's Sources and Influences: *Ratio Fidei* and *Fruitio*" in this volume, pp. 35–66, esp. 36–39.

112   I rely here on the omission in *Dictionnaire de spiritualité*, vol. 3, s.v. "Divinisation," 1289–1459, of any 12th-century scholars, but the inclusion of 13th-century theologians (cols. 1413–1432).

113   *Enarrationes in Psalmo* 146.5.11: CCSL 40, line 45. See n. 92 above. On Augustine and deification, see Norman Russell, *The Doctrine of Deification in the Greek Patristic Tradition* (Oxford: University Press, 2004), Appendix 1, 321–32, and Gerald Bonner, s.v., "Deification, divinization," *Augustine through the Ages: An Encyclopedia*, (ed.) Allan D. Fitzgerald, OSA (Grand Rapids, MI: Eerdmans, 1999), 265–66.

114   *Dictionnaire de spiritualité*, vol. 3, 1399–413. Rupert of Deutz, for example, wrote in his *Liber de diuinis officiis*, Book 6, the book in which William found a 'small blemish' which he corrected in his *De sacramento altaris*, that: "Igitur sicut supra dicere coepimus ut participatione mortis Christi iustificaremur in morte ipsius baptizati sumus consepulti," CCCM 7:224.

115   William, *Epistola ad domnum Rupertum abbatem Tuitiensem* (*Letter to Rupert of Deutz*), CCCM 88:47–52.

116   E.g., *Enarrationes in Psalmos* 49.2 and 117.11.

117   *Sermo in dominica infra octauam assumptionis beatae Mariae*, 1, "Absorpta videtur in deitatem humanitas, non quod sit mutata substantia, sed affectio deificata," SBOp 5:262, and *De diligendo Deo*, 28, "Sic affici, deificari est," SBOp 3:143.

Twelfth-century theologians who moved beyond the devil's right wrote of justification by faith or penal substitution. William mentioned justification in passing in two very early works[118] and, not surprisingly, treated it at length in his *Commentary on the Epistle to Romans*. Yet while at both Saint-Thierry and Signy, he coupled justification with the unity of spirit which leads to love, holiness, and glorification.[119] *Satisfactio*, a word linked by Anselm of Canterbury with justice by substitution, however, was a term William used only in a single work[120] and a theory with which he seems to have been unfamiliar. He did not regard the blood of Christ as a pay-off to Satan, or to God, and he mentioned it almost exclusively in a Eucharistic context.[121] His heightened emphasis on participation in Christ at Signy may perhaps reflect his concern that, if salvation is thought to depend on the grisly suffering of Christ, then Abelard would have been right in questioning why a loving God would forgive humankind's self-serving disobedience because of their brutal execution of his Son.

William implied that the peripatetic of Paris was one of the "many persons who do not love [God, but] ponder *about him* [whereas] no one ponders *him* and does not love him."[122] Critical of those who sought to go beyond what is rationally discernible and verbally explicable,[123] Abelard interpreted *similitudo* (likeness) to mean that the mind of man is "similar," analogous, to the mind of the Creator, and from this he concluded that the human mind is incapable of comprehending the mystery, the *res*, of the Godhead except through analogy

---

118   Contemp, 17, CCCM 88:164, and Nat am, 9, CCCM 88:184.

119   Contemp, 17, "Qui, ut dictum est, conformans sibi et uniens spiritum nostrum, spirat in nobis quando uult, quomodo uult, quantum uult; cuius sumus factura, creati in operibus bonis, exsistens sanctificatio nostra, iustificatio nostra, amor noster," CCCM 88:164. Exp Rom, V.8.31-33, "Praedestinatio nostra non in nobis facta est, sed in occulto apud ipsum in eius praescientia. Tria uero reliqua in nobis fiunt: uocatio, iustificatio, glorificatio," CCCM 86:127.

120   Exp Rom, IV.8.29-33, CCCM 86:127.

121   E.g. Exp Rom, II.3.1 (CCCM 86:40, ln. 262), III.4.3-4 (CCCM 86:78, ln. 642), and IV.8.33-34 (CCCM 86:129, ln. 690); *Excerpta de libris beati Ambrosii super Cantica Canticorum* (Cant Amb), 66, 85, 125 (CCCM 87:284–285, 315, 359–362); and Sac alt, 14 (CCCM 88:90).

122   Spec fid, 113, "De ipso enim multi cogitant qui non amant. Ipsum autem nemo cogitat et non amat," CCCM 89A:124. Italics mine.

123   Peter Abelard, *Theologia christiana,* III.20, "Ad quod tanto facilius professores dialecticae pertrahi solent, quanto se amplius rationibus armatos esse autumant, et tanto securiores liberius quidlibet aut defendere aut impugnare praesumunt; quorum tanta est arrogantia, ut nihil esse opinentur quod eorum ratiunculis comprehendi atque edisseri non queat, contemptis que uniuersis auctoritatibus, solis sibi credere gloriantur," CCCM 12:ln. 252. On Abelard, see Constant J. Mews, "Man's Knowledge of God according to Peter Abelard," in *L'homme et son univers au moyen age; actes du septième congrès international de philosophie médiévale (30 aout-4 septembre 1982)* (Leuvain-la-Neuve, 1986), 391–426.

(*similitudine*).[124] In William's terms, Abelard was seeking *scientia*: knowledge. William himself was seeking *sapientia*: wisdom. He was convinced that likeness means being-like-God and that, although severely deformed, the likeness bestowed at creation is reparable, not by human effort, but by divine action and human choice. God reveals himself in the natural world, in scripture, and most fully in the Incarnate Son, and invites each person to cooperate in reformation. William, therefore, believed, unlike Abelard in his opinion, that the Incarnation was utterly necessary to the renewal of likeness of God and salvation.[125]

If Abelard had been aware of William's role in his second condemnation or of the treatises written afterwards,[126] or if one of his students had sought to defend him on this point, yet another question might have been raised:

> If all human beings share in being *homo*, and if incarnate Christ is the *homo* perfectus, and if at the final judgment a single human being willfully persists in ignorance or disobedience, has *humanitas* really been renewed?

Whether, in 12th-century terms, *homo* is understood as a divine idea realized imperfectly in individual human beings or an aggregative term without metaphysical reality, is there no renewal, no hope of eternal life for those who do not (to use a modern phrase) 'accept the Lord Jesus Christ'? And if some humans have no hope, does anyone? William wavered on this point, writing at one time that those "without the grace of Christ ... [are] strangers to salvation and eternal life."[127] Yet, despite the great value he placed on free choice, he also counseled that "There be no despair about those who ... have not yet believed, because they shall believe and shall be freed from the servitude of death, as

---

124   *Theologia christiana*, III.57, "Quicquid itaque de hac altissima philosophia disseremus, umbram, non veritatem esse profitemur, et quasi similitudinem quamdam, non rem," CCCM 12:ln. 742.

125   William would have been unaware that "At the conclusion of 'Book Three' of the first version of *Theologia*, Abelard [had] ... pointed out that St Augustine said [that] ... the mystery of the Incarnation, in which it is certain that the whole sum of human salvation consists and without which all the rest is believed in vain' (Clanchy, *Abelard: A Medieval Life*, 272, n. 54). See *Theologia Summi Boni*, p. 110, CCCM 13:201, ln. 671–75. Abelard did not specify why.

126   There is no evidence that he was aware of William's role in his second condemnation or of his writings, or indeed of his existence.

127   Referring to unbaptized children, he wrote in Exp Rom, III.5.16, "...paruulos sine accepta Christi gratia defunctos intrare non posse ipsi etiam haeretici confitentur; uerum et a salute ac uita aeterna facit alienos,...," CCCM 86:73.

were we who are now sons of God, although it has not yet appeared what we shall be."[128] He was convinced that before the final judgment the Jews[129]—and probably, if he had been aware of them, other unbelievers—would recognize and choose to love and accept the truth of Christ, and so be saved.[130]

6   Conclusion

How then would William have answered Abelard's unanswered question? How could the Apostle say that humankind is reconciled by the death of the Son of God to a God who ought to be so much the more enraged against men in that men transgressed in crucifying his Son than by disobeying his commandment and eating that one lone piece of fruit? William would (and did, though not concisely) say that "the first man was created with free will, that is, having the freedom to have perpetual justice with immortality if he so willed, [but] he consented freely to the enemy's suggestion" and fell into unlikeness, ignorance, and alienation; all this God, who is perfect justice, justly permitted.[131] The consequences of this choice—deformity of will and deviation of love, forgetfulness of God, misuse of reason, spiritual blindness, and physical death—are shared by every descendant of Adam.

---

128   Exp Rom, V.8.20-21, "...de ipsis non est desperandum, qui nondum uocantur filii Dei, quia nondum crediderunt, sed tantum sunt creatura, quia et ipsi credituri sunt, et liberabuntur a seruitute interitus, quemadmodum nos qui iam filii Dei sumus, quamuis nondum apparuerit quod erimus," cccm 86:118. Origen, whose thought may have influenced William (see Exp Rom, Pref., cccm 86:3) was also of two minds on *apokatastasis*, the renewal of all creation. In *Peri archon* 3.5.7 (on 1 Cor 15:24-28), he posits the restoration of those who have been lost; and in *Peri archon* 3.6.1-2, he emphasizes free will and the necessity of "earnest efforts to imitate Christ." William did not identify which work of Origen he consulted. A 12th-century copy of various homilies and scriptural commentaries by Origen survives (Charleville BM mss 207) but no copy of *De principiis*, although it was available, having been translated by both Rufinus and Jerome. Fragments of Jerome's lost work and Rufinus' translation appear in *Die Griechischen Christlichen Schriftsteller* (gcs) *Origenes* and PG 11:111-414. According to J.T. Muckle, "translations" attributed by Jerome (Ep 84.7) to Hilary, Ambrose, and Victorinus refer probably to "treatises based on Origen" (Muckle, "Greek Works Translated Directly into Latin before 1350," *Medieval Studies* 4 (1942): 33–42, here 40).
129   Exp Rom, VI.11.26-27, "ante iudicium in ultimo tempore Iudaeos in dominum Iesum esse credituros," cccm 86:157.
130   Spec fid, 19, "Cur enim non credis, o infidelis? Vtique quia non diligis ... Incipe diligere, hoc est age ut uelis; et incipies credere; et tantum credes quantum uoles, hoc est quantum diliges," cccm 89A:89.
131   Adv Abl, 7, "Primus siquidem homo cum conditus esset liberi arbitrii, hoc est liberum habens si uellet perpetuam habere cum immortalitate iustitiam, sponte consensit inimico suggerenti...," cccm 89A:44–45.

Yet out of the boundless charity by which the divine persons love one another, the triune God has provided humankind with a means of re-education, re-formation, and renewal. The eternal Word of God was made man without taint of lust and so did not inherit 'original sin.' As man, he possessed intact the full image and likeness of God, as had Adam before the fall. He renewed memory and liberated reason. In obedience and love, he freely chose to die, although his human nature, untainted by sin, was not subject to mortality. By choosing to share the mortality of fallen humankind, he freed the will which Adam and Eve had enslaved by negligent disobedience and perverse self-love.

By the renewal of human nature in Christ Jesus and the grace of the indwelling Holy Spirit, the Love of God, human beings are able to re-order wills made perversely self-centered by sin[132] by choosing to respond to God in the degree of love of which each person is capable.[133] The residual "likeness to God" in Adam's offspring can again become "unity of spirit," the ability freely and in love "to will what God wills" and, even in this life, to become incapable of willing otherwise.[134] In the life to come, human beings who have freely chosen to respond in love to Love will share in the perfection of a human nature restored by and in Christ. They will become, in a manner appropriate to their created nature, "not God ... but by grace what God is by nature."[135] They will become what God Incarnate was, is, and ever shall be by nature. At this God does not rage but rejoices.

---

132   Ep frat, 252, CCCM 88:280.

133   Ep frat, 257, "Magna enim uoluntas ad Deum, amor est; dilectio, adhaesio siue coniunctio; caritas, fruitio," CCCM 88:281—a rare instance in which William does not order love by degrees.

134   Ep frat, 262, "...non iam similitudo, sed unitas spiritus nominetur; cum fit homo cum Deo unus spiritus, non tantum unitate idem uolendi, sed expressiore quadam ueritate uirtutis, sicut iam dictum est, aliud uelle non ualendi," CCCM 88:282.

135   Ep frat, 263, "...in summa illa unitate ueritatis et in ueritate unitatis, hoc idem fit homini suo modo ad Deum, quod consubstantiali unitate Filio est ad Patrem uel Patri ad Filium ... cum modo ineffabili et incogitabili, fieri meretur homo Dei, non Deus, sed tamen quod Deus est: homo ex gratia quod Deus est ex natura," CCCM 88:282.

CHAPTER 6

The Trinity's Glorifying Embrace: *Concientia* in William of Saint-Thierry

Thomas X. Davis, OCSO

1 Introduction

There have been various quests striving to respond to the challenging question of Jesus, "Who do you say that I am?"[1] One notable quest stemming from the Enlightenment era has taken an historical approach over the years extending even until today. This quest strives to know the historical Jesus who lived in the 1st-century CE, and consequently questions the reliability of the four Gospels. Another quest arose from the earliest centuries of Christianity through pilgrimage to the Holy Land in search of the actual sites where Jesus lived and walked to experience the 'world' of Jesus and to deepen their devotion.

William of Saint-Thierry, on the contrary, offers a different type of quest. His is to encounter, to run up against, Christ dwelling within a person by faith and grace with the surprising effect of a comprehensive, far-reaching restoration and transfiguring of one's life in terms of image and likeness to the divine Trinitarian mystery.[2] This quest is found in the realm of experience, in the depths of one's *conscientia*,[3] and not in the realm of history or locality. The degree and intensity of this experience results in a union of wills between a person and

---

1 Matt 16:13; Mark 8:27; Luke 9:18.

2 In the last paragraphs of *The Nature and Dignity of Love,* William compares a person's eternal happiness as a glorification like being bathed in the brightness, splendor, and glory of the sun. Grace transfiguring a person, body and soul, is God's gift of glorification. This glorification begins in this life manifesting itself in a profound transparency of *conscientia* shining out through the body and a grace of a communal life that is nothing other than the beginning of future glory. These paragraphs are an extremely condensed presentation for William's ascent into the Trinitarian mystery and the basis for this chapter. (*The Nature and Dignity of Love,* trans. Thomas X. Davis, CF 30 [Kalamazoo, MI: Cistercian Publications, 1981], 105ff, CCCM 88:210ff). Unless noted otherwise, reference numbers to William of Saint-Thierry's works are from English translations (when available) in the Cistercian Father series (Cistercian Publications) and to the Corpus Christianorum Continuatio Mediaevalis (Brepols) for the Latin text.

3 *Conscientia* for William means what today we would call both conscience and consciousness. At times, *conscientia* can mean both conscience and/or consciousness depending on its context. The Latin word is retained in this article so as to convey the profound significance of this embrace involving both conscience and consciousness.

the Divine will, a unity of spirit, *unitas Spiritus*. William emphasizes Trinitarian unity and one's call to enter into its depths. This unity is the ultimate transfiguring of a person into God's likeness, making this person "one with God, one spirit, not only with the unity which comes of willing the same thing but with a greater fullness of virtue ... the inability to will anything else. It is called unity of spirit not only because the Holy Spirit brings it about ... but because it is the Holy Spirit."[4] For William and contemporary people of faith, a quest of this nature brings peace and happiness and progress toward one's ultimate goal. This quest is truly a glorifying embrace, mystic and contemplative.

Contemporary relevance of William rests precisely in his insight into this union as revealing the great Trinitarian mystery of Christ and its transfiguring effect in the life of a Christian, the comprehensive purpose God has for each individual and the the whole of humanity. This mystery comprises this eternal purpose and the medium through which it is revealed by the Incarnate Christ. For William, an authentic Christian implies an ongoing process of deepening identity with an Christ in his mystery.[5] This insight reveals William as a Cistercian spiritual master whose significance is still quite contemporary. To read, study, and embrace William's teaching is to set out on a spiritual journey that is ascent into the Trinitarian mystery of Christ.

2   *Conscientia* as the Inner Self

While aspects of his thought in different treatises reveal development over time, the transfiguring role of a well-composed *conscientia* by the Mystery of Christ in its Trinitarian dimension remains consistent in William's writing. William offers a refreshing concept of the human person with the ability to recognize and acknowlede one's inner self (*conscientia*). Inherent in such recognition and acknowledgment is a relationship with the Divine Persons, culminating in participation in the mystery of the Trinity.[6]

---

4   *The Golden Epistle* (Ep frat), 262–63, CCCM 88:282. ET: *The Golden Epistle: Letter to the Brethren of Mont Dieu*, trans. Theodore Berkeley, OCSO, CF 12 (Kalamazoo, MI: Cistercian Publications, 1980), 95–96. The phrase *Unitas Spiritus*, Unity of Spirit, is used only some ten times in William's writings. He uses it in *On Contemplating God* (Contemp, 7), considered by some to be his first work; ET: *On Contemplating God, Prayer, Meditations*, trans. Sister Penelope [Lawson], CF 3 (Kalamazoo, MI: Cistercian Publications, 1977), 47ff, CCCM 88:159. In his last treatise, the *Golden Epistle*, William brings to maturity his understanding of this unity.

5   *Exposition on the Epistle to the Romans* (Exp Rom), II.2.21. CCCM 86:37. ET: *Exposition on the Epistle to the Romans*, trans. John Baptist Hasbrouck, CF 27 (Kalamazoo, MI: Cistercian Publications, 1980), 59.

6   William's various ascent themes developed over the years come from the perspective of the human person depending upon the ordering of either the will or love. William

William articulates powerfully the depth of life-changing experiences a person undergoes when truly encountering Christ. A person with an authentic thirst for the living God, allured by grace, runs up against the God-Man, Jesus Christ, the Image of the invisible God.[7] The Latin word William uses for "runs up against" (*offendit*) expresses the idea of a totally unexpected encounter with Christ of such magnitude that the Spirit of the Lord transfigures one into the image and likeness of the Triune God whose glory one beholds. This formidable encounter brings joy and life to a person, whose mind dances with joy, and who can proclaim, "we have heard and seen and our hands have handled something of the Word of Life."[8] The depths of these experiences are highly nuanced and more than transformative. They coalesce into a glorifying embrace that transfigures[9] a person. Encountering Christ face to face in the rich context of faith offers an experience far more satisfying than other quests for Christ. God's creating grace and illuminating grace penetrate into the depths of a person's good *conscientia*. Here in one's *conscientia* a person enters into the glorifying embrace of the Father and Son in the Holy Spirit.[10]

At the end of his commentary on St. Paul's *Epistle to the Romans*, William clarifies how the mystery of Christ is revealed.[11] This Trinitarian mystery is the fullness of the Incarnation that consists of the entire life of Christ, the Word made flesh among us, consisting of Jesus' early life, public life, and especially

---

accepts the definition of a Divine Person as one "whose particular form is the ability to recognize and acknowledge" ("cuius pro sui forma certa sit agnitio") in the *Enigma of Faith* (Aenig), 34, CCCM 89A:152–153. ET: *The Enigma of Faith*, trans. John D. Anderson, CF 9 (Kalamazoo, MI: Cistercian Publications, 1973), 65–67 and n. 150. See also Odo Brooke, *Studies in Monastic Theology*, CS 37 (Kalamazoo, MI: Cistercian Publications, 1980), 78–80. This definition may have also influenced his concept of the human person.

7   *Mirror of Faith* (Spec fid), 26, CCCM 89A:118. ET: *The Mirror of Faith*, trans. Thomas X. Davis, CF 15 (Kalamazoo, MI: Cistercian Publications, 1979), 70.

8   1 John 1:1. Nat am, 30. The Latin actually uses the idea of dancing: "ita ut cum quodam mentis tripudio...," CCCM 88:200. ET: *On the Nature and Dignity of Love*, CF 30:90.

9   The word "transfiguring" is used deliberately to capture William's concept of a type of spiritual *eucrasis*, which appears to have been first used by Hippocrates to define a harmony or balance between mind and body. Although William only used this word twice, once in *The Nature of the Body and Soul* (Phys corp, 1, CCCM 88:104–105; ET: *Three Treatises on Man*, (ed.) Bernard McGinn, CF 24 [Kalamazoo, MI: Cistercian Publications, 1977], 106) and again in Spec fid, his consistent thought is a harmonious integration of body and soul. He sees a spiritually well-composed soul as living out its faith in good works, its hope in a consolation that embraces all things, and its charity in a tenderness of devotion (Spec fid, 17, CCCM 89A:103 [ET: CF 15:43]). In other words, a powerful inner experience needs to shine through (transfigure) and not just change (transform) a person's life style and behavior.

10   Spec fid, 32, CCCM 89A:123. ET: *Mirror of Faith*, CF 15:80.

11   Exp Rom, VII.16.21-27, CCCM 86:196. ET: *Exposition on the Epistle to the Romans*, CF 27:267–268.

the passion, death, and glorification of the resurrection.[12] Although the Hebrew Bible prophets prepared for its eventual revelation, according to the Divine will, the mystery was kept secret for many ages until the Annunciation at Nazareth.[13] For William, a person enters into this mystery with Christ through the power of the Holy Spirit, a grace coming from faith, Sacraments, and virtues that bring about various likenesses to God, the whole of a person's perfection.[14]

When two people meet one another for the first time, it is important to know and address each other by one's proper name. If the relationship is to unfold into one of an enduring nature, it is also important that people come to know and understand one another. William uses this relationship example to explain how to develop a relationship with Jesus Christ. To hear Christ's name brings joy and happiness to a person of faith and proceeds to open one's inner depths for entrance into the mystery of Christ. *Jesus* has the meaning of "Savior," bearing within it all the goodness God generously pours forth upon all peoples. *Christ* evokes the "anointing" that Jesus received making him King and Priest showing his vocation as the one interceding and leading all towards the Father. Jesus and Christ coalesce into the concept of "Lord," an overseer who orchestrates nothing but good, enabling us to become sons and daughters of God. As brothers and sisters of Christ, we can cry out, "Abba, Father."[15]

The historical events in the life of Jesus along with his teaching, as revealed in the Gospels, accepted in faith, are resources to know who and what Christ is. Making a lovely and profound comment on Song of Songs 2:3, "In his shadow, I delight to sit," William says that the shadow is the body of Christ, the bond between the divinity of Christ and an individual person. This is the 'place' where one modestly and humbly sits, that is, to contemplate the mystery of his Incarnation. A person is called to enter into and sit in the shadow, Christ's human life, with all its events and his teachings.[16]

Sitting in the shadow of Christ's human life is not the same as pursuing the historical Jesus. William's use of the word "contemplate" makes this distinction. While meditation and reflection may express considering and pursuing

---

12   *Enigma of Faith* (Aenig), 10, CCCM 89A:135–136. ET: *The Enigma of Faith*, trans. with intro. John D. Anderson, CF 9 (Kalamazoo, MI: Cistercian Publications, 1973), 43.

13   Luke 1:26–35.

14   Ep frat, 259–262, CCCM 88:281–282. ET: *Golden Epistle*, CF 12:95.

15   *Exposition on the Song of Songs* (Cant), 39–40, Cant CCCM 87:38. ET: *Exposition on the Song of Songs*, trans. Mother Columba Hart, OSB, CF 6 (Kalamazoo, MI: Cistercian Publications, 1970), 31–32.

16   *Brevis commentatio* (Brev com), XXI, "Vmbra inter deitatem Christi et nos, corpus eius est. Sub qua sedet sponsa, dum modeste et humiliter mysterium incarnationis eius contemplatur," CCCM 87:189.

some topic within oneself, contemplation implies a vitality influenced by divine grace, to give oneself, to go out of oneself, and ascend into something beyond oneself.[17] Contemplative vitality contains no self-reservations nor permits anything to divide or separate one from the object being contemplated, and this meaning is implied in the events and words of Christ. To contemplate the life of Christ challenges a person to enter more deeply into Christ's Body so as to experience its real meaning.

Furthermore, William explains that the Resurrection of Christ is pivotal for this process. Christ's Resurrection has glorified his entire life and now has the power to transfigure a person who enters into the life of Christ because of Christ's divinity manifested in his Resurrection.[18] This contemplative ascent into the mystery of Trinitarian Divinity itself requires a personal abasement on the part of one ascending, similar to the abasement of Christ's Incarnation.[19] This is the ultimate reason underlying contemplative reflection on the life of Christ using mental or physical images. By means of these images relative to the life of Christ and with the fiercely devoted love that comes to be in one's good *conscientia*, grace makes it possible for a person today to have an experience and understanding similar to that of the apostles in their relationship with Christ. Williams writes, "This is the taste, which the Spirit of understanding gives us in Christ, namely, the understanding of Scripture and of the Sacraments of God."[20] Christ himself opens up his life and its full significance for those devoted to him. Contemplative quest of this nature bestows a deep personal peace. Purely historical quests cannot do this.

William has a further significance and contemporary importance in his teaching on knowing Christ in an entirely different way or manner due to the transfiguring effect the Trinitarian mystery of Christ has on a person's *conscientia*. Williams lays this out in his letter to the Carthusian brothers of Mont Dieu (*The Golden Epistle*).[21] Both the role of Christ and the Holy Spirit lead a person to ascend into the heart of the Trinity through unity of spirit which begins and progresses in one's *conscientia*: "Christ in your conscience is the treasure that you will possess."[22] In view of the freedom of conscience that is so

---

17   This is a theological *res* or meaning or implication beyond some thing or event.

18   *De sacramento altaris* (Sac alt), 11, CCCM 88:55, Nat am, 31, CCCM 88:201; ET: *On the Nature and Dignity of Love*, CF 30:91, and Brev com, XXXIV, CCCM 87:194.

19   Contemp, 3, CCCM 88:154. ET: *On Contemplating God*, CF 3:38.

20   Nat am, 31, CCCM 88:201. ET: *On the Nature and Dignity of Love*, CF 30:91.

21   Ep frat, 5, CCCM 88:225. ET: *Golden Epistle*, CF 12:4–5.

22   *Meditation* (Med), 10.9, CCCM 89:60. ET: *On Contemplating God, Prayer, Meditations*, trans., Sr. Penelope [Lawson], CF 3 (Kalamazoo, MI: Cistercian Publications, 1977), 155. At present I am working on a new translation of William's *Meditations*.

vehemently—and rightly—defended today, the spirituality of Christ in one's *conscientia* is definitely relevant and contemporary for a proper understanding of this great freedom.

The Latin *conscientia* derives from two Latin words: *Cum* meaning "with" and *scire* meaning "to know." Conscience and consciousness together constitute the ability or faculty of being aware and knowing oneself and others because one is always in relationship with someone, something, and with oneself. It is not uncommon to be asked, "Were you aware of this or that?" A person wakening from the state of unconsciousness is asked, "Are you awake?" "Do you know your name or know this or that?" These two, conscience and consciousness, form the foundation for one's primary relationship, that is, one's relationship with God. The more common and general understanding of conscience in this dimension is the ability to know right from wrong (sometimes styled "the voice of God" within a person).

Conscientia embraces the general moral knowledge that comes from God speaking to an individual. Based on this moral knowledge, ascent to good, by means of grace that liberates one from sin, is the initial foundation for faith.[23] And faith is one way Christ is present in a person's life. *Conscientia* can be understood in another perspective as clear and precise moral dictates challenging one to do or not to do something.[24] Finally, *conscientia* embraces within oneself the awareness of some external object, fact, or situation. As a person develops and ascends, a delicate sensitivity to the various graces coming from the sevenfold Spirit.[25] The development of *conscientia* as both conscience and consciousness is integral to developing a sense of self-knowledge—"Who and What am I"—for any spiritual ascent. *Conscientia*, in these three dimensions becomes the matrix for self-knowledge, an essential element in Cistercian teaching.

The ability to know good from evil is the crucial starting point for developing a good *conscientia*[26] proper to William's ascent program into the mystery of the Trinity, into the midst of a glorifying embrace of Father, Son, and Holy Spirit. The gift of creating grace, to use William's precise term, is to have created *conscientia* for this experience. This gift is further developed by illuminating grace[27] leading to a clearer understanding and finding of God—Father, Son, and Holy Spirit—within oneself.[28] This implies that every person owes to God

---

23   Spec fid, 5, CCCM 89A:86–87. ET: *Mirror of Faith*, CF 15:13–14.

24   Contemp, 3, CCCM 88:154. ET: *On Contemplating God*, CF 3:39.

25   Cant, 39, CCCM 87:37. ET: *Exposition on the Song of Songs*, CF 6:31. See Isaiah 11:2, "The spirit of the Lord shall rest upon him: a spirit of wisdom and understanding, a spirit of counsel and of strength, a spirit of knowledge and of fear of the Lord."

26   Spec fid, 32, "bonae conscientiae suavitas," CCCM 89A:123. ET: *Mirror of Faith*, CF 15:80.

27   Spec fid, 24–25, CCCM 89A:112. ET: *Mirror of Faith*, CF 15:59.

28   *Prayer of Dom William* (Orat), 4–6, CCCM 88:170. ET: David N. Bell, "The Prayer of Dom William: A Study and New Translation," in *Unity of Spirit: Studies on William of Saint-Thierry in*

a good *conscientia* and to one's neighbor a good reputation.[29] For to be like God is to see and recognize God, which is, of course, the goal and *raison d'être* of a person's *conscientia*. One's image and likeness to God means one is capable of good and of living this goodness in one's life by virtue and wisdom, for God is the fullness of good.[30]

William's own experience of being intensely involved in the dynamic of *conscientia* leads to the understanding of *what* he is as distinguished from *who* he is as developed in his *Meditations*. In *Meditation* 3, William speaks about Moses' intimate relationship with God and suggests that Moses would have done better if he had asked to know what God is rather than who God is.[31] However, as Moses approaches the end of his life, he does request to see the glory of God, that is, to see what God is. There are four characteristics of what God is: *qualis, quantas, quantus, qualitas*. These four philosophical Latin terms can be rendered: (1) What sort of God does one have? (2) What is the measure (how great) of God? (3) What is God's power? How powerful is God? (4) What is the precise quality of God?[32] In the process of discerning his experience of his own *conscientia*, William actually confronts his own *qualis, quantas, quantus, qualitas* in terms of his relationship with God, a relationship as image and likeness that he is keenly aware his own personal sins have severely damaged. Especially in his *Meditations*, William describes at great length his *conscientia* and his experiences as a result of entering deeply into himself by the process of recognizing and acknowledging.[33]

3   Metaphors for *Conscientia*

First for William, *conscientia* is his personal house or place, *locus*, where he belongs. He sees this place or house with a distinction between his deepest self (the "I") and the place where this deepest self is to be found.[34] True, this

---

Honor of E. Rozanne Elder, (eds.) F. Tyler Sergent, Aage Rydstrøm-Poulsen, and Marsha L. Dutton, CS 268 (Collegeville, MN: Cistercian Publications, 2015), 34–35 and CF 3:73.

29   Exp Rom, VII.12.17-16, 13.3-4, CCCM 86:169–170, 172. ET: *Exposition on the Epistle to the Romans*, CF 27:235–236, 239.

30   Phys corp, 7, CCCM 88:133. ET: *The Nature of the Body and Soul*, CF 24:138. Here is a good example of behavior as a consequence of *eucrasis*.

31   Med, 3.1-2, CCCM 89:14. ET: *Meditations*, CF 3:102.

32   Med, 3.1, CCCM 89:14. ET: *Meditations*, CF 3:102.

33   William appears to consider a human person as a form giving knowledge of itself, thus "what" with its four characteristics *qualis, quantas, quantus, qualitas* is appropriate. This concept of person in itself tends towards union with another.

34   Cant, 155, CCCM 87:106–107; ET: *Exposition on the Song of Songs*, CF 6:127 and Contemp, 3, CCCM 88:154; ET: *On Contemplating God*, CF 3:39.

house or place is full of problems and has been corrupted by sin and victim-ized by concupiscence. A beginner on the journey seeking intimacy with God must begin by destroying all forms of self-deception and have an honest understanding of the deepest self.

A rather unique image for *conscientia* is that of a house evicting its owner. The owner in this case is the "I." When this house evicts its owner, the owner falls from the house into "the self" (mistakenly the self tends to see itself as identified with its *conscientia*) and even tumbles from the self into lower depths due to the damage caused by sin. One's personal misery is so great that rescue and restoration seem next to impossible.[35] Human misery opens into the hu-man tendency to hide, disguise, or even excuse negative things about oneself, which leads to creation of all kinds of dark corners, nooks, and crannies in one's conscience or consciousness. A spiritual ascent demands casting off any tendency or 'garment' to hide one's disgrace and shame. One must show and expose the self before God's presence as one honestly and truly is. But there is a counterbalance to this profound misery: God's goodness to a person. "Behold my wounds; new and old, I hide nothing. I expose everything, both your ben-efits conferred on me and my own bad actions."[36] For William, human misery can have a positive result: openness to God.

William offers another powerful image of *conscientia* as a house, but this time a house that is dark, foggy on the inside, and full of flies. This is the op-portunity to take to heart that gospel admonition to make peace with one's neighbor before offering a gift at the altar[37]—in this case, make peace with oneself. In William's words, "giving myself an angry shake, I kindle the lamp of the Word of God, and in wrath and bitterness of soul; I enter the dark house of my *conscientia*."[38] William, using scriptures in a discerning way, re-enters his house to discover the source of its darkness with its shadows and fogginess. This "hateful fog" constitutes and forms a wall between him and the "light of his heart," namely, God. And what happens as he walks into his house? "A kind of plague of flies erupts into my eyes, and almost drives me out of my house!"[39]

Here we see the elements of the subtleties of *conscientia*. Consciousness can form a wall blocking the grace of illuminating Divine light. This happens when one's proliferating thoughts run rampant, constituting a dense swarm of flies and forming a barrier making any kind of divine illumination difficult if

---

35   Med, 9.1, CCCM 89:52. ET: *Meditations*, CF 3:145. Med 9 is the source of this entire section.

36   Med, 9.5, "Ecce vulnera mea recentia et antiqua. Nihil subtraho, omnia tibi expono, et bona tua et mea mala," CCCM 89:54. ET: *Meditations*, CF 3:147.

37   Matt 5:24.

38   Med, 9.2, CCCM 89:52. ET: *Meditations*, CF 3:146.

39   Med, 9.2, CCCM 89:52. ET: *Meditations*, CF 3:146.

not impossible. Discernment and control of one's thoughts has always been an essential ingredient for any spiritual progress.[40] As important as it is to control, if not to eliminate, bad and wrong thoughts, it is always necessary for 'harmless' thoughts not to eclipse Divine light, the voice of God speaking within a person. William states that it is imperative to put one's house in order by discerning one's thoughts, condemning and banishing some, correcting others, being strict with certain ones, and exercising control to make proper use of others.

The principal goal for all this discerning, watching, disciplining one's thoughts—so essential to any serious spiritual formation—is to arrive at the source of these thoughts, that is, a person's many affections. What or whom does a person really love? A clarion cry for William is that a person has as many faces as affections,[41] a situation far worse than being simply two-faced. Progress and ascent toward unity of spirit consists in having the 'Prince' of a person's affections controlling the crowd of these thoughts, seen as flies, to bondage under God who strengthens a person by Divine grace.

Regardless of the consistency and density of these thoughts, this fog and swarm of flies, or the thickness of this wall that consciousness tends to create, a person maintains the use of reason, which implies that God never ceases speaking to that person's conscience. Moreover, reason is a fundamental element in the formation of *conscientia* and for its ascent. Even if a person could eventually forget every thought, this forgetting is not the aim of such an ascetic discipline (*ascesis*). Thoughts do not perish from one's *conscientia*, William claims. Eventually they return to act as accuser, witness, and judge against the person.[42] The aim in confronting one's numerous thoughts, or thought process, is to discern and establish one's will as a strong, steady impulse towards good, although at this initial stage good may be an authentic good or one that simply appears as authentic. Consequently, a really good person is one whose will is becoming a straightforward desire for good, a simple *affectus*,[43] steady and firm in its seeking goodness.

---

40   See, e.g., Evagrius of Pontus, *The Praktikos*, and John Cassian, *The Institutes*, on the eight thoughts, and Cassian, *Conference* 10, on controlling thoughts in general.

41   Med, 8.1, CCCM 89:46. ET: *Meditations*, CF 3:139.

42   Exp Rom, II.2.14-16, CCCM 86:34–35. ET: *Exposition on the Epistle to the Romans*, CF 27:56.

43   *Affectus* is another of William's term having no adequate English translation capturing the comprehensiveness of its implications. In conscience's formation, at this stage, it is a person's strong, steady, always constant, impulse towards good, either real or apparent. As progress is made in one's spiritual ascent, the *affectus* takes on different characteristics. Cf. David N. Bell, *The Image and Likeness: The Augustinian Spirituality of William of St Thierry*, CS 78 (Kalamazoo, MI: Cistercian Publications, 1984), 131–32.

William uses another striking metaphor, a dog, to illustrate an essential aspect of *conscientia*.[44] Normally, one would not consider a dog as a good image of one's *conscientia*: conscience and consciousness. William, however, sees himself in the context of the Gospel account of the Canaanite woman who is initially rebuffed by the Lord.[45] Due to his deep personal misery, William cries out to the Lord in prayer, "Speaking as to a dog, you reproach my sullied conscience with its past impurity and present shame. And you drive your dog from your table unfed and famished and beaten by the rebukes of his conscience. Should I draw near again when this occurs? Yes, surely, Lord, for whelps that are chased with blows ... return immediately and, hanging watchfully about the place, receive their daily bread."[46] Regardless of the condition of one's *conscientia*, it was made by God, for God, and accordingly is always capable of the presence of God. *Conscientia*, by nature, "hangs around" God who never ceases to speak in one's conscience.

There is a second quality of conscience that this metaphor of a dog illustrates. *Conscientia* is made for a distinctive companionship, intimacy, with God. A dog is a faithful companion. As mentioned, the essence of *conscientia* is to be capable of God, *capax Dei*. In this resides one's image to God. To be *capax Dei*, capable of God, simply means that a person can be enlightened by God's illuminating grace so as to continue one's ascent into the mystery of the Trinity. "A dog cannot live without human companionship (*contubernium*), nor can my soul without the Lord her God. Open to me, therefore, Lord, that I may come to you and be enlightened by you."[47]

Similar to the metaphor of a house for one's *conscientia* is that of one's inner cell, an apt comparison for one truly seeking God. It comes from William's *Golden Epistle* to the Carthusian monks, hermits who spent the great part of their day in their individual monastic cells in absolute solitude. First, William explains that such a person has two cells.[48] There is the outward cell of one's life style. This is the cell of one's conduct, one's behavior, and the manner in which one lives. In this cell dwell both one's body and soul. Obviously, the challenge is to live one's exterior life in such a manner as to have a very good reputation, a reputation of a person who is truly seeking God. William proceeds then to explicate a person's inner cell as one's *conscientia*. This is a most private cell and here one's spirit dwells alone with God. God is more interior to one than all else that is within a person. This is a cell of profound intimacy with God.

---

44   Med, 2.3, CCCM 89:9. ET: *Meditations*, CF 3:96.
45   Matt 15:21–28.
46   Med, 2.3, CCCM 89:9. ET: *Meditations*, CF 3:96.
47   Med, 2.3, CCCM 89:9. ET: *Meditations*, CF 3:96. The term *contubernium* indicates a special type of intimate bonding. Its importance will be developed below.
48   Ep frat, 105, CCCM 88:250. ET: *Golden Epistle*, CF 12:47.

This doctrine of a person's two cells has profound implications in challenging today's contemporary life styles where exterior behavior is often rooted in what is superficial and expedient. William understands that the core of one's life is a profound intimacy with God. This intimacy is something extremely personal, rooted in the depths of one's being, the place where the "I" encounters the presence of the living God, namely, *conscientia*. The challenge is one of sincere honesty and radical integrity flowing from a genuine commitment to the goodness that is divine because it comes from God. This is what God is asking of a person if one's image of God, damaged by sin, is to be restored.

Related is also the arena of freedom of conscience, albeit given an authentic and objective formation of conscience. Freedom of conscience is not to be translated into "I can do whatever I want." Divine goodness touches the very spirit of a person as God dwells in the very depth of a person's spirit, the noblest part of a person.[49] This doctrine of the two cells precludes any degree of separation between one's inner life and exterior life. The firm bonding between these two depends on the degree of the intensity of focus within one's inner life (cell).

On a same note, William maintains that what goes on outwardly, in the exterior cell, will definitely affect the interior cell, *conscientia*. Exterior observance of the norms of morality and holiness is more than simple conformity, provided one does this for the sake of God. In reality, a person is entrusting one's will to be formed by God's divine goodness. Such a process with its motivation brings to birth tremendous inner simplicity that William describes as "a will that is wholly turned to God, seeking one thing from the Lord with all earnestness, without any desire to disperse its energies in the world."[50]

This doctrine of the two cells with its implications for intimacy with God in simplicity, as understood by William, lays the groundwork for a final metaphor of *conscientia* as a flowery bed—an uncommon metaphor in contemporary Christian spirituality. Yet, the point is that the mystery of *conscientia* coming to perfection consists in an intimate exchange, in the Holy Spirit, between the soul and the Incarnate Word of God. This union, William describes, "is nothing else than the Unity of the Father and the Son of God, their Kiss, their Embrace, their Love, their Goodness and whatever in that supremely simple Unity is common to both."[51] For in this unity, "the Creator Spirit infuses itself into the human spirit as It wills, and that person becomes one spirit with God,"[52] Unity

---

49   Ep frat, 105, "…interior est conscientia tua, quam inhabitare debet omnium interiorum tuorum Deus, cum spiritu tuo," CCCM 88:250. ET: *Golden Epistle*, CF 12:47. The concept of two cells is another consequence of *eucrasis*.

50   Ep frat, 49, CCCM 88:238. ET: *Golden Epistle*, CF 12:28.

51   Cant, 95, CCCM 87:71. ET: *Exposition on the Song of Songs*, CF 6:78.

52   Cant, 95, CCCM 87:70–71. ET: *Exposition on the Song of Songs*, CF 6:77–78.

of Spirit, *Unitas Spiritus*. This is nothing other than God's glorifying embrace of a person through a love so intimate that it makes the person one spirit with God.[53] This unity of spirit reveals a person not only who wills what God wills but who is unable to will or even want anything else.[54] To will what God wills is not uncommon, but there is a greater fullness of virtue in this inability to will otherwise—a transforming union of wills that culminates a person's ascent into the Triune God, a treasure kept in the depths of one's *conscientia*.[55]

This detailed presentation and teaching on the nature of *conscientia* can be summarized into one basic tenet: *conscientia* witnesses that a person belongs to and is oriented towards God.[56] This belonging and orientation breathes of intimacy and wholesome familiarity with the Divine. *Conscientia* gives witness to another basic tenet of ascent, William will go so far as to say, that a person will arrive at authentic self-knowledge to the degree this person will call upon and invoke the name of the Lord.[57] *Conscientia,* then, is the foundation and dynamic for the understanding and ongoing ascent of one's life in the image and likeness of God. Here grace is at work.[58] To quote again William's well-known dictum: "one becomes through grace what God is by nature."[59]

4   *Animalis, Rationalis, Spiritualis*: Dimensions of Spiritual Progress

Anyone acquainted with William's treatises and spirituality will know his presentation of a spiritual progress in terms of *homo animalis, homo rationalis, homo spiritualis* and the well-known concept of the soul as *anima, animus*, and *spiritus*. Because these Latin terms, so integral to William's thought, challenge translators to render them properly in English, they are sometimes conveyed in infelicitous translations as the "animal man, the rational man, and the spiritual man" or simply "animal, rational, and spiritual." Their context is not so much anthropological or even theological. Rather, these three descriptions capture the way people live, pray, and experience life and God working in their daily lives. Suggestions of this threefold dimension of human experience are scattered throughout William's works. In his later works, namely, the preface

---

53   Spec fid, 30–32, CCCM 89A:122–124. ET: *Mirror of Faith*, CF 15:75–80.
54   Ep frat, 262, CCCM 88:282. ET: *Golden Epistle*, CF 12:95.
55   Ep frat, 300, CCCM 88:289. ET: *Golden Epistle*, CF 12:105.
56   Cant, 163, CCCM 87:111. ET: *Exposition on the Song of Songs*, CF 6:133.
57   Spec fid, 5, CCCM 89A:87. ET: *Mirror of Faith*, CF 15:14.
58   Throughout his treatises, William presents grace as taking various forms: creating, prevenient, supervening, liberating, working, affecting, cooperating, illuminating, gratuitous, hidden, charitable, and hospitable.
59   Ep frat, 263, CCCM 88:282. ET: *Golden Epistle*, CF 12:96.

to his *Exposition on the Song of Songs*[60] and, more articulately, in the *Golden Epistle*,[61] William develops in more detail continual ascent and progress of a person's life according to these dimensions.

The undercurrent of William's spiritual ascent into the Trinitarian mystery of God is unwaveringly seeking the face of God, with all its challenges, that gradually and steadily transfigure a person. This is William's understanding of the nature of prayer: seeking the face of God by an on-going opening of oneself to the Divine face, which William describes as composed of all the qualities that makes God lovable.[62] These qualities could be spelled out as goodness, charity, justice, peace, mercy and so on. He proceeds to make a subtle distinction between the Divine *face* and Divine *countenance*, the latter being a kind of divine facial expression shining on a person, by grace, to assist and attract one to the Divine face.[63] The human face composes the characteristic aspects of a person's inner and outer life, one's *conscientia* and how it affects the way a person lives by wanting one thing, then another. One has many faces, each corresponding to the many affections, loves, and miseries one has in life.[64]

In its ascent towards the Divine, the human face unfolds into the three dimensions of *animalis, rationalis,* and *spiritualis.* These aspects are not three levels or steps of ascent, as if one could definitively leave one level and move onto the next or because of some failure one returns to the previously level. Instead, they constitute characteristics and dimensions of real life for anyone truly seeking God, forming a spectrum or continuum of spiritual ascent into the mystery of God. As such, a person may reasonably function simultaneously in both the *animalis* and *rationalis* and enter from time to time into the *spiritualis.* The limits of human imperfection experienced in the *animalis* and *rationalis* dimensions are never better understood than in the light of God's countenance shining on a person, assisting and attracting one to God's goodness, charity, justice, peace, mercy, and unity of spirit.[65]

One accurate translation for the concept of *homo animalis*, or soul as *anima*, is 'Body Person.' The life (*anima*) or *conscientia* of this type of person is on the level of "experience of sensible objects coming in through the five bodily senses,"[66] meaning that one's life-flow goes out through the five physical senses, for better or for worse. For worse—unhealthy life experiences—the will seeks and desires complete satisfaction and gratification in life through

---

60   See esp. Cant, Pref. 12ff, CCCM 87:24ff. ET: *Exposition on the Song of Songs*, CF 6:11ff.
61   See esp. Ep frat, 41ff, CCCM 88:236ff. ET: *Golden Epistle*, CF 12:25ff.
62   Contemp, 4, CCCM 88:155. ET: *On Contemplating God*, CF 3:40.
63   Ep frat, 195, CCCM 88:269. ET: *Golden Epistle*, CF 12:78.
64   Med, 8.1, 9.1, CCCM 89:46, 52. ET: *Meditations*, CF 3:139, 145.
65   Ep frat, 268–269, CCCM 88:284. ET: *Golden Epistle*, CF 12:97.
66   Ep frat, 285, CCCM 88:287. ET: *Golden Epistle*, CF 12:101–102.

sensual fulfillment. Present day consumerism is built on this type of life flow in which capitalism creates needs so life can be experienced as fulfilled on the level of physical sensory input. Yet what is physical is temporal and passing and must be constantly replenished. Another example of sensual fulfillment has a digital dimension when life is acted out by a simple touch on a screen or keyboard, compelled by the fear that one is out-of-touch or not up-to-date. The effect of a globalized digital world is that one's life, in terms of physical senses, can now be drawn 'anywhere' in the entire world. Life's flow in this respect has a person caught up in vicious circles that eventually "reap the fruits of the flesh, which are fornication, uncleanness, impurity, feuds, quarrels, jealousies, outbursts of anger, factions, dissensions, rivalries, debauchery, drunkenness and such like."[67] These are elements of contemporary news headlines in any daily paper or other news source.

5   Will and Prayer

William offers an alternative to one's life flowing out through the five physical senses by emphasizing the importance of the will (*voluntas*) in making choices. This alternative way, still in the realm of the physical senses, starts a gentle and subtle change of direction in the course of one's life, leading to good fruits such as "charity, joy, peace, patience, kindness, forbearance, generosity, gentleness, faith, temperance, chastity, continence, and the piety which promises well both for this life and for the next."[68] These virtues are aspects of God's face. To initiate this change and to navigate properly through sense experiences, William maintains the importance of a focus on the physical senses but with a healthy obedience to authority that directs a person's will in discerning and making choices. Obedience of this nature is not pure conformity. It educates the will to take responsibility for one's life in the magnitude of demands fostering sense gratification. This type of training comes from obedience and replaces *apparent* good with *authentic* good. With this new direction in discerning authentic good, the will begins to seek and choose those things that truly lead to God. Creating grace (*gratia creans*) is at work bringing to fulfillment a will created according to the image and likeness of God.[69] This new direction towards virtue is a corrective for consumerism in today's terminology or the feeling that 'real life' is just a screen-touch or click away.

---

67   Ep frat, 60, CCCM 88:240. ET: *Golden Epistle*, CF 12:32.
68   Ep frat, 60, CCCM 88:240. ET: *Golden Epistle*, CF 12:32–33.
69   Cant, 22, CCCM 87:28. ET: *Exposition on the Song of Songs*, CF 6:16–17.

Obedience of this nature leads to imitating and learning from the obedience of Christ. Reflecting and meditating with mental images on the life and teachings of Christ renders it possible to attain some insight into the raison d'être of Christ's obedience. This simple reflection or meditation—later to become a more profound understanding through illuminating grace (*gratia illuminans*)—encourages a person to imitate Christ in choosing and accomplishing the God's will. Fidelity and consistency in this type of formation brings to birth a good *conscientia* coming from grace that makes possible for a person to have an experience and an understanding similar to that of the apostles in their relationship with Christ. In addition, a person is blessed with the simplicity of a good will that is nothing other than a will turned totally toward God.[70] This simplicity is more than just good intention; it is an initial transfiguring change in life direction of the 'body person' (*homo animalis*).

This change manifests itself in the way a person begins to pray. The enticement of a 'body person' is to pray for something or for things apart from God or what might lead to God, things that a person believes are essential or needed for life. While there is certainly nothing wrong in prayer requests or petitions, to remain immersed in this form of prayer could result in a distorted understanding of Divinity, conforming the Divine to one's needs and wants, thus conformed to the person making the requests.[71] In contrast, prayer should seek an innocent *conscientia*, a heart pure from perverse thought, a will that seeks to be like God and, thus, to conform itself in simplicity to God's will.

The process of a will seeking God alone in simplicity frequently returns a person to the house of *conscientia* to be instructed, purified, cleansed of vices, richly adorned with virtue, with a gradual transfiguring of one's will to be prepared for the fullness of divine intimacy. For William, detachment and discipline generate a clear focus on the divine goodness. The successful formation of a 'body person' is, at its core, an authentic good will truly devoted to authentic good. And this is simplicity: a good will, the essential element in any spiritual ascent or progress, gradually possessing and knowing God to the degree one is possessed and known by God, and living accordingly.[72] For the 'body person,' this experience of possessing and knowing, leads to becoming rational, as one's life flow follows and lives according to the aegis of reason rather than under the dictates of the physical senses.

Contemporary culture obsessively holds body maintenance in high regard. William's unique role for the physical body in a spiritual ascent challenges

---

70   Cant, 64, CCCM 87:50. ET: *Exposition on the Song of Songs*, CF 6:51–52.
71   Cant, 23, CCCM 87:28–29. ET: *Exposition on the Song of Songs*, CF 6:17–18.
72   Ep frat, 252, CCCM 88:280. ET: *Golden Epistle*, CF 12:93.

contemporary culture. The body is not to be denied, suppressed, heavily disciplined, and plunged into austerity, as happens in some spiritual programs, due to its physical and sensual nature. On the other hand, spiritual life and devotion cannot rest on the physical senses, as if the spiritual life were something purely exterior with observances and practices tailored to a body-dimension. Spiritual ascent, for William, means life-changing experiences resulting from an encounter with Christ, a 'running up against' him in the sacrament of the Paschal Mystery.[73]

This primary encounter must take place with the perspective of Christ's humanity,[74] for human nature and the human body are essential in a bonding between Christ and a 'body person.' Furthermore, life in the body of Christ[75] always remains for transfiguration into the Trinitarian mystery of Christ. William writes, "What better preparation, what happier arrangement could have been made for one who wanted to ascend to God ... one should walk calmly and smoothly over the level of one's own likeness, to a Human like oneself, who tells that person ... 'I and the Father are one.'"[76] Or, as William addresses Christ directly, "one who enters by you, O Door, walks on smooth ground and comes to the Father, to whom no one may come, except by you."[77] This is the 'place' where one is modestly and humbly to sit, that is, to contemplate the mystery of the Trinity.

Near the end of his life, William integrated more fully his teaching on a person's spiritual life in the threefold dimension of *homo animalis, homo rationalis, homo spiritualis.* As stated, his letter to the Carthusian monks of Mont Dieu (*The Golden Epistle*) and the preface to his *Exposition on the Song of Songs* contain substantial outlines of his thought. While his presentation in the former fits the perspective of the Carthusian monastic observance, nevertheless, we can recognize a basic structure for spiritual growth applicable to anyone. The virtue of obedience challenges the 'body person,' with a focus on externals,

---

73 Med, 10.7 "...de mirabili passionis tuae sacramento...," CCCM 89:60. ET: *Meditations*, CF 3:154, "...the wonderful sacrament of your passion...."

74 Contemp, 3, CCCM 88:154. ET: *On Contemplating God*, CF 3:38.

75 Although there are various passages in William's treatises where he states the importance of living in the body of Christ, precisely what this means and how it is to be accomplished, two good references are Med 10 and the entire treatise *On the Sacrament of the Altar* (Sac alt, CCCM 89:53–91), a translation of which is in progress from Cistercian Publications: *Letter to Rupert of Deutz, On the Sacrament of the Altar, and On the Errors of William of Conches*, trans. with intro. F. Tyler Sergent and Nathaniel Peters, CF 82 (Collegeville, MN: Cistercian Publications, forthcoming).

76 Med, 10.8, CCCM 89:60. ET: *Meditations*, CF 3:154. The English translation revised by the author to accommodate inclusive language.

77 Med, 10.7, CCCM 89:60. ET: *Meditations*, CF 3:154.

to develop a will with a taste for goodness. The practical effect is reshaping one's mind in terms of learning to control emotions, guiding one's actions and rectifying behavior, avoiding excesses, conferring dignity and self-respect. What happens here is that this new focus of a person's life, due to an encounter with Christ, begins to enhance reason by restoring its proper role as the supreme evaluator and coordinator of all activity,[78] interior or exterior.

Each rational soul, a spiritual immortal substance, is created by God to be the life-giving font of a person's life, which is shaped by virtues and established in Christ.[79] This is William's concept of a rational person, one who is also consistent with the concept of *eucrasis* ("balance"). William sees virtues as characteristics of the Divine face that are given as gifts or graces from God— William calls these graces perfumes to illustrate their charisma[80]—that allure a person towards unity of spirit, enhancing one's *conscientia* to be well-disposed (*devotio conscientiae bene affectae*),[81] more perceptive and receptive of God's gracious goodness and union with divinity. For William, then, the 'rational person,' as distinguished from the 'body person,' is one whose life is under the guidance of enhanced reason. To become a rational person is not an end or goal in itself. Reason does give stability to a person's inner and outer life, to one's consciousness and behavior. A person's life, however, continues to ascend and be transfigured into a 'spiritual person,' that is, one entering more closely into the Divine will or *Unitas Spiritus*.

6   God's Face and Countenance

William uses God's face and God's countenance as metaphors for ascent into and union with the mystery of Divinity. William possibly picked up these metaphors with their distinction from his familiarity with the psalter in the ancient monastic *praxis* of praying the psalms daily. William would have been familiar with the Vulgate of St. Jerome, which uses the Latin *facies* ("face") some sixty-six times and *vultus* ("countenance") some twenty times.

As his *Meditations* reveal, William places the drama of his own personal life, with its tensions and anguish, in this context of 'face' and 'countenance' as the presence of God. The drama of his life, like any human life, had its adverse,

---

78   Phys an, 3, CCCM 88:125. ET: *The Nature of the Body and Soul*, CF 24:129.

79   Phys an, 1, CCCM 88:121. ET: *The Nature of the Body and Soul*, CF 24:125.

80   One example of this understanding of virtue is Cant, 32–43, CCCM 87:33–40; ET: *Exposition on the Song of Songs*, CF 6:26–34. Another reference for this dynamic of virtue is Nat am, 44, CCCM 88:211–212; *On the Nature and Dignity of Love*, CF 30:107–108.

81   Cant, 31, CCCM 87:35.

confrontational, emotional struggles. But with the positive connotations William gives to God's face and countenance, it remains encouraging and inspiring to see the drama unfold in the divine presence, itself leading to an intimacy with God: "I have seen ... his face shine upon me; I have perceived the gladness of his countenance; I have felt the grace poured abroad in his lips."[82] Although these words in the *Song of Songs* are put into the mouth of the bride, undoubtedly, William speaks from his own prayer experience.

William, in his *Meditations* and *Exposition on the Song of Songs*, sums up the essence of the Divine face: "...the Face of Your goodness is always bent on me to work my good, the face of my misery, bowed down to the dull earth is so enshrouded in the fog of its blindness..."[83] This divine goodness is laid out by means of various figures of speech such as knowledge of all truth,[84] God's ability to adapt to human needs,[85] font of all grace,[86] God's hiding place and our hiding place,[87] the font of our alacrity to understand,[88] and finally, Christ in his Incarnation and in his Passion,[89] which is the knowledge of all truth.[90] Thus the Face of God represents the goal of ascent into the divine mystery, that is, to be transfigured by grace to such an extent that a person "looks just like God!"

While the Face of God is not subject to change, the human face, by contrast, is radically subject to change. The human face is a person's *conscientia*, that is conscience and consciousness, with all its emotions and affections of humility, love, contrition, confusion, sinfulness, masks, thoughts, ideas, phantasms, etc.; everything that one opens up and presents to God when coming face to face with the Divine in the mystery of *capax Dei*: the human capacity of receiving the transfiguring grace of God's glory.[91]

The countenance of God entices a person to such transfiguration. Countenance, typically, is a facial expression appropriate to a person, a distinctive appearance of one's face that expresses a mood or emotion. The Divine countenance touches and transfigures the deepest part of a person, one's *conscientia*, so that one lives and behaves in a manner truly befitting God. "I seek

---

82   Cant, 30, CCCM 87:33. ET: *Exposition on the Song of Songs*, CF 6:25.

83   Med, 9.1, CCCM 89:52. ET: *Meditations*, CF 3:145.

84   Med, 7.6-7, CCCM 89:44. ET: *Meditations*, CF 3:137.

85   Med, 8.1, CCCM 89:46. ET: *Meditations*, CF 3:139.

86   Cant, 185, CCCM 87:122. ET: *Exposition on the Song of Songs*, CF 6:149.

87   Cant, 198, CCCM 87:129; ET: *Exposition on the Song of Songs*, CF 6:159 and Med, 4.11, CCCM 89:25; ET: CF 3:116.

88   Cant, 185, CCCM 87:122. ET: *Exposition on the Song of Songs*, CF 6:149.

89   Med, 10.7, CCCM 89:59. ET: *Meditations*, CF 3:154.

90   Med, 7.6, CCCM 89:44. ET: *Meditations*, CF 3:137.

91   This is the tenor of Med, 8 and 9, CCCM 89:46–56. ET: *Meditations*, CF 3:139–150.

your countenance, O Lord; my face seeks your face. For you give keenness to my interior eyes, that I may contemplate you and give attention to myself."[92] The self-actualization of a rational person, guided by reason enhanced by illuminating grace, is the splendor of the highest good attracted to the Divine face.

Three other aspects are integral to an orientation proper for the *homo rationalis*, rational person. They are the development of one's understanding (*ratio fidei*), of one's love (*affectus*) and of a life fully alive (*sensus vitae, Spiritus vitae*).[93] These developments offer a refreshingly profound insight into a human person grasped by God.

William states that reason is the soul's eye,[94] thereby emphasizing that reason, once restored to its proper role in human life, should orchestrate a person's life in all its aspects. Furthermore, as a person progresses and comes face to face with Christ's revelation and teaching in the Gospels—plus development in ecclesiastical dogmas and doctrine, all of which constitutes faith—reason is challenged and can either rebuff or uphold this faith and say: You are the Christ, the Son of God.[95] The choice to uphold faith demonstrates reason that functions spiritually and not as the 'body person' who functions corporeally.[96] Spiritually, used here, denotes a sense of experience and understanding in a non-corporeal manner as opposed to the experience and understanding rising out of physical senses.

Upholding faith relates to another concept of William, namely *ratio fidei*. 'Reasoning of faith' is one translation, for reason itself, along with its rational understanding, can only lead a person in the direction God. Neither reason nor rational understanding, however, can attain or participate in what God is.[97] Reasoning of faith performs two very important tasks. First, it supports and elucidates faith, in so far as it can. Second, for a person now guided by reason, it maintains a focus that is dead-set on God. The power inherent in this type of reason is a well-directed, unadulterated, and unhindered gaze on Christ. This gaze, foundational for the virtues of faith, hope, and charity, enables reason to attain its full purpose of a happy life.[98]

---

92   Cant, 183, CCCM 87:122. ET: *Exposition on the Song of Songs*, CF 6:149.

93   Ep frat, 195–196, CCCM 88:269. ET: *Golden Epistle*, CF 12:78.

94   Spec fid, 1, CCCM 89A:82. ET: *Mirror of Faith*, CF 15:4.

95   Spec fid, 11, "Requisitus fidem: Tu es, inquit, Christus Filius Dei...," CCCM 89A:94. ET: *Mirror of Faith*, CF 15:29. Cf. Matt 16:16.

96   Spec fid, 11, CCCM 89A:94. ET: *Mirror of Faith* CF 15:29. Terms used are *spiritualiter* as opposed to *carnaliter et animalis*.

97   Med, 3.10, CCCM 89:18. ET: *Meditations*, CF 3:107. The terms are *intellectus naturalis, ratio,* and *ratio fidei*.

98   Spec fid, 1, CCCM 89A:2. *Mirror of Faith*, CF 15:4–5.

Inherent in reason and its reasoning process is a 'rational understanding' (*intellectus rationalis*) that has a heightened ability of perception to grasp an object that leads to human insight. There is another type of understanding, however, a "spiritual understanding" (*intellectus spiritualis*) brought about by illuminating grace. Coming from above, "from the Father of Lights from whom is every good and perfect gift" (James 1:17), illuminating grace enters the believing mind and, William says, "takes reason to itself and makes it like itself; by it a person's faith is also imbued with life and light."[99] William designated this second understanding as 'spiritual' because it comes directly from the Holy Spirit as a pure gift. Through spiritual understanding, a person's intellectual life is enlightened by illuminating grace that bestows insight into the mysteries of faith, with special emphasis given to the mystery of Christ's life, penetrating into the depths of a devout *conscientia*.[100]

This is a small taste and beginning of a *transitus*, that passing over into everlasting happiness, sweetness, and love proper to eternal life in the Trinity. As William says, it is one thing to recognize God as a person recognizes a friend. It is another thing to recognize God as Divinity recognizes or knows itself. The role of illuminating grace is glorifying[101] a person in order that such a person may participate by grace in what God is by nature and come to know God in this manner.[102] Illuminating grace is a manifestation of the Divine Countenance enabling a person to enter into the "knowing" God in the mystery of the Divine Face.

William distinguishes between these two modes of understanding, rational and spiritual. He uses reason (*ratio*) when speaking about human understanding, for reason is its foundation and grounding. When referring to spiritual understanding, he speaks in terms of the human soul (*anima*), that is, a person's entire life, one's *conscientia,* and its physical body. The inference is that through illuminating grace, spiritual understanding affects a person's entire life in both its intellectual and behavioral dimensions. This distinction is consistent with William's understanding of 'person' in the Trinity. William admits there are two possible definitions of person: one is an individual substance of a rational nature, the other the concept whereby a form gives knowledge of itself.[103] The Persons within the Trinity offer knowledge of themselves to

---

99   Med, 2.8-9, CCCM 89:12. *Meditations*, CF 3:100.

100   One reference where these two types of understanding are developed is Cant, 80, CCCM 87:61–63. ET: *Exposition on the Song of Songs*, CF 6:66–67.

101   "Glorifying" in the sense as given in n. 1 above.

102   Spec fid, 26–31, CCCM 89A:118ff. ET: *Mirror of Faith*, CF 15:70ff.

103   Aenig, 25, "Cuius pro sui form certa sit agnitio," CCCM 89A:152–153. ET: *Enigma of Faith*, CF 9:65–67.

one another, and each one is able to answer what the three are. This latter definition places the focus on relationship and on a relationship with the human person via grace.[104] It also clarifies why William sees the development of *conscientia* in a dimension of understanding. Use of the word 'person' in these paragraphs strives to maintain this distinction and clarification.

7   Will and *Affectus*

The development and transfiguring of the will is a major life-changing experience a person undergoes. The will in itself is a simple *affectus*.[105] This Latin term is pivotal to William's concept of spiritual ascent into the mystery of God. Moreover, William's use of this term is complex and technical to the extent that English translations of any sort, like affection, may not adequately render William's nuanced thought. To say that the will is a simple *affectus* means that the will is an ordinary desire for or inclination towards something or someone. The fundamental aspect of a will is to reach out for something or someone and/ or to be influenced or attracted to or fascinated by something or someone, and the possibility of experiencing both of these movements simultaneously. For William, this fundamental aspect is the concept of simple *affectus*.

The more ardent or passionate the will, the more the will becomes love. For ardor and passion transform a simple will into love.[106] For example, a 'body person' obediently accepts faith with a sincere and devout good will and savors this faith by means of the physical senses,[107] i.e., by means of images, exterior devotions, etc. Then temptation surfaces to challenge this faith. In the midst of temptation, reason and the reasoning process, under the God's influence, moves a person of sincere good will to affirm a strong commitment to faith: "You are the Christ, the Son of God" (Matt 16:16). When temptation against this commitment is challenged, the firm response is: "You know that I love you. I will lay down my life for you."[108] William uses this example in his *Mirror of Faith* to show how an *affectus* of a good will becomes an *affectus* of love. This subtle process deepens the quality of a person's life-flow from a physical to a

---

104   This definition of person in the dimension of recognition and acknowledgement with implied relationship suggests a matrix for that famous dictum occurring in Cistercian writings: "love itself is understanding" (*amor ipse intellectus est*).

105   Nat am, 4, CCCM 88:180. ET: *Nature and Dignity of Love*, CF 30:56.

106   Nat am, 4, CCCM 88:180. ET: *Nature and Dignity of Love*, CF 30:56.

107   Spec fid, 11, CCCM 89A:94. ET: *Mirror of Faith*, CF 15:29. The descriptive words are *animalis* and *carnaliter* usually translated as "animal" and "physically."

108   Spec fid, 11, CCCM 89A:94. ET: *Mirror of Faith*, CF 15:29.

more interior expression. This power or force of love leads a person forward in the spiritual ascent.[109]

Indispensable for the on-going ascent towards God is for the *affectus* of love (*amor*) to become an *affectus* of charity (*caritas*): "For God is charity."[110] Illuminating grace performs this change, for as grace leads a person deeper into the mysteries of faith, one senses the goodness and selfless, generous love of God flowing through the Incarnate Christ—this love of God is charity (*caritas*).[111] This sensing changes human love (*amor*) into this divine charity (*caritas*). William describes this change as joy of illuminating grace working in an enlightened *conscientia* beholding the glory of God and putting on the mind of Christ and as the "place" where it is good for a person to be and live.[112] He describes this "place" as well as the sacrament of the Will of God, the hidden and highest of all the sacraments, where love becomes understanding.[113]

In the *Golden Epistle,* believed to be William's last treatise, which gives the maturity of his thought and doctrine, William describes wisdom in his favorite yet unusual way: "For wisdom is indeed piety, that is, the worship [*cultus*] of God, the love by which we yearn to see God and, seeing God, in a mirror obscurely, believe and hope in God and advance even to see God as God chooses to be revealed to a person."[114] Wisdom is a piety that is the worship of God. Piety here is to be understood not in the context of pious devotions, a more contemporary connotation. Rather, piety is a fierce, selfless devotion; an authentic, steadfast love for God that brings about likeness to God since love has taken on the qualities of charity, the selfless charity that is God. This kind of wisdom is a vision of God taking place in this life and changing one's entire life style with its behavior. Anyone who is both penetrated and grasped by God's selfless charity has some experience or vision of what God is.

Two dimensions of wisdom are contained here in William's thought. First, due to charity, wisdom is an experiential way of seeing and understanding

---

109 Nat am, Prol. 1, CCCM 88:177. ET: *Nature and Dignity of Love*, CF 30:47.

110 I John 4.8 (Vlg.), "*quoniam Deus caritas est.*"

111 Charity can have various meanings, but with illuminating grace, charity (*caritas*) has this precise meaning.

112 Med, 3.8ff, CCCM 89:17ff. ET: *Meditation*, CF 3:106ff; and Spec fid, 30, CCCM 89A:119–120. ET: *Mirror of Faith*, CF 15:72–73.

113 Spec fid, 20, CCCM 89A:105–107. ET: *Mirror of Faith*, CF 15:48–51.

114 Ep frat, 279, "Sapientia enim pietas est, hoc est cultus Dei, amor quo eum videre desieramus, et videntes eum in speculo et in aenigmate, credimus et speramus et iam in hoc proficimus ut eum videamus in manifestatione," CCCM 88:286. ET: *Golden Epistle*, CF 12:100. Translation modified for inclusive language. The Latin is more powerful in placing emphasis on worship as a cult, vision in this life as a mirror, and one's ongoing progress towards a clearer vision of God. See *Golden Epistle*, 100, n. 36, for background for William identifying wisdom, piety, and worship of God as one and the same.

what God is. Secondly, wisdom is a cult—worship, veneration—that is a life style based on selfless charity that results from this experiential understanding of God. It might be noted here, that this latter concept of wisdom is also biblical in so far as wisdom in the Old and New Testaments is interpreted as a way of living, a life style, in accordance with God's Word.

8   Sense of Life and Spirit of Life

Sense of life (*sensus vitae*) and the Spirit of life (*Spiritus vitae*) are technical terms that are integral to the concept of progress in William's doctrine. However, they do not appear often and can easily be overlooked. *Sensus* contains the concept of sensation, nuanced by the fact that a person's life is changed into what it senses, through a simple understanding. This concept of sense has powerful implications for the 'body person' who lives entirely in the domain of physical sensation, where love is not free from corruption and understanding is basically sensual and corporeal. This concept of sense also has implications for the rational person in whom reason seeks knowledge and understanding. William describes this mental faculty as a kind of 'sense,' analogous to a physical sense. When the mind goes out into the things of God, the mind's desire to know and understand will become love due to the gift of illuminating grace, as explained above.

The development of a 'sense of life' is another transfigurative experience. The sense of life (*sensus vitae*) is given as a gift from the Spirit of life (*Spiritus vitae*), the Holy Spirit.[115] This sense is integral to a proper orientation of the rational person's (*homo rationalis*) ascent into the Trinity, and the purpose of this gift is to draw one into the Trinitarian mystery. The sense of life is capable of accomplishing this, since as gift it is love, free of corruption, and it is understanding of life, a knowing God in an intimate manner. The sense of life, coming as it does from the Holy Spirit, reveals this love as understanding.

In his work, *Physics of the Soul*, William presents seven aspects of human life that establish its ascent to God, four of which are directly relevant to *sensus vitae*.[116] The very first aspect is the soul (*anima*) in a person's physical body that holds the body together and integrates all bodily activities in harmony and beauty—thus a person lives and has life. The second aspect of ascent to God is the ability of this soul to reach out through the senses in physical sensation. In addition to reaching out, the soul has the ability to desire, to foster

---

115   Cant, 1, CCCM 87:19. ET: *Exposition on the Song of Songs*, CF 6:4 and n. 3.

116   Phys an, 14, CCCM 88:141–144. ET: *On the Nature of the Soul*, CF 24:147–150. Cf. Augustine, *De quantitate animae*, 33.70–76; see *Three Treatises on Man*, 147, n. 38.

companionship and love, and to delight in this ability. The third aspect is life's ability to remember what has entered through the senses and to use this information to reflect, understand, and create. The self deliberately reflects and understands its own life-giving ability in producing harmony and beauty in itself and in creation. Human life, in the domain of *conscientia*, now opens up to what harmony and beauty imply, namely, goodness. The fourth aspect of ascent to God is life's progress in focusing towards God. Thus, human life glimpses something of the nature of God, something spiritual beyond the material. The sense of life has come to be and is ready for transfiguration by illuminating grace. In this way, human life is penetrated, transfigured, by divine life through the the Holy Spirit, who is the profound and supreme unity and knowledge between Father and Son.

The process of transfiguration is that the Spirit of life (*Spiritus vitae*)—the Holy Spirit—frees a person from sin, for the Holy Spirit is a Spirit of sanctification.[117] This Spirit reveals within the depths of a person's *conscientia,* both as consciousness and conscience, the awareness that one is a child of God. Illuminating grace, that light of God's countenance, initiates this awareness within a person, which William explains, "No one knows the Father except the Son, and the one to whom the Son chooses to reveal the Father."[118] The significance of these words is clear, William writes, "These are the Lord's words. The Father and the Son reveal this [knowing] to certain persons then, to those to whom They will, to those to whom They make it known, that is, to whom They impart the Holy Spirit who is the common knowing or the common will of both. (These persons) to whom the Father and Son reveal (Themselves) recognize Them as the Father and Son recognize Themselves"[119] because these persons have within themselves the Father and the Son's mutual knowing. A person becomes more and more like God by this knowledge from the Holy Spirit. Such is the fullness of the Spirit of life; this Trinitarian transfiguring of human life is progress or ascent and also the summit or goal that is unity of spirit.

Irenaeus of Lyons famously wrote, "The glory of God is a living person. The life of this person is a vision of God."[120] While this saying was not necessarily know to William, it captures William's conceptualization of the Spirit of life giving a sense of life. God's glory is a person fully alive with the Divine Spirit. This person's life is nothing other than an authentic vision of God. The Incarnation of the Christ is the exemplar of this teaching with its delicate accent on

---

117   Exp Rm, VI.11.2-7, CCCM 86:150. ET: *Exposition on the Epistle to the Romans*, CF 27:209.

118   Matt 11:27.

119   Spec fid, 31, CCCM 89A:121–122. ET: *Mirror of Faith* CF 15:75–76.

120   Irenaeus of Lyons, *Adversus Haereses*, 4:20, "Gloria Dei est vivens homo. Vita hominis visio Dei." The translation is my own. Unfortunately, this quotation is used on occasion to promote a cult of self-fulfillment that was not the intention of Irenaeus.

ascent into unity of spirit. The so-called last discourse of the Gospel of John in its entirety unravels this mystery of the Incarnation.[121]

The rational soul (*animus*) also has a dimension as spirit (*spiritus*), as refined by William in the *Golden Epistle*.[122] This characteristic of the rational soul provides efficacious perception for seeking the good because, as *animus* is created in the image of its Creator, the rational soul is set free by the proper use of reason,[123] allowing one to live a daily life that flows from a proper use of reason with memory, understanding, and love.[124] From the viewpoint of the *spiritus*, illuminating grace sets one's gaze or focus on goodness as a vision of God's divine life, and out of this vision shares this goodness with others.[125] Now the spiritual person is gradually coming to birth.

"Perfection of the rational person is the beginning of the spiritual person; its progress is to look upon God's glory with face uncovered; its perfection is to be changed into the same likeness, going from splendor to splendor by the Lord's Spirit."[126] This is William's description of passing from the rational person to the spiritual person. William uses the word 'spiritual' with various nuances and definitions. One tendency is to think of 'spiritual' as implying 'supernatural.' For William, however, a 'spiritual person' is distinguished from a 'body person' and 'rational person' by each one's *modus operandi* and the source from which this mode of operating flows. As noted, the 'body person' is rooted in the physical senses, good or evil, depending on the quality of the will. A rational person's life flows under the aegis of reason with a will shaped by faith perceived by a rational soul (*animus*) and focus provided by the *spiritus*. A spiritual person's life flows entirely from a will under the profound influence of the Holy Spirit. These three aspects, whereby human life becomes like the Divine life, bring out the incredible richness of William's teaching on unity of spirit with dimensions of a good will progressing into love, then maturing into charity and finally becoming wisdom.

9   Wisdom

The gift of Divine Wisdom allures and attracts a person to respond freely and joyfully with a profound *affectus*, namely, an ardent and passionate "yes," to

---

121   John 13:21–17:25.
122   Ep frat, 198ff, CCCM 88:270ff. ET: *Golden Epistle* CF 12:79ff.
123   Ep frat, 199, CCCM 88:270. ET: *Golden Epistle* CF 12:79.
124   Ep frat, 249, CCCM 88:279. ET: *Golden Epistle* CF 12:92. Following Augustine, *De Trinitate*, William also writes of memory, understanding, will; see, e.g., Ep frat, 248.
125   An entire section in the *Golden Epistle* develops the full implications of this *animus/spiritus* concept; see, Ep frat, 198ff, CCCM 87:269–279. ET: *Golden Epistle*, CF 12:79–91.
126   Ep frat, 45, CCCM 88:237. ET: *Golden Epistle* CF 12:27.

want to become one with God. William perceives wisdom as a manifestation of the Divine. Wisdom, personified, comes to meet a person, revealing itself to in ascent and progress toward union with God.[127] In this capacity, wisdom displays its characteristic of selfless love (*caritas*). Wisdom is a gift from the Holy Spirit that enables a person to taste, enjoy, and cleave to God in sweetness.[128] Wisdom is the capacity to comprehend and understand God as a result of this tasting, enjoying, and cleaving. Wisdom is the ability to touch Divinity through the Trinitarian mystery of Christ.[129]

Wisdom accomplishes this, William says, by leading one "with the hand of experience" to understand the "inner meaning" of scripture and the Sacraments—understood as life of Christ and his body as the Church—so as to come to know Jesus in a most intimate way,[130] grasping the full implication of his Passion, death, and resurrection, within one's consciousness and conscience.[131] Christ, the personified Wisdom of God, bestows on a person this relish for Divinity.[132] Ultimately, one comes to the awareness that Wisdom is both Christ and his Spirit. This Holy Spirit unites with the will, and the person, truly loving God, is unexpectedly and entirely transformed by grace into what God is by nature. This unity of spirit[133] brings to perfection in this life the prayer of Jesus: "Father, my will is that as I and you are one, so they too may be one in us."[134]

10   The School of Charity and Communal Life

In *The Nature and Dignity of Love,* William highlights the powerful transfiguration a person experiences in community, a transfiguration whose effectiveness is in proportion to one's *affectus* in adhering indissolubly to God and living the virtues that come from the light of the divine countenance. A primary premise

---

127   Ep frat, 195, CCCM 88:269. ET: *Golden Epistle,* CF 12:78. William quotes Wis 6:14 here.
128   Nat am, 28, CCCM 87:189–200. ET: *Nature and Dignity of Love,* CF 30:88.
129   Nat am, 40ff, CCCM 87:208ff. ET: *Nature and Dignity of Love,* CF 30:102ff.
130   Nat am, 31, CCCM 87:201–202. ET: *Nature and Dignity of Love,* CF 30:91–92.
131   Spec fid, 30, CCCM 89A:119–120. ET: *Mirror of Faith,* CF 15:72–74; cf. Ep frat, 286, CCCM 88:287. ET: *Golden Epistle,* CF 12:102.
132   Nat am, 30, CCCM 88:200. ET: *Nature and Dignity of Love,* CF 30:90.
133   Glenn E. Myers presents a magnificent development of the nine aspects of *Unitas Spiritus* in his article, "Manuscript Evidence of the *Golden Epistle*'s Influence in the Sermons of Johannes Tauler," *Cistercian Studies Quarterly* 48.4 (2013): 479–501 and with greater detail in his chapter, "William of Saint-Thierry's Legacy: Progress Toward Trinitarian Participation in the *Unio Mystica* in Johannes Tauler's Sermons" in this volume, pp. 199–228.
134   John 17:21; Ep frat, 288, CCCM 88:287. ET: *Golden Epistle,* CF 12:102.

for William is that the quality of one's union with God determines the quality and appropriateness of a person's life style and behavior: a profound harmony, concord, and unanimity in community. One's union with God mirrors one's work for a unity and charity in community that also reflects Trinitarian unity and charity. The challenge for the school of charity (*schola caritatis*)[135] is handling the turmoil and hardships of life—in particular those of a communal nature, what William calls baggage[136]—in such a way as to ascend into wisdom's joy of the Lord.[137]

William uses the phrase *schola caritatis* only once and in a very early treatise, possibly his first, *The Nature and Dignity of Love*.[138] With it, he paints a somewhat ideal concept of living together in community with all its components essential for unity. Unity is the heart of this phrase, charity its bonding. In his other writings, William presents features of this school of charity using powerful expressions—e.g., *vita communis, communis intitutio, vita socialis, contubernium,* and *communitas*—to reveal the great depths of this phrase. To form this bond in communal living requires a personal ascent, by the help of grace, from the enticements of physical, external things to a union of one's will with the Divine Will, expressed in this present life by the manner in which one lives with other people.

A foundational phrase, *Vita communis*, "communal life," gives emphasis to a profession of holiness through communal living. Each person is summoned by God, through the Gospel message, to this profession. For William, people who respond to this call are "holy poor people for this very reason that they had made profession of holiness and the common life, impoverishing themselves to that end."[139]

Latin words *communis institutio* illustrate another aspect of communal life. *Institutio* is usually translated "institution." In this context, however, the word suggests an arrangement of customs and norms basic to educating a person for a special responsibility. The communal *institutio* challenges the 'body person' to develop a focus from the bodily dimension to a more spiritual, immaterial

---

135 This phrase, "school of charity," is special to the Cistercians who tend to use it as an expression for community. See Étienne Gilson, "Schola Caritatis," in *The Mystical Theology of Saint Bernard*, trans. A.H.C. Downes (London/New York: Sheed & Ward, 1940; rpt., Kalamazoo, MI: Cistercian Publications, 1990), 60–84.

136 For William, baggage (*sarcina*) would be whatever threatens—exterior events and inner personal thoughts—fraternal charity, the *schola caritatis*. Nat am, 26, CCCM 88:198. ET: *Nature and Dignity of Love*, CF 30:86.

137 Nat am, 23–27, CCCM 88:195–198. ET: *Nature and Dignity of Love*, CF 30:80–87.

138 Nat am, 26, CCCM 88:198. ET: *Nature and Dignity of Love*, CF 30:86.

139 Ep frat, 162, CCCM 88:261. ET: *Golden Epistle*, CF 30:63.

dimension and thus toward God. This is the process of learning the truth about oneself, an authentic understanding of who and what one is. For William, this *initial* understanding—essential to the concept of personhood—is foundational and preparatory for *spiritual* understanding that comes from God who is love.[140]

Another feature of communal living is accented by the word *socialis* that describes persons living together in amiable and compatible fellowship. William sees this aspect of common life as the ground for fraternal charity. Persons well advanced in their progress or ascent, William argues, prefer nothing to this feature of communal life, "the sweetness of fraternal charity."[141]

Infrequently used in William's works is the word *contubernium*. In Classical Latin it referred to some eight men living very closely together in a Roman army tent, bonding in fellowship on their military expedition.[142] Rare as its use may be William always maintains the concept of an intimate bonding by dwelling together in community. The implication is that the quality of any communal life together is contingent on the quality of life lived intimately with God. A remarkable use of this word by William is in his *Meditations* where he states that the highest knowledge a person can have here and now consists in knowing God in what way one does not know God. Yet, this human darkness and ignorance, a secret place that hides the Divine Face, is luminous and full of light precisely because of bonding intimately (*contubernium*) with divine light and divine fire.[143] *Contubernium* situates human experience of knowing and not knowing as the apex of understanding: knowing in a way one does not know. The concept of *contubernium* fittingly expresses what William describes as Peter's desire to live intimately with the Christ, "in the fellowship of our Lord and the citizens of heaven," in the Transfiguration passage of the Gospel of Matthew.[144]

Surprisingly, William appears to use the word *communitas* only four times, three of which express the Holy Spirit's relationship in the Trinity.[145] Consequently, this use of *communitas* as limited to the role of the Holy Spirit is significant. Generally *communitas* is correctly translated as "community." However,

---

140   Ep frat, 77–79, 105–107, cccm 88:243–244, 250–251. ET: *Golden Epistle*, CF 30:37–38, 47–48.

141   Ep frat, 190, cccm 88:268. ET: *Golden Epistle*, CF 30:76.

142   *Oxford Latin Dictionary*, s.v. "contubernium, -i, n."

143   Med, vii.8, cccm 89:44. ET: *Meditations*, CF 3:137.

144   Ep frat, 12, cccm 88:230. ET: *Golden Epistle*, CF 30:12; see Matt 17:4.

145   Spec fid, 32, cccm 89A:123, ET: *Mirror of Faith*, CF 15:79; Exp Rom, iii.5.5-6, cccm 86:63; ET: *Exposition on the Epistle to the Romans*, CF 27:95; Adv Abl, 4, cccm 89A:29; and Ep frat, 133, cccm 88:256; ET, *Golden Epistle*, CF 30:55 (§ 134). The usage in Ep frat refers to community life.

a first meaning of this word is "joint possession, participation, or sharing."[146] This meaning presents a powerful insight into William's understanding of community. The Holy Spirit makes possible God's divine wish that humanity be bound together by participation in a communal unity, the body of Christ, by conferring that selfsame Holy Spirit who is the *communitas* of the Trinity. Thus, communal living on earth is a temporal inauguration of the Holy Spirit's unifying role in eternal communal life of the Trinity through the transfiguration of a person that the Holy Spirit brings about. In addition, because the Holy Spirit brings people together into a unity of wills in *communitas—Unitas Spiritus—* this act of participation is itself an ascent into eternal Trinitarian life. Thus is realized the school of charity's ideal.

11   Conclusion

This ascent, this *transitus*, to God,[147] is absolutely impossible for anyone of faith without first having entered into the abasement of the Incarnate Christ. The surprising outcome of this comprehensive, far-reaching restoration and transfiguring of one's entire life through the embrace coming from the Trinitarian mystery of Christ results in an image and likeness through the unity of spirit. Such an ascent requires an intense disciplined asceticism of willingness to allow grace to transfigure a free will into a will that is thoroughly good, then into one that is love, and this loving becoming charity, which unfolds into divine wisdom of unity of spirit. This progressive ascent, extremely intimate and personal, takes place and evolves in the depths of one's *conscientia,* in a profound silence that even the person experiencing it may not be able to articulate nor even comprehend. One can only rest at peace in the shadow of the Scriptural words of the Prophet Isaiah, "My secret is my own, my secret is my own."[148]

---

146   *Oxford Latin Dictionary*, s.v. "communitas, -atis, f."
147   This is the phrase William uses to express the passing over into eternal joy and happiness. See, Nat am, 45, CCCM 88:211. ET: *Nature and Dignity of Love*, CF 30:108.
148   Ep frat, 300, CCCM 88:289. ET: *Golden Epistle*, CF 12:105. Isaiah 24:16 are the last words of William's *Golden Epistle*, William's final thoughts of this last treatise.

CHAPTER 7

The Eucharistic Theology of William of Saint-Thierry

Nathaniel Peters

1 Introduction

William of Saint-Thierry is best known for his writings on the journey of the soul toward God and for his Trinitarian theology. It is curious, then, that in *The Cistercian Heritage*, Louis Bouyer calls William's Eucharistic doctrine "the keystone of his own spiritual teaching."[1] Should not that pride of place go to William's doctrine of *unitas spiritus*, his emphasis on the Holy Spirit as both the substantial love of God and the gift of grace by which human beings participate in that love, or his understanding of human faculties as a real image of the Trinity? While these are all vital elements of his theology, Bouyer is correct, for a keystone caps the arch as its peak—it holds the other stones in place, but its shape is determined by the architectural logic of the arch as a whole. Likewise, William's Eucharistic theology caps his theological system and serves as the meeting point for many aspects of his thought according to the shape provided by his understanding of the Trinity.

For William, human beings are brought into the relationship with God for which they were created by participating in the relations of the Trinity. This participation takes place in a Trinitarian way, through movements of the Son and the Spirit that mirror their relations in the Godhead. This Trinitarian pattern or 'logic' (to use Matthieu Rougé's term) consists of the order in which the persons proceed in their endless exchange of self-giving love, while remaining one substance, and that love desires to incorporate human beings into its exchange.[2] The immanent gift of love provides the template for the economic

---

1 Louis Bouyer, *The Cistercian Heritage*, trans. Elizabeth A. Livingstone (Westminster, MD: The Newman Press, 1958), 107.

2 To offer a brief summary, William's Trinitarian theology emphasizes the unity of the divine essence and its attributes, even as it distinguishes the persons by their relations. Those relations are inherent in the divine essence and cannot be distinguished without reference to the other persons. This unity of essence is reflected in the Trinity's unity of operation. When God acts to create or save, all persons of the Trinity act together in a way that mirrors the order of the relations. The Son proceeds from the Father and the Spirit from the Father and

gift of love: just as God is one substance that has the relations of three persons inherent in it, so the Trinity's one operation of salvation uniting humankind to God mirrors the order of those substantial relations. This takes place according to two dynamics, Rougé argues, both present in the Eucharist: the logic of the Incarnation and the logic of grace or the gift of the Spirit. These are not rivals, but they are carried together by the logic of the Trinity.[3] The logic of the Trinitarian relations forms the logic of the Trinitarian missions, these being the Incarnation and the gift of the Spirit, which reach a peak in the Eucharist.

This chapter builds on this volume's previous accounts of William's mystical and Trinitarian theology, focusing on how that theology shapes his thought on the Eucharist by examining William's understanding of particular questions in the Eucharistic theology of his day, such as how the body and blood of Christ are present under the appearance of bread and wine and the significance of Eucharistic reception, two areas to which William made significant theological contributions. I draw on Rougé's definitive treatment of William's Eucharistic theology to give an account of William's thought on the Eucharist from his early treatise, *De sacramento altaris* (*On the Sacrament of the Altar*), to his last, the *Epistola ad fratres de Monte Dei* (*Epistola aurea*) (*Letter to the Brethren at Mont Dieu* [the *Golden Epistle*]). At the same time, I explore further the arguments of Bouyer and Rougé regarding the Trinitarian nature of William's Eucharistic theology.[4]

How does Trinitarian logic inform William's arguments for the need for Christ's body and soul to be present in the Eucharist, arguments that parallel his understanding of the necessity of Christ's presence in the Incarnation? In both the Incarnation and the Eucharist, Christ becomes present in the way necessary for incorporating human beings into the life of the Trinity. The necessity of Christ's bodily and spiritual presence, in turn, drives William's argument on the metaphysics of that presence. However, the Trinitarian dimensions of his Eucharistic theology become most visible in his theology of bodily and spiritual Eucharistic reception, including spiritual reception through meditation on

---

Son. Therefore, salvation comes by a gift of the Son and, through the Son, a gift of the Spirit. Those who are saved are drawn to the Father, through the Son, and in the Spirit. This Trinitarian logic shapes the logic of the missions of the Son and Spirit, including their work in the Eucharist. For a detailed analysis, see David N. Bell's chapter in this volume, pp. 67–92.

3 Matthieu Rougé, *Doctrine et experience de l'eucharistie chez Guillaume de Saint-Thierry* (Paris: Beauchesne, 1999), 304.

4 Bouyer, *The Cistercian Heritage*, 108–09, 118–19. Connections between the Trinity and the Eucharist are also present in Isaac of Stella and Baldwin of Forde. See also Nathaniel Peters, "The Trinitarian Dimensions of Cistercian Eucharistic Theology," Ph.D. diss., Boston College, Boston, MA, 2017.

the Passion or the Mass. In both, the faithful are joined to the members of the Trinity and participate by grace in their relations. They are bound to the Son in the Spirit, making them part of the Son's offering of himself to the Father. Unity with Christ in the Spirit also makes them part of the body of Christ, the Church, and gives them a foretaste of that union with God that will be experienced fully only in the beatific vision. William's use of imagery of a kiss, based on the Song of Songs, ties together each theme: Trinity, Incarnation, Eucharist, Church, and eschatology.

2   Why Christ's Physical Body Must be Present in the Eucharist

William of Saint-Thierry's thought on the Eucharist first appears in an early treatise as a *Letter to Rupert of Deutz* in response to Rupert's *De officiis*, which Paul Verdeyen dates to 1126 or shortly thereafter.[5] While William writes as one monk to another, he also writes as a man who attended the schools and was formed there. His primary critique of Rupert is that he makes use of ambiguous vocabulary, the kind of reproach made by someone who had been a student in the schools and learned dialectic, to someone who had not.[6] William begins his letter to Rupert with compliments, and his tone remains friendly throughout. Yet there is a problem he has with Rupert's treatise, one mole he sees on its otherwise pretty face:[7] the separation Rupert makes between the body of sacrifice offered on the altar and the body of the Lord that was crucified and now reigns in heaven. When William reads *De officiis*, therefore, he questions whether Rupert holds that the human body of Christ is truly present in the sacrament.

William relates two of Rupert's arguments for such a separation. First, because the body of sacrifice that is offered in the Eucharist does not have the

---

5   Paul Verdeyen, "Introduction," in *Guillelmi a Sancto Theodorico Omnia Opera: Opera Didactica et Spiritualia*, CCCM 88 (Turnhout: Brepols, 2003), 22. For alternative dating of this letter to 1112–1114, see John van Engen, "Rupert of Deutz and William of St. Thierry," *Revue bénédictine* 93 (1983): 327–36.

6   Jean Châtillon, "William of Saint Thierry, Monasticism and the Schools: Rupert of Deutz, Abelard, and William of Conches," in *William, Abbot of St. Thierry: A Colloquium at the Abbey of St. Thierry*, CS 94 (Kalamazoo, MI: Cistercian Publications, 1987), 165, 169.

7   *Letter to Rupert* (Ep Rup), "in facie pulchri operis naeuum unum," CCCM 88:47 (ln. 8–9). All English translations of Ep Rup and *De sacramento altaris* are my own. An English translation of Ep Rup and Sac alt is in progress: William of Saint-Thierry, *Letter to Rupert of Deutz, On the Sacrament of the Altar, and On the Errors of William of Conches*, trans. with intro. F. Tyler Sergent and Nathaniel Peters, CF 82 (Collegeville, MN: Cistercian Publications, forthcoming).

characteristics of a living body (life, sense, mobility), it is not the body of the Lord.[8] Second, the body of the Lord contains animal and spiritual life. The animal life is engaged with the senses, while spiritual life is what gives the wisdom and grace of Christ in the Eucharistic sacrifice.[9] The spiritual life, then, is present in the body of sacrifice apart from the animal life, "as the light of the sun is apart from its heat in the body of the moon."[10] But the animal life, which is not needed for conveying grace and does not visibly appear, remains absent. Although Rupert puts the first argument in the mouth of an adversary—which William does not acknowledge in his response—he more clearly adopts the second argument as his own, more nuanced view.

In response to the first of these claims, William argues that the Eucharist operates in a manner analogous to the miracle at the wedding feast at Cana. As he turned water into wine, the Word of God, operating invisibly through the prayers of the Eucharist, truly transforms the substance of bread into the substance of his body. At Cana, the water visibly became wine, but the appearance of bread remains in the Eucharist because of the horror that would result from eating human flesh, as Ambrose said.[11] Moreover, William continues, this teaching is confirmed in the recent condemnation of Berengar of Tours, whose theory of impanation argued that the body of the Lord becomes present in the bread, even though it remains bread at the same time.[12] And finally, he concludes, Scripture itself rejects the idea that Christ's body is not at all sacrificed in the Eucharist, as is apparent from those who depart from Christ when he teaches this in John 6.[13] The body of sacrifice must be nothing less than the body of the Lord.

In addition, Rupert must be more specific about what he means by "animal life." According to the common sense of scripture, soul (*anima*), body, and spirit (*spiritus*) exist in a person. When the soul and body serve the spirit, that person's life is said to be spiritual. When the spirit serves the body and soul, it is said to be animal, and those who live an animal life do not receive the things of God. To say that the body of Christ lives by animal life, then, is impermissible. But if we narrow the sense of "animal life" to that life by which all animal bodies live, then whoever says that the body of Christ after the resurrection has no animal life, even though he seeks to bring glory to Christ, destroys the hope

---

8   Ep Rup, CCCM 88:47 (ln. 13–18).
9   Ep Rup, CCCM 88:47–48 (ln. 19–28).
10   Ep Rup, "Haec autem uita spiritualis sic est in corpore sacrificii absque eius uita animali, quomodo lux solis absque calore eius in corpore lunae," CCCM 88:47 (ln. 26–28).
11   Ep Rup, CCCM 88:47 (ln. 29–38).
12   Ep Rup, CCCM 88:47 (ln. 39–47).
13   Ep Rup, CCCM 88:47 (ln. 39–47).

that Christ's human body was resurrected, which in turn destroys the hope
that the members of the body of which he is the head might be as well. Moreover, suggesting that the body of Christ on the altar does not have human life
within it goes against Rupert's own words, when he argues that the one who
receives the visible bread of the Eucharist without receiving the invisible bread
of Christ's body by faith, separates life from the one who was vivified and is for
this reason "guilty of the body and blood of the Lord." Therefore, Rupert must
clarify what he means by the body of sacrifice and the animal life of Christ not
being present in it.[14]

In addition to his *Letter to Rupert*, William penned a Eucharistic treatise of
his own, *On the Sacrament of the Altar*, focused on the clarification of potential ambiguities, this time with respect to the writings of the Fathers. Different
sententiae of the Fathers seem to make conflicting claims about the presence
of Christ in the Eucharist and its significance. William structures his work as
a treatise on how to read these *sententiae* and resolve any apparent conflicts
based on the Fathers' understanding of the Eucharist, as he sees it.[15] The work
does act as a manual for exegesis, but it is more than that. Indeed, *On the Sacrament of the Altar* and the *Letter to Rupert* argue that just as Christ became
present by taking on human flesh once in history for the salvation of the world,
so he becomes present now in the Eucharist under the visible species of bread
and wine for the salvation of the world. Since Christ came to unite himself
to the whole person, body and soul, he needed to take on both in history and
must become present in his full humanity now on the altar.

William begins this argument for the necessity of Christ's bodily presence
in the Eucharist by writing that "just as the necessity of human salvation made
him be present where it was beneficial [in the Incarnation], so it also made his
body be present in this [Eucharistic] way where it is beneficial."[16] Since Christ
needed to be crucified in order to redeem human nature from death, he had

---

14   Ep Rup, CCCM 88:47 (ln. 109–135).
15   Déchanet argues that although William's method of listing patristic *sententiae* in Sac alt
      resembles Abelard's, *Sic et Non* was not yet composed by 1128, the latest date likely for
      Sac alt. Ergo, he is unlikely to have taken his method from Abelard. In the decades since
      Déchanet's work, however, scholars have determined that Abelard wrote *Sic et Non* in
      multiple recensions, the earliest of which may date from the 1120s and 1130s. Thus, it is
      possible that William is trying to demonstrate a better way to account for apparent dis-
      crepancies in the Fathers than Abelard's. See Jean-Marie Déchanet, *Guillaume de Saint-
      Thierry: L'homme et son œuvre* (Bruges: Éditions Charles Beyaert, 1942), 166 and Constant
      J. Mews, "On Dating the Works of Peter Abelard," *Archives d'histoire doctrinale et littéraire
      du moyen âge* 52 (1984): 73–134.
16   Sac alt, III, "Sicut enim exigit necessitas salutis humanae ut adsit ubi opus est, sic etiam
      exigit ut sic adsit corpus eius sicut opus est," CCCM 88:59 (ln. 3–4).

to take on that human nature in such a way that it was visible and could suffer and be crucified. After the crucifixion and resurrection, Christ need not appear among us visibly, but his presence is still necessary for salvation, now in the form of food that sustains us and prepares us to share in his life:

> And as by the communal food that a person desires so that he might live, he reaches that life by which one truly lives only through that food, so he only reaches this life by this food. For this food was prepared for bringing the soul to eternal life, not for prolonging the catastrophes of this miserable life....
>
> Therefore, this way is that by which the presence of his body is necessary for us for salvation and life, namely that it might be eaten by us, having become our daily bread.[17]

William presses the point further when he writes that Christ became incarnate "so that his flesh would be eaten."[18] This means that the Eucharist is one of the reasons for the Incarnation, like the crucifixion, and plays a central role in the economy of salvation. It is, in a sense, a continuation of Christ's presence on earth and action for salvation. Hence, William uses the same verb *fio* to describe Christ becoming incarnate and appearing under the species of bread and wine.[19] In both cases, the Word becomes flesh, first visible flesh and then invisible flesh. With this in mind, we can see the Eucharistic overtones in a passage from his *Expositio super Cantica Canticorum* (*Exposition on the Song of Songs*), where he writes that "the Word of God 'in the form of God,' born inseparably of God, comes to be [*fit*] in the Bride in what he does [*facit*] in the Bride; and he comes to be [*fit*] not in an unlike manner. For whatever God the Father does [*facit*], this the Son also does [*facit*] in a like manner."[20]

---

17 Sac alt, III, "Et sicut communi cibo id appetitur ut uiuatur, sic ad eam uitam qua uere uiuitur, solummodo per hunc cibum peruenitur. Cibus enim hic ad uitam aeternam animae conferendam collatus est, non ad ruinas sustentandas huius miserae uitae, quae uapor est ad modicum parens. Hic ergo modus est quo necessaria nobis est ad salutem et uitam praesentia corporis eius, uidelicet ut manducetur a nobis, factus panis noster cotidianus," CCCM 88:60 (ln. 17–23).

18 Sac alt, III, "Oportebat autem ut, sicut cum necessaria nobis fuit uisibilis eius praesentia, inuisibile in suis uisibile factum est in nostris Verbum caro factum sic cum res exigit salutis nostrae ut manducetur caro eius, quod non est ipsa caro in natura sua, fiat in aliena, manducabilis scilicet," CCCM 88:60 (ln. 24–28).

19 Cf. Sac alt, III and IV, CCCM 88:60 (ln. 25–30), CCCM 88:61 (ln. 8).

20 *Expositio super Cantica Canticorum* (Cant), XXVIII.137, "Sic et Verbum Dei, in forma Dei natum de Deo inseparabiliter, fit in sponsa in eo quod facit in sponsa; et fit indissimiliter, quia quaecumque facit Deus Pater, haec et Filius facit similiter," CCCM 87:96–97 (ln. 55–58).

"Therefore," William concludes in his Eucharistic treatise, "by this worthiness and piety he deigned to lift the lost sheep on his shoulders, that is, to assume our corrupt nature in the unity of his person, and now in the same way, taking the earthly substance of bread in the strength of the divine power to which he is near, in, and through all things (since he desired that it be possible), he changes that substance into the truth of his flesh."[21]

In both the Eucharist and the Incarnation, the flesh of Christ serves as a medium for union with him and the Father. Rougé writes that Christ's humanity is to his divinity what the *sacramentum* is to the *res*.[22] The Eucharist, for William, is a particular instance of the principle that we are reconciled to God and receive beatitude through the flesh of Christ.[23] With our humanity joined to Christ's, we enter into his union with the Father. In Rougé's words, the flesh of the sacrament and of Jesus unites us to him so that we can enter into glory and, in him, pass into the Father.[24] This is all the more true of Christ's body, which as *res et sacramentum* serves as the flesh through which we receive the

---

ET: *Exposition on the Song of Songs*, trans. Mother Columba Hart, CF 6 (Kalamazoo, MI: Cistercian Publications, 1970), 113 (§141). Rougé comments, "Ce '*fit*' évoque immanquablement la 'confection' eucharistique du corps du Christ, qui est bel et bien 'fait' chaque fois que le sacrement de l'autel est célébré selon les formes prescrites, mais qui n'est 'fait pour' les fidèles que lorsqu'ils communient avec foi," Rougé, *Doctrine et experience*, 306. This connection to confection does not obscure the more verifiable connection between the Eucharist and the Incarnation in William's use of *fio*.

21   Sac alt, III, "Qua igitur dignatione et pietate dignatus est in humeros suos leuare ouem perditam, id est in unitatem personae suae assumere corruptam naturam nostram, eadem nunc terrenam substantiam panis suscipiens, in uirtute diuinae potentiae cui in omnibus et per omnia subest cum uoluerit posse, transmutat in ueritatem carnis suae," CCCM 88:60–61 (ln. 32–37).

22   Rougé, *Doctrine et experience*, 280.

23   *Expositio super Epistolam ad Romanos* (Rom), III.5:7-11, "NON SOLVM AVTEM, SED ET GLORIAMVR IN DEO PER DOMINVM NOSTRVM IESVM CHRISTVM, non iam in sacramentis, sed in ipsa re omnium sacramentorum; non in mysteriis, sed in ipsa luce manifestae ueritatis; quia, etsi nouit Iesum secundum carnem, sed nunc iam non nouit. Per carnem tamen transit in Deum, per dominum nostrum Iesum Christum; PER QVEM NVNC interim ACCIPIMVS RECONCILIATIONEM, ibi cum eo habituri beatitudinis unitatem," CCCM 86:65. ET: *Exposition on the the Epistle to the Romans*, trans. John Baptist Hasbrouk, CF 27 (Kalamazoo, MI: Cistercian Publications, 1980), 96: "'**Not only so; but also we glory in God, through our Lord Jesus Christ**, no longer in sacraments but in the very reality of all the sacraments, not in mysteries but in the light of revealed truth.' Because, even if that man knew Jesus according to the flesh, now he no longer knows him thus [2 Cor 5:16]. He has passed through the flesh into God, **through our Lord Jesus Christ, by whom we now** in the meantime **receive reconciliation**. There with him we shall have blessed union." Boldface in original.

24   Rougé, *Doctrine et experience*, 281.

res of union with Christ in the Spirit. The metaphysics of Christ's real presence on the altar is analogous to the unity of his humanity and his divinity.[25] In both cases, Christ's humanity is the medium of spiritual union between those joined to it and the Father. Those who receive that humanity in the Eucharist are joined to Christ and with Christ to the Father.

As we will see in greater detail, this union takes place in the Holy Spirit. In receiving Christ in the Eucharist with love, the faithful receive his Spirit. As William writes in *De natura et dignitate amoris* (*On the Nature and Dignity of Love*), the Eucharistic recipient "eats and drinks the Body and Blood of his Redeemer ... and while eating it he is transformed into the nature of the food he eats. For to eat the Body of Christ is nothing other than to be made the Body of Christ and the temple of the Holy Spirit."[26] The Spirit prepares this temple by hallowing the sacraments and is the person of the Trinity who sanctifies external, material things so that they can convey interior, spiritual realities. The Spirit purifies the soul through the outward washing with water in baptism, and refreshes it with incorruptible food when it consumes the corruptible species of the Eucharist.[27] Hence it would seem that for William, the Holy Spirit enables Christ to be truly present in the sacrament of the altar. The Spirit makes Christ present so that through that presence, we might receive more of the Spirit, love God better, and thereby, share more in the divine life.

In summary, William's primary concern in his letter to Rupert—also present in other works—is that the human body of Christ is truly present in the Eucharist. This presence occurs in a manner analogous to the events of salvation history because it is one such event. The Eucharist is a miracle effected by the same Christ who took flesh, turned water into wine, and communed with his disciples after the resurrection.[28] This takes place according to the same economy in which the Word of God takes on human nature so that he may join his humanity to ours in a union of love, which is the Holy Spirit, and thereby

---

25   Hence debates about the Eucharist are not so much about what Christ did before, but who he is and how he saves us now (Rougé, *Doctrine et experience*, 278–79).

26   *De natura et dignitate amoris* (Nat am), 38, "Manducat et bibit corpus et sanguinem Redemptoris sui, manna caeleste, panem angelorum, panem sapientiae; et manducans transformatur in naturam cibi quem manducat. Corpus enim Christi manducare nichil est aliud quam corpus Christi effici, et templum Spiritus sancti," CCCM 88:206. ET: *The Nature and Dignity of Love*, trans. Thomas X. Davis, CF 30 (Kalamazoo, MI: Cistercian Publications, 1981), 100.

27   *Speculum fidei* (Spec fid), 62–64, CCCM 89A:105–106. ET: *The Mirror of Faith*, trans. Thomas X. Davis, CF 15 (Kalamazoo, MI: Cistercian Publications 1979), 49–50 (§20–21).

28   Rougé, *Doctrine et experience*, 278.

draw us into union with the Father. As William later writes in *Speculum fidei* (*The Mirror of Faith*), God establishes the sacraments to lead our inmost being to his inmost being through the outer being, the body and its senses. He adds, "Through the workings of the physical sacraments he gradually incites in us spiritual grace. It is for this purpose that he humbled himself to fellowship with our humanity: that he might make us partakers of his divinity."[29] Christ became present in flesh in history for the same reason he becomes present in flesh on the altar: the deification of bodies and souls. The two doctrines go hand in hand, and William's understanding of Christ's first coming forms his understanding of Christ's Eucharistic presence.

3   Metaphysics of Presence

William's understanding of the metaphysics of Christ's Eucharistic presence is also marked by this continuity with the way in which the incarnate Christ was present on earth. In the incarnation, human and divine natures united in such a way that "neither divine things could be acted on without humanity nor human things without God, and through this unity even in the days of his flesh Christ the man could do divine things."[30] After the Resurrection, Christ's glorified body passed through walls and appeared to his disciples. This serves as a metaphor of the Incarnation itself, William explains, in which "he proceeded from the bridal chamber of the virgin's womb to run the way of the human dispensation with the doors of nature closed."[31] Or, as he discusses at length, consider Christ's entombment. Because of the union of humanity and divinity in him, Christ could be in multiple places at the same time. In his body, he was in the tomb; in his spirit, he was liberating hell; and in his deity, he was sitting

---

29 Spec Fid, 63, "Omnibus enim interioribus nostris interior Deus in exterioribus nostris, hoc est in sensibus corporis, exteriora nobis condidit sacramenta, per quae interiora nostra ad sua introduceret interiora, per corporalium sacramentorum operationem paulatim suscitans in nobis gratiam spiritualem; qui etiam ad hoc inclinauerat se ad consortium humanitatis nostrae, ut participes nos efficeret diuinitatis suae," CCCM 89A:106. ET: *The Mirror of Faith*, 49 (§20).

30 Sac alt, II, "Et si natura carnis ex quo illi naturae summae unita est, in tanta unitate ei ab ipso conceptu uirginis est conserta, ut nec sine homine diuina nec sine Deo agerentur humana, et per hanc unitatem etiam in diebus carnis suae homo Christus potuit diuina...," CCCM 88:56 (ln. 30–33).

31 Sac alt, II, "Nam quod de humanitate eius, per resurrectionem glorificata, saecularis philosophiae ratiocinationibus uidetur insusceptibile, ut clausis ad discipulos ianuis intraret, etiam passibilis et mortalis exercuit, dum de thalamo uteri uirginalis ad currendam uiam dispensationis humanae clausis naturae ianuis processit," CCCM 88:56 (ln. 36–40).

at the right hand of the Father.[32] In these miracles, divine power allows human flesh to deviate from the normal created order according to a particular act of God. These acts take place according to the law of creating nature, i.e. God, not the law of created nature. This should not be seen as a deviation from the order that God instituted, "since it is the nature of created nature to obey all laws of creating nature," especially in the case of Christ's human nature, which was joined to the Word through which all that has been made was made.[33] Miracles are not violations of that order, but suspensions of its normal processes by acts of divine power to accomplish salvation.

Likewise, during the Eucharist, Christ's humanity and divinity become present by an act of divine power that suspends the normal course of the laws of creation. William explains by arguing that through the prayers of the rite, a real, substantial change takes place whereby the bread and wine on the altar become the body and blood of Christ. In the Incarnation, as William has written, Christ's humanity and divinity are joined such that they remain distinct, but predicate different attributes to the same subject. In an analogous— but not at all identical—way, when the substantial change takes place in the Eucharist, the accidents of bread and wine remain. As we have already seen, William uses the same verb to describe Christ's appearance on the altar as his appearance in history: *fio*. Thus, his body becomes (*fiat*) edible and able to be carried, essential attributes for its purpose as the food of regeneration. But by a miracle that, like the miracle of the incarnation, runs contrary to secular philosophy, the accidents do not inhere in the substance. Christ's body may appear white and round under the form of bread, and it may be near whiteness and roundness, but it does not actually have them in it.[34] The integrity of Christ's substance remains together with the integrity of the bread's accidents. As the humanity and divinity are joined without mixture in the Incarnation, so these are joined without inherence.

---

32   Sac alt, II, CCCM 88:59 (ln. 111–112).

33   Sac alt, II, "Sic ergo constat in diuersis locis uno horae momento esse posse corpus Christi, sed lege creatricis naturae, non creatae. Cum autem naturae creatae natura sit creatricis naturae legibus in omnibus obedire, si haec aliquando pacta sua resoluenda illi permittit qui ea instituit et ordinat, non debet uideri errare uel deuiare ab ordine suo, maxime in illa natura quae in unitate personae coniuncta est illi Verbo, per quod facta est omnis facta natura, et praeter quod non posset aliquo modo esse, nisi, sicut dicit Euangelista, *in ipso uita esset*," CCCM 88:58 (ln. 80–89).

34   Sac alt, IV, CCCM 88:61 (ln. 1–16). Ten years later, in his *Disputatio adversus Petrum Abaelardum*, William offers this argument against Abelard's idea that the Eucharistic accidents remain in the air after substantial change (see Rougé, *Doctrine et experience*, 85–86).

William probes still further, asking whether the Eucharistic change not only suspends the rules of nature, but breaks them as well. He determines that it bends them, but does not break them completely, according to Boethius's understanding of the process of substantial change in *De persona et duabus naturis*. There Boethius writes that things that can be transformed into each other must have the same material. For example, air cannot be changed into stone or grass, but wine can become water if a drop of it can be mixed in a much larger quantity.[35] As a result, William notes, "the body of the Lord has the common subject of one material with the bread. In as much as the body of the Lord can both be generated and die, it seems to have a common matter with this earthly bread. In as much as bread truly has common matter with the body of Christ, it has the possibility of being transmuted into it, and when this happens, it is not withdrawn altogether from nature."[36] For William and Boethius, the change between bread and body would be natural in the sense that it is possible according to the ordinary laws of nature. That such a change actually takes place and that the accidents of the bread remain without inhering in the body is possible by the power of Christ "by which Jesus Christ the man is one with God the Father."[37] And it is Christ in his representative, the priest, who effects this change through the words of the Mass. In short, the Eucharistic change in no way violates the laws of nature, but by the miraculous power of God surpasses them for the sake of the economy of salvation.

William echoes these arguments in his *Letter to Rupert* where he writes that irrespective of what Rupert means by "body of sacrifice," what he says about it is not fitting for the body of the Lord. That body is Jesus himself in his body, William argues, which is both available to the faithful on the altar and at the right hand of the Father. It is fully human in all things, even if it has a superhuman glory. If by "body of sacrifice" Rupert means the visible species of bread,

---

35   Boethius, *De persona et duabus naturis* (*Contra Eutychen et Nestorium*) 6, in *Opuscula sacra*, (eds.) Claudio Moreschini, trans. Alain Galonnier, 2 vols. (Leuven, 2007–13); Sac alt, V, CCCM 88:62 (ln. 11–16). As Rougé notes, William owes much of his philosophical vocabulary to Boethius (Rougé, *Doctrine et experience*, 34, n. 1).

36   Sac alt, V, "Corpus autem Domini cum pane unius habet commune materiae subiectum. In quantum enim corpus Domini et generari potuit et mori, communem cum pane isto terreno uidetur sortiri materiam. In quantum uero panis cum corpore Christi communem habet materiam, possibile habet in illud transmutari, nec cum hoc fit, a natura usquequaque receditur," CCCM 88:63 (ln. 35–40).

37   Sac alt, V, "Si enim multitudini maris modicam uini guttam in suam transformare naturam, in tantum ut de ea nichil penitus uideatur residuum, est possibile multitudini uel magnitudini uirtutis Christi, qua cum Deo Patre unum est homo Christus Iesus, omnipotenti Creatoris actione et obedientissima creaturae passione panem in suum transmutare corpus erit impossibile?" CCCM 88:63 (ln. 40–46).

then obviously that lacks the characteristics of living things. For though the substance of bread changes into that of Christ's body, the accidents remain. Though this is contrary to the law of nature, it is not outside the power of God, who created the world.[38] Again, William appeals to Christ's glorified body after the resurrection. We see in Scripture that the resurrected Christ could pass through closed doors into the room where his disciples gathered, then distribute himself to them in the Eucharist. In a similar way, Christ in his body is at the Father's right hand, sacrificed on the altar, and distributed to the faithful.[39] This reflection serves as a springboard to a further reflection on the nature of Christ's Eucharistic presence. The Eucharist is not like a magician's trick, William writes, in which the eyes are deceived about the reality of the thing before them. Rather, the substance of bread goes away and the substance of Christ's body becomes present under its accidents. The accidents of bread do not inhere in the substance of the body as accidents normally do, but they remain so that they can convey the substance of Christ's body to the faithful.[40]

The point of these reflections is clear. Because they are both part of the Son's mission, the Incarnation and the Eucharist share the same Trinitarian logic and other patterns of logic, even down to the particular ways in which Christ makes himself present. Both are part of the one mission of the Son for salvation. As Rougé puts it,

> Just as it is the *res* of human salvation that determines the mode of the presence of the Lord that is necessary from now on, so it is the *res* of the sacrament that demarcates the transformation that the species must know. The Word, in the occurrence, does not maintain the substance of bread except insofar as necessary "according to the rite of the mystery, so that it can be touched and tasted."[41] What the ritual and liturgical economy needs so that the flesh of Christ can be eaten, is that the nature by which the Word makes itself food could be seized in a sensible manner. These are the exterior characteristics, the accidents of bread and wine that, alone, are required by the reality of the mystery.[42]

---

38   Ep Rup, CCCM 88:49 (ln. 58–75).

39   Ep Rup, CCCM 88:49–50 (ln. 75–84).

40   Ep Rup, CCCM 88:50 (ln. 92–101).

41   Sac alt, IV, "...ut secundum mysterii ritum tractabile foat et gustabile ex illa natura, quod non erat ex sua," CCCM 88:61 (ln. 8–9).

42   Rougé, *Doctrine et experience*, 47: "De même que c'est la 'res salutis humanae' qui détermine le mode de présence du Seigneur désormais nécessaire, de même, c'est la *res* du sacrement qui délimite la transformation que l'espèce droit connaître. Le Verbe, en l'occurrence, ne conserve de la substance du pain que ce qui est nécessaire 'pour, selon le

Then and now, God sometimes suspends the normal laws of creation for the sake of redemption. While incarnate, Christ performed miracles to show his divinity and the reality of his new life after the resurrection. This same logic is at work in the Eucharist, in which the relationship between substance and accidents is suspended so that Christ can become present and be joined to the faithful under the accidents of bread and wine received as food for the salvation of their bodies and souls.

4   Bodily Reception of the Eucharist

Like many medieval thinkers, William distinguishes between physically or bodily receiving the Eucharistic elements and spiritually receiving them by being joined to Christ in charity. Both the virtuous and vicious alike can receive bodily, but only the virtuous can receive both bodily and spiritually to their benefit. William places greater emphasis on spiritual reception, going so far as to say that it alone suffices for salvation, but only if necessity compels one not to receive bodily.[43] Still, because our souls and bodies must both be joined to Christ, they must both receive the Eucharist. Each doorpost of the house, he writes, must be marked by the blood of the lamb, and just as sin entered the human race by one food, so it must be cured by the antidote of another food.[44] But William's concerns are more than tropological or exegetical. For just as spiritual reception conforms the soul to Christ through the purification of love, so bodily reception makes the body more like Christ's glorified body. Unlike regular food, which becomes part of the body that ingests it, the Eucharistic

---

rite du mystère, pouvoir être touché et goûté.' Ce dont l'économie rituelle et liturgique a besoin pour que la chair du Christ soit mangée, c'est que la nature par laquelle le Verbe se fait nourriture puisse être saisie de manière sensible. Ce sont les caractéristiques extérieurs, les accidents, du pain et du vin qui, seuls, sont requis par la réalité du mystère."

43   William quotes Fulgentius of Ruspe in this regard who writes that one is made a part of the body of Christ by baptism (Sac alt, IX, CCCM 88:70–71 [ln. 11–18]). For the original, see *Letter* 12.26 (PL 65:392; CCSL 91:380–381). Therefore, those who die before they can receive the sacrament are not cut off from the body of Christ or the benefits of the Eucharist.

44   Sac alt, IX, "Non est tamen negligenda sacramenti perceptio, quia uterque domus nostrae postis, id est corpus et anima, signandus est Agni sanguine, ne ab exterminatore uastetur, et ne flagellum appropinquet tabernaculo nostro. Sed et natura nostrae carnis, quae in primo parente suo cibo uitiata illicito, originali propagine, peccato et poena peccati tota erat infecta et morti aeternae et corruptioni contradita, alterius cibi curanda erat antidoto, sicut pulcherrime Christianus poeta dicit Sedulius: Qui pereuntem hominem uetiti dulcedine pomi / Instauras meliore cibo, potu que sacrati / Sanguinis infusum depellis ab angue uenenum," CCCM 88:71 (ln. 19–29); Cf. Sedulius, *Paschale Carmen* I.70–72, CSEL 10:21.

meal "turns our body into its nature, and prepares and joins it to the future resurrection and perpetual incorruption."[45]

William then pushes this logic to a startling conclusion: "[the Eucharist] turns our body into its nature ... and it is in us, and where it was, namely at the right hand of the Father.... Therefore, the same Christ is in us through the flesh, and we are in him, while this, which we receive, is with him in God. Therefore, this is the cause of our life, for we have Christ remaining in us carnal people through the flesh—in us who will conquer through him by this condition, by which he lives through the Father."[46] In the physical reception of the Eucharist, the body of Christ is both in the recipient and with God in heaven. This unites the recipient to God and prepares the recipient to join Christ at the end time, but also means that Christ is alive in the recipient as he is alive in the Father.[47] In other words, there is a two-fold participation in the Trinitarian relations in physical reception. The recipient stands with Christ—conformed by reception to Christ's body—in relationship to the Father, and at the same time, stands in a manner analogous to the Father in relationship to Christ, because Christ now also abides in the recipient.

5   Spiritual Reception of the Eucharist

This strong argument for the necessity of Christ's presence in the Eucharist and the physical reception of that presence seems to conflict with William's more famous theology of spiritual Eucharistic reception, especially in his later

---

45   Sac alt, IX, "Quae, ut multa breuiter concludam, non est aliud quam ponere corda in uirtute eius, et rem ducere in opus et affectum. Iam que ipse rei ordo uidetur exigere, ut etiam de corporali aliqua disseramus. Corporalis autem manducatio est corpus Domini corporaliter percipere, siue digne siue indigne, siue ad uitam siue ad mortem. Licet enim illa sufficiat, si sic ineuitabile cogat necessarium, tamen et haec non est omittenda," CCCM 88:70 (ln. 4–10).

46   Sac alt, IX, "Hic est cibus qui non uadit in corpus, quia nequaquam, sicut alii cibi, in naturam uertitur corporis, sed corpus nostrum in suam uertit naturam, et futurae resurrectioni et perpetuae incorruptioni illud praeparans et coaptans, et in nobis est, et ubi erat, scilicet in dextera Patris. Sic enim naturalis per sacramentum proprietas perfectae sacramentum fit unitatis, cum haec accepta atque hausta id efficiunt, ut et nos in Christo, et Christus in nobis sit. Est ergo in nobis ipse per carnem, et sumus in eo, dum se cum hoc, quod nos sumus, in Deo est. Haec ergo uitae nostrae causa est, quod in nobis carnalibus per carnem Christum manentem habemus; uicturis nobis per eum ea conditione, qua uiuit ille per Patrem," CCCM 88:71–72 (ln. 34–45).

47   Paul Verdeyen, *La Théologie mystique de Guillaume de Saint-Thierry* (Paris: FAC-éditions, 1990), 170.

works. Yet that theology begins in *De sacramento altaris*. There William asks an important question: What makes the Eucharist necessary food for eternal life? He answers with the following argument. Bodily reception alone is not enough for salvation, since Scripture warns against such presumption and gives examples of those who have received badly, to a bad end. Moreover, the Eucharist is not for the nourishment of the body but of the soul. The one who receives it seeks more of the life of the soul. As the life of the soul is the body, so God is the life of the soul. Since God is love, the life of the rational soul is the love of God. The Eucharist exists to increase our love for God, "who is his love itself and who is possessed where he is loved."[48]

William cites Augustine's *Confessions* and uses explicitly Augustinian language to describe the way in which the Eucharist augments and purifies our love. This love is a matter of turning from the world and the devil to God.[49] Christ's incarnation makes him like us so that we can trust in him, and his embrace of death in the face of the fallen angels' spite draws us to God "in chains of love."[50] Given that the Holy Spirit is the love of the Father and Son, these passages are pneumatological. They describe a reception of the Holy Spirit and the healing and ordering effect that that has on the soul and its own loves. We also see these Trinitarian dynamics present in Augustine's sermons on the Gospel of John, which William uses in formulating his Eucharistic theology. In Sermon 27 on the bread of life discourse in John 6, Augustine instructs his flock that they are members of the body of Christ, which is animated and held together by the Holy Spirit in the same way that the soul animates a human body. He tells them to receive the Eucharist not only sacramentally but also to "eat and drink to the extent of a participation in the Spirit, staying in the Lord's body as members, and being energized by his Spirit...."[51] Elaborating how the Spirit does this, Augustine writes,

---

48   Sac alt, VI, "Vt igitur ille ametur, qui est ipse amor suus et qui habetur ubi amatur, ad hoc enutrire nos debet cibus iste. Quicquid enim Redemptor noster in carne fecit, ob hoc utique fecit, ut amaretur a nobis; non quod egeret ipse nostro amore, qui bonorum nostrorum non eget, per omnia sufficiens ipse sibi, sed quia, quos beatos facere susceperat, nisi eum amando non poterant esse beati," CCCM 88:64–65 (ln. 15–20).

49   Sac alt, VI, "Ideo quippe descenderat ad nos, ut amorem nostrum, in terrenis dispersum et putrefactum, beneficia pietatis exhibendo, in se recolligeret et in nouitatem uitae reformaret; et abstractum et emundatum a faece earum rerum, quae cum ipso pariter amari non possunt, se cum sursum leuaret," CCCM 88:65 (ln. 25–29). See Augustine, *Confessions* VII.21, 27 (CCSL 27:111).

50   Sac alt, VI, "Sic enim, ut ait propheta Osee, adtrahendi eramus *in uinculis caritatis*," CCCM 88:66 (ln. 53–54).

51   Augustine, *Iohannis Euangelium Tractatus* 27, "sed usque ad spiritus participationem manducemus et bibamus, ut in domini corpore tamquam membra maneamus, ut eius

Now we abide in him when we are his members, while he abides in us when we are his temple. But for us to be his members, we have to be bonded together by unity. What makes unity bond us together? What else but charity? And where does the charity of God come from? Question the apostle. *The charity of God,* he says, *has been poured out in our hearts through the Holy Spirit who has been given to us* (Rom 5:5). So then, *the Spirit gives life;* it is the Spirit after all who makes sure that the members are alive, unless they are in the body which the spirit itself animates.[52]

For Augustine and William, the spiritual fruit of the Eucharist is a gift of the Holy Spirit that comes through receiving Jesus into oneself.

This theme appears again in *Meditatio* 10, where William writes that picturing the Passion of Christ teaches us to love God, the highest good.[53] Our love for the Father comes through the way and door of the Son. The one who seeks to ascend to God and desires

to offer gifts and sacrifices according to the precepts of the Law ... should walk calmly and smoothly over the level of his own likeness, to a Man like himself, who tells him on the very threshold: 'I and the Father are one.' And he is forthwith gathered up to God in love through the Holy Spirit and receives God coming to him and making his abode with him, not spiritually only but corporally too, in the mystery of the holy and life-giving body and blood of our Lord Jesus Christ.[54]

---

spiritu uegetemur..." *Corpus Augustinianum Gissense,* (ed.) Cornelius Mayer (Basel: Schwabe, 1995), 27.11, 276/13–15 (CAG). ET: Edmund Hill, *Homilies on the Gospel of John (1–40)* (Hyde Park, NY: New City Press, 2009), 475.

52   *Iohannis Euangelium Tractatus,* 27.6, "Manemus autem in illo, cum sumus membra eius; manet autem ipse in nobis, cum sumus templum eius. Ut autem simus membra eius, unitas nos compaginat. Ut compaginet unitas, quae facit nisi caritas? Et caritas dei unde? Apostolum interroga. 'caritas,' inquit, 'Dei diffusa est in cordibus nostris per spiritum sanctum qui datus est nobis.' Ergo 'spiritus est qui uiuificat'; spiritus enim facit uiua membra. Nec uiua membra spiritus facit, nisi quae in corpore quod uegetat ipse spiritus, inuenerit," (CAG), 272/4–13. ET: *Homilies on the Gospel of John,* 470.

53   As Rougé puts it, "C'est bien le Christ, et non l'eucharistie, qui constitue notre trésor. Mais c'est grâce à l'eucharistie que ce trésor peut, en toute vérité, être en notre possession." Rougé, *Doctrine et experience,* 69.

54   *Meditationes* (Med) X.10, "Quid enim melius praeparatum, quid suauius potuit esse dispositum, quam quod ascensuro homini ad Deum suum offerre dona et sacrificia secundum praeceptum legis, non sit ei ascendendum per gradus ad altare eius, sed per planum similitudinis, placide et pede inoffenso, eat homo ad hominem similem sibi, in primo ingressu limine dicentem sibi: Ego et Pater unum sumus. Statim que per Spiritum sanctum affectus assumptus in Deum, et ipse Deum in semetipsum excipiat uenientem et

In receiving and loving Christ by meditating on the Passion and sacramental reception, we receive his Spirit. This reception binds us to Christ, uniting us and our loving sacrifices and works to his self-offering to the Father.

This connection between the sacrifice of Christ for redemption and the redeemed joining in that sacrifice also appears in William's *Expositio super epistolam ad Romanos* (*Exposition on the Epistle to the Romans*). In Romans 8:3–4, Paul writes, "For God has done what the law, weakened by the flesh, could not do: sending his own Son in the likeness of sinful flesh and for sin, he condemned sin in the flesh, in order that the just requirement of the law might be fulfilled in us, who walk not according to the flesh but according to the Spirit." William comments that because the infirmity of the law comes through the flesh, the only-begotten Son comes from the Father so full of grace that it overflows from him to the faithful. They receive from Christ faith, hope, and charity, the latter being poured into their hearts through the Holy Spirit.[55] The Son then joins the believer to his own self-sacrifice to the Father. Living a life of faith, hope, and love in union with the Son who offered himself on the cross is what redemption and justification entail.

Eucharistic reception plays an explicit role in this process. William writes: "[Jesus] put his faith and charity into [the believer's] heart, the saving confession of himself into his mouth, and his body and blood into his hand. In this way, he presents him to God the Father as his own, a culprit yet redeemed. With the sin of the presumer condemned and the sin of the penitent destroyed, he restored him, pleasing and acceptable, to a part in the sacrifice of his justice."[56] The Trinitarian dimensions we have already seen appear again here. Christ bestows the Spirit on the believer, which unites the believer to the Son. The Son then presents the believer to the Father, as he does his own self. The Eucharist is put forward as an important part of justification, along with the infusion of the theological virtues by the Holy Spirit. Together, they join the believer's life

---

mansionem apud eum facientem, non tantum spiritualiter sed etiam corporaliter per mysterium sancti et uiuifici corporis et sanguinis Domini nostri Iesu Christi," CCCM 89:60. ET: *On Contemplating God, Prayer, Meditations*, trans. Sr. Penelope [Lawson], CF 3 (Kalamazoo, MI: Cistercian Publications, 1970), 154–55.

55   Exp Rm, IV.Rom 8:3–4. CCCM 86:108.

56   Exp Rom, IV.8:3–4, "Ipse uero innocentis mortis suae iustitiam dans peccatori paenitenti, fidem suam et caritatem posuit ei in corde, confessionem ad salutem in ore, corpus suum et sanguinem in manu; sic que reum et redemptum suum Deo Patri repraesentans, de peccato praesumptoris damnato et destructo peccato paenitentis, placitum et acceptum eum reddidit in sacrificium iustitiae suae," CCCM 86:108. ET: *Exposition on the Epistle to the Romans*, 153.

to the Son's in sacrifice to the Father. This, William continues, is the redemption, justice, and work of God.[57]

6   Meditation, Memory, and Eucharistic Reception

Memory and meditation also play an important role in William's theology of spiritual reception. William holds strongly to Augustine's psychological analogy according to which the memory, understanding, and will serve as an image of the Father, Son, and Holy Spirit. As the Father is the source of the other persons of the Trinity, so memory is foundational to the soul's being. Yves-Anselme Baudelet outlines how memory functions as the parchment on which the stylus of the *animus* inscribes, or as a tablet of wax on which images of material objects from the corporeal senses are imprinted. The soul that wants to be the spouse of God must purify its memory by meditating on the things that will conform it to the divine image.[58] What a person remembers forms who that person is. Thus, William understands memory to be "one of the privileged places of the presence of God"[59] and even, in David Bell's words, "the latent presence of God in the soul, and (what comes to the same thing) the latent participation of the soul in God."[60]

The Eucharist is a means of receiving Christ into the soul through the memory, and Eucharistic meditation a kind of eating and drinking. Christ heaps up a great matter (*materiam*) of love in his flesh by suffering and dying out of love

---

57   Rougé summarizes the interplay between the Trinity and the Eucharist in William's theology of reception in this way. Christ gives himself to us in giving us a share of his Spirit. His food is to do the will of the Father, to live on the "substantial will" that is the Spirit. Christ never ceases to offer himself to the Father, eternally presenting to him his glorified human flesh, and he is heard because of his piety. The Spirit is himself the piety of those who worship rightly, in spirit and in truth. Rougé concludes: "Tout le 'jeu' de l'eucharistie, manifestation visible de l'humanité du Christ qui introduit dans la profondeur invisible de sa divinité, don de l'Esprit qui permet de reconnaître le Christ, don du Christ qui donne part à son Esprit, chemin vers le souvenir veritable et l'adoration du Père, tout ce jeu, tout ce mouvement, rend témoinage à la circumincession des Personnes divines, au mouvement et à l'unité de leur amour." Rougé, *Doctrine et experience*, 304.

58   Yves-Anselme Baudelet, *L'Expérience spirituelle selon Guillaume de Saint-Thierry* (Paris: Les Éditions du Cerf, 1985), 47–48. For more on the medieval understanding of memory, see Mary J. Carruthers, *The Book of Memory: A Study of Memory in Medieval Culture* (New York: Cambridge University Press, 2008).

59   Baudelet, *L'Expérience spirituelle*, 46: "La mémoire est l'un des lieux privilégiés de la présence de Dieu."

60   David N. Bell, *The Image and Likeness: The Augustinian Spirituality of William of Saint Thierry*, CS 78 (Kalamazoo, MI: Cistercian Publications, 1984), 26.

for us. This love is "the wonderful nourishment of life for our souls," which we then "take in with greedy mouths, when we recognize it sweetly, and we put away in the stomach of memory whatever things Christ did or suffered for us. And this is the banquet from the flesh and blood of Jesus; for the one who receives, has life abiding in him."[61] Receiving the flesh of Christ in the Eucharist stores in our memory the deeds of that flesh on our behalf, and this brings as its fruit an increase in the *affectus* of our love for him. This, in turn, compels us to offer ourselves to the one who offered himself. By works of faith and charity, the faithful recipient puts back on the Lord's table those kinds of things he or she took from it.[62] One "abides in Christ by the banquet of Christ through the affect of pious love, and has Christ abiding in him through the effect of this holy work [*sanctae operationis*]."[63] The more one loves, the more one eats, and the more one is built into a greater mass of the love of which one has but a pledge now, with the promise of fulfillment in the life to come. This exchange of love, William concludes, is what Jesus means when he says that "Whoever eats my flesh, abides in me and I in him."[64] In this metaphorical language, William is outlining the Trinitarian logic of the Eucharist. The one who receives the Eucharist has the Holy Spirit operating in oneself and is able to offer back Christ-like works to the Father. By the Spirit one is joined to Christ, and one's offering can be joined to Christ's because the person acts with the love of the Spirit, which is Christ's love.

William examines the Trinitarian dynamic of spiritual reception again in *Meditatio* VIII, focusing this time on the way in which meditation on the Eucharist serves as a form of that reception. William asks God to receive his own spirit, which he offers him, and then asks for an infusion of the Holy Spirit so that he may permeate him. This happens, he says,

> when we eat and drink the deathless banquet of your body and your blood. As your clean beasts, we there regurgitate the sweet things stored within our memory, and chew them in our mouths like cud for the renewed and ceaseless work of our salvation. That done, we put away again

---

61   Sac alt, VI, "Quam tunc auidis faucibus sumimus, cum dulciter recolligimus et in uentre memoriae recondimus, quaecumque pro nobis fecit uel passus est Christus. Et hoc est conuiuium de carne Iesu et sanguine; cui qui communicat, habet uitam in se manentem," CCCM 88:66 (ln. 66–70).

62   Sac alt, VI, CCCM 88:66–67 (ln. 70–74).

63   Sac alt, VI, "Sicque in Christo manet bonus conuiua Christi per piae dilectionis affectum, habetque Christum in se manentem per sanctae operationis effectum," CCCM 88:67 (ln. 78–80). See also, Rougé, *Doctrine et experience*, 50.

64   Sac alt, VI, CCCM 88:67 (ln. 87–88); cf. John 6:57.

in that same memory what you have done, what you have suffered for our sake. When you say to the longing soul: "Open your mouth wide and I will fill it," and she tastes and sees your sweetness in the great Sacrament that surpasses understanding, then she is made that which she eats, bone of your bone and flesh of your own flesh. Thus is fulfilled the prayer that you made to your Father on the threshold of your passion. The Holy Spirit effects in us here by grace that unity which is between the Father and yourself, his Son, from all eternity by nature; so that, as you are one, so likewise we may be made one in you. This, O Lord, is the face with which you meet the face of him who longs for you. This is the kiss of your mouth on the lips of your lover; and this is your love's answering embrace to your yearning bride who says: "My beloved is mine, and I am his; he shall abide between my breasts." And again, "My heart has said 'My face has sought you.'"[65]

Here we see many themes from *De sacramento altaris* echoed again, with a more explicit connection to the Trinity. The Eucharist stores memories of Christ's saving work, and when we meditate on them, these memories increase our love for him. This loving, spiritual reception of Christ further conforms the recipient to him. It is a nuptial act, Rougé notes, which William signifies by echoing Adam's encounter with the newly created Eve in Genesis 2:23: "This is bone of my bone, and flesh of my flesh."[66] This conformation takes place by grace, with the Holy Spirit giving himself to us, and in so doing gives us the same unity as that between the Father and the Son, thereby binding those who receive worthily to each other and to Christ and the Father. It is a strong, high

---

65   Med, VIII.7-9, "Hoc est quod agitur cum facimus quod *in tui commemorationem nos fa-cere* praecepisti, quo in salutem filiorum tuorum nil dulcius, nil potuit prouideri poten-tius, cum manducantes et bibentes incorruptibile epulum corporis et sanguinis tui, sicut munda animalia tua, ab intestino memoriae cogitandi dulcedine, quasi ad os reducimus, et in nouum et perpetuum salutis nostrae officium, nouo semper pietatis affectu rumi-nantes, rursum suauiter in ipsa recondimus memoria quid pro nobis feceris, quid fueris passus. Vbi dicis animae desideranti: *Dilata os tuum et ego adimplebo illud.* Et illa gustans et uidens suauitatem tuam sacramento magno et incomprehensibili, hoc efficitur quod manducat, *os ex ossibus tuis et caro de carne tua,* ut sicut orasti Patrem iturus ad passio-nem, hoc Spiritus sanctus operetur in nobis per gratiam, quod in Patre et te, Filio eius, est ab aeterno per naturam, ut *sicut uos unum estis, ita et nos in uobis unum simus.* Haec est, Domine, facies tua ad faciem te desiderantis; hoc est osculum oris tui ad os te amantis; hic est amplexus dilectionis tuae ad amplexum sponsae tuae suspirantis tibi et dicentis: *Dilectus meus mihi, et ego illi; in medio uberum meorum commorabitur. Et: Tibi dixit cor meum: Exquisiuit te facies mea,"* CCCM 89:48–49. ET: *Meditations,* 142–43.

66   Rougé, *Doctrine et experience,* 251.

doctrine of spiritual union or deification: Through the grace mediated by the Eucharist, human beings can enjoy the relationship that the persons of the Trinity enjoy by nature.

William's most significant writing on Eucharistic reception through medita-tion occurs in his celebrated letter to the Carthusian brothers of Mont-Dieu (*The Golden Epistle*). Here he offers counsel on the basics of living the monastic life. In his discussion of reading, prayer, and meditation, he treats the Eucha-rist. It is beneficial and important to devote at least one hour of the day, he writes, "to an attentive passing in review of the benefits conferred by his Pas-sion and the Redemption he wrought, in order to savor them in spirit and store them away faithfully in the memory. This is spiritually to eat the Body of the Lord and drink his Blood in remembrance of him who gave to all who believe in him the commandment: 'Do this in remembrance of me.'"[67] Here William makes more explicit the connection we have already seen between meditation and spiritual reception. In the *Golden Epistle*, they are effectively identical. Be-cause meditation on the Passion allows a person to grow in love of Christ and store that love in one's memory, it produces the same spiritual fruit as receiving the Eucharist in the sacrament.

William continues to exhort meditation on the Passion as a form of Eucha-ristic reception, in particular, as safer and more accessible. Only a few, by vir-tue of their priestly ordination, are allowed to celebrate the mystery of this commemoration, he notes:

> But the substance of the mystery can be enacted and handled and re-ceived for salvation at all times and in every place where God rules, in the way in which it was given, that is, with due sentiments of devotion, by all those to whom are addressed the words: "You are a chosen race, a royal priesthood, a consecrated nation, a people God means to have for himself; it is yours to proclaim the exploits of the God who has called

---

67   Ep frat, 115, "Scit etiam quicumque *habet sensum Christi* quantum christianae pietati expediat, quantum seruum Dei, seruum redemptionis Christi deceat, et utile ei sit una saltem aliqua diei hora passionis ipsius ac redemptionis attentius recolligere beneficia, ad fruendum suauiter in conscientia et recondendum fideliter in memoria; quod est spiri-tualiter manducare corpus Domini et bibere eius sanguinem, in memoriam eius qui om-nibus in se credentibus praecepit dicens: *Hoc facite in meam commemorationem*," CCCM 88:252. ET: *The Golden Epistle*, trans. Theodore Berkeley, CF 12 (Kalamazoo, MI: Cistercian Publications, 1971), 49–50. Baudelet draws attention to the significant role memory plays in William's theology; meditation on things of God further conforms the soul to the divine likeness. Baudelet, *L'Expérience spirituelle*, 46–48.

you out of darkness into his marvellous light." [1 Pet 2:9] The substance is only received by the man worthy of it and prepared. The sacrament without substance brings death, but the substance even without sacrament, brings eternal life.

Now if you wish, and if you truly desire it, this is at your disposal in your cell at all hours both of day and of night. As often as you stir up sentiments of piety and faith in recalling to mind what he did when he suffered for you, you eat his body and drink his blood. As long as you remain in him through love and he in you through the sanctity and justice he works in you, you are reckoned as belonging to his Body and counted as one of his members.[68]

Unlike when physically receiving the sacrament, there is no danger of unworthy reception when receiving the sacrament's spiritual benefit by meditation. Any monk can meditate on the Passion at any time of day as part of his share in the priesthood of all believers. One need not wait until the celebration of Mass to receive its spiritual fruits. The extent to which William equates meditation and Eucharistic reception seems shocking, and yet the conclusion is entirely consistent with his theology of spiritual reception. By receiving Christ in the Eucharist, a person is reminded of Christ's saving work and grows in love by a gift of the Spirit. Yet such a memorial and increase of love are possible by meditation as well, and hence the fruits of each are the same. This does not denigrate or radically relativize the uniqueness of the sacrament. As we have seen, in previous works William has written of the necessity of the sacrament for the deification of the body and the importance of joining oneself to the

---

68   Ep frat, I.117-119, "Siquidem sanctae huius ac reuerendae commemorationis mysterium, suo modo, suo loco, suo tempore celebrare licet paucis hominibus, quibus in hoc creditum est ministerium; rem uero mysterii in omni tempore *et in omni loco dominationis Dei*, modo quo traditum est, hoc est debitae pietatis affectu agere et tractare et sumere sibi in salutem, omnibus in promptu est, quibus dicitur: *Vos autem genus electum, regale sacerdotium, gens sancta, populus adquisitionis, ut uirtutes adnuntietis eius qui de tenebris uos uocauit in admirabile lumen suum.* Nam et sacramentum, sicut accipit ad uitam dignus, sic ad mortem suam et iudicium temerare potest indignus; rem uero sacramenti nemo percipit nisi dignus et idoneus. Sacramentum enim sine re sacramenti sumenti mors est; res uero sacramenti, etiam praeter sacramentum, sumenti uita aeterna est. Si autem uis et uere uis, omnibus horis tam diei quam noctis, haec tibi in cella tua praesto est. Quotiens in commemorationem eius qui pro te passus est, / huic facto eius pie ac fideliter fueris affectus, corpus eius manducas et sanguinem bibis; quamdiu in eo manes per amorem, ipse uero in te per sanctitatis et iustitiae operationem, in eius corpore et in membris eius computaris," CCCM 88:252–253. ET: *The Golden Epistle,* 50–51.

sacrifice of Christ offered in the Mass. But why does he not mention these here? Why the interiorization of liturgy and sacrament?

There are two reasons. First, William derives his theology of spiritual reception from Origen, who saw the scriptures as an incarnation of the Word of God into the letter analogous to the Word's incarnation in the flesh. Most of Origen's theological themes express the interiorization of Christ the Word into the Christian, particularly through the means of the scriptures. By reading and meditating on the words of Scripture, the Word that it contains is appropriated to the one reading and meditating.[69] The purpose of both spiritual study and the Eucharist is to reveal the Word of God again,[70] to bring Christ's presence in history in the Incarnation into the present life of the believer. Hans Urs von Balthasar sums up this core view: "In the platonism of Origen, spiritual presence and eating equal real presence and eating."[71] Activities such as meditation and study that increase the presence of Christ in the memory by the power of the Spirit are logically, for Origen, other forms of spiritual reception.

Second, Rougé suggests that the answer lies in the letter's context. William, he says, is addressing Carthusians, whose vocation is to remain in their cell and whose liturgical life is diminished compared to more cenobitic monastics. At the same time, he is also conscious of the monastic practice of accumulating private Masses for the intentions of the deceased: "A warning against limiting all of the spiritual life to the celebration of the sacrament of the altar should not be interpreted too quickly as a complete denigration of the Eucharist as

---

69   Henri Crouzel, *Origen*, trans. A.S. Worrall (San Francisco: Harper & Row, 1989), 70, 76.

70   Henri de Lubac, *Histoire et esprit: L'intelligence de l'écriture d'après Origène* (Paris: Les Éditions du Cerf, 2002), 365: "L'attention d'Origène se porte avant tout sur la function que remplissent et l'Écriture et le sang du Verbe dans l'économie de notre salut. Or, leur function à l'une et à l'autre est analogue. Elle est d'exprimer et de révéler le Verbe de Dieu. L'une et l'autre le font selon un schéma semblable et l'Écriture le fait en fin de compte avec une supériorité qui permet de la considérer, non sans doute en sa matérialité, mais prise en son essence secrète, comme la vérité dont l'Eucharistie serait le symbole." For more on William's use of Origen in his theology of reception, see Verdeyen, *La Théologie mystique de Guillaume de Saint-Thierry*, 172ff.

71   Hans Urs von Balthasar, *Parole et mystère chez Origène* (Paris: Les Éditions du Cerf, 1957), 105. Crouzel adds, "The birth of Christ in the soul is essentially bound up with the reception of the Word and in a certain way Jesus is thus being continually born in souls…. The birth of Jesus at Bethlehem is only effective in the order of Redemption if Jesus is also born in every man, if each adheres personally to this advent of Jesus into the world, and thereby into him…. It can even happen that some accord Him such a place within them that he walks in them, lies down in them, eats in them, with the whole Trinity" (Crouzel, *Origen*, 125).

such."[72] Rougé also points to the fact that grace procured in meditation is named *res mysterii*, that is specifically the grace that the Eucharist brings. It is not that meditation on the Passion could replace the Eucharist; rather, it serves as another way to receive the grace that the celebration of the Eucharist makes available: "Therefore if William establishes a real distinction between the materiality of the exterior celebration and the interior participation in its virtue, he maintains no less that the grace that a person must acquire is the grace of the Eucharist. If the discursivity of the sacrament is relativized in part, it is only to better value the grace of the sacrament itself."[73] In short, William is more attempting to enhance the meditation and affective life of his readers than to make reductive dogmatic statements about the Eucharist. His words in the *Golden Epistle* should be read together with *De sacramento altaris* and the *Letter to Rupert*, where he emphasizes that Christ's body must be truly present to save those bodies physically receiving it. Meditation may be a form of spiritual eating, but it does not replace physical eating.

7   Sacrifice

The purpose of the Eucharist is not just for its recipients to have the Holy Spirit dwelling in them; it is to unite them in the Spirit to Christ in his sacrifice to the Father, and to unite their sacrifices and lives to his own. In *De natura et dignitate amoris*, William treats the Eucharist during a section in which he constructs a conversation between the persons of the Trinity on the need for redemption of the human race. As "the medium between God and man,"[74] Christ addresses humanity and the Father and tells them what he has done for each: "Taking his own Body and Blood in his hand, he said: 'Eat this! Drink this! And live by it!' And presenting it to the Father, he says: 'Behold, Father, the price of my blood. If you require a price for sin, see here is my Blood for it. Lord

---

72   Rougé, *Doctrine et experience*, 103: "Une mise en garde contre la limitation de toute la vie spirituelle à la célébration même du sacrement de l'autel ne doit pas être interpretée trop vite comme un dénigrement complet de l'eucharistie en tant que telle." For more on Masses for the dead and Cistercian liturgical reforms, see Marie-Gérard Dubois, "L'Eucharistie à Cîteaux au milieu du XIIe siècle," *Collectanea Cisterciensia* 67 (2005): 269–76.

73   Rougé, *Doctrine et experience*, 104: "Si donc Guillaume établit une distinction réelle entre la matérialité de la célébration extérieure et la participation intérieure à sa vertu, il n'en maintient pas moins que la grâce qu'il s'agit d'accueillir en soi, c'est la grâce de l'eucharistie. Si la discursivité du sacrement est en partie relativisée, ce n'est que pour mieux mettre en valeur la grâce du sacrement lui-même."

74   Nat am, 35, "...inter Deum et hominem medium se faciens...," CCCM 88:204. ET: *On the Nature and Dignity of Love*, 96.

Father, you have bestowed liberality, and the earth of my Body has produced its fruit. Now righteousness will walk before you and you will set your feet on the path of human salvation..."[75]

William goes on to describe further the fruits of redemption as reconciliation with God, but more than reconciliation. Receiving redemption through the Eucharist brings wisdom, for the one who receives savors well what is eaten and becomes conformed to the one eaten, who is Wisdom itself: "He eats and drinks the Body and Blood of his Redeemer, the heavenly manna, the bread of angels, the bread of wisdom, and while eating it he is transformed into the nature of the food he eats. For to eat the Body of Christ is nothing other than to be made the Body of Christ and the temple of the Holy Spirit."[76]

These passages echo many of the themes we have already seen in William's Eucharistic writings. First, the Eucharist serves as a means of deification whereby the recipient becomes conformed to the one he receives. Rougé identifies this as a Christological theme, which is true enough.[77] But it is even more a Trinitarian theme. For this conformity to the one he receives accompanies an infusion of the Holy Spirit so that the recipient, in sharing the life of the Son, can become part of the offering of the Son to the Father. That offering takes a particular form in the economy of salvation, where the Son assumes human flesh and offers his life on behalf of sinners. But it is part of the eternal exchange of love between the two.

The Eucharist is not only a matter of increasing love, but it also serves as a sacrifice of Christ's body, offered by Christ to the Father. William describes Christ as the one who blesses the Eucharistic bread and changes it into his body with the words of institution.[78] In the Eucharist, Christ bears the flesh that he assumed for us to the Father for our sake.[79] William offers an extensive quotation of Chrysostom's (cited as Ambrose's) homilies on the letter to the

---

75   Nat am, 37, "Positoque corpore suo et sanguine in manu eius: Hoc, inquit, manduca, hoc bibe, hinc uiue. Patrique eum repraesentans: En, inquit, Pater, sanguinis mei pretium. Si de peccato huius requires, en pro eo meus sanguis. Domine Pater, dedisti benignitatem, et terra corporis mei dedit fructum suum. Iam iustitia ante te ambulabit, et tu pones in via saluationis humanae pedes tuos," CCCM 88:206. ET: *On the Nature and Dignity of Love*, 99.

76   Nat am, 38, "De fructu ergo huius operas satiates homo, mediante sapientia Dei, non solum reconciliatur, sed etiam sapiens efficitur. Sapit enim ei quod manduact. Manducat et bibit corpus et sanguimen Redemptoris sui, manna caeleste, panem angelorum, panem sapientiae; et manducans transformatur in naturam cibi quem manducat. Corpus enim Christi manducare nichil est aliud quam corpus Christi effici, et *templum Spiritus sancti*," CCCM 88:206. ET: *On the Nature and Dignity of Love*, 100.

77   Rougé, *Doctrine et experience*, 30.

78   Sac alt, v, CCCM 88:64 (ln. 48–52).

79   Sac alt, xi, CCCM 88:77 (ln. 28–29).

Hebrews explaining that the Eucharistic sacrifice is the *exemplum* of Christ's self-offering on the cross. The two are always together, so that the Eucharist is completely a sacrifice.[80] And both are a sacrifice by which the Son incorporates human beings into his self-offering to the Father. As Rougé puts it, "The glorious Christ offers the flesh that he took from our nature to the Father; we offer this flesh with the same piety when we recognize it as holy and sanctifying and when we recognize that we present it to Him from whom all holiness comes (cf. Heb. 2:11). This is the profound reality of the sacrament of the altar."[81]

Two implications arise from this. First, while the Eucharist serves as a memorial, it is also an enactment of the Son's offering to the Father in heaven now and forever. It points to the present and future as much as the past.[82] Second, our offering of the Eucharist is efficacious because it is joined by faith to Christ's self-offering in heaven.[83] William writes:

> Indeed, we do this humbly here on earth through him, which he does powerfully for us in heaven, as the Son who must be heard on account of his reverence, where he intercedes before the Father as an advocate for us. It is his to intercede for us: to bear the flesh, which he assumed for us and from us, to God the Father in a certain way for our sake. Therefore, let us sacrifice the body of Christ, since we believe it to be holy and sanctifying with certain piety of faith, and we offer this faith for his honor, from which, whoever sanctifies and whoever are sanctified, all are from one.[84]

---

80   Sac alt, XI, CCCM 88:78 (ln. 35–50).

81   Rougé, *Doctrine et experience*, 56: "Le Christ glorieux offer au Père pour nous la chair qu'il a prise de notre nature; nous offrons cette chair avec la mème piété quand nous la reconnaissons sainte et sanctifiante et que nous la présentons à Celui de qui provient toute sainteté (cf. Heb. 2:11). Voilà la réalité profonde du sacrement de l'autel."

82   Rougé, *Doctrine et experience*, 178.

83   Rougé, *Doctrine et experience*, 179: "Notre sacrifice du corps du Seigneur procède, par la médiation de la foi, du sacrifice que le Christ fait lui-même de son propre corps. Ce qui rend notre offrande effective, c'est notre foi en la puissance sanctifiante de la chair glorifiée de Jésus. Cette foi, vécue dans la célébration du sacrement lui-même, est la mise en oeuvre de la médiation sanctifiante du Fils, à la louange de la gloire du Père. Notre sacrifice est authentique parce que nous croyons à l'unique véritable sacrifice du Fils." Rougé also notes that all of our offerings and sacrifices are only a secondary response to the primary iniative of God, which gives us all we could ever offer back. Rougé, *Doctrine et experience*, 169.

84   Sac alt, XI, "Hoc enim hic per eum humiliter agimus in terris, quod pro nobis ipse potenter, sicut Filius *pro sua reuerentia* exaudiendus, agit in caelis, ubi apud Patrem pro nobis quasi aduocatus interuenit. Cui est pro nobis interuenire: carnem, quam pro nobis et de nobis sumpsit, Deo Patri quodammodo pro nobis ingerere. Sacrificamus ergo corpus Christi, dum certa fidei pietate sanctum illud credimus et sanctificans, et hanc fidem

Not only the priest but all those participating in the sacrament become joined to Christ's offering of himself to the Father. Their deification through the sacrament entails an entrance into that Trinitarian relationship. And, as William's subsequent quotation of Augustine makes clear, the faithful offer themselves to Christ at the same time as they participate in his self-offering to the Father. They are one with him in his act and make a similar act of their own. Indeed, it is through Christ's sacrifice to the Father that those united to his body and indeed now its members have the sacrifices of their lives brought into the eternal offering of the Son to the Father in the Spirit.[85]

8   The Eucharist as the Body of Christ, the Church

In *De sacramento altaris*, William turns more explicitly to the question of how to understand the Fathers' apparently conflicting *sententiae* about the body of Christ. From these *sententiae*, William finds three ways in which the Fathers speak of the body of Christ according to layers of sacramentality: "A sacrament is a sign of a sacred thing ... it makes something come into the mind."[86] The visible species of bread on the altar makes the faithful think of the physical body of Christ. William emphasizes that the sacramentality of the visible species depends not only on the spoken words of the priest, but on the fact that the bread is broken, laid down, and raised, which call to mind Christ's death, burial, and ascension.[87] The physical or material flesh of Christ in the sacrament is then received by the faithful. But Christ's body received is also a sacrament of the third sense of the body of Christ, his spiritual body, the Church. As William puts it, "Indeed that flesh or body must be understood in one way, which hangs on the cross and is sacrificed on the altar; that flesh or body that whoever eats it has life abiding in him in another way; and his flesh or blood which is the

---

offerimus ad honorem eius, ex quo, qui sanctificat et qui sanctificantur, ex uno omnes," CCCM 88:77 (ln. 24–31).

85   Rougé, *Doctrine et experience*, 164–65: "Le Christ offre et est offert, comme l'homme qui est appelé à s'offrir lui-même mais aussi à rapporter à Dieu l'offrande qu'il lui présente. Seul le Christ, grand prêtre du sacrifice universel permet à l'homme d'être, en vérité, le prêtre du sacrifice de sa propre vie"; and Rougé, 182: "L'eucharistie n'est pas le seul sacrifice que nous ayons à célébrer. C'est par toute notre vie que nous sommes appelés à render à Dieu le culte et la louange qui lui sont dûs. Mais l'eucharistie ouvre la porte et montre le chemin de l'action de grâce véritable. L'eucharistie est le sacrifice visible qui nous introduit dans l'offrande éternelle et invisible de l'amour."

86   Sac alt, x, "Sacramentum enim est sacrae rei signum. Signum autem est, quod praeter speciem quam ingerit, facit aliquid in mentem uenire," CCCM 88:73 (ln. 32–34).

87   Sac alt, x, CCCM 88:74 (ln. 39–44).

church in another way…. For this trinity of the body of the Lord must not be understood as other than that body of the Lord, thought of according to its essence, strength, and effect. For the body of Christ, which is so much in itself, presents itself to all as the food of eternal life, and it truly makes those receiving it faithfully one with it, and by the love of the Spirit and the communion of nature, appears as the head of his body the Church."[88]

A similar parallel exists, then, between the unity of the persons of the Trinity and the unity of the members of the body of Christ.[89] William writes that the Father and the Son are each in the other, bound together by the Holy Spirit "who exists as such by virtue of his unity of being with you both."[90] Likewise, the Spirit creates and orders the unity that makes those in the Church one among themselves and in God, as sons. The sonship the Spirit brings is not by nature, as with the Son, but by an adoption of grace: "The former birth is not something that happens, nor does it effect a unity; it is itself a oneness in the Holy Spirit. The latter birth, however, has no existence of itself, but comes to being through the Holy Spirit, in so far as it is stamped with the likeness of God."[91] This union is perfected in the beatific vision, which will make the faithful like God: "For the Father to see the Son is to be

---

88　Sac alt, XIII, "Aliter enim cogitanda est caro illa uel corpus, quod pependit in ligno et sacrificatur in altari; aliter caro eius uel corpus, quod qui manducauerit, habet uitam in se manentem; aliter caro uel corpus eius, quod est ecclesia. Nam et ecclesia caro Christi dicitur, ut ibi: *Hoc nunc os ex ossibus meis, et caro de carne mea. Sacramentum hoc*, inquit Apostolus, *magnum est; ego autem dico, in Christo et in Ecclesia.* Non quod tricorpor a nobis Christus describatur, sicut de Geryone illo ferunt fabulae, cum unum esse corpus Christi testetur Apostolus; sed quodam fidei respectu intellectus uel affectus facit diuersitatem hanc, res uero ipsa simplicitatis suae puram obtinet ueritatem. Haec enim trinitas corporis Domini non est aliud intelligenda quam ipsum Domini corpus, cogitatum secundum essentiam, secundum uirtutem, secundum effectum. Nam corpus Christi, quantum in se est, omnibus se praebet cibum uitae aeternae, et fideliter se sumentes unum uere se cum efficit, et amore spiritus et ipsius consortio naturae, *caput* exsistens *corporis Ecclesiae*," CCCM 88:84 (ln. 25–41).

89　For more on the way in which the same term, *unitas spiritus*, is used to describe Trinitarian and ecclesial unity, see F. Tyler Sergent, "*Unitas Spiritus* and the Originality of William of Saint-Thierry," in *Unity of Spirit: Studies on William of Saint-Thierry in Honor of E. Rozanne Elder*, (eds.) F. Tyler Sergent, Aage Rydstrøm-Poulsen, and Marsha L. Dutton, CS 268 (Collegeville, MN: Cistercian Publications, 2015), 144–70.

90　Med, VI.11, "Nostra ergo, ut uideo, in te, uel tua in nobis habitatio nobis caelum est; *caelum uero caeli* tua aeternitas tibi, qua es quod es in teipso, Pater in Filio, Filius in Patre, et unitas qua Pater et Filius unum estis, id est Spiritus sanctus, non quasi aliunde ueniens et medium se faciens, sed coessendo in hoc ipsum existens," CCCM 89:36. ET: *Meditations*, 128.

91　Med, VI.13, "Natiuitas uero Filii de Patre, aeternitatis natura est; natiuitas in nobis, gratiae adoptio est. Illa nec fit, nec facit unitatem, sed ipsa in Spiritu sancto unitas est; ista non

what the Son is, and vice versa. For us, however, to see God is to be like God. This unity, this likeness is itself the heaven where God dwells in us, and we in him."[92]

9   The Eschatological End of Eucharist

The Eucharist is a real participation in the union of the Trinity, but it is only a foretaste of the real union to come in the beatific vision. In *De natura et dignitate amoris*, William describes the glorification of the body in beatitude and its reception of the beatific vision. He does not think that God will be seen by physical eyes, but the glorification of the body will show it the presence of divinity through some kind of grace, in a way similar to the way in which grace makes God present to our senses now through the sacraments: "Even in this life the religion of the physical sacraments is effective for this. Since we understand scarcely anything besides bodies and physical things while we are passing through as an image, we are bound by the physical sacraments lest we draw away from God."[93] Rougé notes the eschatological and anthropological point at work here.[94] This union with Christ's body is accomplished now through sacraments and is real, but not as full as it will be in the beatific vision, when the body is glorified and material things have passed away. Until that time, the Eucharist serves as a physical bond to God for physical beings who need it and as a real foretaste and participation in the union that is to come.

William returns to this topic in *Meditatio devotissima* VI, where he describes the joy of the blessed, the inter-Trinitarian relations of God in heaven, and his own longing for beatitude. The second of these is most pertinent here for its echoes with William's treatment of Eucharistic reception. William quotes John

---

est, sed fit per Spiritum sanctum, in quantum similitudine Dei insignitur, equidem ultra modum humanae naturae, sed citra essentiam diuinae," CCCM 89:36. ET: *Meditations*, 129.

92   Med, VI.13-14, "Similitudinem autem Dei ipsam conferet nobis uisio eius, qua Deum uidebimus, non quod est, sed sicut est, et ipsa similitudo qua similes ei erimus. Nam uidere Patri Filium, hoc est esse quod Filius, et e contrario. Nobis autem uidere Deum, hoc est similes esse Deo. Haec unitas, haec similitudo ipsum est caelum, quo Deus in nobis habitat, et nos in Deo," CCCM 89:36-37. ET: *Meditations*, 129.

93   Nat am, 44, "...sic in illa vita videbitur Deus a singulis in omnibus, et ab omnibus in singulis; non quod corporalibus oculis videatur diuinitas, sed praesentiam duinitas glorificatio corporum demonstrabit manifesta quaedam sui gratia. Ad hoc etiam in hac vita corporalium sacramentorum ualet religio; quia cum uix aliquid nisi corpora et corporalia intelligamus, quamdiu in imagine pertransimus, corporalibus religamur sacramentis, ne a Deo recedamus," CCCM 88:211. ET: *On the Nature and Dignity of Love*, 107.

94   Rougé, *Doctrine et experience*, 30.

1:38, in which Andrew and another disciple ask Jesus where he lives, and an-swers the question with Jesus' words in John 14:20, "In that day you will know that I am in my Father, and you in me, and I in you." He understands this to mean that the Father is the *locus* of Christ, and Christ the *locus* of the Father, but also that we are the *locus* of Christ and Christ is ours. He continues: "Since, then, Lord Jesus, you are in the Father and the Father is in you, O most high and undivided Trinity, you are yourself the place of your abode, you are your-self your heaven…. When, therefore, you dwell in us, we are your heaven, most assuredly. Yet you are not yourself sustained by dwelling in us; no, it is your sustaining that makes a dwelling for you. And you too are our heaven, to which we may ascend, and in which we may dwell."[95]

10   Imagery of the Kiss

William's most complex connections between the Trinity, Christ, and the Eu-charist appear when he characterizes each of these as a kiss or embrace, bor-rowing the image from the opening verse of the Song of Songs, "Let him kiss me with the kiss of his mouth." In his *Brevis commentatio* on the Song of Songs, he calls these the kiss of nature, the kiss of doctrine, and the kiss of grace.[96] William writes that there is a *conversio* from the Father to the Son, and from the Son to the Father. This takes place in a kiss of mutual knowledge and an embrace of mutual love. The Holy Spirit is this kiss and embrace, the love of the Father to the Son and the Son to the Father.[97] The Holy Spirit reveals the truth of God's trinity and unity to us. Hence, we are said to be touched by the

---

95   Med, VI.10-11, "Locus ergo tuus Pater est, et tu Patris, et non solum, sed etiam nos locus tuus sumus, et tu noster. Cum ergo, o Domine Iesu, tu es in Patre, et Pater in te, o summa et indiuisa Trinitas, tu tibi locus es, utique tu tibi locus es, tu tibi caelum es, sicut non habens ex quo, sic non indigens in quo subsistas, nisi ex teipso in teipso. Cum autem nos inhabitas, caelum tuum sumus utique, sed non quo sustenteris, ut inhabites, sed quod sustentes ut in|habitetur, tu quoque caelum nobis exsistens ad quem ascendamus et in-habitemus," CCCM 89:35–36. ET: *Meditations*, 128.

96   *Brevis commentatio* (Brev com), VII.28-30, CCCM 87:163.

97   Brev com, VI.17-26 "Et est quaedam conuersio a Patre ad Filium, et a Filio ad Patrem. Sed prima est Patris ad Filium, quia Filius a Patre est, non Pater a Filio. Prima autem non tempore, sed quasi quadam relatione, sicut Pater ad Filium. Conuersio autem ista est in osculo et amplexu. Osculum est mutua de se cognitio; amplexus est mutua dilectio. Vnde dicit Filius in euangelio: Nemo nouit Patrem nisi Filius, et nemo nouit Filium nisi Pater. Osculum igitur Patris et Filii, et amplexus, est Spiritus sanctus ab utroque procedens, amor Patris ad Filium, et amor Filii ad Patrem," CCCM 87:161.

kiss of the mouth when God reveals himself to us by the Spirit.[98] This characterization of the Holy Spirit as a kiss between the Father and the Son appears in William's other works as well. In his *Disputatio adversus Petrum Abelardum*, he writes that the Spirit is common to the Father and the Son, and is their community (*communitas*). He also characterizes the Spirit as "charity, embrace and kiss, goodness, sweetness and joy … and their divinity."[99] In the *Golden Epistle*, he calls the Spirit "the God who is Charity. He who is the love of Father and Son, their Unity, Sweetness, Good, Kiss, Embrace and whatever else they can have in common in that supreme unity of truth and truth of unity."[100]

The Incarnation is a second kiss in which humanity and divinity are joined in union (*coniunctio*).[101] This kiss intensifies in the Passion, which William describes as a kiss and an embrace and Rougé characterizes as "the kiss of the cross."[102] The third kiss is the union of the Holy Spirit and the soul in particular gifts of grace. William describes these latter two in greater detail in his *Commentary on the Song of Songs*:

> A kiss is a certain outward loving union of bodies, sign and incentive of an inward union. It is produced by use of the mouth and aims, by mutual exchange, at a union not only of bodies but of spirits. Christ the Bridegroom offered to his Bride the Church, so to speak, a kiss from heaven, when the Word made flesh drew so near to her that he wedded her to himself; and so wedded her that he united her to himself, in order that God might become man, and man might become God. He also offers this same kiss to the faithful soul, his Bride, and imprints it upon her, when from the remembrance of the benefits common to all men, he gives her own special and personal joy and pours forth within her the grace of his

---

98 Brev com, VI.37-40: "Cui igitur Filius per Spiritum reuelat, non dicendus est osculari ore suo Deus, sed osculo oris sui. Non enim os tangimus, sed osculo tangimur. Osculo tangimur, cum amor et cognitio nobis infunditur," CCCM 87:161.

99 *Disputatio adversus Petrum Abelardum* (Adv Abl), IV, "Cum ergo Pater etiam sit spiritus et sanctus, Filius quoque spiritus et sanctus, oportuit censeri aliquo nomine quod commune esset amborum, ipsum qui communis et communitas est amborum; et commune amborum quidquid commune est eorum: caritas, amplexus et osculum, bonitas, suauitas et gaudium, et ut totum concludam, diuinitas amborum," CCCM 89A:29 (ln. 85–90). The translation is my own.

100 Ep frat, 263, "Deus caritas; cum qui est amor Patris et Filii, et unitas et suauitas, et bonum et osculum, et amplexus et quicquid commune potest esse amborum," CCCM 88:282. ET: *The Golden Epistle*, 96.

101 Brev com, VII.5–6, 26–27: "Coniunctio enim Verbi et audientis, diuinitatis et humanitatis, quasi quoddam osculum est caritatis…. Haec igitur coniunctio diuinae et humanae naturae quoddam est osculum sponsi et sponsae," CCCM 87:162–163.

102 Med, V.8, V.17, VIII.5; Rougé, *Doctrine et experience*, 310.

love, drawing her spirit to himself and infusing into her his spirit, that both may be one spirit.[103]

Here it becomes clear that, for William, a kiss is a movement of love and knowledge by a person of the Trinity toward another person, human or divine. In the kiss of nature, this movement takes place within the existing unity of the Trinity and thus is a *conversio*, a turning toward. In the kisses of doctrine and grace, however, these movements go out toward human beings to form a *coniunctio*, a union that did not previously exist. In the same pattern of logic we have seen before, the Son unites himself to human nature and bestows the Spirit on particular persons so that they may have his love in them. The Spirit unites them to Christ, which incorporates them into his self-offering to the Father and into the life of the Trinity. In Rougé's words, "The kiss of the humanity and the passion of Jesus bear witness and lead to the still more surprising and wonderful kiss of the Trinity itself."[104] *Coniunctio* leads to a share in *conversio*.

Furthermore, in this passage William describes the kisses of doctrine and grace in sacramental, even Eucharistic, language. First, like the sacraments, a kiss is an outward sign of a corresponding inner spiritual reality in which the outward sign not only signifies but effects that reality. Indeed, the Eucharist is obviously one of the kisses of grace that Christ gives through the Holy Spirit. Second, the purpose of the union of the kiss of the Incarnation is for God to become human so that humanity might become divine. Here again William uses *fio*, the verb he regularly employs for the Word taking on flesh and becoming present on the altar during the Eucharist. This reflects logic common to both the mission of the Son in the Incarnation and the mission of the Spirit in gifts of grace, such as the Eucharist. Finally, Christ imprints the kiss on the soul when he infuses it with the grace of his love and draws its spirit to himself. In so doing, he gives the soul its own joys from the *memory* of the good things common to all, a clear reference to the way in which meditation on the Passion

---

103   Cant, IV.27, "Osculum amica quaedam et exterior coniunctio corporum est, interioris coniunctionis signum et incentiuum. Quod oris ministerio exhibetur, ut non tantum corporum, sed ex mutuo contactu etiam spirituum coniunctio fiat. Sponsus uero Christus sponsae suae ecclesiae quasi osculum de caelo porrexit, cum Verbum caro factum in tantum ei appropinquauit, ut se ei coniungeret; in tantum coniunxit, ut uniret, ut Deus homo, homo Deus fieret. Ipsum etiam osculum fideli animae sponsae suae porrigit et imprimit, cum de memoria communium bonorum, priuatum ei et proprium commendans gaudium, gratiam ei sui amoris infundit, spiritum eius sibi adtrahens et suum infundens ei, ut inuicem *unus spiritus sint,*" CCCM 87:33. ET: *Exposition on the Song of Songs*, 25–26. For more on how this union takes place in thoughts and feelings, knowledge and love, see Cant, XXVII.

104   Rougé, *Doctrine et experience*, 311: "Le baiser de l'humanité et de la passion de Jésus rend témoignage et mène au baiser, plus surprenant et admirable encore, de la Trinité elle-même."

and spiritual reception of the Eucharist increase love in a particular person based on remembering what Christ has done for all. This is made explicit in the passage of *Meditatio* VIII mentioned above, in which William describes spiritual reception of the Eucharist and the union of grace it produces as the kiss of the lover on the mouth of the beloved.

The role of the Eucharist becomes even more explicit when William elaborates on the work of God. He writes:

> Your work is made true for us when we sacrifice to you this your sacrifice. When we remember with the sure sacrament of faith and a pious affection of heart what you have done for us, faith, as it were, receives it with its mouth, hope chews it, and charity cooks into salvation and life the blessed and beatifying food of your grace. There you show yourself to the soul which desires you, accepting the embrace of her love and kissing her with the kiss of your mouth. As happens in a loving kiss, she pours out to you her spirit [*anima*, soul], and you pour in your spirit [*spiritum*], so that you are made one body and one spirit when she receives in this way your body and blood.[105]

As Rougé notes, this is not metaphorical language about a general way in which the soul is justified. Rather, it is explicitly Eucharistic language tying together some of William's favorite themes.[106] Eucharistic offering and meditation make Christ present to the soul, which then receives him through faith, hope, and charity. That act of reception is depicted metaphorically in the opening passage of the Song of Songs, as William wrote earlier in his *Meditations*. It is an exchange in which the believer offers his or her

---

105   Exp Rm, IV.8:3-4, "Verum quippe nobis fit opus tuum, cum sacrificamus tibi hoc sacrificium tuum; cum certo fidei sacramento et pio cordis affectu recolentibus nobis quid pro nobis fecisti, fides quasi ore suscipit; spes ruminat, caritas excoquit in salutem et uitam beatam et beatificum gratiae tuae cibum. Ibi enim te exhibes animae desideranti, acceptans amplexum amoris sui, et osculans eam osculo oris tui, ubi sicut in osculo amoris solet, ipsa tibi effundit spiritum suum, et tu ei infundis tuum, ut efficiamini unum corpus et unus spiritus, cum hoc modo sumit corpus et sanguinem tuum," CCCM 86:108. ET: *Exposition on the Epistle to the Romans*, 153.

106   Rougé, *Doctrine et experience*, 83: "Il semble pourtant qu'en insistant sur la nécessaire conjonction du 'véritable sacrement de la foi' et d'une 'pieuse affection du coeur' ainsi qu'en parlant explicitement du corps et du sang du Seigneur, notre auteur se situe délibéré dans le registre sacramental.... De manière peu inopinée, Guillaume fournit donc aux lecteurs de son commentaire une brève synthèse de ses themes eucharistiques favoris: participation au mystère de la Rédemption, memorial intérieur, nourriure spirituelle, échange intime avec le Christ."

soul to Christ and receives the Spirit of Christ in return. In this way, the soul's reception of Christ's body and blood unites the believer to Christ in body and spirit. Given what William has written previously in *De sacramento altaris* about physical reception deifying the body, he seems to imply spiritual and physical reception here. Offering and receiving the Eucharist, then, are important parts of justification and union with God. Hence Rougé comments, "If man and his Lord can form 'one single body and one single spirit,' it is because one food at once corporal and spiritual is received in communion."[107]

William repeatedly emphasizes the way in which the kiss of the Spirit, by grace, brings human beings into the kiss of nature that takes place between the persons of the Trinity. In the *Golden Epistle*, his characterization of the Holy Spirit as the kiss of the Father and the Son is situated in the middle of a passage describing how the Spirit "becomes for man in regard to God in the manner appropriate to him what he is for the Son in regard to the Father or for the Father in regard to the Son through unity of substance. The soul in its happiness finds itself standing midway in the Embrace and the Kiss of the Father and Son. In a manner which exceeds description and thought, the man of God is found worthy to become not God but what God is, that is to say man becomes through grace what God is by nature."[108]

This incorporation into the life of the Trinity through union with the Spirit takes place in part in this life through the sacraments but comes to fulfillment only in heaven. In his *Exposition on the Song of Songs*, William writes that this embrace of the Holy Spirit who is the embrace of the Father and Son is begun here, but perfected elsewhere. The sweetness experienced here foretells a future sweetness. The essence of that future good and this present good are the same, but the aspect is different. This present union belongs to wayfaring in mortal life, the other to the journey's end in eternal life. Then, when mutual knowledge shall be perfect, it will be the full kiss and the full embrace.[109] Only the wall of mortal life holds back the Bridegroom, Christ, from his bride, the

---

107   Rougé, *Doctrine et experience*, 83: "Si l'homme et son Seigneur peuvent former 'un seul corps et un seul esprit,' c'est bien parce qu'une nourriture à la fois corporelle et spirituelle est reçue en communion."

108   Ep frat, 263, "...in summa illa unitate ueritatis et in ueritate unitatis, hoc idem fit homini suo modo ad Deum, quod consubstantiali unitate Filio est ad Patrem uel Patri ad Filium. Cum in osculo et amplexu Patris et Filii mediam quodammodo se inuenit beata conscientia; cum modo ineffabili et incogitabili, fieri meretur homo Dei, non Deus, sed tamen quod Deus est: homo ex gratia quod Deus est ex natura," CCCM 88:282. ET: *The Golden Epistle*, 96.

109   Cant, XXVII.128. ET: *Exposition on the Song of Songs*, 106 (§ 132).

Christian soul, in the full kiss of union in the Spirit.[110] While that wall remains, the sacraments serve to mediate the reception of the Spirit so that that union can come about. In heaven, however, "the Reality [*res*] which is veiled by all the sacraments will utterly put an end to all sacraments. In the sacraments of the New Testament, it is true, the day of new grace began to break; but in that end of perfect consummation will come the full noonday when glass and riddle and that which is in part shall be done away, but there shall be the vision face to face and the plenitude of the highest good."[111] The *res* of union with the Spirit that the sacraments, especially the Eucharist, make available is only a foretaste of the fulfillment of that union to come.

In the *Mirror of Faith*, William also connects memory to the Holy Spirit's meditation of union with God. We recognize God as we recognize a friend. We have *affectus* derived from faith in our memory, which makes God present to us when he is absent. But the Father and Son recognize each other in their unity, which is the Spirit and the substance by which they are what they are. The Father and Son reveal this recognition by imparting the Spirit, who is their common knowledge and will. This enables one who has received the Spirit to recognize them as the Father and Son recognize each other, because that person has within mutual knowledge and love. In this kiss of the Spirit the person receives a partial recognition of God, which will become perfect in the beatific vision.[112] The preparation of memory by right faith and Eucharistic reception imprints the recognition of God on one's memory, conforming it to God and preparing one's mind to receive the fullness of the image of God.

11   Conclusion

As much as William did not seek theological novelty, he made significant contributions to the development of medieval Eucharistic thought. As Gary Macy has noted, William's metaphysics of Eucharistic presence made sense of how Christ could be really present in complete substantial integrity and still have the accidents of bread and wine. It was adopted by Peter Lombard and subsequently became accepted as the most popular conception in the 13th

---

110   Cant, XXXIII.151. ET: *Exposition on the Song of Songs*, 127–28 (§ 155).

111   Cant, XXXVII.172, "In sacramentis quippe Noui Testamenti cepit aspirare nouae gratiae dies; in illo uero omnis consummationis fine erit meridies, ubi non erit speculum et aenigma et ex parte, sed uisio faciei ad faciem, et summi boni plenitudo," CCCM 87:117. ET: *Exposition on the Song of Songs*, 142 (§ 176).

112   Spec fid, 105–112. ET: *Mirror of Faith*, 74–79 (§ 31–32).

century.[113] William's articulation of spiritual reception offers a detailed account of how the Eucharist and meditation on the Passion are means of union with Christ through the love (*caritas*) that is the Spirit. Indeed, his understanding of the relations and substantial unity of the persons of the Trinity gives shape to his Eucharistic theology which, to clarify Bouyer's metaphor, serves as the keystone of the Trinitarian arch of his thought.

The Eucharist is part of the missions of the Son and the Spirit, which are themselves part of the unified operation of the Trinity and take place according to the order of the three persons. The Eucharist is the climax of those missions, the place where the Son is received most intimately and bestows the Spirit on those who receive him. Those who receive it have the Son abiding in them, as the Father does, and are united to the Father in the Spirit with the Son. In order for this union to take place, it must encompass the whole person, body and soul. Hence Christ must be completely present under the Eucharistic species, as he was present body and soul in his Incarnation. By the Spirit living in and inspiring their actions, the faithful become conformed to the one whom they have received and live as members of the one body of Christ, the Church. Joined to Christ, they are also able to offer their lives as Christ did and to join that offering of themselves to Christ's own offering of himself to the Father. This self-offering reaches its perfection in the beatific vision, where they will know and love the Father, the Son proceeding from him, and the Spirit proceeding from the Father through the Son. Moreover, they have been brought to that vision with the Spirit uniting them to the Son, and the Son drawing them to the Father. Therefore, they participate in the divine life in a manner analogous to that life, with the Eucharist providing a true foretaste of that union in this life even as it furthers those who receive it toward that perfection.

---

113   Gary Macy, *The Theologies of the Eucharist in the Early Scholastic Period: A Study of the Salvific Function of the Sacrament according to the Theologians c.1080–c. 1220* (Oxford: Clarendon Press, 1984), 97.

CHAPTER 8

William of Saint-Thierry's Legacy: Progress toward Trinitarian Participation in the *Unio Mystica* in Johannes Tauler's Sermons

Glenn E. Myers

1 Introduction

William of Saint-Thierry (c. 1085–1148) helped to shape the understanding of spiritual formation from his day to our own. Especially through his *Epistola ad fratres de Monte Dei* (*Letter to the Brethren at Mont Dieu*), known as the *Epistola aurea* (*Golden Epistle*), William's thought was carried far and wide. By the end of the 12th century, manuscripts of the *Golden Epistle* were spreading across Europe—in monastic collections as well as city libraries—as has been traced by Volker Honemann.[1] By the 14th century it was published exclusively in collected works under the name of William's close friend, Bernard of Clairvaux.[2]

One notable example of William's influence is found in the 14th-century German preacher, Johannes Tauler (c. 1300–1361). The Dominican's eighty-some extant sermons show evidence of the Cistercian's influence regarding both the process of spiritual formation and the framing of the *unio mystica*

---

1 See Volker Honemann, *Die 'Epistola ad fratres de Monte Dei' des Wilhelm von Saint-Thierry: Lateinische Überlieferung und mittelalterliche Übersetzungen*, Münchener Texte und Untersuchungen zur deutschen Literatur des Mittelalters 61 (Zürich, München: Artemis, 1978); Honemann, "Eine neue Handschrift der deutschen 'Epistola ad fratres de Monte Dei,'" in *Überlieferungsgeschichtliche Editionen und Studien zur deutschen Literatur des Mittelalters*, (eds.) Konrad Kunze, Johannes Mayer, Bernhard Schnell (Tübingen: Niemeyer, 1989), 332–49; and Honemann, "The Reception of William of St Thierry's *Epistola ad fratres de Monte Dei* during the Middle Ages," in *Cistercians of the Middle Ages*, CS 64, (ed.) E. Rozanne Elder (Kalamazoo, MI: Cistercian Publications, 1981), 5–18. See also Jean-Marie Déchanet, "Les manuscrits de la Lettre aux Frères du Mont-Dieu du Guillaume de Saint-Thierry et le problème de la 'Preface' dans Charleville 114," *Scriptorium* 8 (1954): 236–71.

2 See Jean-Marie Déchanet, "Introduction," *The Golden Epistle: A Letter to the Brethren at Mont Dieu*, trans. Theodore Berkeley, CF 12 (Kalamazoo, MI: Cistercian Publications, 1980), ix–x. The German Preacher cites Bernard throughout his sermons; see Louise Gnädinger, "Der minnende Bernhardus: Seine Reflexe in den Predigten des Johannes Tauler," *Cîteaux – Commentarii Cistercienses* 31 (1980): 387–409.

as the culmination of that growth in terms of participation in Trinitarian communion.

For some years, Tauler's acquaintance with the *Golden Epistle* has been postulated—especially regarding the three-person paradigm that presents not only three states of the spiritual life but also three persons, as it were, within each person—although not all scholars have been convinced of William's influence.[3] This chapter seeks to demonstrate Tauler's dependence on William, offering passages from the Dominican's sermons that so closely follow the *Golden Epistle* as to be difficult to explain otherwise. Moreover, it highlights the influence that the Cistercian Father had on Tauler's theological synthesis. The first section presents the manuscripts of the *Golden Epistle* to which Tauler most likely had access. The second shows William's stamp on Tauler's concept of spiritual progress, demonstrating the German Preacher's direct reliance on various passages of the *Golden Epistle*. The final section describes the *Golden Epistle*'s influence on Tauler's understanding of the *unio mystica* as the culmination of spiritual formation. In that union with the divine, referred to as the "unity of spirit," the spiritual person is not only deified but also participates in the very Intra-Trinitarian communion of the Godhead. Such a Trinitarian understanding of the apex of the spiritual life is William's most profound imprint on Tauler's theology.

---

3 Alois Haas attributes Tauler's paradigm to William (Haas, *Nim din Selbes war: Studien zur Lehre der Selbsterkenntnis bei Meister Eckhart, Johannes Tauler und Heinrich Seuse* [Freiburg: Universitätsverlag, 1971], 134–39). Bernard McGinn maintains it is likely that Tauler is following William (McGinn, *The Harvest of Mysticism in Medieval Germany*, The Presence of God: A History of Western Christian Mysticism, vol. 4 [New York: Crossroad, 2005], 252, 590, n. 54). Louise Gnädinger asserts that Tauler was probably acquainted with William's work and adds the names of Bernard of Clairvaux and William of Saint-Thierry as potential sources for the German Preacher's "Christian-Neoplantonic imprinted mystical theology" (Gnädinger, *Johannes Tauler: Lebenswelt und mystische Lehre* [München: Verlag C.H. Beck, 1993], 122, n. 29, 368). Regarding Tauler's three-person paradigm, however, she lists William as only one of many potential sources (Gnädinger, *Johannes Tauler*, 135–36). Marie-Madeleine Davy claims that William influenced Tauler (Davy, *Un traité de la vie solitaire: Lettre aux frères du Mont-Dieu de Guillaume de St-Thierry*, Études de philosophie médiéval 29, part 2 [Paris: Traduction Française, 1940], 42–48). Georg Steer follows Davy's attribution of Tauler's thought to William, finding the foundation for both in Bernard's *Sermon 20 on the Song of Songs* (Steer, "Bernhard von Clairvaux als theologische Autorität für Meister Eckhart, Johannes Tauler und Heinrich Seuse," in *Bernhard von Clairvaux: Rezeption und Wirkung im Mittelalter und in der Neuzeit*, (ed.) Kasper Elm [Wiesbaden: Harrassowitz, 1994], 246–47). I agree with Dietrich Schlüter who wonders whether this three-person paradigm might serve as a prevailing feature in Tauler's thought, despite the fact that the terminology is in a limited number of sermons; see Schlüter, "Philosophische Grundlagen der Lehren Joahnnes Taulers," in *Johannes Tauler, ein deutscher Mystiker: Gedenkschrift zum 600. Todestag*, (ed.) Ephrem Filthaut (Essen: Hans Driewer Verlag, 1961), 126.

2   Tauler's Potential Manuscripts of the *Epistola aurea*

In his *Instructiones de officiis ordinis*, Humbert of Romans (c. 1200–1277), the fifth master general of the Order of Preachers, suggested a reading list for Dominican novices that included the *Golden Epistle*, attributed to Saint Bernard.[4] Thus, along with other Dominicans of the 14th century, Tauler should have been acquainted with the *Golden Epistle*, at least by name. Living and ministering along the Rhine valley his whole life, Tauler would have had access to at least eight manuscripts of the *Golden Epistle* in the early 14th century.[5] Born to a burgher family in Strasbourg, Tauler received his education with the Dominican Order in that city and was ordained around the year 1325. As a Dominican friar he served in the *cura monialium* among Dominican convents, hearing confessions and providing spiritual direction to nuns, as well as preaching and celebrating daily Mass. From 1338/39–1342/43 Tauler and his fellow Friars Preachers from Strasbourg moved to Basel along the upper Rhine.[6] Tauler continued his care of Dominican nuns in the environs of Basel, as well as households of Beguines and other devout women, covering a circuit that extended to the Dominican convent of Maria Medingen near Dillingen an der Donau, where he and Heinrich von Nördlingen visited in 1339.[7] In the same

---

4   Humbert of Romans, *Instructiones de officiis ordinis*, 5 *De officio magistri novitiorum*, 18 (*Opera de Vita Regulari*, vol. 2, (ed.) Joachim-Joseph Berthier [Turin, 1956], 230), as quoted in Cédric Giraud, *Spiritualité et histoire des textes entre Moyen Âge et époque moderne: genèse et fortune d'un corpus pseudépigraphe de méditations* (Paris: Institut d'études augustiniennes, 2016), 34.

5   The most thorough discussion of Tauler's life and ministry is Gnädinger, *Johannes Tauler*, 9–103. Overviews in English include Bernard McGinn, *The Harvest of Mysticism*, 240–43; Oliver Davies, *God Within: The Mystical Tradition of Northern Europe* (Hyde Park, NY: New City, 2006), 73–78; James M. Clark, *The Great German Mystics: Eckhart, Tauler and Suso* (New York: Russel, 1949; rpt., 1970), 36–44; Josef Schmidt, "Introduction," *Johannes Tauler Sermons*, trans. Maria Shrady, Classics of Western Spirituality (Mahwah, NJ: Paulist Press, 1985), 2–9.

6   The Dominicans were exiled by the city council of Strasbourg for refusing to offer the Mass during the interdict by the Avignon Pope John XXII in his political contest with the HRE Ludwig of Bavaria. For a discussion of Tauler's time in Basel, see Gnädinger, *Johannes Tauler*, 34–43. It is likely that during these four years Tauler first became acquainted with the loose association known as the *Gottesfreunde*. An informal matrix of spiritual renewal of the time, the Friends of God included monks, nuns, Beguines, secular priests, as well as married men and women. A concise description of the movement can be found in English in McGinn, *The Harvest of Mysticism*, 407–31. Likely becoming acquainted with them through the secular priest Heinrich von Nördlingen, Tauler spread their spiritual emphases across German-speaking territories.

7   Evidence from the Dominican convent of Klingenthal bei Basel confirms Tauler's ministry there; cf. Gnädinger, *Johannes Tauler*, 34.

year Tauler made a four-month trip to Cologne on the lower Rhine, preaching in this key city and most probably to convents along the way.[8] After returning to Strasbourg in 1342/43, Tauler continued his traveling ministry, visiting Basel and Cologne again in 1346 and Maria Medingen in 1347. During his lifetime, Tauler's sermons were compiled by his listeners.[9] His fame as a preacher and leader in spiritual renewal associated with the Friends of God—a lay spiritual movement originating in 14th-century Basel—spread far and wide until his death on 16 June 1361.[10]

According to Honemann, there were eight extant manuscripts of the *Golden Epistle* within the territory where Tauler ministered by the early 14th century, to which Tauler would have had reasonable access.[11] Four of these belonged to Dominican houses.[12] Although we do not know what contact Tauler had with his fellow Dominican houses, the presence of the *Golden Epistle* in each demonstrates its transmission in Dominican circles by this time.[13]

Of the eight manuscripts potentially available to Tauler, two present strong possibilities of Tauler's acquaintance. The first is Ms. 181, which, since the

---

8   It is doubtful that Tauler attended the *studium generale* in Cologne. Instead, he almost certainly received his full education with the Dominicans in Strasbourg. See Kurt Ruh, *Geschichte der abendländischen Mystik*, vol. 3, *Die Mystik des deutschen Predigerordens und ihre Grundlegung durch die Hochscholastik* (Munich: Beck, 1996), 478–79.

9   Three collections of his sermons were made during Tauler's lifetime, with the oldest compilation made by the Dominican nuns of Saint Gertrude's in Cologne, for whom Tauler gave some oversight; see Gnädinger, *Johannes Tauler*, 110–15. Although Davies believes the written sermons to be *reportationes* (Davies, *God Within*, 75, 201–02, n. 4), Ruh convincingly argues that Tauler's sermons were read, and what seems to be an "off the cuff" style is simply how Tauler preached (see Ruh, *Geschichte der abendländischen Mystik*, 3:487, 512–15).

10 Tauler's fame is evidenced in the praise accorded him by another Dominican nun, Christine Ebner, from the Engelthal convent near Nürnberg; see Gnädinger, *Johannes Tauler*, 43.

11 These manuscripts are found throughout Honemann, *Die 'Epistola ad fratres de Monte Dei,'* 1–201.

12 Citing Déchanet, Honemann notes that extant manuscripts of the *Golden Epistle* were not numerous enough for Déchanet to posit a "Dominican family" of manuscripts; cf. *Die 'Epistola ad fratres de Monte Dei,'* 198; Déchanet, "Les manuscrits," 236–71.

13 Manuscript 70 with the Dominican friars at Leipzig by 1300 is a complete manuscript and attributed to Bernard; cf. Honemann, *Die 'Epistola ad fratres de Monte Dei,'* 37. Ms. 70: Leipzig, Universitätsbibliothek Ms. F. p. 145 nr. 11 (Katalog Nr. 377). Two other manuscripts were found during the 14th century in Dominican houses in Italy: Ms. 47 in Florence and Ms. v 8 in Bologna; cf. Honemann, *Die 'Epistola ad fratres de Monte Dei,'* 197. However, it is unlikely that Tauler had contact with either.

latter half of the 13th century, was in the possession of the Dominican nuns at Saint Barbara's convent near Trier, situated halfway between Strasbourg and Cologne.[14] Given Tauler's ministry among Dominican nuns, it is possible that Tauler visited Saint Barbara's convent to hear confessions and celebrate the Mass. Even if Tauler never visited Saint Barbara's, he could have encountered this manuscript through the known exchange of books and devotional materials between Dominican convents.[15] It is thus possible that Tauler had access to Saint Barbara's copy of the *Golden Epistle*, whether directly or through mutual contacts.

The second manuscript—and perhaps the strongest possibility for Tauler's acquaintance—is a copy of the *Golden Epistle*, Ms. 6, in the library of the Carthusian house in Basel where Tauler and his fellow Dominicans resided while in exile from Strasbourg. During the 14th century, the Charterhouse of Basel obtained a full manuscript of William's work, though again attributed to Bernard.[16] This manuscript would have been available for Tauler to read during his four years in Basel when Tauler also appears to have become acquainted with an array of spiritual writings, including Mechthild of Magdeburg's *Fliessende Licht der Gottheit* (*The Flowing Light of the Godhead*), Hildegard of Bingen's visions, and probably Heinrich Suso's *Horologium Sapientiae* (*The Clock of Wisdom*). Gnädinger summarizes Tauler's exile as an expanding season of ministry and a time when he "procured manuscripts that could be adopted for the circle of the Friends of God."[17] It would have been à propos for the Dominican Preacher to have acquired a copy of the *Golden Epistle* during this period when he was gathering various writings for those in his growing spiritual movement.[18]

---

14   Honemann, *Die 'Epistola ad fratres de Monte Dei,'* 75. Ms. 181: Trier, Stadtbibliothek, Ms. 198. Honemann lists this as a complete manuscript attributed to Bernard.

15   For example, in addition to the correspondence and books spread by Heinrich von Nördlingen, letters and personal messengers traveled between the Dominican convent of St. Gertrude in Cologne and that of Maria Medingen near Dillingen; cf. Gnädinger, *Tauler*, 34–43. William's work could have been loaned to one of the eight Dominican convents in Strasbourg that Tauler visited repeatedly, including Saint Nicholas am Giessen, where Tauler's sister was a nun. Another possible connection would have been the convent of Saint Gertrude am Neumarkt in Cologne. Both Saint Nicholas and Saint Gertrude had scriptoria for the copying of loaned manuscripts, and Tauler was closely associated with both. Tauler spent his dying days in the garden house at Saint Nicholas, being nursed by his sister and other nuns; cf. Gnädinger, *Johannes Tauler*, 77–79.

16   Honemann, *Die 'Epistola ad fratres de Monte Dei,'* 14. Ms. 6: Basel, Öffentliche Bibliothek der Universität Ms. B X 26.

17   Gnädinger, *Johannes Tauler*, 42.

18   It should also be noted that by the early 16th century the Carthusians in Basel copied a three-volume bound collection of Tauler's sermons. See Gnädinger, *Johannes Tauler*,

A third manuscript that initially appears to have strong possibilities of Tauler's usage is Ms. Ü2, a *Mittelhochdeutsch* (MHD, Middle High German) translation of the *Golden Epistle*. The manuscript originated in the early 14th century and found its way to the cloister of Dominican nuns at Donaueschingen during the 15th century.[19] Honemann places the copyist in the environs north of Augsburg and posits the likelihood of its being copied at the scriptorium of the Cistercian abbey of Kaisheim. If Honemann is correct, the Ü2 manuscript was in the very matrix of Tauler's ministry and friendships.[20] Given the network of relationships connecting Tauler with Margareta Ebner and the abbey of Kaisheim,[21] the MHD translation of the *Golden Epistle* appears to hold reasonable possibilities of being the source of Tauler's contact with William's thought.

Arguing against Ü2 as Tauler's source, however, are key passages where the Dominican follows the *Golden Epistle* and cites material included in the Latin manuscripts but absent from the MHD text. First, in sermon V 60a Tauler

---

116 and Johannes Mayer, "Tauler in der Bibliothek der Laienbrüder von Rebdorf," in *Überlieferungsgeschichtliche Editionen und Studien zur deutschen Literatur des Mittelalters*, (eds.) Konrad Kunze, Johannes Mayer, Bernhard Schnell (Tübingen: Niemeyer, 1989), 388–90.

19   Honemann, *Die 'Epistola ad fratres de Monte Dei*,' 119–48. Ms. Ü2: Fürstliche Fürstenbergischen Hofbibliothek, Ms. 421. The MHD translation provides no introduction or attribution of authorship. Although it has lacunae throughout, it is an excellent translation of the Latin, according to Honemann, *Die 'Epistola ad fratres de Monte Dei*,' 119–28.

20   Abbot Ulrich III of Kaisheim maintained an ongoing correspondence with the mystic Margareta Ebner, a Dominican nun at the nearby convent of Maria Medingen; cf. Honemann, *Die 'Epistola ad fratres de Monte Dei*,' 139; Gnädinger, *Johannes Tauler*, 37–52. Tauler and Heinrich von Nördlingen visited Margareta in 1339. Tauler sent a letter and several cheeses to Margareta and her prioress, Elisabeth Scheppach, in 1346 and visited her again the following year. This correspondence is Tauler's one extant letter; cf. Philipp Strauch, *Margaretha Ebner und Heinrich von Nördlingen: Ein Beitrag zur Geschichte der deutschen Mystik* (Freiburg-im-Breigau/Tübingen: Mohr, 1882), 270–71.

21   Heinrich von Nördlingen held an extensive correspondence with Margareta, and introduced Tauler, Margareta, the Kaisheim abbey, and others to his MHD translation of Mechthild of Magdeburg's *Fliessende Licht der Gottheit*. Indeed a copy of his translation went back and forth between Maria Medingen and Kaisheim. Heinrich sent a copy of Mechthild's work to Margareta and the sisters at Maria Medingen, from where it was loaned to the abbey of Kaisheim to be copied. After the ms. was taken to Maria Medingen, Heinrich asked Margareta to return it after they had enough time to copy it as well, so it could be lent to the Dominican convent in Engelthal, where Christine Ebner lived. In addition, Heinrich sent a copy of Suso's *Horologium Sapientiae* to Abbott Ulrich of Kaisheim. Gnädinger traces the movement of Mechthild's work through the explicit statements in Heinrich's correspondence with Margareta (Gnädinger, *Johannes Tauler*, 34–43). In English, see Bernard McGinn, *The Flowering of Mysticism: Men and Women in the New Mysticism 1200–1350*, The Presence of God, vol. 3, A History of Western Christian Mysticism (New York: Crossroad, 1998), 223, 308–15.

follows Sections 173–176 of the *Golden Epistle* quite closely; however, three of the key terms or phrases that Tauler cites from William's work are absent from manuscript Ü2, as detailed below.[22] Second, Tauler often quotes from the *Golden Epistle*, 170: "God loves Godself in the person, making one [with Godself] the person and his spirit and his love",[23] but Section 170 of the *Golden Epistle* is missing from Ms. Ü2. Third, in sermon V 70 Tauler follows Section 112 from a manuscript of the *Golden Epistle* with the variant *scabendo*, while Ü2 translates from a manuscript that must have read *scopendo*.[24] Therefore, it is almost impossible that Tauler worked from the MHD manuscript Ü2.[25]

Aside from these three main manuscripts, five others remain within the realm of possibility, two of which were in Dominican houses within Tauler's likely vicinity of travel.[26] The remaining three manuscripts are remote

22   See below for the detailed comparison of Latin and MHD texts. Honemann notes that the lacunae in the MHD manuscript do not correspond with those in any of the extant Latin manuscripts (*Die* 'Epistola ad fratres de Monte Dei,' 140); therefore, the translation was likely made from a full Latin text.

23   Ep frat, 170, "amans semetipsum de homine Deus, unum secum efficit et spiritum eius et amorem eius," CCCM 88:263. Translations are my own. Cf. below Tauler's use of this passage in sermons V 26, V 37, V 39, V 41 and V 60d.

24   The MHD manuscript reads "*geist...reinigen*" for "*scopendo spiritum*," Honemann, *Die* 'Epistola ad fratres de Monte Dei,' 331.

25   According to Honemann, *Die* 'Epistola ad fratres de Monte Dei,' 140, Ms. Ü2 is a copy of an original MHD translation, given the specific corrections on the extant manuscript which are appropriate to correcting scribal errors rather than translation errors. Since his original work, Honemann has uncovered a further MHD manuscript; see Honemann, "Eine neue Handschrift der deutschen," 332–49. Referred to as the Roth's Manuscript, this document came from lower Bavaria and was copied by someone from the environs of Augsburg. Neither MHD manuscript was copied from the other, according to Honemann; both come from the "Branche Monte Cassino." Because this manuscript contains the same lacunae as Ms. Ü2, it could not be Tauler's source.

26   Ms. 212, found in the library of the Dominican friary at Würzburg by the 14th century, is a complete manuscript and attributed to Bernard. See Honemann, *Die* 'Epistola ad fratres de Monte Dei,' 86–87. Ms. 212: Würzburg, Universitätsbibliothek M. p. th. f. 10. Würzburg would have been a potential stop for Tauler, depending on his route from Maria Medingen to Cologne. Given Tauler's travels and the exchange of correspondence and books among the Dominican convents, this is a potential source. Ms. 177 from the library at the Dominican house in Ghent also presents a possibility. Honemann, *Die* 'Epistola ad fratres de Monte Dei,' 74. Ms. 177: Stuttgart, Württembergische Landesbibliothek Ms. theol. et phil. qu. 159. Given Tauler's close proximity to Ghent—and Tauler's possible visit to the Lowlands to meet Jan van Ruusbroec—the Ghent manuscript is a further potential source for Tauler. Some scholars believe that Tauler visited the Low Lands in order to see Jan van Ruusbroec; see Ruh, *Geschichte der abendländischen Mystik*, 481 and McGinn, *The Harvest of Mysticism*, 243.

possibilities.[27] Ms. 49 was housed in the cathedral church at Frankfurt am Main.[28] Ms. 9 was at the Cistercian abbey of Himmerod, where a copy of William's work arrived directly from Clairvaux by the end of the 12th century.[29] Ms. 63 was available in Cologne at the convent of Saint Clara, of the Order of Saint Clare.[30]

Thus, of the extant manuscripts of William's masterpiece, eight would have been realistically available to Tauler and two present the strongest possibilities of his usage: Ms. 181 at Saint Barbara's Dominican convent near Trier and Ms. 6 with the Carthusians in Basel. Further research is needed to compare Tauler's citations to the various manuscripts of the *Golden Epistle* to see if any textual variant would resolve the question of Tauler's source.[31]

3   Spiritual Progression: Three-Person Paradigm

William and Tauler continually draw their audience toward spiritual maturity, and both recognize a gradual progression toward that end, honoring the

---

27   Honemann denotes this area as the middle- to lower-Rhine region and notes that the spread of the *Golden Epistle* generally stayed within regions. Moreover, Honemann observes that within such regions, copies of William's work were shared and copied among the various religious orders. Both are complete manuscripts and attributed to Bernard (Honemann, "The Reception of William of St. Thierry's *Epistola ad fratres*," 197–211).

28   Honemann, *Die* 'Epistola ad fratres de Monte Dei,' 30. Ms. 49: Frankfurt/Main, Stadt- und Universitätsbibliothek Ms. Barth. 167. Tauler's travels along the Rhine would have brought him into the vicinity of Frankfurt, where he would have had access to the cathedral library.

29   Honemann, *Die* 'Epistola ad fratres de Monte Dei,' 15. Ms. 9: Berlin, Staatsbibliothek Preussischer Kulturbesitz Ms. lat. fol. 752. Being 150 km south of Cologne, this would have been accessible to the Dominican Preacher.

30   Honemann, *Die* 'Epistola ad fratres de Monte Dei,' 34. Ms. 63: Cologne, Historische Archiv Ms. W. 146. Given the conflict between the two mendicant orders at this time—with Henry of Virneburg, the Franciscan Archbishop of Cologne, placing the Dominican leader Meister Eckhart on trial for heresy in 1326—it is doubtful that Tauler would have had interaction with the nuns of the Franciscan Order. Ghent is some 250 km from Cologne where Tauler preached on various occasions and where he had close connections with the Dominican nuns at Saint Gertrude's convent. In addition, some forms of MHD would have been quite close to the Middle Flemish of Ghent; see Saskia Murk-Jansen, "Hadewijch and Eckhart: *Amor intellegere est*," in *Meister Eckhart and the Beguine Mystics*, (ed.) Bernard McGinn (New York: Continuum, 1994), 18.

31   Because William's *Golden Epistle* was bound to collections of Bernard's works, verifying a specific manuscript could also shed light on Tauler's citations attributed to Bernard and help to clarify the precise imprint of Bernard's thought on Tauler. Gnädinger calls for more research to see if we can uncover which manuscript(s) Tauler was using (*Johannes Tauler*, 408–09). See also Louise Gnädinger, "Der minnende Bernhardus," 392–409.

states of spiritual growth along the way.[32] Both mystagogues follow the classic three-fold way of the spiritual life, and both do so under the rubric of the animal, rational, and spiritual person. William asserts in the *Golden Epistle* that "when we discuss the carnal or the animal sense, or the rational knowledge, or the spiritual wisdom, we describe a single person…as well as three kinds of persons, each according to these properties of that state".[33] More than in this one quote, however, William employs the three-person structure throughout the *Golden Epistle* to describe the states of spiritual progress, as Haas notes.[34] William's paradigm presents a Neoplatonic tripartite anthropology as well as a three-fold itinerary for spiritual progress, culminating in mystical union.

Tauler follows suit in various sermons, depicting every person as comprised of three persons: "The one is the outer person. / The second is the rational person. / And the third is the most noble, God-formed, innermost hidden person. And this is nevertheless all one person".[35] Tauler employs this paradigm in seven sermons, v 64–v 70, and alludes to it in another seven sermons.[36] More generally, this three-person paradigm is interwoven throughout Tauler's numerous sermons following a three-way progression of the spiritual life, and provides the context for Tauler's theology of mystical union in the third and highest person.[37] The following passages regarding various aspects of spiritual progress highlight Tauler's reliance on the *Golden Epistle*.

---

32   Although Tauler follows Meister Eckhart in many concepts and terms for the spiritual life, here Tauler breaks with the great Dominican on spiritual formation as a process. See Alois Haas, *Nim din Selbes war: Studien zur Lehre der Selbsterkenntnis bei Meister Eckhart, Johannes Tauler und Heinrich Seuse* (Freiburg, Schweiz: Universitätsverlag, 1971), 83, n. 20.

33   Ep frat, 140, "cum de carnali uel de animali sensu, uel de rationali scientia, uel de spirituali sapientia disserimus, et unum hominem describimus…et tria hominum genera, singula secundum statuum horum proprietates," CCCM 88:257. All translations are my own.

34   Cf. Haas, *Nim din Selbes war*, 139 n. 173.

35   v 68 (373.8-12), "Der eine ist der usser mensche. / Der ander der vernünftige mensche. / Und der dritte das ist der hoch edel gotformiger aller innerlichste verborgen mensche. Und ist doch alles ein mensche."

36   v 64 (348.21-25); v 65 (357.16-358.13); v 66 (363.4-11); v 67 (365.30-366.9); v 68 (373.8-12, 374.28-375.28, 376.18-22); v 69 (377.3-378.21); v 70 (382.20-22). Sermons more generally assuming or implying the three-person paradigm include v 4 (21.9-12); v 10 (50.15); v 15 (67.28-68.2, 69.37-70.15, 71.16-17); v 23 (92.20-27); v 24 (97.13-16, 101.1-4); v 60e (305.31-306.8); v 60h (322.1-10).

37   Gnädinger, *Johannes Tauler*, 356, highlights the connection of Tauler's three-way progression of the spiritual life and his three-person paradigm. Likewise, M. Engratis Kihm, "Die Drie-Wege-Lehre bei Tauler," in *Johannes Tauler, ein deutscher Mystiker: Gedenkschrift zum 600. Todestag*, (ed.) Ephrem Filthaut (Essen: Hans Driewer Verlag, 1961), 273–75, 286, correlates the two.

4   Overcoming Our Vices

The beginner's state in the threefold progression is one of detachment from fleshly desires and overcoming vices. Although both William and Tauler desire their hearers to arrive at mystical union with the divine, they recognize the necessity of this first state of spiritual progress and give ample space to the battle against disoriented passions. William asserts that sin comes from two sources: "every vice comes from some evil will of desire or evil habit".[38] In sermon v 52 Tauler follows William's teaching in the *Golden Epistle* (222–225) on vices that have become rooted within us, describing both sources of our faults. First, he attributes sin to our "will" and "desire" and appears to remember the *Golden Epistle*'s Latin quite closely as he declares that such faults derive from both "their heart with free will and their desire turned toward created things".[39] Second, Tauler addresses the force of bad habit: "these evil vices...have remained in his [inner] ground from evil habit".[40]

In their respective passages, William and Tauler continue to connect these "vices" and this "evil habit" with pride. William offers a list of vices and other pestilences of the spirit, "that usually flow from the puffing-up and habit of pride".[41] Tauler asserts that although people claim their vice is actually a virtue, to do so is hypocrisy, "for pride lies hidden in their [inner] ground".[42]

Ultimately both assert that once vice is so firmly rooted in us, it can "hardly be overcome." Regarding such vice, William avers that "it can hardly be shaken off from [our] nature",[43] and again, "it can hardly be overcome".[44] Tauler uses the same formula of "hardly" being able to gain victory over such vices: "the fault which is rooted so deeply in the person that the person, with all his diligence, can hardly overcome the fault".[45] The parallels in William's and Tauler's passages—especially the turn of phrase, "hardly be overcome," in their teaching on deeply-rooted vices—can best be explained by Tauler's reliance on William.

---

38   Ep frat, 224, "omnia genera uitiorum, ex aliquo malae uoluntatis affectu uel malae consuetudinis usu," CCCM 88:275.

39   V 52 (235.15), "ir herzen mit frijem willen und ir lust kerent zů den creaturen."

40   V 52 (235.27-30), "dise bőse untugende...sint in dem grunde beliben von der bőser gewonheit."

41   Ep frat, 223, "quae profluere solent ex tumore et usu superbiae," CCCM 88:274.

42   V 52 (235.31), "da hofart in dem grunde lit verborgen."

43   Ep frat, 222, "uix eam a se excutiat natura," CCCM 88:274.

44   Ep frat, 225, "uinci uix potest," CCCM 88:275.

45   V 52 (236.16-18), "der gebreste der wurzelt also tief in den menschen das der mensche mit allem seinem flisse kume den gebresten úberwinden mag."

5   **Devotion at Night**

Both spiritual teachers present the middle of the night as an opportune time
to cultivate devotion. In his discussion of the rhythm of prayer throughout
the day, William highlights that "even in our night vigils, when we arise in the
middle of the night", we can come face to face with God.[46] Closely following
the *Golden Epistle* (111–115), Tauler shifts the time to the middle of the night just
after vigils as an opportune time to cultivate devotion that leads to contemplative union with God, which he refers to as the unity of the spirit: "The most
help and practice is at night after matins, while the night is long".[47]

William asserts that in prayer during this time we should meditate in two
ways. On the one hand, we acknowledge our shortcomings as we "find our distress and sorrow regarding ourselves in ourselves".[48] On the other hand, we
meditate on Christ's redemption for us through "his passion".[49] Continuing
in sermon V 70, Tauler presents meditation on both our redemption through
Christ's suffering and our shortcomings as valuable spiritual exercise: "exercises that the person has used, be it the suffering of our Lord or his own faults".[50]

As we practice the spiritual exercises of meditating on Christ's suffering and
our faults, William asserts that we "strike sparks in our spirit until it ignites"
(...*scabendo spiritum nostrum donec incalescat*...).[51] As a dynamic preacher,
Tauler expands on this idea and paints a picture of igniting a fire: "And should
the person thus stir his love higher—as from much coal and wood comes a great
fire and the flames break through and leap to the heights—so should these

---

46   Ep frat, 111, "Qui etiam in nocturnis uigiliis nostris, quibus media nocte surgimus," CCCM
       88:251.
47   V 70 (382.4-5), "Die meiste helfe und ůbunge ist des nachtes nach mettin die wile die nacht
       lang ist."
48   Ep frat, 112, "tribulationem et dolorem nobis de nobis ipsis inuenire," CCCM 88:251.
49   Ep frat, 115, "passionis ipsius," CCCM 88:252.
50   V 70 (382.23-24), "ůbungen die der mensche vor geůbet hat, es si das liden unsers herren
       oder sin gebreste." Although the MHD sentence is awkward, "sin gebreste" likely refers to
       the faults of the one praying rather than Christ's wounds because *gebresten* (*Gebrechen*)
       is the standard term used by Tauler to refer to human faults or vices, never otherwise to
       Christ's passion. This interpretation is confirmed by the MHD manuscript of the *Golden
       Epistle* that renders "tribulationem et dolorem nobis" (Ep frat, 112) as "vnser gebresten
       erkennen"; see Honemann, *Die* 'Epistola ad fratres de Monte Dei,' 331.
51   Ep frat, 112, CCCM 88:251. The use of *scabendo* rather than *scopendo* also follows Theodore
       Berkeley's amendment of the Latin text in his translation, *The Golden Epistle: A Letter to
       the Brethren at Mont Dieu*, trans. Theodore Berkeley, CF 12 (Kalamazoo, MI: Cistercian
       Publications, 1980), 49. As mentioned above, the MHD manuscript reads "geist...reinigen"
       for "scopendo spiritum"; see Honemann, *Die* 'Epistola ad fratres de Monte Dei,' 331, mak-
       ing it almost certain that Tauler did not follow Ms. Ü2.

good practices ignite the spirit".[52] Of particular note is this double formula of striking "sparks/flames" that results in "igniting our spirit." Ultimately, both William and Tauler are following Cassian's *Conferences* in the assertion that compunction causes one's mind to be both "inflamed and set afire, prompted to pure and most fervent prayers."[53] While Tauler probably knew Cassian's *Conferences*,[54] and while it is possible that he could have followed Cassian directly or through another source, Sections 111–15 of the *Golden Epistle* are the most likely source, since in this sermon Tauler follows the progress of multiple themes from William's discussion.[55]

Finally, William declares: "I will sing with the spirit"[56] as well as with the mind. Tauler similarly concludes his passage on midnight prayer by asserting that such are the true worshipers, "who worship the Father in the spirit".[57] Singing or worshiping in the spirit is not a necessary inclusion—or a foregone conclusion—of either man's train of thought. William is quoting 1 Cor 14:15 while Tauler is following John 4:24. For Tauler to relate the phrase from the Fourth Gospel "in spirit and in truth" to prayer is not an inevitable application of this passage on worship. However, precedence is found in Evagrius Ponticus's *Chapters on Prayer*, where Evagrius exhorts his readers to move toward imageless prayer, referring to John 4:23 four times.[58]

Thus, William and Tauler invite their audience to cultivate spiritual growth by practicing contemplative prayer at night. Both move their discussion of

---

52 V 70 (382.16-18), "Und sol der mensche sine minne hie mitte reissen also: als von vil koln und holtz wirt ein gros fúr und die flamme tringet do durch und slecht uf in die hôhi, also súllent dise gůten ůbunge dis gemůte enzúnden."

53 Cassian, *Conference* 9.26.1, "...quibus inflammata mens atque succensa ad orationes puras ac feruentissimas incitatur," *Collationes XXIIII*, (ed.) Michael Petschenig, CSEL 13 (Vindobonae: C. Geroldi and Sons, 1886; rpt., 2004), 273. Quoted in Columba Stewart, *Cassian the Monk*, Oxford Studies in Historical Theology (New York: Oxford University Press, 1998), 115.

54 Gnädinger argues that Tauler would have been acquainted directly with the *Conferences* given their place of high regard among the German Dominicans of the time, as well as Tauler's several references to the Desert Fathers; see Gnädinger, *Johannes Tauler*, 403–10 and Gnädinger, "Das Altväterzitat im Predigtwerk Johannes Taulers," in *Unterwegs zur Einheit: Festschrift für Heinrich Stirnimann*, (eds.) Johannes Brantschen and Pietro Selvatico (Freiburg: Univeristätsverlag, 1980), 253–67.

55 As well as prescribing such prayer for the night and discussing worship in the spirit, Tauler and William both refer to meditation on Christ's passion as a source of devotion, none of which Cassian mentions in his passage. For analysis of William's connection between meditation on Christ's Passion and the Eucharist, see Nathaniel Peters's chapter, "The Eucharistic Theology of William of Saint-Thierry" in this volume, pp. 160–95.

56 Ep frat, 113, "Psallam spiritu...," CCCM 88:252.

57 V 70 (382.34), "die den vatter anbettent in dem geiste."

58 Evagrius, *De oratione*, 58, 59, 77, 146.

night prayer to the double formula of "sparks/flames" that "ignite our spirit," then to the concept of worship/singing in the spirit. For these parallels to appear within a few paragraphs in William's work as well as Tauler's sermon, suggest that the latter was acquainted with the *Golden Epistle*, consciously following it to some degree as he preached.[59]

6   The Rational Faculty Ruling over the Animal

Progressing from the beginner's state to the rational state in their three-person paradigm, both William and Tauler contend that the reasoning faculties must bring the sensate desires under control.[60] For example, William asserts that when the soul begins to be rational, it "discards the characteristics of weakness and becomes spirit endowed with reason, suited to rule the body, or spirit having [control of] itself".[61]

Tauler likewise states that "the reason itself undoes itself and discards itself and changes itself into the pure, bare spirit".[62] In at least ten sermons, the Dominican stresses the importance of the sensate or animal person coming

---

59   Also following Ep frat, 111–15, Tauler, in sermon v 42, exhorts his listeners to pray, asserting that a genuine Christian "should always take a good span of time, day or night...a good hour," ("sol under nacht und tag iemer ein gůte zit nemen...ein gůte stunde"), for devotion, "each according to his means" ("ein ieklichs nach siner wise"), v 42 (179.24-29). It is possible that Tauler is making a conflation of William's teaching in Ep frat 115 and 174, asserting that each Christian should "use at least some hour/time of the day" ("utile ei sit una saltem aliqua diei hora"), Ep frat, 115, cccm 88:252, "according to their own mode/ means" ("iuxta modum suum"), Ep frat, 174, cccm 88:264. One wonders if Tauler's inclusion of both "good span of time" and "good hour" is his attempt to render the Latin *hora* into German, offering both a narrower and broader translation of the term.

60   Emphasis on reason ruling over the sensate passions is found throughout Christian and Platonic writings, tracing back to Plato's allegory of the charioteer (*Phaedrus*, 246a-254e). What argues for Tauler's reliance on the *Golden Epistle* is the specific phraseology that he employs.

61   Ep frat, 198, "...abdicat a se notam generis feminini, et efficitur animus particeps rationis, regendo corpori accommodatus, uel seipsum habens spiritus," cccm 88:270.

62   V 4 (21.32-33), "die vernunft irs selbes entwúst und sich ires selbes verlöukent und wandelt sich in den lutern blossen geist." It should be noted that although Tauler articulates the role of the rational faculties in various sermons, overall, he places less stress on the role of reason than does William. The German Preacher is quite cautious regarding the "theologians in Paris" and their overly-rational faith; see, for example v 78 (421.1-9) and v 81 (432.2-5). In his sermons, Tauler moves quickly past the rational person because he is perennially focused on leading his audience toward the climactic encounter of deification and mystical union. Most of all, the Dominican believes that transformation comes more from the season of the dark night, trial, and abandonment—which he inserts as a

under the control of reason, and he exhorts his listeners to employ their rational capabilities to master their animal faculties.[63] Similarly, in sermon v 68 Tauler asserts that rational persons "become just like the princes of the world, who are free and under no one.... They rule over all the movements of their inner and outer persons".[64] Tauler's passage is reminiscent of William's assertion that a human spirit moved by reason "freely uses itself".[65] In the following sermon, the German Preacher contends that "the rational person should with diligence be ruler over the animal person".[66]

7   Using Means of Devotion

William and Tauler share an ambivalence toward the use of mental images in prayer. Recognizing the process of growth, both make concession for those less advanced to meditate or pray discursively, while expressing their desire for everyone to "pray spiritually," employing this phrase as a technical term to refer to imageless contemplation.[67] William asserts that beginners must be instructed to raise their heart on high "to pray spiritually.... However, for such people it is better and safer" to meditate on the Lord's image.[68]

---

necessary transitional step before the third and highest stage of spiritual union—than from one's own conscious efforts to curb one's animal nature.

63   Sermons describing the rational person ruling over the animal person include: v 4 (21.17-33); v 7 (30.1-5); v 24 (97.13-17); v 60e (305.31-306.4); v 64 (350.30-32); v 65 (357.17-18, 358.1-4); v 66 (363.4-11); v 67 (365.30-66.3); v 68 (374.28-375.21, 376.18-22); v 69 (377.3-378.12).

64   v 68 (374.29-375.5), "vernúnftigen menschen...werdent recht als die fúrsten der welte, di fri sind und under nieman ensint.... si herschent über all die bewegunge irs usseren und inren menschen." Tauler's passage is reminiscent of William's assertion that a human spirit moved by reason "freely uses itself" ("hoc est seipso libere utens"), Ep frat, 201, CCCM 88:271. In the following sermon, the German Preacher contends that "the rational person should with diligence be ruler over the animal person" ("Der vernúnftige mensche der sol mit flisse meister sin über den vehelihen menschen"), v 69 (377.17-18).

65   Ep frat, 201, "hoc est seipso libere utens," CCCM 88:271.

66   v 69 (377.17-18), "Der vernúnftige mensche der sol mit flisse meister sin über den vehelihen menschen."

67   William clarifies that to pray in the spirit means to stay away "from bodies or corporeal images" ("a corporibus, uel corporum imaginibus"), Ep frat, 173, CCCM 88:264. Likewise, Tauler continually calls his listeners to turn within to God "without image and without form" ("an bilde und an formen"), v 42 (179.27), clarifying in another sermon that to pray "without any...image" is "to maintain the unity of the spirit" ("sunder alle...bilde...si behalten die einikeit des geistes"), v 53 (244.8-9), a phrase used by Tauler in connection with praying in the spirit.

68   Ep frat, 173–74, "spiritualiter orare.... Huiusmodi tamen homini oranti uel meditanti, melius ac tutius," CCCM 88:264.

Making an extended allusion to the *Golden Epistle* in sermon v 60a, Tauler makes the same argument: "All people cannot pray in the Spirit, but must pray with words".[69]

William clarifies that the "better and safer" discursive prayer would be meditation on "an image of our Lord's humanity, especially his birth, passion, and resurrection".[70] Tauler follows suit by telling his hearers, as they take before them "the suffering or the wounds of our Lord," to pray that the heavenly Father would give them "through his only begotten Son an image in the most pleasing manner".[71] Both use meditation on the image of our Lord's humanity—especially his Passion—as a stepping stone toward the desired "spiritual" prayer.

Such an image helps beginners stir up devotion. William wants them to "have something to which they can apply themselves," and specifically something that is "according to their own mode/means of devotion to which they can cling".[72] In sermon v 60a, the Dominican Preacher exhorts: "And when you find a mode/means that stirs you to devotion the most and is most pleasing... remain there and choose these".[73] This terminology of clinging to a personal mode/means of devotion argues strongly for Tauler's reliance on the *Golden Epistle*.[74]

Finally, William continues his discussion of prayer in terms of Jesus' metaphor from Luke 11:9-10 (cf. Matt 7:7-8): "asking, seeking, knocking until...it is opened".[75] Tauler, in the next sentence of sermon v 60a, alludes to the same passage and states that clinging to a mode that stirs inner devotion is what it

---

69   v 60a (280.12-14), "Alle menschen enkúnnent nút in dem geiste betten, sunder mit worten mûssent si betten." Here the MHD *Golden Epistle* does not translate *oranti,* which is the precise concession that both William and Tauler are making for those less advanced in prayer (Honemann, *Die* 'Epistola ad fratres de Monte Dei,' 359).

70   Ep frat, 174, "...imago dominicae humanitatis, natiuitatis eius, passionis et resurrectionis," CCCM 88:264.

71   v 60a (280.11-18), "von dem liden oder von den wunden unsers herren...durch sinen einbornen sun gebe...einen fúrwurf in der aller bevellichester wise." In MHD *fúrwurf* carries the sense of being a "model," "image" or "object," as in Thomistic philosophy, the sun was seen to be an image or object of the eye.

72   Ep frat, 174, "habeat aliquid cui se afficiat; cui iuxta modum suum pietatis intuitu inhaereat," CCCM 88:264.

73   v 60a (280.18-20), "Und als du denne vindest ein wise die dich aller meist zŭ andacht reisset und aller gevellichest ist ... do bi blib nnd [sic] kús sú us." Tauler seems to follow this same passage of William's in sermon v 42 when he again encourages his listeners to pray "each according to his means" ("ein ieklichs nach siner wise"), v 42 (179.26).

74   That reliance, however, is not on the MHD *Golden Epistle*, which does not even translate *modum*. See Honemann, *Die* 'Epistola ad fratres de Monte Dei,' 359.

75   Ep frat, 176, "pententes, quaerentes, pulsantes, donec...aperiatur eis," CCCM 88:265.

means when "one seeks...and knocks with perseverance".[76] In fact, his entire sermon is based on the text from Luke 11.

Thus, within a few paragraphs, both authors exhort their audience to pray by offering a line of reasoning based on the same four assertions in essentially the same order: (1) desiring all to pray in the spirit while conceding that not everyone is able; (2) employing the image of our Lord's earthly body, especially his passion; (3) holding on to one's own means of devotion; and (4) seeking and knocking. These parallel passages demonstrate both mystagogues' emphasis on the necessary progression in the life of prayer, as well as Tauler's dependence on William.

8   Beyond the Carnal Love of Christ

In order to progress toward such imageless devotion, William and Tauler maintain that monks must release their physical or carnal love of Christ. In the *Golden Epistle*, the Cistercian Father avers that those making spiritual progress "begin to know Christ no longer according to the flesh".[77] In various sermons, the German Preacher builds on the theme of moving past a sensate, emotional love of Christ. Four times he uses the illustration of the disciples who needed to relinquish their physical love of Christ in order for them to receive the Holy Spirit. In sermon v 38, he declares that if one is to receive the Holy Spirit in overflowing measure, one must become like the disciples who "now indeed had to let go of the Lord, his most-loved presence".[78]

Likewise in sermon v 24, Tauler exhorts his audience not to cling to their initial experience of spiritual sweetness, as tempting as that might be. Rather, like Jesus' disciples having let go of the Lord's physical presence in order to receive the Holy Spirit, souls moving on to maturity must release their physical love of Christ: "The holy disciples were so entirely filled—inwardly and outwardly—with the presence of our Lord Jesus Christ, and so completely filled—all the corners, heart, soul, senses and faculties, inwardly and outwardly—that this

---

76   v 60a (280.21-22), "man sûche...und klophe mit emziger volhertunge." The MHD *Golden Epistle* lacks the entirety of Ep frat, 176–81, thus excluding Jesus' discussion of asking, seeking, and knocking; see Honemann, *Die 'Epistola ad fratres de Monte Dei,'* 361–63. This lacuna is one of the strongest arguments against Tauler's use of Ms. Ü2, since Tauler would have needed independently to continue his discussion of prayer with the exact same passage from Luke 11 as did William.

77   Ep frat, 175, "incipunt eum iam non secundum Deum carnem cognoscere," CCCM 88:265.

78   v 38 (152.17-18), "Nu mûsten doch die jungern unsern herren lossen, die aller minneklichsten engegenwúrtkeit." See also v 16 (75.12-14) and v 76 (411.6-9).

had to be dispossessed and unpossessed, were they to come to the true spiritual inward consolation. This had to be cut from them—no matter how sour and bitter it ever would be for them—were they ever to move forward. They would otherwise always remain in the lowest [level] and in their senses."[79]

Those who release their sensate love of Christ, however, eventually experience new consolation that comes as such persons are filled with the Spirit, like the disciples, and come into mystical union with the divine. They begin "praying in the Spirit...true, essential prayer",[80] which are two of Tauler's synonyms for the unity of the spirit. Here a new "sweetness sinks in"[81] beyond the earlier sweetness connected with a physical love of Christ. The human "spirit has gone immediately into God...there alone is true union".[82] The human spirit melts into "the love, the same that God is naturally and by essence".[83] Here the person enters "a completely God-like life".[84]

9   Restoring What Was Lost

Ultimately, William and Tauler both see spiritual progress in terms of recovering that which was lost when humanity turned away from God in the Garden of Eden. Regarding fallen human nature, the *Golden Epistle* states: "if it has been turned to God, it quickly recovers ... all that was lost turning away".[85] Tauler echoes in sermon v 56: "But a great, noble master said: 'As soon as the person turns with his spirit ... into God's spirit ... , so all will be brought back in an instant, whatever was lost.'"[86]

---

79   v 24 (100.28–101.1), "Die heiligen jungern worent also gar besessen von innan und von ussen mit der gegenwertikeit unsers herren Jhesu Christi, und also refúllet alzúmole alle ire winkel, hertze, sele, sinne, krefte, indewendig und ussewendig, daz daz besessen uz múste und abe múste, soltent sú zú dem woren geistlichen indewendigen troste komen. Diz múste in abgesnitten werden, wie sur und wie bitter es in iemer wurde, soltent sú iemer fúrbas kommen; sú werent anders zúmole verbliben in dem nidersten und in den sinnen."
80   v 24 (101.12-25), "bettent in dem gieste...woren wesentlichen gebette."
81   v 24 (101.33–102.1), "sich die sússekeit inversencket." Quoting Ps 46:4 (45:5 Vlg), William describes this as "abundant sweetness" ("abundantiae suauitatis"), Ep frat 273, CCCM 88:237.
82   v 24 (101.17-29), "der geist and daz gemúte unmittellichen in Got gon...do wore einikeit alleine ist."
83   v 24 (102.8-9), "der minnen, die selber Got ist wesenlichen und natúrlich."
84   v 24 (102.6-7), "ein zúmole gôttelich leben."
85   Ep frat, 88, "si ad Deum fuerit conuersa, recuperat cito...quaecumque perdidit auersa," CCCM 88:246.
86   v 56 (263.1-4), "Aber ein gros edel meister sprach: 'also schiere als sich der mensche wider kert mit sinem gemúte...in Gotz geiste...so wirt alles das wider bracht in dem ôgenblicke

In two of his sermons on Pentecost, the Dominican elaborates on this restoration. The first sermon for Pentecost (v 60e) asserts that the coming of the
Holy Spirit restores what we lost in the Fall. "Today is the beloved day that
the noble, valuable Treasure is restored, which was harmfully lost in Paradise
by sin."[87] In his second sermon for Pentecost—v 26, which will be discussed
at length below—Tauler clarifies that it is precisely the gift of the Holy Spirit
himself that is restored. That restoration of the Holy Spirit is vitally important
because, for both William and Tauler, the Holy Spirit is the agent of Christian
maturity and perfection. For both mystagogues, the Spirit brings the soul into
the very intimacy of Intra-Trinitarian communion, the *unio mystica*.

10   *Unio Mystica*: Participation in Intra-Trinitarian Communion

In the *Golden Epistle*, William of Saint-Thierry challenges his readers to move
ever forward toward the spiritual state and the experience of mystical union.
Referred to as *unitas spiritus*, William depicts this encounter with the divine in
terms of Intra-Trinitarian love. While William also describes various dynamics
of the *unio mystica*, here we will focus on those five elements most pertinent to
Tauler's sermons. The first three of these elements come directly from Section
263 of the *Golden Epistle*. William describes the spiritual person's participation in divine intimacy and the transformation that is effected in the human
person:

> It is called this unity of the spirit...rather because (1a) it is the Holy Spirit
> himself, God [who is] love; who is the love of the Father and the Son,
> and their unity and sweetness, goodness, kiss and embrace.... The blessed
> consciousness somehow finds itself in the middle of the Father and Son's
> kiss and embrace. In an ineffable, incomprehensible manner, the person
> of God (2) merits to become not God, but what God is: (3) the person
> [becomes] by grace what God is by nature.[88]

---

das ie verlorn wart.'" Déchanet asserts that Tauler is referring here to William (assumed to
be Bernard) as the "great, noble master" ("Introduction," *The Golden Epistle*, xiii, n. 13). On
restoring what was lost, see also sermons v 26 (103.6-11) and v 49 (219.24-29).

87   v 60e (304.13-15), "der minnencliche tag ist húte, daz der edel túre schatz ist widergeben
der so schedeliche waz verlorn in dem paradise mit den súnden."

88   Ep frat, 263: "Dicitur autem haec unitas spiritus...sed quia (1a) ipsa ipse est Spiritus
sanctus, Deus caritas; cum qui est amor Patris et Filii, et unitas et suauitas, et bonum et
osculum, et amplexus.... Cum in osculo et amplexu Patris et Filii mediam quodammodo
se inuenit beata conscientia; cum modo ineffabili et incogitabili, (2) fieri meretur homo

In this union, William's Trinitarian mysticism insists that spiritual persons (1a) experience divine sweetness and goodness. Created in the image of the Trinity, and now returned to the Trinity, they find themselves wrapped "in the middle of the Father and Son's kiss and embrace" (*in osculo et amplexu Patris et Filii mediam*) in an encounter that is beyond human comprehension or expression.[89] Such encounter takes place in what William calls the "unity of the spirit" (*unitas spiritus*) precisely because the Person of the Holy Spirit is the divine "unity, sweetness, goodness, kiss and embrace" (*unitas et suauitas, et bonum et osculum, et amplexus*). Thus in the ineffable ecstasy of mystical union, spiritual persons share in the mutual love of the Father and the Son. (2) Such an experience of divine *amor* is transformative. William asserts that the human person becomes divinized and "merits to become not God, but what God is" (*fieri meretur homo non Deus, sed tamen quod Deus est*). Here the Cistercian describes deification in the strongest possible language without compromising orthodoxy. (3) Guarding against accusations of pantheism or panentheism, William follows his statement of deification immediately with the traditional formulation that the person becomes "by grace what God is by nature" (*ex gratia quod Deus est ex natura*). The human person remains a created being but by grace comes to share in God's divine nature. Thus elements (1a), (2) and (3) of mystical union are interconnected in the *Golden Epistle*.

(1b) Before examining the last two elements, we should note that in the *Golden Epistle* (170) William offers another description of the soul's experience of Trinitarian love. By the infusing of the Holy Spirit, says the Cistercian Father, "God loves Godself in the person, making one [with Godself] the person and his spirit and his love."[90] The Intra-Trinitarian communion between the Father and Son expresses itself in the human spirit, and the human person thereby participates in this relationship of divine Persons. This alternative description of the encounter with Intra-Trinitarian love is significant because Tauler refers to it in some thirteen sermons, frequently substituting it for element (1a) when he follows Section 263 of the *Golden Epistle*.

(4) In mystical union, a soul at times goes into ecstatic *raptus*, according to William, in which the spiritual person is "sometimes shown the light of God's

---

Dei, non Deus, sed tamen quod Deus est: (3) homo ex gratia quod Deus est ex natura," CCCM 88:282. Numbers are added throughout to William's and Tauler's quotations to highlight the five key elements.

89   On William's theological foundation for *unio mystica*, see Odo Brooke, *Studies in Monastic Theology*, CS 37 (Kalamazoo, MI: Cistercian Publications, 1980), esp. 12–62.

90   Ep frat, 170, "amans semetipsum de homine Deus, unum secum efficit et spiritum eius et amorem eius," CCCM 88:263.

face".[91] God "snatches the soul out of himself and raptures him into what is, from tumultuous events, into silent joys".[92] (5) Finally, this deified person will not fall from grace. For the one who has come into the divinized life, according to William, "it is not possible to will anything except what God wills".[93] In the *unitas spiritus*, concludes David Bell, "to love God and to will what he wills are both inseparable from participation in the Holy Spirit, who is himself the substantial Will/Love of Father and Son."[94] Therefore, William maintains that these spiritual persons will never persist in willful rebellion against God. For such a soul, living in God's likeness, "in its ardent adherence to the unchangeable good, it seems no longer possible to be changed from that which is".[95]

Thus William presents a mystical union founded upon participation in Intra-Trinitarian love in the unity of the Spirit. That experience is relational and transformative, as Anne Hunt summarizes, the human soul's "entry into the Trinitarian communion, is grounded in the very person of the Holy Spirit as bond of union, mutual love *and knowledge* of Father and Son, their kiss and embrace, their very oneness; and that too for the human person in union with God."[96]

11 Tauler's *Unio Mystica* and Intra-Trinitarian Love

In his sermons, Tauler repeatedly leads his hearers toward the climax of the *unio mystica*, where the innermost human spirit—the human "ground/innermost depths" (*grunde*) or "abyss/fathomless depths" (*abgrunde*)[97]—is so

---

91   Ep frat, 268, "aliquando lumen quoddam uultus Dei ostenditur," cccm 88:283.

92   Ep frat, 269, "eripit eum sibi, et rapit in diem qui est, a tumultu rerum, ad gaudia silentii," cccm 88:283. For a discussion of William's concept of ecstasy, see David N. Bell, *The Image and Likeness: The Augustinian Spirituality of William of St. Thierry*, CS 78 (Kalamazoo, MI: Cistercian Publications, 1984), 196–215.

93   Ep frat, 257, "ut non possit uelle nisi quod Deus uult," cccm 88:281.

94   Bell, *Image and Likeness*, 185. For a fuller discussion of William's assertion that those who arrive at the unity of spirit cannot persevere in sin, see Bell, 184–96.

95   Ep frat, 276, "ut ex ardentissima boni incommutabilis adhaesione, nullatenus iam uideatur posse mutari ab eo quod est," cccm 88:285.

96   Anne Hunt, *The Trinity: Insights from the Mystics* (Collegeville, MN: Liturgical Press, 2010), 20.

97   Tauler refers to the innermost realm of the person using a variety of terms, including *grunde/grunt*, *abgrunde/abgrunt*, *mens* and *gemûte*. For a discussion of Tauler's terminology, see Paul Wyser, "Taulers Terminologie vom Seelengrund," in *Altdeutsche und altneiderländische Mystik*, (ed.) Kurt Ruh (Darmstadt: Wissenshaftliche Buchgesellschaft, 1964), 324–52; Gnädinger, *Johannes Tauler*, 241–51; McGinn, *The Harvest of Mysticism*, 254–64, 591, n. 67; and Loris Sturlese, "Tauler im Kontext: Die philosophischen Voraussetzungen des 'Seelengrundes' in der Lehre des deutschen Neuplatonikers

unified with the divine abyss that the two become "one single one" (*ein einig ein*).[98] In fact, the majority of the Dominican's sermons call his listeners into oneness with God, employing a wide variety of imagery and terminology to depict union with the divine. Such an invitation to experience mystical union is so widespread in his preaching that Louise Gnädinger concludes, "Tauler's language regarding the encounter, the uniting and the union of the person with God is found in his sermons—strikingly constant and ubiquitous, yes almost intrusiveness of the theme—to be extremely diverse and frequently varied."[99]

Seventeen sermons follow the *Golden Epistle*, employing at least three of the five elements of mystical union. Such usage demonstrates William's imprint on the Dominican's theological construction of the *unio mystica*. Often, however, Tauler's wording is less precise than his Cistercian predecessor. In good homiletic fashion, the German Preacher expresses these elements in his own words, at times embellishing or illustrating them. In addition, Tauler is rendering William's Latin passages from the *Golden Epistle* into *Mittelhochdeutsch*.[100] Thus the Preacher's terminology is diverse. In the midst of that variety, though, he unmistakably follows William's concepts of the *unio mystica*. Below I will first describe Tauler's general use of these five elements. Second I will examine six sermons in which the Dominican employs these elements at length and which demonstrate the degree to which Tauler references the *Golden Epistle* Section 263.

(1a) Tauler describes the soul's encounter with God in the *unio mystica* using William's language of the divine sweetness, kiss, and embrace. In three sermons, the German Preacher invites his listeners to move toward this unitive ecstasy in which the human person participates in Intra-Trinitarian intimacy.[101] In various other sermons, he offers a more general description of sweetness and savoring God's presence in the encounter of mystical union.[102]

(1b) Tauler likewise asserts that in mystical union, God "loves" (*minnet*), "knows" (*kennt/bekennet*), "understands" (*verstat*), and/or "enjoys/savors"

Berthold von Moosburg," *Beiträge zur Geschichte der deutschen Sprache und Literatur* 109 (1987): 422–26.

98   V 41 (176.9). The same formula of "ein einig ein" is found in V 39 (156.20), V 45 (201.6), and V 53 (245.17).

99   Gnädinger, *Johannes Tauler*, 241: "Die Redeweise über die Begegnung, die Vereinigung und die Einheit des Menschen mit Gott gestaltet sich in seinen Predigten—bei auffallender Konstanz und Allgegenwart, ja beinahe Aufdringlichkeit des Themas—äußerst abwechslungsreich und vielfach variiert."

100   In MHD there is little concern for consistency of spelling, making any uniformity of translation unlikely.

101   Sermons V 38 (153.8-9, 14–18), V 39 (160.25, 34), and V 53 (245.13-15).

102   For example, cf. sermons V 6 (27.17), V 7 (33.20-23), V 12 (57.2-10), V 15 (70.29-34), V 21 (87.33-88.4), V 24 (101.3-6), V 54 (248.9-249.32), V 67 (368.28-32), and especially V 70 (382.1–383.26).

(*gebrucht/smacket*) Godself in the spiritual person. Here the Dominican follows the *Golden Epistle* Section 170 where William states that in the human person, God loves Godself. The divine Intra-Trinitarian communion between the Father and Son expresses itself in the human spirit, and the human spirit thereby participates in this divine relationship of Persons. This formula of Trinitarian self-knowledge is employed in no less than thirteen of Tauler's sermons.[103] Thus, the Dominican articulates Intra-Trinitarian love and knowledge of the divine Persons, doing so predominantly in the context of the human soul's experience of this love in mystical union with the divine.

Tauler often substitutes this description of the soul's encounter of Intra-Trinitarian love from the *Golden Epistle* Section 170 for element (1a) of Section 263 in his presentation of the *unio mystica*. Of particular note are sermons V 26, V 37, V 39, V 41 and V 60d, presented below, in which the German Preacher inserts (1b)—God's knowing, loving, understanding, and/or savoring Godself—in passages where he is closely following elements (2) and (3) from the *Golden Epistle* Section 263. Tauler certainly would have known Augustine's discussion of God's loving Godself from *De Trinitate*, as well as Eckhart's passages that frame the divine birth in the soul in the theological discussion of the Trinitarian procession of Persons.[104] Nevertheless, the fact that Tauler's depiction of God's knowing Godself is woven into passages that follow Section 263 of the *Golden Epistle* in these five sermons, argues strongly for William as the immediate source of Tauler's concept of the human spirit's participation in Intra-Trinitarian communion.[105]

---

103   Cf. sermons V 1 (8.32-35) *bekennen, bekant, verstanden het*; V 26 (109.19-20) *bekennet, verstat, smacket*; V 37 (146.19-20) *mint, bekent, gebrucht* ; V 39 (156.24-29) *bekentnisse, gebruchen, niessen*; V 41 (175.21) *gebruchet*; V 55 (258.2-3) *kenne, minne, gebruche*; V 57 (266.11) *gebruchet*; V 60 (278.16) *bekant*; V 60d (299.7-10) *bekentnisse, gebruchende* and (300.21) *gebruchet*; V 62 (340.26) *minnet*; V 67 (367.25) *gebruchet*; V 74 (402.26-27) *gebruchet*; and V 76 (411.25) *minnet*. For example, in sermon V 55 (258.2-3) Tauler describes those in union with God: "Regarding these one can say that in them God knows and loves and savors Godself" ("Von disen mag man sprechen das sich Got in disen kenne und minne und gebruche"). A few of these passages refer to God the Father's self-knowledge in eternity in the eternal generation of the Son; however, for Tauler that eternal self-knowledge is never far removed from God's self-knowledge and self-love encountered in the human spirit, as demonstrated in sermon V 60d (299.7-10, 300.17-25). While some scholars, including Bernard McGinn (*The Harvest of Mysticism*, 586), believe sermon V 1 to belong to Eckhart, others have maintained it as part of Tauler's corpus. See Gnädinger's summary of the debate, *Johannes Tauler*, 140, esp. n. 44.

104   Cf. McGinn, *The Harvest of Mysticism*, 293.

105   While William makes similar statements regarding the kiss and embrace of the Father and Son in the union of the Holy Spirit in his *Exposition on the Song of Songs* (95) and *Mirror of Faith* (32), Tauler's repeated interweaving of all three elements points to his direct dependence on the *Golden Epistle*, 263.

(2) Tauler expands on the concept of becoming not God, but what God is. He uses an array of terms to describe deification: "deified" (*vergottet*), "God-hued" (*gotvar*), "godly" (*gottig*), "God-like" (*gótlich*), "God-formed" (*gotformig*), "God-imaged" (*gotbildig*), and "god in God" (*got in gotte*). These and related terms are used in more than half of the Dominican's sermons. To flesh out the concept of a divinized life, Tauler asserts that such persons become "so God-hued ... and transformed ... that God works this person's work".[106] The German Preacher employs a version of 'God's working a person's works' in some twelve sermons.[107] This phrase of 'God's working the person's work' is used synonymously with statements of deification, as seen in sermon v 39: "there the person becomes so deified that all that the person is and works, God works and is in him".[108] Likewise, sermon v 68 explains that, in the third and highest person, who is "God-imaged, God-formed, ...God...works all his works".[109] In two passages that closely follow *Golden Epistle* Section 263, Tauler utilizes the phrase of 'God's working their works' as his statement of deification, v 26 (109.25-26) and v 6od (300.21).[110]

(3) Tauler qualifies his concepts of deification by asserting that the soul becomes "by grace what God is by nature" at least ten times in his extant sermons.[111] The Dominican likely includes such a guardrail against any pantheistic interpretation in light of the charges brought against Meister Eckhart.[112] More relevant to this study is the fact that in the six sermons below, Tauler

---

106   v 41 (175.17-21), "als gotvar...und úberformet...das Got dis menschen werk wúrket." Kihm recognizes the concept of God's working one's work as an essential dynamic of the divinized life and lists it first in her description of Tauler's "Das göttliche Leben im Menschen" (Kihm, "Die Drie-Wege-Lehre bei Tauler," 296). Gnädinger, likewise, situates this theme of 'God's working the person's works' in Tauler's discussion of the *unio mystica* (Gnädinger, *Johannes Tauler*, 359–60).

107   Sermons v 1 (9.33), v 26 (109.25-26), v 37 (146.20), v 38 (153.26-27), v 39 (162.8-9), v 41 (175.18-22), v 54 (251.19-20), v 6od (300.21), v 6of (312.7-10), v 62 (340.26-27), v 68 (375.27-28, 376.25), and v 70 (382.20-22).

108   v 39 (162.8-9), "wird do der mensche als vergottet das alles das der mensche ist und wúrket, das wúrket und ist Got in ime."

109   v 68 (375.23-27), "gotbildigen, gotformigen...Got...wúrket alle sine werk." Five of these sermons explicitly identify 'God's working the person's works' with deification: v 37 (146.20), v 38 (153.26-27), v 39 (162.8-9), v 41 (175.18-22), and v 68 (375.27-28, 376.25). Five sermons link the phrase of 'God's working the person's works' directly with element (1b), God's knowing, loving, and/or savoring Godself in the person: v 26 (109.18-26), v 37 (146.20), v 41 (175.18-22), v 6od (300.21), v 62 (340.26-27). All of these except v 62 will be discussed below.

110   See below for a discussion of sermons v 26 and v 6od.

111   v 6 (25.23-24), v 10 (47.20-21), v 24 (102.6-9), v 26 (109.23-24), v 37 (146.21-22, 27), v 38 (153.21-22), v 39 (162.10-11), v 41 (175.20), and v 6od (300.25). See also one sermon not found in Vetter's collection: H 71 from the modern German translation, *Johannes Tauler: Predigten: Vollständige Ausgabe*, (ed.) and trans. Georg Hofmann (Freiburg: Herder, 1961), 551.

112   For a concise discussion of the accusations against Eckhart and the bull, *In agro dominico*, see McGinn, *The Harvest of Mysticism*, 103–07.

connects this qualifying phrase directly to his description of deification, as does William in the *Golden Epistle* Section 263.[113]

(4) More than half of Tauler's sermons describe the ecstasy that may accompany mystical union, using various descriptions of the soul's "going above itself."[114] In Neoplatonic fashion, the German Preacher often employs terminology of surpassing understanding—human and angelic—to describe spiritual persons' ascent in ecstasy, as well as their divinized state.[115] In the following six sermons Tauler weaves a depiction of ecstasy in his passages that follow the *Golden Epistle* Section 263, demonstrating the connection Tauler—as William—saw between ecstasy and the Intra-Trinitarian experience of God's love in the *unio mystica*.[116]

(5) Finally, Tauler asserts: "it is not possible to believe that these people would ever be able to be separated from God".[117] Likewise, regarding one who has experienced mystical union with God, the Preacher maintains, "without any doubt God will not allow him to err, no matter what path he travels".[118]

---

113   Four times the qualification of "by grace what God is by nature" comes immediately after a statement of deification: sermons v 37 (146.22), v 38 (153.21-22), v 39 (162.10-11), and v 41 (175.20). Two additional times it is linked with the substitute phrase for deification, "God works their works": sermons v 26 (109.23-24) and v 60d (300.25).

114   For example, in sermon v 67 (368.33-34) Tauler asserts that the heights of God's love "draws the human spirit so high above itself with love" ("zúhet des menschen gemúte als hoch úber sich mit minnen"). Other sermons clarify that the human spirit or *gemúte* is drawn directly into the divine: "thus exalted God draws the [created] spirit up into Godself" ("also zúhet der hoch Got den geist uf in sich"), v 54 (252.10-11). Gnädinger notes that Tauler uses many more terms for this ecstatic *úbervart* in the various ways he describes *unio mystica* (Gnädinger, *Johannes Tauler*, 357).

115   For example, in v 38 (153.29-30) Tauler asserts that union with God "goes above all senses and all human, yes angelic, understanding" ("gat úber alle sinne und alle menschlich, ja engelschlich verstentnisse"). Thus, the soul goes "far above all thought and reason of humans and angels, and all creatures in heaven and on earth" ("verre úber allen gedang und vernunft menschen und engelen und allen creaturen in himmele und in erden"), v 32 (119.22-24), "because it is too high for all created intelligences, angelic and human" ("wan es ist allen geschaffenen verstentnissen, engelen und menschen, zú hoch,") v 26 (109.29-30).

116   While William is circumspect in his description of ecstasy, he does not avoid the experience, as seen above in Ep frat, 269.

117   v 41 (176.16-17), "Das enist nút ze glóbende das dise lúte iemer von Gotte múgen gescheiden werden."

118   v 74 (402.15), "On allen zwifel so enlat in God nút irren, welichen weg er ouch get." Tauler does not so much assert that a person can no longer sin, but rather that he or she will not fall into permanent error or be separated from God, much as William maintains that it is not possible to persist in sin. Tauler makes similar assertions in other sermons: v 21 (88.18-19), v 26 (109.7), v 37 (147.8), v 39 (160.5-6), v 41 (176.16), and v 74 (402.15). Tauler renders William's claim that "it seems no longer possible to be changed from that which is" ("nullatenus iam uideatur posse mutari ab eo quod est," Ep frat, 276, CCCM 88:285) as "it is not possible to believe" ("das enist nút glóiplich") that such a one would fall or be separated from God (v 39 [160.5] and v 41 [176.17]). Tauler makes an even stronger claim that "it is

While Tauler could have adopted elements (4) and (5) from other Christian Neoplatonic sources, his inclusion of these two elements in passages centered on elements (1) through (3) from the *Golden Epistle* Section 263 suggests that in Tauler's mind they are integrally linked with the first three elements. That linkage is seen most clearly in the following six sermons. In and around the first three elements, Tauler weaves elements (4) and (5), firmly contending for the *Golden Epistle* as Tauler's source for all the elements (1) through (5) and demonstrating how much the Cistercian influenced the Dominican's concept of the *unio mystica*.

12   Sermon V 39

In sermon V 39 Tauler depicts the mystical union experienced by the spiritual person who has attained to the third and highest level of growth. On this "third level...one becomes in truth one with God".[119] Although comprised of three passages distributed across the sermon, this example is significant because Tauler follows all five elements from the *Golden Epistle*, including both (1a) and (1b), weaving the two together:

> The heavenly Father...(1b) in the knowing of himself gives birth to his beloved Son, and both breathe out into each other (1a) the Holy Spirit in an ineffable embrace....
>
> The third [level], that is a (4) transcendence into (2) a God-formed essence in unity of the created spirit in the "being" spirit of God...(5) it is not possible to believe that they would ever be able to fall from God....
>
> (4) And then the bright sun shine rises and lifts the person completely out of all his distress.... In this the Lord takes the person so completely out of himself into Godself ...that God draws the person out of human manner into a godly manner, out of all his turmoil into a divine security, and there the person becomes (2) so deified that all that the person is and works, God works and is in him, and (4) is taken so far up above his natural ways that he truly (3) becomes by grace what God is essentially by nature.[120]

impossible that God would ever forsake these people" ("daz ist unmúgelich das Got disen menschen iemer gelasse"), V 26 (109.6-7).

119   V 39 (162.1, 22), "dritten grat...man in der worheit ein mit Gotte wirt."

120   V 39 (156.23-26, 160.3-6, 162.2-11), "Der himelsche vatter...(1b) in dem bekentnisse sin selbes gebirt sinen geminten sun, und si beide geistend usser in beiden (1a) den heiligen geist in einem unsprechlichen umbevange....

Das dritte das ist ein (4) úbervart in (2) ein gotformig wesen in einikeit des geschaffenen geistes in den istigen geist Gotz...(5) das enist nút glöiplich das si iemer von Gotte múgen gevallen....

First, the Dominican depicts the person's experience of Trinitarian love by combining the themes from Sections 170 and 263 of the *Golden Epistle*, asserting that God the Father (1b) "in the knowing of himself gives birth to his beloved Son, and both breathe out into each other (1a) the Holy Spirit in an ineffable embrace" (*...in dem bekentnisse sin selbes gebirt sinen geminten sun, und si beide geistend usser in beiden den heiligen geist in einem unsprechlichen umbevange*). Such a juxtaposition of quotes from these two sections of the *Golden Epistle* on participation in the Intra-Trinitarian intimacy demonstrates how closely these two passages are linked in Tauler's thought.

Here, in the *unio mystica*, the human spirit becomes what God is, "a God-formed essence" (*ein gotformig wesen*). In that transformation, the person becomes (2) "so deified that all that the person is and works, God works and is in him" (*als vergottet das alles das der mensche ist und würket, das würket und ist Got in ime*). Continuing with the description of union, Tauler depicts the flight of ecstasy and reminds his hearers that this is all by grace. The person (4) "is taken so far up above his natural ways that he truly (3) becomes by grace what God is essentially by nature" (*wirt als verre uf erhaben über sin natürlich wise das er recht wird von gnaden das Got weslichen ist von naturen*).

Tauler reiterates the experience of ecstasy: (4) "And then the bright sun shine rises and lifts the person completely out of all his distress.... In this the Lord takes the person so completely out of himself into Godself...out of all his turmoil into a divine security" (*Und denne gat uf der liechten sunnen schin and hebet in alzemole usser aller siner not.... In disem so fürt recht der herre den menschen usser im selber in sich...usser aller jomerkeit in ein götlich sicherheit*).[121] He then asserts that those who have achieved the third level of perfection need not fear that they will fall from grace: (5) "it is not possible to believe that they would ever be able to fall from God" (*das enist nút glöiplich das si iemer von Gotte mügen gevallen*).

---

(4) Und denne gat uf der liechten sunnen schin and hebet in alzemole usser aller siner not.... In disem so fürt recht der herre den menschen usser im selber in sich...so zúhet Got den menschen us menschlicher wise in ein götliche wise, usser aller jomerkeit in ein götlich sicherheit, und wird do der mensche (2) als vergottet das alles das der mensche ist und würket, das würket und ist Got in ime, und (4) wirt als verre uf erhaben über sin natúrlich wise das er recht (3) wird von gnaden das Got weslichen ist von naturen."

121   As quoted above, William asserts that the spiritual person is "sometimes shown the light of God's face" ("aliquando lumen quoddam uultus Dei ostenditur"), Ep frat, 268, CCCM 88:283. God "snatches him from himself, and catches him up into what is, from tumultuous events, into silent joys" ("eripit eum sibi, et rapit in diem qui est, a tumultu rerum, ad gaudia silentii"), Ep frat, 269, CCCM 88:283. Rendering "a tumultu rerum" as "usser aller jomerkeit," Tauler's language here follows Ep frat 268 and 269 very closely.

Beyond these five elements, it should be noted that the German Preacher describes such mystical union in terms of "unity of the spirit"[122] in which there is a "unity of the created spirit in the 'being' Spirit of God" (*einikeit des geschaffenen geistes in den istigen geist Gotz*). Tauler adopts this terminology of the "unity of the spirit" to describe mystical union of the human soul with God, employing it seven times in five sermons.[123] Interestingly, all of these are among the sermons that follow at least three of William's five elements of the *unio mystica*. While Tauler may have encountered this usage of the *unitas spiritus* in other Neoplatonic writings, his use of the term in sermons V 39 and V 70 clearly points to William since that usage is embedded in passages of material from the *Golden Epistle*.[124] Moreover, Tauler employs the term precisely as does William, who, as Tyler Sergent has demonstrated, is the first in the Western tradition to interpret *unitas spiritus* as a reference to the union between the human soul and the divine.[125] Thus, as well as employing all five elements from the *Golden Epistle*, including both (1a) and (1b), sermon V 39 displays the extent of William's stamp on Tauler's spiritual theology.[126]

---

122   Five times in the *Golden Epistle* William names this spiritual union, *unitas spiritus*: Ep frat, 235, 256, 257, 262, and 263. Playing on this theme, William also asserts that the physical solitude of such a person is transformed into "unity of mind" (*unitatem mentis*) in Ep frat, 288, CCCM 88: 287. He asserts that the transformation of the person in this *unio mystica* is so profound that it is "not just a likeness but [moreover] the unity of the Spirit" ("non iam similitudo, sed unitas spiritus"), Ep frat, 262, CCCM 88: 282.

123   Sermons V 39 (160. 3-4), V 53 (240.5, 244.15, 245.29), V 66 (363.27), V 70 (380.25, 382.4), V 74 (400.12). While three of these are quotations of Eph 4:3, the context shows that the Dominican understands the verse to refer to *unio mystica*.

124   In sermon V 39 Tauler also employs three phrases almost interchangeably with the unity of the spirit: "one-mindedness of prayer" ("einmütkeit des gebettes"): V 39 (162.21); cf. V 39 (154.10) from 1 Pet 3:8; "should pray, that is in the spirit" ("betten sol, das ist in dem geiste"): V 39 (154.18); "prayer that takes place in the spirit" ("gebet, das in dem geiste geschiht"): V 39 (156.1); and "true, spiritual prayer" ("wore geistes gebet"): V 139 (156.11-12). Tauler uses the term "worship in the spirit" ("anbettent in dem geiste"): V 70 (382.34) and V 78 (421.23) as a synonymous phrase. "Prayer in the spirit" ("Gebette des geistes") is likewise employed in sermon V 75 (405.19) and "heartfelt prayer and that is in the spirit" ("herzelicheme gebette und daz in deme geiste") in sermon V 81 (433.26-27).

125   F. Tyler Sergent, "*Unitas Spiritus* and the Originality of William of Saint-Thierry," in *Unity of Spirit: Studies on William of Saint-Thierry in Honor of E. Rozanne Elder*, (eds.) F. Tyler Sergent, Aage Rydstrøm-Poulsen, and Marsha L. Dutton, CS 268 (Collegeville, MN: Cistercian Publications, 2015), 144–70; see also, Sergent, "'Signs of Spiritual and Divine Realities': The Sources and Originality of William of Saint Thierry's Ascetic Language," Ph.D. diss., Roskilde Universitet, Denmark, 2009, 135–77.

126   Earlier in the sermon, Tauler also follows William's threefold spiritual development and his exhortation to use this means of devotion. See Glenn E. Myers, "Manuscript Evidence of the *Golden Epistle*'s Influence in the Sermons of Johannes Tauler," *Cistercian Studies Quarterly* 48.4 (2013): 479–501.

13   Sermon V 38

Sermon V 38 further demonstrates how closely Tauler follows the *Golden Epistle* in his discussion of the human spirit's participation in Intra-Trinitarian love. The Dominican offers an allegorical interpretation of Queen Esther, as the human soul, coming before King Ahasuerus, as God the Father, in his presentation of the *unio mystica*:

> (1a) the heavenly Father...gives her [Esther/the soul] his divine embrace and (4) lifts her up above all her sickness in the divine embrace.
>
> [He]...(1a) gives her his one and only Son...and in the sweetest kiss he pours into her completely the highest, super-essential sweetness of the Holy Spirit...(2) that she [Esther/the soul] would be as Lady all that he is as Lord, and (3) God would be in him by grace what he is and has by nature.[127]

Within thirteen lines of text, Tauler closely follows the first three elements of the *unio mystica* as they are found in the *Golden Epistle* Section 263. Using William's language, the Dominican describes (1a) the soul's experience of the "divine embrace" (*gótlichen umbevang*), the "sweetest kiss" (*aller sússesten kusse*), and "the highest super-essential sweetness of the Holy Spirit" (*die oberste úberweselichen súskeit des heiligen geistes*). In a powerful image of William's assertion that the spiritual person becomes (2) "not God, but what God is" (*non Deus, sed tamen quod Deus est*),[128] Tauler asserts "that she [Esther/the soul] would be as Lady all that he is as Lord" (*das si des alles frówe si des er herre ist*). Thus, the German Preacher offers a word picture for his audience of Dominican nuns—some of whom were ladies of the nobility—that brings alive the concept of becoming not God, but all that God is. Several lines later Tauler adds his further explanation of becoming *vergottet*, that "God works all the person's works" (*Got wúrkt alles des menschen werk*).[129] As in the *Golden Epistle* Section 263, the statement of the divinized life is followed immediately by the qualifying formula, (3) "God would be in him by grace what God is and has by nature" (*Got in ime si von gnaden, das er ist und hat von naturen*). In this *unio mystica*, God (4) "lifts her up above all her sickness in the divine embrace" (*hebt*

---

127   V 38 (153.10-22), (1a) "der himelsche vatter...git ir [Hester] sinen gótlichen umbevang und (4) hebt si uf úber alle ir krankheit in dem gótlichen umbevang.
        [Er]...(1a) git ir sinen einbornen sun...und in dem aller sússesten kusse in gússet er ir alzemole die oberste úberweselichen súskeit des heiligen geistes...(2) das si des alles frówe si des er herre ist, und (3) Got in ime si von gnaden, das er ist und hat von nature."

128   Ep frat, 263, CCCM 88:282.

129   V 38 (153.26).

si uf über alle ir krankheit in dem götlichen umbevang). Thus, although sermon v 38 does not contain element (5) of the *unio mystica*, it parallels elements (1a), (2), (3) and (4) from the *Golden Epistle* 263, demonstrating how closely the Dominican knows and follows William's work.

14   Sermon v 37

Sermon v 37 employs five elements from the William's depiction of the spiritual person. The German Preacher declares with regard to the *imago Dei* in the spiritual person:

> (1b) there God loves, there God knows, there God savors Godself; (2) God lives and exists and works in her.
>
> In this one the soul becomes completely God-hued, God-like and godly. (3) She becomes all by grace that God is by nature, in the union with God, in the melting into God, and (4) is snatched above herself into God.... (5) Thus the person will not be able to err.[130]

Tauler depicts the experience of the *unio mystica* in Trinitarian terms: in the inner *imago Dei* (1b) "there God loves, there God knows, there God savors Godself" (*do mint Got, do bekent Got, do gebrucht Got sin selbes*). In the soul (2) "God lives and exists and works in her" (*Got lebt und wesent und wirkt in ir*). Here, the soul becomes what God is, becoming "completely God-hued, God-like, and godly" (*alzemole gotvar, gotlich, gottig*). Again, Tauler immediately asserts that the soul (3) "becomes all by grace that God is by nature" (*wird alles das von gnaden das Got ist von naturen*). In ecstasy, (4) the soul "is snatched above herself into God" (*wirt geholt über sich in Got*).[131] Thus, within five lines Tauler presents elements (1b)-(4) in an unbroken sequence in the same order as the *Golden Epistle*, highlighting how interconnected the dynamics of the mystical union are in the Dominican's thought. Finally, the German Preacher concludes that on this path (5) "the person will not be able to err" (*so enmag er nút verirren*).

---

130   v 37 (146.19-23, 147.8), (1b) "do mint Got, do bekent Got, do gebrucht Got sin selbes; (2) Got lebt und wesent und wirkt in ir.
    In disem wirt die sele alzemole gotvar, gotlich, gottig. (3) Sie wird alles das von gnaden das Got ist von naturen, in der vereinunge mit Gotte, in dem inversinkende in Got, und (4) wirt geholt über sich in Got....
    (5) so enmag er nút verirren."

131   Tauler restates the ecstasy several sentences later, v 37 (147.5-6), asserting that the soul "goes farther above all senses and understanding than one can say or think" ("gat verre über alle sinne und verstentnisse und das man geworten oder gedenken mag").

15   Sermon V 41

Sermon V 41 likewise incorporates all five elements of the *unio mystica*, keeping (1b)-(4) in an unbroken grouping.

> (4) For God has drawn this person so completely into Godself that the person (2) becomes so God-hued that all that is in him becomes—by a super-essential means—infused and transformed, that God works this person's work. And this is surely called a God-formed person, for whoever would correctly see the person, would see him as God, (3) not except by grace, (2) for God lives and exists and works in him all his works and (1b) savors Godself in him….
>
>   (5) And it is not to be believed that these people could ever be separated from God.[132]

Tauler begins with element (4), describing how "God has drawn this person so completely into Godself that the person (2) becomes so God-hued that all that is in him becomes—by a super-essential means—infused and transformed, that God works this person's work" (*Got hat disen menschen als gar in sich gezogen das der menschen wirt als gotvar das alles das in im ist, das wirt von einer überweselicher wise durchgossen und überformet, das Got dis menschen werk wúrket*). Fleshing out William's concept of becoming what God is, Tauler avows that the divinized person "is surely called a God-formed person, for whoever would correctly see the person, would see him as God" (*heisset wol ein gotformiger mensche, wan wer den mensche recht sehe, der sehe in als God*). As in the *Golden Epistle* Section 263, the second element is followed immediately by an abbreviated qualifying statement: (3) "not except by grace" (*nút denne von gnaden*). To these assertions Tauler adds a description of the person's participation in the Intra-Trinitarian communion, substituting the wording from the *Golden Epistle* 170, stating that (1b) God "savors Godself in him" (*gebruchet sin selbes in ime*).

After a few paragraphs Tauler includes element (5): "it is not to be believed that these people could ever be separated from God" (*das enist nút ze glöbende*

---

132   V 41 (175.16-22, 176.16-17), (4) "Wan Got hat disen menschen als gar in sich gezogen das der mensche (2) wirt als gotvar das alles das in im ist, das wirt von einer überweselicher wise durchgossen und überformet, das Got dis menschen werk wúrket. Und dis heisset wol ein gotformiger mensche, wan wer den menschen recht sehe, der sehe in als God, (3) nút denne von gnaden, (2) wan Got lebet und weset und wúrket in im alle sine werk und (1b) gebruchet sin selbes in ime… .
(5) Und das enist nút ze glöbende das dise lúte iemer von Gotte múgen gescheiden werden."

das dise lúte iemer von Gotte múgen gescheiden werden). Finally, it should be noted that for Tauler this experience of the *unio mystica* takes place in the "inward-dwelling person" (*inwonende menschen*),[133] alluding to the innermost of three persons within one person.

16   Sermon v 26

The whole of sermon v 26, Tauler's second exposition for Pentecost, is structured around the Spirit's work that brings a person into the *unio mystica*. In that union, according to the Dominican, the Holy Spirit fills the human spirit, that highest and innermost third person within each person. Tauler makes reference to all five elements, asserting that:

> (5) it is impossible that God would ever forsake these people.... (1b) God knows Godself and understands Godself and savors God's own wisdom and essence.... (3) [B]y grace God gives the [human] spirit what he is by nature,...(2) there, in the [human] spirit, God must work, know, love, praise and savor all his works...(4) for it is too high for all created intellects, angelic or human, by nature or also by grace.[134]

Again, Tauler follows the three elements of the *Golden Epistle* Section 263. Regarding the Intra-Trinitarian relationship, he substitutes the phrase from Section 170 on God's self-knowledge: In the divine abyss within the human person, (1b) "God knows Godself and understands Godself and savors God's own wisdom and essence" (*Got sich selber bekennet und verstat sich selber und smacket sin selbes wisheit und wesenlicheit*). In all of this (3) "by grace God gives the [human] spirit what he is by nature" (*von genaden git Got dem geiste daz das er ist von naturen*). Referring to deification, the Preacher employs the phrase seen many times, (2) "there, in the [human] spirit, God must work, know, love, praise and savor all his works" (*do mûs Got in dem geiste alle sine werg wúrken, bekennen, minnen, loben und gebruchen*). Introducing these elements, he declares: (5) "it is impossible that God would ever forsake these

---

133   v 41 (174.29).

134   v 26 (109.6-30), (5) "daz ist unmúgelich das Got disen menschen iemer gelasse.... (1b) Got sich selber bekennet und verstat sich selber und smacket sin selbes wisheit und wesenlicheit.... (3) [v]on genaden git Got dem geiste daz das er ist von naturen,...(2) do mûs Got in dem geiste alle sine werg wúrken, bekennen, minnen, loben und gebruchen.... Von diseme mag man also wenig gesprechen...(4) wan es ist allen geschaffenen verstentnissen, engelen und menschen, zû hoch von naturen and ouch von genaden."

people" (*daz ist unmúgelich das Got disen menschen iemer gelasse*). Finally, asserting that it is difficult even to speak about this mystical union, Tauler employs the phrase that he often uses to describe ecstasy: (4) "for it is too high for all created intellects, angelic or human, by nature or also by grace" (*wan es ist allen geschaffenen verstentnissen, engelen und menschen, zů hoch von naturen and ouch von genaden*).

17   Sermon v 60d

Finally, sermon v 60d depicts mystical union following the contours of *Golden Epistle* Section 263. Here Tauler asserts that in the ground of the soul where God's image lies—as opposed to the "sensate, animal, outward person" (*sinnelich tierlich uswúrkliche mensche*)[135]—the spiritual person can encounter the Intra-Trinitarian love of the divine:

> ...in the most hidden, deepest ground of the soul, there they have God essentially and actively and existentially, in which (2) God works and exists and (1b) savors Godself in it [the ground of the soul] and (5) one is able to be separated from God as little as from himself...so this ground (3) possesses all by grace that God has by nature....
>
> (4) Then comes the [heavenly] Father's power and calls the person into Godself...so the person is born in the Son by the Father and flows back into the Father with the Son and becomes one with [God].[136]

In the hidden, deepest part of the soul, (1b) God "savors Godself in it" (*gebruchet sin selbes in dem*). Employing his frequently-used description of deification, Tauler maintains that (2) God "works and exists...in him" (*wurket and weset... in dem*). (5) Such a "one is able to be separated from God as little as from himself" (*man môhte Got also wenig dannan abegescheiden also von ime selber*). This spiritual person's ground (3) "possesses all by grace that God has by

---

135   v 60d (301.7-8).

136   v 60d (300.19-25, 301.25-29), "...in dem allerverborgensten tieffesten grunde der selen, do sú daz in dem grunde hat Got wesentlichen und wúrklich und isteklich, in dem (2) wurket and weset Got und (1b) gebruchet sin selbes in dem, und (5) man môhte Got also wenig dannan abegescheiden also von ime selber...so hat diser grunt (3) alles das von genaden daz Got von naturen hat... .

(4) Denne kummet die vetterliche kraft und rüffet den menschen in sich...also wurt dis mensche in dem sune von dem vatter geborn und flússet wider in den vatter mit deme sune und wurt eine mit ime."

nature" (*alles das von gnaden daz Got von naturen hat*). Thus elements (1b)-(3) and (5) are presented within seven lines of text. Finally, some lines later the Dominican describes the ecstasy of such a union: "the heavenly Father's power comes and calls the person (4) into Godself...so the person becomes...one with [God]" (*kummet die vetterliche kraft und rüffet den menschen in sich...also wurt dis mensche...eine mit ime*). This sermon, along with the ones above, demonstrates how significantly William's concept of the *unio mystica* impacted Tauler's sermons.

18   Conclusion

William of Saint-Thierry's thought spread through the dissemination of his writings, especially the *Epistola ad fratres de Monte Dei*, as it was bound in collections of Saint Bernard's works. With manuscripts across Europe by the 14th century, a copy of the *Golden Epistle* most certainly found its way into the hands of the German Friar Preacher, Johannes Tauler, who further propagated William's ideas of spiritual progress through sermons delivered to the religious women to whom he ministered, and, in modern times, to interested Protestants and Catholics alike.

Closely following the Cistercian Father's thought, Tauler depicts spiritual formation in terms of the three states of spiritual progress, corresponding to our animal, rational, and spiritual faculties. Both authors honor the stages along the journey and assign spiritual practices appropriate to each given state. Yet, both mystagogues continually call their audience to further progress in the spiritual life, culminating in the *unio mystica*, which both discuss under the heading of "unity of the Spirit." In such union with the divine, the human spirit is taken above itself at times in ecstasy into God where it participates in the Intra-Trinitarian communion and experiences the sweetness of the divine kiss and embrace. Here the human person is deified, becoming by grace all that God is by nature.

Bibliography

Works of William of Saint-Thierry

Listed alphabetically with possible date of composition, Latin editions, and recent translations.

Ænigma fidei (PL 180:397–440), 1142–1144.

    Guillelmi a Sancto Theodorico Opera Omnia, V: Opuscula adversus Petrum Abaelardum et de Fide. (Ed.) Paul Verdeyen, SJ, 130–91. Corpus Christianorum Continuatio Mediaevalis 89A. Turnhout: Brepols, 2007.

    Guillaume de Saint-Thierry, Deux traités sur la foi: Le miroir de la foi, l'enigme de la foi. Edited and trans. M.-M. Davy, 92–179. Paris: J. Vrin, 1959.

    William of Saint Thierry: The Enigma of Faith. Transl. John D. Anderson. Cistercian Fathers 9. Kalamazoo, MI, and Spencer, MA: Cistercian Publications, 1973.

Brevis commentatio (PL 184:407–36), 1125 (?)

    Guillelmi a Sancto Theodorico Opera Omnia, II: Brevis Commentatio. (Ed.) Stanislaus Ceglar, SDB, and Paul Verdeyen, SJ, 155–96. Corpus Christianorum Continuatio Mediaevalis 87. Turnhout: Brepols, 1997.

De contemplando Deo (PL 184:365–80), 1119–1120.

    Guillelmi a Sancto Theodorico Opera Omnia, III: De Contemplando Deo. (Ed.) Paul Verdeyen, SJ, 153–73. Corpus Christianorum Continuatio Mediaevalis 88. Turnhout: Brepols, 2003.

    Guillaume de Saint-Thierry, La contemplation de Dieu, L'Oraison de Dom Guillaume. (Ed.) and trans. Dom Jacques Hourlier. Sources chrétiennes 61 bis. Paris: Les Éditions du Cerf, 1959; revised edition, 1977; corrected edition, 1999, 2005.

    Prière de Guillaume, Contemplation de Dieu. (Ed.) and trans. Robert Thomas. Pain de Cîteaux 23. Roybon, France: Abbaye de Chambarand, 1965.

    Guillaume de Saint-Thierry, Deux traités de l'amour de Dieu: De la contemplation de Dieu. (Ed.) M.-M. Davy, 31–67. Paris: J. Vrin, 1953.

    William of St Thierry: On Contemplating God, Prayer, Meditations. Trans. Sr. Penelope [Lawson], CSMV, and intro. Jacques Hourlier, OSB, 36–64. Cistercian Fathers 3. Kalamazoo, MI: Cistercian Publications, 1977.

Disputatio adversus Petrum Abaelardum (PL 180:249–82), 1140.

    Guillelmi a Sancto Theodorico Opera Omnia, V: Opuscula adversus Petrum Abaelardum et de Fide. (Ed.) Paul Verdeyen, SJ, 17–59. Corpus Christianorum Continuatio Mediaevalis 89A. Turnhout: Brepols, 2007.

Epistola ad domnum Rupertum (to Rupert of Deutz) (PL 180:341–46), 1120–1123.

    Guillelmi a Sancto Theodorico Opera Omnia, III: Epistola Guillelmi ad Rupertum Tuitiensem. (Ed.) Stanislaus Ceglar, SDB, and Paul Verdeyen, SJ, 47–52. Corpus Christianorum Continuatio Mediaevalis 88. Turnhout: Brepols, 2003.

William of Saint-Thierry: *Letter to Ruper of Deutz, On the Sacrament of the Altar, and On the Errors of William of Conches.* Trans. and intro. F. Tyler Sergent and Nathaniel Peters, Cistercian Fathers 82. Collegeville, MN: Cistercian Publications, *in progress.*

Epistola de erroribus Guillelmi de Conchis (to Bernard of Clairvaux) (PL 180:333–40), 1141.

> *Guillelmi a Sancto Theodorico Opera Omnia, V: De Erroribus Guillelmi de Conchis.* (Ed.) Paul Verdeyen, SJ, 61–71. Corpus Christianorum Continuatio Mediaevalis 89A. Turnhout: Brepols, 2007.

> Leclercq, Jean, (ed.) "Les lettres de Guillaume de Saint-Thierry à saint Bernard." *Revue Bénédictine* 79 (1969): 375–91.

> *William of Saint*-Thierry: *Letter to Ruper of Deutz, On the Sacrament of the Altar, and On the Errors of William of Conches.* Trans. and intro. by F. Tyler Sergent and Nathaniel Peters. Cistercian Fathers 82. Collegeville, MN: Cistercian Publications, *in progress.*

Epistola ad fratres de Monte-Dei (PL 184:307–64), 1144–1145.

> *Guillelmi a Sancto Theodorico Opera Omnia, III: Epistola ad fratres de Monte Dei.* (Ed.) Paul Verdeyen, SJ, 223–89. Corpus Christianorum Continuatio Mediaevalis 88. Turnhout: Brepols Publishers, 2003.

> *Guillaume de Saint-Thierry, Lettre aux frères du Mont-Dieu (Lettre d'Or).* (Ed.) and trans. Jean Déchanet, OSB. Sources chrétiennes 223. Paris: Les Éditions du Cerf, 1975; revised and corrected edition, 2004.

> *Lettre aux frères du Mont-Dieu.* (Ed.) and trans. Robert Thomas. Pain de Cîteaux 33–34. Roybon, France: Abbaye de Chambarand, 1968.

> *William of St Thierry, The Golden Epistle: A Letter to the Brethren at Mont Dieu.* Trans. Theodore Berkeley, OCSO, and intro. J.-M. Déchanet, OSB. Cistercian Fathers 12. Kalamazoo, MI: Cistercian Publications, 1980.

Epistola ad Gaufridum Carnotensem episcopum et Bernardum abbatem Clarae-vallensem (Preface to Adv Abl) (PL 182:531–533), 1138.

> *Guillelmi a Sancto Theodorico Opera Omnia, V: Epistola Willelmi.* (Ed.) Paul Verdeyen, SJ, 13–15. Corpus Christianorum Continuatio Mediaevalis 89A. Turnhout: Brepols, 2007.

> Leclercq, Jean, (ed.) "Les lettres de Guillaume de Saint-Thierry à saint Bernard." *Revue Bénédictine* 79 (1969): 377–91.

Excerpta de Libris Beati Ambrosii super Cantica Canticorum (PL 15:1851–1962), 1128–1130 (?)

> *Guillelmi a Sancto Theodorico Opera Omnia, II: Excerpta de libris beati Ambrosii super* Cantica canticorum. (Ed.) Antony van Burink, 205–384. Corpus Christianorum Continuatio Mediaevalis 87. Turnhout: Brepols, 1997.

Excerpta ex Libris Beati Gregorii super Cantica Canticorum (PL 180:441–74), 1128–1130 (?)

Guillelmi a Sancto Theodorico Opera Omnia, II: Excerpta ex libris beati Ambrosii super Cantica canticorum. (Ed.) Paul Verdeyen, SJ, 393–444. Corpus Christianorum Continuatio Mediaevalis 87. Turnhout: Brepols, 1997.

Expositio super Cantica Canticorum (PL 180:473–546), 1138.

Guillelmi a Sancto Theodorico Opera Omnia, II: Expositio super Cantica Canticorum. (Ed.) Paul Verdeyen, SJ, 17–133. Corpus Christianorum Continuatio Mediaevalis 87. Turnhout: Brepols, 1997.

Guillaume de Saint-Thierry, Exposé sur le Cantique des Cantiques. (Ed.) J.-M. Déchanet, OSB, and trans. M. Dumontier, OCSO. Sources chrétiennes 82. Paris: Les Éditions du Cerf, 1962; 2nd edition, 1998.

Commentaire sur le Cantique des cantiques. (Ed.) and trans. Robert Thomas. Pain de Cîteaux 9–12. Roybon, France: Abbaye de Chambarand, 1961.

William of Saint Thierry, Exposition on the Song of Songs. Trans. Columba Hart, OSB, and intro. J.-M. Déchanet, OSB. Cistercian Fathers 6. Kalamazoo, MI: Cistercian Publications, 1970.

Expositio super Epistolam ad Romanos (PL 180:547–694), 1137.

Guillelmi a Sancto Theodorico Opera Omnia, I: Expositio super Epistolam ad Romanos. (Ed.) Paul Verdeyen, SJ, 1–196. Corpus Christianorum Continuatio Mediaevalis 86. Turnhout: Brepols, 1989.

Guillaume de Saint-Thierry, Exposé sur l'Épître aux Romains, I (Books I–III). (Ed.) Paul Verdeyen, SJ, and trans. Yves-Anselme Baudelet, OSB. Sources chrétiennes 544. Paris: Les Éditions du Cerf, 2011.

Exposé sur l'Épître aux Romains. (Ed.) and trans. Antoine Bru. Pain de Cîteaux. Paris: OEIL, 1986.

William of St Thierry, Exposition on the Epistle to the Romans. Trans. John Baptist Hasbrouk, (ed.) John D. Anderson. Cistercian Fathers 27. Kalamazoo, MI: Cistercian Publications, 1980.

Meditativae orationes (PL 180:205–48), 1128–1132.

Guillelmi a Sancto Theodorico Opera Omnia, IV: Meditationes Devotissimae. (Ed.) Paul Verdeyen, SJ, 1–80. Corpus Christianorum Continuatio Mediaevalis 89. Turnhout: Brepols, 2005.

Guillaume de Saint-Thierry, Oraisons méditatives. (Ed.) and trans. Dom Jacques Hourlier. Sources chrétiennes 324. Paris: Les Éditions du Cerf, 1985.

Oraisons méditées. (Ed.) and trans. Robert Thomas. Pain de Cîteaux. Roybon, France: Abbaye de Chambarand, 1964.

William of St Thierry, On Contemplating God, Prayer, Meditations. Trans. Sr. Penelope [Lawson], CSMV, and intro. Jacques Hourlier, OSB, 87–178. Cistercian Fathers 3. Kalamazoo, MI: Cistercian Publications, 1977.

The Meditations of William of St Thierry: Meditativae Orationes. Trans. A Religious of CSMV [Sr. Penelope Lawson]. London: A.R. Mowbray, 1954.

William of Saint-Thierry: Meditationes. Trans. Thomas X. Davis. *In progress.*

De natura corporis et animae (PL 180:695–726), c. 1138 (?)

> *Guillelmi a Sancto Theodorico Opera Omnia, III: De Natura Corporis et Animae.* (Ed.) Paul Verdeyen, SJ, 101–46. Corpus Christianorum Continuatio Mediaevalis 88. Turnhout: Brepols, 2003.

> *William of St Thierry: The Nature of the Body and Soul.* In *Three Treatises on Man: A Cistercian Anthropology.* (Ed.) Bernard McGinn and trans. Benjamin Clark, OCSO, 101–52. Cistercian Fathers 24. Kalamazoo, MI: Cistercian Publications, 1977.

De natura et dignitate amoris (PL 184:379–408), 1119–1122.

> *Guillelmi a Sancto Theodorico Opera Omnia, III: De Natura et Dignitate Amoris.* (Ed.) Paul Verdeyen, SJ, 175–212. Corpus Christianorum Continuatio Mediaevalis 88. Turnhout: Brepols, 2003.

> *Nature et dignité de l'amour.* (Ed.) and trans. Robert Thomas. Pain de Cîteaux 24. Roybon, France: Abbaye de Chambarand, 1965.

> *Guillaume de Saint-Thierry, Deux traités de l'amour de Dieu: De la nature et de la dignité de l'amour.* (Ed.) M.-M. Davy, 69–137. Paris: J. Vrin, 1953.

> *William of St Thierry, The Nature and Dignity of Love.* Trans. Thomas X. Davis and intro. David N. Bell. Cistercian Fathers 30. Kalamazoo, MI: Cistercian Publications, 1981.

Oratio domni Willelmi, 1128–1132.

> *Guillelmi a Sancto Theodorico Opera Omnia, III: Oratio Domni Willelmi.* (Ed.) Paul Verdeyen, SJ, 169–71. Corpus Christianorum Continuatio Mediaevalis 88. Turnhout: Brepols, 2003.

> *Guillaume de Saint-Thierry, La contemplation de Dieu, L'Oraison de Dom Guillaume.* (Ed.) and trans. Dom Jacques Hourlier. Sources chrétiennes 61 bis. Paris: Les Éditions du Cerf, 1959; 2nd edition, 1968; revised edition, 1977; corrected edition, 1999, 2005.

> *Prière de Guillaume, Contemplation de Dieu.* (Ed.) and trans. Robert Thomas. Pain de Cîteaux 23. Roybon: Abbaye de Chambarand, 1965.

> Bell, David N. "The Prayer of Dom William: A Study and New Translation." In *Unity of Spirit: Studies on William of Saint-Thierry in Honor of E. Rozanne Elder.* (Eds.) F. Tyler Sergent, Aage Rydstrøm-Poulsen, and Marsha L. Dutton, 21–36. Cistercian Studies 268. Collegeville, MN: Cistercian Publications, 2015.

> *William of St Thierry, On Contemplating God, Prayer, Meditations.* Trans. Sister Penelope [Lawson], CSVM, and intro. Jacques Hourlier, OSB, 71–74. Cistercian Fathers 3. Kalamazoo, MI: Cistercian Publications, 1977.

Prologus ad Domnum Bernardum abbatem Claravallis (Prologue to Sac alt) (PL 180:344–45), 1122–1123.

Guillelmi a Sancto Theodorico Opera Omnia, III: Prologus [*Ad Domnum Bernardum Abbatem Claravallis*]. (Eds.) Stanislaus Ceglar, SDB, and Paul Verdeyen, SJ, 53. Corpus Christianorum Continuatio Mediaevalis 88. Turnhout: Brepols, 2003.

*William of Saint-*Thierry: *Letter to Ruper of Deutz, On the Sacrament of the Altar, and On the Errors of William of Conches*. Trans. with intro. F. Tyler Sergent and Nathaniel Peters. Cistercian Fathers 82. Collegeville, MN: Cistercian Publications, *in progress*.

Responsio abbatum auctore Willelmo abbate Sancti Theoderici (to Cardinal Matthew), 1131/32.

Guillelmi a Sancto Theodorico Opera Omnia, IV: Responsio Abbatum Auctore Willelmo Abbate Sancti Theoderici. (Ed.) Paul Verdeyen, SJ, 103–12. Corpus Christianorum Continuatio Mediaevalis 89. Turnhout: Brepols, 2005.

Responsio Abbatum (*Suessione, 1132*) *Auctore Willelmo Abbate Sancti Theodorici*. In *William, Abbot of Saint-Thierry: A Colloquium at the Abbey of St. Thierry*. Trans. Jerry Carfantan, 87–112. Cistercian Studies 94. Kalamazoo, MI: Cistercian Publications, 1987.

Documents inédits pour servir l'histoire ecclésiastique de la Belgique. (Ed.) Dom Ursmer Berlière, I: 103–10. Maredsous: Abbaye de Saint-Benoit, 1894.

De sacramento altaris (PL 180:345–66), 1122–1123.

Guillelmi a Sancto Theodorico Opera Omnia, III: De Sacramento Altaris. (Eds.) Stanislaus Ceglar, SDB, and Paul Verdeyen, SJ, 53–91. Corpus Christianorum Continuatio Mediaevalis 88. Turnhout: Brepols, 2003.

*William of Saint-*Thierry: *Letter to Ruper of Deutz, On the Sacrament of the Altar, and On the Errors of William of Conches*. Trans. with intro. F. Tyler Sergent and Nathaniel Peters. Cistercian Fathers 82. Collegeville, MN: Cistercian Publications, *in progress*.

Speculum fidei (PL 180:365–98), 1142–1144.

Guillelmi a Sancto Theodorico Opera Omnia, V: Speculum Fidei. (Ed.) Paul Verdeyen, SJ, 81–127. Corpus Christianorum Continuatio Mediaevalis 89A. Turnhout: Brepols, 2007.

Guillaume de Saint-Thierry, Le miroir de la foi. (Ed.) and trans. Jean Déchanet, OSB. Sources chrétiennes 301. Paris: Les Éditions du Cerf, 1982.

Guillaume de Saint-Thierry, Deux traités sur la foi: Le miroir de la foi, l'enigme de la foi. (Ed.) and trans. M.-M. Davy, 24–91. Paris: J. Vrin, 1959.

William of Saint Thierry, The Mirror of Faith. Trans. Thomas X. Davis and intro. E. Rozanne Elder. Cistercian Fathers 15. Kalamazoo, MI: Cistercian, 1979.

Vita prima Sancti Bernardi, Liber Primus (PL 185:225–68), 1145–1147.

Vita Prima Sancti Bernardi Claraevallis Abbatis. (Ed.) Paul Verdeyen, SJ, 29–85. Corpus Christianorum Continuatio Mediaevalis 89B. Turnhout: Brepols, 2011.

William of Saint-Thierry, Arnold of Bonneval, Geoffrey of Auxerre, *The First Life of Bernard of Clairvaux.* Trans. Hilary Costello, OCSO. Cistercian Fathers 76. Collegeville, MN: Cistercian Publications, 2015.

Bernard of Clairvaux: Early Biographies, Volume I by William of St. Thierry. [Trans. Martinus Cawley.] Centennial Edition: 1090–1990. Guadalupe Translations. Lafayette, OR: Abbey of Our Lady of Guadalupe, 1990.

The Life of William of Saint-Thierry

Vita antiqua (MS Lat. 11782, fols. 340–41, Bibliotèque Nationale, Paris, France).

Guillelmi a Sancto Theodorico Opera Omnia, IV: Vita Antiqua. (Ed.) Paul Verdeyen, SJ, 117–22. Corpus Christianorum Continuatio Mediaevalis 89. Turnhout: Brepols, 2005.

Bell, David N. "The *Vita Antiqua* of William of St. Thierry." *Cistercian Studies [Quarterly]* 11 (1976): 246–54. English translation from MS Lat. 11782 BNP.

Verdeyen, Paul. *Guillaume de Saint-Thierry, Premier auteur mystique des anciens Pays-Bas*, 138–50 Turnout: Brepols, 2003. Latin text and French translation.

Works Cited: Ancient, Medieval, Modern

Adam, André. *Guillaume de Saint-Thierry. Sa vie et ses oeuvres.* Bourg: Impr. du Journal de l'Ain, 1924.

Agobard of Lyons. *On the Baptism of Slaves of Jews (De baptismo mancipiorum Judaeorum).*

Alcuin of York. *Opusculum Septimum: Tractatus super Tres S. Pauli ad Titum, ad Philemonem, et ad Hebraeos Epistolas.*

Ambrose of Milan. Letter 49.

Anderson, John D. Introduction to *William of St. Thierry, The Enigma of Faith.* Trans. John D. Anderson. Cistercian Fathers 9. Kalamazoo, MI: Cistercian Publications, 1973.

Anderson, John D. "The Use of Greek Sources by William of St Thierry Especially in the *Enigma Fidei*." In *One Yet Two: Monastic Tradition East and West.* (Ed.) M. Basil Pennington, 242–53. Cistercian Studies 29. Kalamazoo: Cistercian Publications, 1976.

Athanasius of Alexandria. *Ad Serapionem.*

Augustine of Hippo. *Against Julian.*

Augustine of Hippo. *The City of God.*

Augustine of Hippo. *Confessions.*

Augustine of Hippo. *Contra Fortunatum Manichaeum.*

Augustine of Hippo. *De doctrina Christiana.*

Augustine of Hippo. *Enarrationes ad Psalmos.*

Augustine of Hippo. *In evangelium Johannis tractatus.*

Augustine of Hippo. Letters, 92, 120, 147, 155, 169, and 170.

Augustine of Hippo. *De libero arbitrio.*

Augustine of Hippo. *On the Literal Meaning of Genesis.*

Augustine of Hippo. *On the Merits and Forgiveness of Sins.*

Augustine of Hippo. *De peccatorum meritis et remissione.*

Augustine of Hippo. *De quantitate animae.*

Augustine of Hippo. *Retractationes.*

Augustine of Hippo. Sermon 255 *In Diebus Paschalibus.*

Augustine of Hippo. *Tractates on John.*

Augustine of Hippo. *On the Trinity.*

Augustine of Hippo. *On True Religions.*

Augustine through the Ages: An Encyclopedia. (Ed.) Allan D. Fitzgerald. Grand Rapids, MI: Eerdmans, 1999.

von Balthasar, Hans Urs. *Parole et mystère chez Origène.* Paris: Les Éditions du Cerf, 1957.

Baudelet, Yves-Anselme. *L'Expérience spirituelle selon Guillaume de Saint-Thierry.* Paris: Les Éditions du Cerf, 1985.

Bavaud, Georges. "Guillaume de Saint-Thierry, docteur de l'Assomption?" *Revue Bénédictine* 70 (1960): 641–51.

Bede. *In evangelium Lucae.*

Bede. *Homilia LVII in die Assumptionis Mariae.*

Bell, David N. "The Alleged Greek Sources of William of St. Thierry." In *Noble Piety and Reformed Monasticism.* (Ed.) E. Rozanne Elder, 109–22. Studies in Medieval Cistercian History VII. Cistercian Studies 65. Kalamazoo, MI: Cistercian Publications, 1981.

Bell, David N. "Greek, Plotinus, and the Education of William of Saint-Thierry." *Cîteaux – Commentarii cistercienses* 30 (1979): 221–48.

Bell, David N. *The Image and Likeness: The Augustinian Spirituality of William of St. Thierry.* Cistercian Studies 78. Kalamazoo, MI: Cistercian Publications, 1984.

Bell, David N. "The Prayer of Dom William: A Study and New Translation." In *Unity of Spirit: Studies on William of Saint-Thierry in Honor of E. Rozanne Elder.* (Eds.) F. Tyler Sergent, Aage Rydstrøm-Poulsen, and Marsha L. Dutton, 25–28. Cistercian Studies 268. Collegeville, MN: Cistercian Publications, 2015.

Bell, David N. "The *Vita Antiqua* of William of St. Thierry." *Cistercian Studies* [*Quarterly*] 11 (1976): 246–55.

Bell, David N. "William of St Thierry and John Scot Eriugena." *Cîteaux – Commentarii cistercienses* 33 (1982): 5–28.

Berengar of Tours. *Rejoinder against Lanfranc (Rescriptum contra Lanfrannum).*

Bernard of Clairvaux. *An Apologia to Abbot William.*

Bernard of Clairvaux. *De consideratione.*

Bernard of Clairvaux. *De gratia et libero arbitrio.*

Biblia Sacra Iuxta Vulgatam Versionem. Stuttgart: Deutsche Bibelgesellschaft, 1983.

Blythe, Reginald H. *Zen in English Literature and Oriental Classics.* Tokyo: The Hokuseido Press, 1942.

Boethius. *De persona et duabus naturis (Contra Eutychen et Nestorium)*.

Boethius. *One Person and Two Natures*.

Boethius. *On the Trinity*.

Bondéelle Souchie, Anne. *Bibliothèques cisterciennes dans la France Médiévale: Répertoire des Abbayes d'hommes*. Paris: CNRS, 1991.

Bouyer, Louis. *The Cistercian Heritage*. Trans. Elizabeth A. Livingstone. Westminster, MD: The Newman Press, 1958.

Bredero, Adriaan. "William of Saint Thierry at the Crossroads of the Monastic Currents of His Time." In *William, Abbot of St. Thierry: A Colloquium at the Abbey of St. Thierry*. Trans. Jerry Carfantan, 113–37. Cistercian Studies 94. Kalamazoo, MI: Cistercian Publications, 1987.

Brooke, Odo. *Studies in Monastic Theology*. Cistercian Studies 37. Kalamazoo, MI: Cistercian Publications, 1980.

Brooke, Odo. "The Theology of William of St Thierry: A Methodological Problem." *Cistercian Studies [Quarterly]* 6.3 (1971): 261–68.

Brooke, Odo. "Towards a Theory of Connatural Knowledge." *Cîteaux – Commentarii cistercienses* 18 (1967): 275–90.

Brooke, Odo. "William of St. Thierry's Doctrine of the Ascent to God by Faith." *Recherches de Théologie ancienne et médiévale* 30 (1963): 181–204; 33 (1966): 283–318.

Le Brun, Freddy. "*Vita Antiqua Willelmi Sancti Theoderici* d'après le manuscrit latin 11782 de la Bibliothèque Nationale de Paris." In *Signy l'Abbaye et Guillaume de Saint-Thierry. Actes du Colloque international d'Études cisterciennes 9, 10, 11 septembre 1998, Les Vieilles Forges (Ardennes)*. (Ed.) Nicole Boucher, 444–45. Signy l'Abbaye: Association des Amis de l'Abbaye de Signy, 2000.

Burnaby, John. *Amor Dei. A Study of the Religion of St. Augustine*. London: Hodder & Stoughton, 1938; reprint, 1947.

Cappuyns, Maieul J. "Le '*De imagine*' de Grégoire de Nysse traduit par Jean Scot Érigène." *Recherches de théologie ancienne et médiévale* 32 (1965): 205–62.

Carruthers, Mary J. *The Book of Memory: A Study of Memory in Medieval Culture*. New York: Cambridge University Press, 2008.

Cartwright, Steven R. *Peter Abelard: Commentary on the Epistle to the Romans*. Fathers of the Church, Mediaeval Continuation 12. Washington, DC: Catholic University of America Press, 2011.

Cartwright, Steven R. "Twelfth-century Pauline Exegesis: William of St. Thierry's Monastic Rhetoric and Peter Abelard's Scholastic Logic." In *A Companion to St. Paul in the Middle Ages*. (Ed.) Steven R. Cartwright, 205–34. Leiden: Brill, 2012.

Cassian (John). *The Conferences*.

Cassian (John). *The Institutes*.

Cassiodorus. *De anima*.

Cavallera, Ferdinand. "La doctrine de saint Augustin sur l'Esprit saint à propos du *De Trinitate*." *Recherches de théologie ancienne et médiévale* 2 (1930): 365–87.

Cavallera, Ferdinand. "La doctrine de saint Augustin sur l'Esprit saint à propos du *De Trinitate.*" *Recherches de théologie ancienne et médiévale* 3 (1931): 5–19.

Ceglar, Stanley [Stanislaus]. "The Date of William's Convalescence at Clairvaux." *Cistercian Studies Quarterly* 30.1 (1995): 27–33.

Ceglar, Stanislaus. "William of St.-Thierry: The Chronology of His Life with a Study of His Treatise *On the nature of love,* His Authorship of the *Brevis commentatio,* the *In lacu,* and the *Reply to Cardinal Matthew.*" Ph.D. diss., Catholic University of America, Washington, DC, 1971.

Ceglar, Stanislaus. "William of Saint Thierry and His Leading Role at the First Chapters of the Benedictine Abbots (Reims 1131, Soissons 1132)." In *William, Abbot of Saint Thierry: A Colloquium at the Abbey of St. Thierry,* 34–49. Trans. Jerry Carfantan. Cistercian Studies 94. Kalamazoo, MI: Cistercian Publications, 1987.

Châtillon, Jean. "William of Saint Thierry, Monasticism and the Schools: Rupert of Deutz, Abelard, and William of Conches." In *William, Abbot of St. Thierry: A Colloquium at the Abbey of St. Thierry.* Trans. Jerry Carfantan, 153–80. Cistercian Studies 94. Kalamazoo, MI: Cistercian Publications, 1987.

Cicero. *De Officiis.*

Cistercians and Cluniacs: St. Bernard's Apologia to Abbot William. Trans. Michael Casey. Cistercian Fathers 1A. Kalamazoo, MI: Cistercian Publications, 1970.

Clanchy, M.T. *Abelard: A Medieval Life.* Oxford, UK: Blackwell, 1997.

Clark, James M. *The Great German Mystics: Eckhart, Tauler and Suso.* New York: Russel, 1949; reprint, 1970.

Clogan, Paul M. Preface to *Medievalia et Humanistica: Studies in Medieval and Renaissance Culture.* Denton: North Texas State University, 1973.

Como, Giuseppe. *Ignis amoris Dei. Lo Spirito Santo e la transformazione dell'uomo nell'esperienza spirituale secondo Guglielmo di Saint-Thierry.* Milan: Editio Glossa, 2001.

Constable, Giles. *The Letters of Peter the Venerable,* vol. 1. Cambridge, MA: Harvard University Press, 1967.

Costello, Hilary, OCSO. Introduction to *The First Life of Bernard of Clairvaux.* Cistercian Fathers 76. Collegeville, MN: Cistercian Publications, 2015.

Courcelle, Pierre. *Les lettres grecques en occident de Macrobe a Cassiodore.* 2nd edition. Paris, 1948.

Crouzel, Henri. *Origen.* Trans. A.S. Worrall. San Francisco: Harper & Row, 1989.

Davies, Oliver. *God Within: The Mystical Tradition of Northern Europe.* Hyde Park, NY: New City, 2006.

Davis, Thomas X. Appendix to *William of St. Thierry: The Mirror of Faith,* 93–95. Cistercian Fathers 15. Kalamazoo, MI: Cistercian Publications, 1979.

Davy, Marie-Madeleine. *Un traité de la vie solitaire: Lettre aux frères du Mont-Dieu de Guillaume de St-Thierry.* Études de philosophie médiéval 29, Part 2. Paris: Traduction Française, 1940.

Déchanet, Jean-Marie. "Autour d'une querelle fameuse, de l'Apologia à la Lettre d'or." *Recherches de théologie ancienne et médiévale* 20 (1939): 3–34.

Déchanet, Jean-Marie. *Aux sources de la spiritualité de Guillaume de Saint-Thierry. Première série d'études.* Bruges: Charles Beyaert, 1940. Originally published as "Aux sources de la doctrine spirituelle de Guillaume de Saint-Theirry: 1, Saint Grégoire de Nysse." *Collectanea O.C.R.* 5 (1938–39): 187–98, 262–78.

Déchanet, Jean-Marie. "Guillaume et Plotin." *Revue de Moyen Age Latin* 2 (1946): 246–60.

Déchanet, Jean-Marie. *Guillaume de Saint-Thierry, aux sources d'une pensees.* Paris: Beauchesne, 1978.

Déchanet, Jean-Marie. "Les manuscrits de la Lettre aux Frères du Mont-Dieu du Guillaume de Saint-Thierry et le problème de la 'Preface' dans Charleville 114." *Scriptorium* 8 (1954): 236–71.

Déchanet, Jean-Marie. *William of St.-Thierry: The Man and His Work.* Trans. Richard Strachan. Cistercian Studies 10. Spencer, MA: Cisterican Publications, 1972. Originally published as *Guillaume de Saint-Thierry, l'homme et son oeuvre.* Bruges: Charles Beyaert, 1942.

DelCogliano, Mark. "A Fresh Look at William of Saint-Thierry's Excerpts from the Books of Blessed Ambrose on the Song of Songs." In *Unity of Spirit: Studies on William of Saint-Thierry.* (Eds.) F. Tyler Sergent, Aage Rydstrøm-Poulsen, Marsha L. Dutton, 37–59. Cistercian Studies 268. Collegeville, MN: Cistercian Publications, 2015.

Delesalle, Jacques. "La Vierge Marie dans les œuvres de Guillaume de Saint-Thierry." In *La Vierge dans la tradition cistercienne. 54 session de la Société Française d'Études Mariales, Abbaye Notre-Dame d'Orval, 1998.* (Eds.) Jean Longère, et al., 97–107. Paris: Éditions Médiaspaul, 1999.

Deutsch, S. Martin. *Die Synode von Sens.* Berlin, 1880.

Dubois, Marie-Gérard. "L'Eucharistie à Cîteaux au milieu du XIIe siècle." *Collectanea Cisterciensia* 67 (2005): 269–76.

Du Roy, Oliver. *L'Intelligence de la foi en la Trinité selon saint Augustin: Genèse de sa théologie trinitaire jusqu'en 391.* Paris: Études augustiniennes, 1966a.

Elder, E Rozanne. "Christologie de Guillaume de Saint-Thierry et vie spirituelle." In *Signy l'Abbaye et Guillaume de Saint-Thierry. Actes du Colloque international d'Études cisterciennes 9, 10, 11 septembre 1998, Les Vieilles Forges (Ardennes).* (Ed.) Nicole Boucher, 575–87. Signy l'Abbaye: Association des Amis de l'Abbaye de Signy, 2000.

Elder, E. Rozanne. "The Christology of William of Saint-Thierry." *Recherches de théologie ancienne et médiévale* 58 (1991): 79–112.

Elder, E. Rozanne. "Guillaume de Saint-Thierry et le chapitre bénédictin de 1131." In *Signy l'abbaye et Guillaume de Saint-Thierry.* (Ed.) Nicole Boucher, 487–504. Signy l'Abbaye: Association des amis de l'abbaye de Signy, 2000.

Elder, E. Rozanne. "The Image of the Invisible God: The Evolving Christology of William of Saint-Thierry." Ph.D. diss., University of Toronto, Canada, 1972.

Elder, E. Rozanne. "The Influence of Clairvaux: The Experience of William of Saint-Thierry." *Cistercian Studies Quarterly* 51.1 (2016): 55–75.

Elder, E. Rozanne. Introduction to *William of St. Thierry, The Mirror of Faith*. Trans. Thomas X. Davis, OCSO. Cistercian Fathers 15. Kalamazoo, MI: Cistercian Publications, 1979.

Elder, E. Rozanne. "William of Saint Thierry and the Greek Fathers: Evidence from Christology." In *One Yet Two: Monastic Tradition East and West*. (Ed.) M. Basil Pennington, 254–66. Cistercian Studies 29. Kalamazoo: Cistercian Publications, 1976.

van Engen, John. *Rupert of Deutz*. Berkeley: University of California Press, 1983.

van Engen, John. "Rupert of Deutz and William of St. Thierry." *Revue Bénédictine* 93 (1983): 327–36.

Expositiones Pauli epistularum ad Romanos, Galathas et Ephesios e codice Sancti Michaelis in periculo Maris, Expositiones Pauli epistularum. (Ed.) G. de Martel. Corpus Christianorum Continuatio Mediaevalis 151. Turnout: Brepols, 1995.

Evagrius of Pontus. *De oratione*.

Evagrius of Pontus. *The Praktikos*.

Fiske, A. "William of St. Thierry and Friendship." *Cîteaux – Commentarii cistercienses* 12 (1961): 5–27.

Gerson, Jean. *Sermo de humilitate factus in coena Domini (Joannis Gersonii opera omnia)*, vol. 3. Antwerp, 1706.

Gioia, Luigi. *The Theological Epistemology of Augustine's De Trinitate*. Oxford: Oxford University Press, 2008.

Gilson, Étienne. *Christian Philosophy in the Middle Ages*. London: Sheed and Ward, 1955.

Gilson, Étienne. *Introduction à l'étude de saint Augustin*. 2nd edition. Paris: J. Vrin, 2003.

Gilson, Étienne. *The Mystical Theology of Saint Bernard*. Trans. A.H.C. Downes. London/New York: Sheed & Ward, 1940; reprint, Kalamazoo, MI: Cistercian Publications, 1990.

Giraud, Cédric. *Spiritualité et histoire des textes entre Moyen Âge et époque moderne: genèse et fortune d'un corpus pseudépigraphe de méditations*. Paris: Institut d'études augustiniennes, 2016.

Gnädinger, Louise. "Das Altväterzitat im Predigtwerk Johannes Taulers." In *Unterwegs zur Einheit: Festschrift für Heinrich Stirnimann*. (Eds.) Johannes Brantschen and Pietro Selvatico, 253–67. Freiburg: Univeristätsverlag, 1980.

Gnädinger, Louise. *Johannes Tauler: Lebenswelt und mystische Lehre*. München: Verlag C.H. Beck, 1993.

Gnädinger, Louise. "Der minnende Bernhardus: Seine Reflexe in den Predigten des Johannes Tauler." *Cîteaux – Commentarii cisterciensis* 31 (1980): 387–409.

Gregory the Great. *Epistola contra Agnoetas.*

Gregory the Great. *Moral Reflections on the Book of Job (Moralia in Iob).* Volumes 1–5. Trans. Brian Kerns and intro. Mark DelCogliano, OCSO. Cistercian Studies 249, 257H, 258H, 259H, 260H. Collegeville, MN: Cistercian Publications, 2014–2019.

Gregory of Nyssa. *De hominis opificio.*

Haas, Alois. *Nim din Selbes war: Studien zur Lehre der Selbsterkenntnis bei Meister Eckhart, Johannes Tauler und Heinrich Seuse.* Freiburg: Universitätsverlag, 1971.

Heinrich Suso. *Horologium Sapientiae (The Clock of Wisdom).*

Hilary of Poitiers. *Tractate on Psalms.*

Hilary of Poiters. *De Trinitate.*

Holopainen, Toivo J. *Dialectic and Theology in the Eleventh Century.* Leiden: Brill, 1996.

Honemann, Volker. *Die 'Epistola ad fratres de Monte Dei' des Wilhelm von Saint-Thierry: Lateinische Überlieferung und mittelalterliche Übersetzungen.* Münchener Texte und Untersuchungen zur deutschen Literatur des Mittelalters 61. München: Artemis, 1978.

Honemann, Volker. "Eine neue Handschrift der deutschen *'Epistola ad fratres de Monte Dei.'*" In *Überlieferungsgeschichtliche Editionen und Studien zur deutschen Literatur des Mittlealters.* (Eds.) Konrad Kunze, Johannes Mayer, and Bernhard Schnell, 332–49. Tübingen: Niemeyer, 1989.

Honemann, Volker. "The Reception of William of St. Thierry's *Epistola ad fratres de Monte Dei* during the Middle Ages." In *Cistercians in the Middle Ages.* Studies in Medieval Cistercian History VI. (Ed.) E. Rozanne Elder, 5–18. Cistercian Studies 64. Kalamazoo, MI: Cistercian Publications, 1981.

Hourlier, Jacques. Introduction to William of St. Thierry, *On Contemplating God, Prayer, Meditations.* Trans. Sister Penelope [Lawson], CSMV, 3–35. Cistercian Fathers 3. Kalamazoo, MI: Cistercian Publications, 1973.

Hugh of Saint-Victor. *De sacramentis Christianae fidei.*

Humbert of Romans. *Instructiones de officiis ordinis.*

Humbert of Romans. *De officio magistri novitiorum.*

Hunt, Anne. *The Trinity: Insights from the Mystics.* Collegeville, MN: Liturgical Press, 2010.

Hunt, Stephen. "'Spirituality': A Word that Everyone Uses and Some Believe that They Know What it Means," *Implicit Religion* 18 (2015): 107–31.

Irenaeus of Lyons. *Adversus Haereses.*

Isidore of Seville. *Etymologies.*

Jaeger, C. Stephen. *Scholars and Courtiers: Intellectuals and Society in the Medieval West.* New York: Routledge, 2002.

James, Bruno Scott. *The Letters of St Bernard of Clairvaux.* Kalamazoo, MI: Cistercian Publications, 1998.

Javelet, Robert. *Image et resemblance au douzième siècle. De saint Anselme à Alain de Lille*. Paris: Letouzey & Ané, 1967.

Jerome. *Commentary on the Letter to Philemon* (*Commentariorum in Epistolam ad Philemon*).

Johannes Tauler: Predigten: Vollständige Ausgabe. (Ed.) and trans. Georg Hoffmann. Freiburg: Herder, 1961.

Johannes Tauler: Sermons. Trans. Maria Shrady. Classics of Western Spirituality. Mahwah, NJ: Paulist Press, 1985.

John Scotus Eriugena. *De Divisione Naturae Libri Quinque*.

Kihm, M. Engratis. "Die Drie-Wege-Lehre bei Tauler." In *Johannes Tauler, ein deutscher Mystiker: Gedenkschrift zum 600. Todestag*. (Ed.) Ephrem Filthaut, 268–300. Essen: Hans Driewer Verlag, 1961.

Kleinz, John P. *The Theory of Knowledge of Hugh of Saint Victor*. Washington, D.C.: Catholic University of America Press, 1944.

Landgraf, Artur M. *Dogmengeschichte der Frühscolastik*. Regensburg: Friedrich Pustet, 1952.

Lange, Marjory. "Mediating a Presence: Rhetorical and Narrative Strategies in the *Vita Prima Bernardi*." In *Unity of Spirit: Studies on William of Saint-Thierry in Honor of E. Rozanne Elder*. (Eds.) F. Tyler Sergent, Aage Rydstrøm-Poulsen, and Marsha L. Dutton, 117–43. Cistercian Studies 268. Collegeville, MN: Cistercian Publications, 2015.

Leclercq, Jean. *L'amour des lettres et le désir de Dieu. Initiation aux auteurs monastiques du Moyen Âge*. Paris: Éditions du Cerf, 1957; reprint, 2008.

Leclercq, Jean. "Les lettres de Guillaume de Saint-Thierry à Saint Bernard." *Revue Bénédictine* 79 (1969): 375–91.

Leclercq, Jean. *The Love of Learning and the Desire for God: A Study of Monastic Culture*. Trans. Catharine Misrahi. New York: Fordham University Press, 1982.

Leclercq, Jean. "The Renewal of Theology." In *Renaissance and Renewal in the Twelfth Century*. (Eds.) Robert L. Benson, Giles Constable, and Carol D. Lanham, 69–87. Toronto: University of Toronto Press, 1991.

The Letters of Peter the Venerable. Vol. 1. (Ed.) Giles Constable. Cambridge, MA: Harvard University Press, 1967.

Leo the Great. Sermon 76 and 77.

Library of Latin Texts (LLT-A). Centre Traditio Litterarum Occidentalium. Turnhout: Brepols, 2001–2018. www.brepolis.net.

de Lubac, Henri. *Histoire et esprit: L'intelligence de l'écriture d'après Origène*. Paris: Éditions du Cerf, 2002.

Mabillon, Jean. *The Life and Works of Bernard of Clairvaux*. 2nd edition. Trans. Samuel Eales. London: John Hedges, 1889.

Macy, Gary. *The Theologies of the Eucharist in the Early Scholastic Period: A Study of the Salvific Function of the Sacrament according to the Theologians c.1080–c.1220.* Oxford: Clarendon Press, 1984.

Marenbon, John. *The Philosophy of Peter Abelard.* Cambridge: Cambridge University Press, 1997.

Mayer, Johannes. "Tauler in der Bibliothek der Laienbrüder von Rebdorf." In *Überliefererungsgeschichtliche Editionen und Studien zur deutschen Literatur des Mittelalters.* (Eds.) Konrad Kunze, Johannes Mayer, and Bernhard Schnell, 388–90. Tübingen: Niemeyer, 1989.

Maximos the Confessor. *Quaestiones ad Thalassium.*

McGinn, Bernard. Introduction to *Three Treatises on Man. A Cistercian Anthropology.* (Ed.) Bernard McGinn, 27–47. Cistercian Fathers 24. Kalamazoo, MI: Cistercian Publications, 1977.

McGinn, Bernard. *The Flowering of Mysticism: Men and Women in the New Mysticism 1200–1350.* The Presence of God: A History of Western Christian Mysticism, Vol. 3. New York: Crossroad, 1998.

McGinn, Bernard. *The Growth of Mysticism.* The Presence of God: A History of Western Christian Mysticism, Vol. 2. New York: Crossroad, 1992.

McGinn, Bernard. *The Harvest of Mysticism in Medieval Germany.* The Presence of God: A History of Western Christian Mysticism, Vol. 4. New York: Crossroad, 2005.

McGuire, Brian Patrick. "Bernard of Clairvaux." In *The History of Western Philosophy of Religion.* (Eds.) Graham Oppy and Nick Trakakis, 109–20. Durham, UK: Acumen, 2009.

McGuire, Brian Patrick. *Jean Gerson and the Last Medieval Reformation.* University Park, PA: Pennsylvania State University Press, 2005.

Mechthild of Magdeburg. *Fliessende Licht der Gottheit (The Flowing Light of the Godhead).*

Mews, Constant J. "The Council of Sens (1141): Abelard, Bernard, and the Fear of Social Upheaval." *Speculum* 77 (2002): 342–82.

Mews, Constant J. "On Dating the Works of Peter Abelard." *Archives d'histoire doctrinale et littéraire du moyen âge* 52 (1984): 73–134.

Mews, Constant J. "The Lists of Heresies Imputed to Peter Abelard." *Revue Bénédictine* 95 (1985): 73–110.

Mews, Constant J. "Man's Knowledge of God according to Peter Abelard." In *L'homme et son univers au moyen age; actes du septième congrès international de philosophie médiévale (30 août-4 septembre 1982),* 391–426. Leuvain-la-Neuve, 1986.

Milis, Ludo. "William of Saint Thierry, His Birth, His Formation and His First Monastic Experiences." In *William, Abbot of St. Thierry: A Colloquium at the Abbey of St. Thierry.* Trans. Jerry Carfantan, 9–33. Cistercian Studies 94. Kalamazoo, MI: Cistercian Publications, 1987.

de Montfaucon, Bernard. *Bibliotheca bibliothecarum manuscriptorum nova*, Vol. 2. Paris, 1739.

Moore, Rebecca. "Hugh of St. Victor and the Authorship of *In Threnos Jeremiae*." The *Journal of Religious History* 22.3 (1998): 255–69.

Muckle, J.T. "Greek Works Translated Directly into Latin before 1350." *Medieval Studies* 4 (1942): 33–42.

Murk-Jansen, Saskia. "Hadewijch and Eckhart: *Amor intellegere est*." In *Meister Eckhart and the Beguine Mystics*. (Ed.) Bernard McGinn, 17–30. New York: Continuum, 1994.

Myers, Glenn E. "Manuscript Evidence of the *Golden Epistle*'s Influence in the Sermons of Johannes Tauler." *Cistercian Studies Quarterly* 48.4 (2013): 479–501.

Novum Testamentum Graece. Nestle-Aland, 27th edition. Stuttgart: Deutsche Bibelgesellschaft, 1996.

Origen of Alexandria. *In Epistulam Pauli ad Romanos explanationum libri*.

Origen of Alexandria. *Peri archon (De principiis)*.

Paschasius Radbertus. *De Fide, Spe et Charitate*.

Paschasius Radbertus. *De corpore et sanguine Domini*.

Peter Abelard. *Apologia contra Bernardum*.

Peter Abelard. *Commentaria in epistulam Pauli ad Romanos*.

Peter Abelard. *Sic et Non*.

Peter Abelard. *Theologia christiana*.

Peters, Nathaniel. "The Trinitarian Dimensions of Cistercian Eucharistic Theology." Ph.D. diss., Boston College, Boston, 2017.

Plato. *Phaedrus*.

Pourrat, Pierre. *La spiritualité chrétienne*, Vols. 1–4. Paris: Gabalda, 1918–1928.

Pseudo-Augustine. *Ad interrogate*.

Rabanus Maurus. *Enarrationum in Epistolas beati Pauli*.

Radl, Karl. "An English Translation of Agobard of Lyons' 'De Baptismo Judaicorum Mancipiorum.'" *Semitic Controversies: A Daily Blog about Jews and Judaism*. Posted 24 March 2013. Http://semiticcontroversies.blogspot.com/2013/03/an-english-translation-of-agobard-of.html. Accessed 2 January 2018.

Rose, Stuart. "Is the Term 'Spirituality' a Word that Everyone Uses, But Nobody Knows What Anyone Means by it?" *Journal of Contemporary Religion* 16 (2001): 193–207.

Rougé, Matthieu. *Doctrine et experience de l'eucharistie chez Guillaume de Saint-Thierry*. Paris: Beauchesne, 1999.

Du Roy, Olivier. *L'Intelligence de la foi en la Trinité selon saint Augustin: Genèse de sa théologie trinitaire jusqu'en 391*. Paris: Études augustiniennes, 1966.

Ruh, Kurt. *Geschichte der abendländischen Mystik*, Vol. 3. *Die Mystik des deutschen Predigerordens und ihre Grundlegung durch die Hochscholastik*. Munich: Beck, 1996.

Rule of the Master (Regula magistri).

Russell, Norman. *The Doctrine of Deification in the Greek Patristic Tradition*. Oxford: Oxford University Press, 2004.

Rydstrøm-Poulsen, Aage. "Research on William of Saint-Thierry from 1998 to 2008." *Analecta Cisterciensia* 58 (2008): 158–69.

Rydstrøm-Poulsen, Aage. "The Way of Descent: The Christology of William of Saint-Thierry." In *Unity of Spirit: Studies on William of Saint-Thierry in Honor of E. Rozanne Elder*. (Eds.) F. Tyler Sergent, Aage Rydstrøm-Poulsen, and Marsha L. Dutton, 78–91. Cistercian Studies 268. Collegeville, MN: Cistercian Publications, 2015.

Saword, Anne. "Man as the Image of God in the Works of William of St. Thierry." In *One Yet Two: Monastic Tradition East and West. Orthodox-Cistercian Symposium, Oxford University, 26 August-1 September 1973*. (Ed.) M. Basil Pennington, 267–303. Cistercian Studies 29. Kalamazoo: Cistercian Publications, 1976.

Saword, Anne. "Notes on William of St. Thierry's Use of Gregory of Nyssa's Treatise *On the Making of Man*." *Cistercian Studies* [*Quarterly*] 9 (1974): 394–97.

Schlüter, Dietrich. "Philosophische Grundlagen der Lehren Joahnnes Taulers." In *Johannes Tauler, ein deutscher Mystiker: Gedenkschrift zum 600. Todestag*. (Ed.) Ephrem Filthaut. Essen: Hans Driewer Verlag, 1961.

Schmaus, Michaël. *Die psychologische Trinitätslehre des hl. Augustinus*. Münster in Westfalen: Aschendorff Verlag, 1927; reprint, 1967.

Schmidt, Josef. Introduction to *Johannes Tauler Sermons*. Trans. Maria Shrady, 2–9. Classics of Western Spirituality. Mahwah, NJ: Paulist Press, 1985.

Sergent, F. Tyler. "A Bibliography of William of Saint Thiery." In *Truth as Gift: Studies in Medieval Cistercian History in Honor of John R. Sommerfeldt*. (Eds.) Marsha L. Dutton, Daniel M. LaCorte, and Paul Lockey, 457–82. Cistercian Studies 204. Kalamazoo, MI: Cistercian Publications, 2004.

Sergent, F. Tyler. "Cassian and William of St. Thierry on the Incarnation and Spiritual Union." Presentation at the Cistercian Studies Conference in the International Conference on Medieval Studies. Western Michigan University, Kalamazoo, 13 May 2011.

Sergent, F. Tyler. "'Signs of Spiritual and Divine Realities': The Sources and Originality of William of Saint Thierry's Ascetic Language." Ph.D. diss., Roskilde Universitet, Denmark, 2009.

Sergent, F. Tyler. "*Unitas Spiritus* and the Originality of William of Saint-Thierry." In *Unity of Spirit: Studies on William of Saint-Thierry in Honor of E. Rozanne Elder*. (Eds.) F. Tyler Sergent, Aage Rydstrøm-Poulsen, and Marsha L. Dutton, 144–70. Cisterican Studies 268. Collegeville, MN: Cistercian Publications, 2015.

Sergent, F. Tyler. "William of Saint-Thierry and the Gendering of the Soul." Presentation at the Southeastern Medieval Association Conference. The University of Tennessee, Knoxville, 6 October 2016.

Southern, R.W. *Scholastic Humanism and the Unification of Europe*. Vol. 1: Foundations. Oxford: Blackwell, 1995.

Steer, Georg. "Bernhard von Clairvaux als theologische Autorität für Meister Eckhart, Johannes Tauler und Heinrich Seuse." In *Bernhard von Clairvaux: Rezeption und Wirkung im Mittelalter und in der Neuzeit*. (Ed.) Kasper Elm. Wiesbaden: Harrassowitz, 1994.

Stewart, Columba. *Cassian the Monk*. Oxford Studies in Historical Theology. New York: Oxford, 1998.

Strauch, Philipp. *Margaretha Ebner und Heinrich von Nödlingen: Ein Beitrag zur Geschichte der deutschen Mystik*. Freiburg-im-Breigau/Tübingen: Mohr, 1882.

Sturlese, Loris. "Tauler im Kontext. Die philosophischen Voraussetzungen des 'Seelengrundes' in der Lehre des deutschen Neuplatonikers Berthold von Moosburg." *Beiträge zur Geschichte der deutschen Sprache und Literatur* 109 (1987): 390–426.

Sullivan, John E. *The Image of God: The Doctrine of St. Augustine and Its Influence*. Dubuque, IA: The Priory Press, 1963.

Tanner, Norman. "Piety in the Middle Ages." In *A History of Religion in Britain: Practice and Belief from Pre-Roman Times to the Present*, 61–76. (Eds.) Sheridan Gilley and W.J. Sheils. Oxford: Blackwell, 1994.

Tauler, Johannes. "Das Altväterzitat im Predigtwerk Johannes Taulers." In *Unterwegs zur Einheit: Festschrift für Heinrich Stirnimann*. (Eds.) Johannes Brantschen and Pietro Selvatico, 253–67. Freiburg, Schweiz: Univeristätsverlag, 1980.

Thomas, Robert. *Notes sur Guillaume de Saint-Thierry*, Vol. 3. Chambarand: Pain de Cîteaux, 1959.

Tomasic, Thomas Michael. "Neoplatonism and the Mysticism of William of St.-Thierry." In *An Introduction to the Medieval Mystics of Europe*, 53–75. Albany, NY: SUNY Press, 1984.

Tomasic, Thomas Michael. "Just How Cogently Can One Argue for the Influence of John Scotus Eriugena on William of Saint-Thierry?" In *Erudition at God's Service*. (Ed.) John R. Sommerfeldt, 185–94. Studies in Medieval Cistercian History XI. Cistercian Studies 98. Kalamazoo: Cistercian Publications, 1987.

Tomasic, Thomas Michael. "Just How Cogently is it Possible to Argue for the Influence of St. Gregory of Nyssa on the Thought of William of Saint-Thierry?" *Recherches de théologie ancienne et médiévale* 55 (1988): 72–129.

Vacandard, Elphège. "Chronologie abélardienne: La date du Concile de Sens: 1140." *Revue des questions historiques* 50 (1891): 235–45.

Verbaal, Wim. "The Council of Sens Reconsidered: Masters, Monks, or Judges?" *Church History* 74.3 (2005): 460–93.

Verdeyen, Paul. "La Chronologie des oeuvres de Guillaume de Saint-Thierry." *Collectanea Cisterciensia* 72.4 (2010): 427–40 [also published in *Ons geestelijk erf* 82.3 (2011): 190–203].

Verdeyen, Paul. "En quoi la connaissance de Guillaume de Saint-Thierry a-t-elle progresse depuis le Collogue de 1976?" *Revue des sciences religieuses* 73 (1999): 17–20.

Verdeyen, Paul. *La Théologie mystique de Guillaume de Saint-Thierry*. Paris: FAC-éditions, 1990.

Vita antiqua (Life of William of Saint-Thierry). See Works of William of Saint-Thierry.

Wainwright, Geoffrey. "Types of Spirituality." In *The Study of Spirituality*. (Eds.) Cheslyn Jones, Geoffrey Wainwright, and Edward Yarnold. Oxford: Oxford University Press, 1986.

Williams, John R. "The Cathedral School of Reims in the Time of Master Alberic, 1118–1136." *Traditio* 20 (1964): 93–114.

Wilmart, André. "La seri et la date des oeuvres de Guillaume de Saint-Thierry." *Revue Mabillon* 14 (1924): 156–67.

Wilmart, André. "La préface de la lettre aux frères de Mont-Dieu." *Revue Bénédictine* 36 (1924): 229–47.

Wyser, Paul. "Taulers Terminologie vom Seelengrund." In *Altdeutsche und Altneiderländische Mystik*. (Ed.) Kurt Ruh. Darmstadt: Wissenshaftliche Buchgesellschaft, 1964.

Zerbi, Piero. "William and His Dispute with Abelard." In *William, Abbot of St. Thierry: A Colloquium at the Abbey of St. Thierry*. Trans. Jerry Carfantan, 181–203. Cistercian Studies 94. Kalamazoo, MI: Cistercian Publications, 1987.

Zwingmann, Wolfgang. "Der Begriff *Affectus* bei Wilhelm von St. Thierry." Ph.D. diss., Pontifical Gregorian University, Rome, 1964.

Zwingmann, Wolfgang. "*Ex affectu mentis*. Über die Vollkommenheit menschlichen Handelns und menschlicher Hingabe nach Wilhelm von St. Thierry." *Cîteaux – Commentarii cistercienses* 18 (1967): 5–37.

Zwingmann, Wolfgang. "*Affectus illuminati amoris*. Über das Offenbarwerden der Gnade und die Erfahrung von Gottes beseligender Gegenwart." *Cîteaux – Commentarii cistercienses* 18 (1967): 193–226.

Index